Symbols of Defeat in the Construction of

If nationalism is the assertion of legitimacy for a nation and its effectiveness as a political entity, why do many nations emphasize images of their own defeat in understanding their history? Using Israel, Serbia, France, Greece, and Ghana as examples, the author argues that this phenomenon exposes the ambivalence that lurks behind the passions nationalism evokes. Symbols of defeat glorify a nation's ancient past, while reenacting the destruction of that past as a necessary step in constructing a functioning modern society. As a result, these symbols often assume a foundational role in national mythology. Threats to such symbols are perceived as threats to the nation itself and consequently are met with desperation difficult for outsiders to understand.

Steven J. Mock is co–lead researcher in the Balsillie School of International Affairs Ideational Conflict Project and teaches courses on nationalism, ethnic conflict, and power sharing in the Political Science Department of the University of Waterloo. Mock is a past chair of the Association for the Study of Ethnicity and Nationalism and a former editor and current member of the international advisory board for the journal *Nations and Nationalism*. Working on issues related to racism, ethnic conflict, and genocide and traveling extensively in Europe, the Balkans, and the Middle East piqued his interest in methods and theories for modeling symbols of identity and the emotions they evoke in conflict situations.

Symbols of Defeat in the Construction of National Identity

STEVEN J. MOCK

Balsillie School of International Affairs

CAMBRIDGE
UNIVERSITY PRESS

CAMBRIDGE
UNIVERSITY PRESS

32 Avenue of the Americas, New York NY 10013-2473, USA

Cambridge University Press is part of the University of Cambridge.

It furthers the University's mission by disseminating knowledge in the pursuit of
education, learning and research at the highest international levels of excellence.

www.cambridge.org
Information on this title: www.cambridge.org/9781107429482

© Steven J. Mock 2012

First published 2012
First paperback edition 2014

A catalogue record for this publication is available from the British Library

Library of Congress Cataloguing in Publication data

Mock, Steven J., 1972–
Symbols of defeat in the construction of national identity / Steven Mock.
p.   cm.
Includes bibliographical references and index.
ISBN 978-1-107-01336-0
1. Nationalism – History.   2. National characteristics – Memory.   3. Crises –
Psychological aspects – History.   4. Memory – Social aspects – History.   5. Collective
memory – History.   6. Political messianism – History.   I. Title.
JC311.M54   2011
320.54–dc22   2011015036

ISBN   978-1-107-01336-0   Hardback
ISBN   978-1-107-42948-2   Paperback

Contents

Acknowledgments

A work such as this, so many years in the making, naturally incurs a large debt of gratitude. I would like to thank, first of all, my family: my father, David Mock; my mother, Karen Mock (who also gave the proofs a final inspection); my brother, Dan, and his wife, Ashley, for always surrounding me in an environment that combined critical thought with a passion for social justice and tolerance, along with models of hard work and creative energy. I am grateful for the intellectual contribution and support of John Breuilly, Montserrat Guibernau, John Hutchinson, Dominic Lieven, and Anthony D. Smith, as well as my colleagues at the Association for the Study of Ethnicity and Nationalism (ASEN): primarily, my perennial co-chair, conference co-organiser, and co-author, Daphne Halikiopoulou; Harcourt Fuller, for helping me locate sources on Ghana; and Gordana Uzelac, for feeding me plum brandy while challenging me to defend the intellectual value of functionalism. The depth and breadth of this work benefitted greatly from the various conferences, debates, and seminars organized by ASEN, affording me opportunities to converse about these ideas with scholars such as Michael Billig, Michael Hechter, Krishan Kumar, Carolyn Marvin, Aviel Roshwald, and many others. The input of the (formerly) anonymous reviewers for Cambridge University Press (Eric Kaufmann and Siniša Malešević), along with the help of my editors, was also of great value.

Thanks go as well to Thomas Homer-Dixon and David Welch, both for preparing me in the early stages of my career with the necessary background in multiple interacting models and paradigms of international relations and peace and conflict studies, and more recently for helping me to secure a base at the Balsillie School of International Affairs (BSIA), from which I completed the final stages of this book. Some of the early research for this work was undertaken at the University of Toronto under the supervision of Thomas McIntire, while Peter Beyer was there to introduce me to the sociology and politics of religion in the modern world. This work could not have been completed without the financial and institutional support of the London School of Economics, Government Department, and the Morrison Fellowship in Peace and Conflict Studies at the BSIA.

Needless to say, all errors and misjudgments are entirely my own.

Steven J. Mock
Balsillie School of International Affairs
Waterloo, ON
September 2011

Introduction

If the proverbial alien from outer space were to be placed, suddenly and unprepared, on the plaza overlooking the Western Wall in Jerusalem, what would he/she/it conclude about the prevailing political situation? One distinct ethnoreligious group would be seen beneath the wall, mourning their destruction and degradation against a meager ruin of what was clearly once a mighty structure. While above them, the location of what was, and indeed still is considered the holiest place in their religion was under the control of another ethnoreligious group, dominated by a glorious gold-plated dome enjoying its 14th century of existence on that spot. Which group would be presumed to be in control of the surrounding territory? Which would be presumed to have the larger army? Which would be presumed dominant, and which dominated?

Viewed in this light, the continued centrality of such a symbol to Israeli and Jewish national identity appears paradoxical. Indeed, one of the first acts of Israeli authorities upon conquering the site along with the whole of Jerusalem's Old City in the 1967 Six Day War was to raze 135 houses in the quarter immediately adjoining the Western Wall, summarily evicting its 650 inhabitants, so that a vast plaza could be constructed, comparable to the sort that a state might build to showcase a national cathedral or public building, so that Jews could mourn their powerlessness and degradation in larger numbers and relative comfort.[1] There is little question that this remnant of the Second Temple complex, destroyed by the Romans during the Judean revolt in 70 C.E., remains Judaism's holiest site – arguably the only holy place universally recognized

---

[1] Wasserstein 2001: 329–30.

as such in the otherwise iconoclastic Jewish religion – as well as Israel's most important national symbol. The only site that has ever contested this latter designation is Masada, the location of the last battle of the Judean revolt against the Romans that ended in 73 C.E., which prior to 1967 had been adopted as secular Zionism's most significant and inspirational monument.[2] A booklet titled "Facts About Israel," published in English by the Israeli Ministry of Foreign Affairs, summarizes the Masada story as follows in a chapter titled "Roots":

> Nearly one thousand Jewish men, women and children who had survived the fall of Jerusalem refused to surrender to Rome. They took over King Herod's fortress on the steep rock-mountain of Masada by the Dead Sea. For three years they managed to hold their own against repeated Roman attempts to dislodge them. When the Romans finally broke through, they found that the Jews had committed suicide so as not to surrender to the enemy.[3]

No one, either within the national tradition or outside of it, would dispute that these are both symbols of defeat. Despite efforts made within the national mythology to transform military defeat into moral victory, both symbols represent a moment when history, according to the normative values of the national ideology, took a wrong turn, yielding disastrous results that would endure for centuries afterward and that the nation exists to reverse.

Israel is not the only nation that places such symbols at the center of its national mythology. The battlefield of Kosovo Polje is the most important symbol to the Serbian national ideology, and the battle that took place there in 1389, considered to be the moment when the Serbian Empire was defeated by the Turks, leading to five centuries of subjugation under the Ottoman Empire, is its most powerful national myth. The day of the battle, June 28 – St. Vitus' Day (Vidovdan) – is the Serbian national holiday, and Kosovo is frequently referred to in political discourse as the "Serbian Zion" or "Serbian Jerusalem."[4] According to the mythic narrative, the leader of the united Serbian forces, Prince Lazar Hrebeljanović, willingly chose to face death fighting against impossible odds rather than submit to Ottoman domination, though the betrayal of one of his key allies, Vuk Branković, was nonetheless a pivotal cause of his defeat. However, before the battle was over, Ottoman Sultan Murad I was killed by a heroic Serbian knight, Miloš Obilić, who was himself killed in the attempt. The

---

[2] Liebman and Don-Yehiya 1983: 158.
[3] Quoted in Ben-Yehuda 1995: 13.
[4] Perica 2002: 8.

defeat led directly to the subjugation of the Serbs under Turkish rule, which they endured for centuries to follow. Virtually any expression of Serbian nationalism, even if it does not directly involve the territory of Kosovo, expresses itself in the language and symbols of this national myth, and appeal to the myth has proven to have tremendous potential for political mobilization at numerous points in modern Serbian history, up to the present day.

Other cases can be found in which the image of defeat, though perhaps less central or overtly commemorated in monument and ritual, nonetheless plays or has played a crucial role in the national construction of history and memory. In France there are, or were during key periods of national mobilization, multiple symbols of universal appeal, if contested meaning, that generated a sense of spiritual victory and moral fortitude out of a moment of political failure and martyrdom. The most enduring and iconic is Joan of Arc, burned as a heretic at Rouen. As Robert Gildea has observed, despite the divided nature of French political culture, with the cult of the Revolution cutting across that of the united nation, virtually all manifestations of French national expression throughout the modern period have had to come to terms with Joan of Arc as their symbolic representative: the royalist, republican, and revolutionary; the Catholic and the anticlerical; even the fascist and the communist.[5] Other symbols of defeat, less contested because they were less central, also came to be elevated in French national consciousness at around the same time, including the epic hero Roland, killed by a horde of Saracens defending Charlemagne's empire, and the historical defeat of Vercingetorix, ruler of the Gauls, at the hands of Caesar's Roman legions.[6]

It has long been recognized that Greek national identity is divided between two sometimes conflicting, sometimes complementary, narratives: the classical model, which associates modern Greek identity with the civilization of the ancient city-states focused on Athens, and the Byzantine model, which connects it to the medieval Christian successor to the Roman Empire centered on Constantinople. As Greek nationalism coalesced into the ideology known as the "Great Idea" toward the end of the 19th century, the moment of the fall of Constantinople to the Ottoman Empire in 1453 developed into a unifying image, elevated as a focal point in folklore, literature, and constructions of historical memory, one that retains at least some of its salience even today.

---

[5] Gildea 1994: 154, 165.
[6] Schivelbusch 2003: 142–6, 166–7.

Although the key martyr–hero figures of Czech national mythology, such as Jan Hus and St. Wenceslas, are identified with the high points of sovereignty and cultural achievement of the Kingdom of Bohemia, the Battle of White Mountain of November 8, 1620, the moment identified as the final defeat of the kingdom at the hands of the Habsburg Empire – along with the cruel public execution of 27 Protestant Czech aristocrats that followed in Prague's main square, and the "300 years of darkness" that ensued for the Czech nation as a consequence – nonetheless holds a prominent and crucial place in the construction of Czech national history.

Examples can be found, as well, among nations that do not enjoy state sovereignty. France's loss to Britain in the Battle of the Plains of Abraham on September 13, 1759, the decisive battle that brought Quebec under British control, provided a later Québécois nationalism a moment from which the struggle to maintain political and cultural sovereignty for a distinct French-Canadian nation could be dated. And the Catalan national movement adopted September 11 as their national day, the date of the fall of Barcelona to the forces of Philip V in 1714, marking the final incorporation of Catalonia into a united Spain under Castillian rule. This moment is described by Montserrat Guibernau as one of the two most emotive historical events for Catalan national consciousness, the other being the War of the Reapers (1640–1652), another national defeat that inspired the Catalan national anthem, *Cant dels Segadors*.[7]

Commemorations and narratives of national defeat display wide variation. Some will be marked in time by national days commemorating pivotal battles, elevated into recurring rituals of the civic calendar such as *Vidovdan* for Serbia or *La Diada* for Catalonia. Some are commemorated in space by means of monuments or landmarks, such as Masada or the battlefield of Kosovo Polje. Some are commemorated through historical or literary narrative, such as in the epic–poetic tradition surrounding the Battle of Kosovo or the fall of Constantinople. Any of these mechanisms for commemoration may be sufficient to elevate a defeat myth to a point of centrality in the national construction of history and identity, though no single one is necessary. Indeed, there are numerous cases in which a sense of tragic defeat pervades national history and identity, without the need for its being localized and commemorated through a specific moment, place, or narrative. Poland's sense of being a "crucified nation," associated primarily with the era of partition, does not

---

[7] Guibernau 2004: 30; Balcells 1996: 13.

require the elevation of any particular battle or tragic hero,[8] nor does the Arab conception of a period of "stagnation," nor does the Chinese notion of "centuries of humiliation." The Hungarian national anthem is rife with allusions to a nation torn apart "for our sins" by multiple enemies, besieged by "Mongol's arrows" and beaten under "the Turks' slave yoke"; and Slovak history, in turn, contains a pervasive sense of subjugation to Hungarians.[9]

National defeat myths are not restricted to a particular region nor to nations with a particular common antecedent. Beyond Europe and the Judeo-Christian framework, we find, in Ghana, the figure of Nana Yaa Asantewaa, often explicitly described as an African Joan of Arc,[10] and the war that she led as the last failed rebellion of the Asante against British colonial rule. In India, images of various heroes such as Shivaji Maharaj and Lakshmibai, the Rani of Jhansi – depicted as having heroically fought ultimately unsuccessful wars against Muslim or British conquerors – have been known to mobilize either national, regional, or religious–communal sentiments, depending on how they are interpreted and presented. And in Mexico, Peru, and other nations of Latin America, the sense of continuity with the defeated civilizations of the Mayas, Aztecs, and Incas rests uneasily with the reality that modern Latin American culture is actually a hybrid between that of the conquered indigenous peoples and their Spanish conquerors.

Myths of defeat can manifest in figures as overtly legendary as Roland or the Latvian epic hero Lāčplēsis, or as scrupulously historical as Yaa Asantewaa. Nor can these memories be said to stem from the common experience of a particular historical era. The destruction of the Temple and the fall of Masada took place in antiquity, as did the defeat and death of Armenian tragic hero Vardan Mamikonian at the hands of the Sasanids at the battle of Avarayr in 451. The fall of Constantinople and the battle of Kosovo Polje took place in late medieval times. The Battle of

---

[8] The concept of the "crucified nation," in the Polish case along with others, is examined in Davies 2008.

[9] Although the centrality of the defeat motif to the construction of history and identity for such nations serves to further highlight the widespread salience of the phenomenon, the lack of empirical material resulting from a relative lack of concrete focal points for commemoration hinders any detailed examination of these as case studies, further to constructing an explanatory model.

[10] For example, in the *Daily Mirror*, June 5, 1950 (cited in Boahen 2003: 115); Asirifi-Danquah (2002: vii) identifies her as well with "Boudica (leader of the British struggle for independence from the Roman Empire), and Ida B. Wells (leader of the crusade against racism in the U.S.)."

White Mountain and the fall of Barcelona occurred in the early modern period. The Ghanaian national myth refers to a defeat suffered during the colonial period at the turn of the 20th century, and Arab and Palestinian nationalisms mobilize around a sense of grievance symbolized by defeats that occurred within the last century.

Both insiders to these nations and scholars examining particular national traditions tend to view this phenomenon as a trait exceptional to the nation in question. But how many of these exceptions must we encounter before we consider that what we are observing is, in fact, a common phenomenon demanding a common explanation?

Contrary to the expectations of both liberalism and Marxism, nationalism, at the beginning of the 21st century, remains one of the most powerful social and political forces in the modern world. It remains the basis of relations within the international system, even as states seek closer economic and political ties in an age of globalization. It has spread to every country in every part of the world, both as a movement of self-assertion against existing distributions of power and as the most compelling basis for state legitimacy. It is perhaps a testament to the pervasiveness of nationalist thinking that the immense power of symbols of defeat in national ideologies is widely recognized, yet there has been little critical inquiry into the reasons why such symbols should wield such power. Why would a national ideology, whose purpose is to reinforce the strength and legitimacy of the nation and its efficacy as a means to identity and political autonomy, mould itself around an image of conquest and humiliation?

Speaking specifically about the importance of Kosovo to Serbian identity, Ernest Gellner, in his last book on the subject of nationalism, recognized the immense problems involved in settling an ethnic dispute in which such symbols were a factor. "Can a nation be expected to separate itself from a piece of land which witnessed its greatest national disaster, even if that land is now largely inhabited by aliens?"[11] Indeed, the problematic nature of such a symbol of national disaster is so obvious to the reader that there is no need for Gellner to explain this point any further; a fact that is itself of interest, as it indicates the extent to which we have internalized the nationalist hierarchy of values. It would be considered unusual, indeed pathological, for an individual to revere and idealize memories and symbols of a past trauma. The expected individual response would be repression. Why, then, do we not presume that

[11] Gellner 1997: 105.

a nation should be similarly inclined to repress moments of defeat from its collective memory and to distance itself from the symbols and territories associated with those defeats? Instead, we take it as a given that such symbols and territories are more likely than any others to acquire a sacred quality to the national ideology, and that it is over such symbols and territories that even avowedly secular national movements are most likely to come to blows. Why should this be so obvious?

Ironically, it is often individuals within the national tradition who have confronted this question more critically than do scholars studying nationalism as a phenomenon. Rachel Yanait Ben-Zvi, an early Zionist leader and the wife of Israel's second president, on a visit to the Western Wall in the 1920s, reacted against the mourning, fasting, and lamentation she observed, given the implied resignation, passivity, and expectation of divine salvation that conflicted with Zionist values. "A desire to cry out to the wall in protest against the weeping arose within me," she wrote, " . . . to cry out against the unfortunate verdict of fate: no longer will we live in the land of destruction, we will rebuild the ruins and regenerate our land."[12] Milovan Djilas once lamented, in a more general sense, the Serb tendency to glorify their defeats. "A strange destiny to be an unlucky people with a great spirit. A people who reckon their defeats as victories . . . A people who sing songs of their defeats. That is the Serbian Idea. A song of misfortune. How long must it be so?"[13]

This work examines the question of why so many nations elevate symbols signifying their own defeat to the center of their national mythology. It is argued that this is a phenomenon that distinguishes nationalism and the nation as a modern ideology and form of social organization, as opposed to earlier and coexisting modes of cultural identity. What's more, these symbols enable the nation to compete with other forms of identity construction insofar as they successfully resolve basic human psychological dilemmas of the sort that any social system must in some way address. Under certain conditions, such myths can even serve as the very signifiers that give the system its structure and meaning and, therefore, the principal test distinguishing insiders from outsiders – the foundation myths of the nation.

Examination of the pivotal role of images of defeat in the mythology, symbolism, and civic ritual of many nations will serve to highlight and to at least partially fill a key gap in the literature on the study of nations

[12] Quoted in Liebman and Don-Yehiya 1983: 54.
[13] Quoted in Cohen 2001: preface.

and nationalism, relating to the centrality of violence and sacrifice to the maintenance of the nation as a form of social order. It is therefore necessary to examine and develop current theories of nations and nationalism at length before the question is to be satisfactorily answered. One of the key points of contention in the study of nationalism is the question of whether the nation is a recent construct, the product of a uniquely modern configuration of social forces, or whether it is dependent on continuity with durable ethnic antecedents. This work offers its own contribution to the debate, and the answer it offers, in short, is: yes. Yes, the nation is a wholly modern construct; and yes, it is dependent on continuity with premodern constructs. In framing my answer in this way, I am not claiming that these two views are reconcilable, nor am I attempting to find a "middle ground" between them. They are two mutually contradictory positions, and yet they are both, in their own ways, completely true. Hence we are left with the nation as a construct burdened with an inherent contradiction, and the strength of a given nation therefore lies in the extent to which the mechanisms that serve to resolve this contradiction are psychologically satisfying. I argue that the elevation of the defeat myth is a product of its unique ability to address this dilemma in the context of modern nation building.

It is my view that the prominence of such symbols first demonstrates the efficacy of theories that place mechanisms of sacrifice at the center of social order but also, more to the point, serves as a convenient way for nations in particular to manage the function that the sacrificial mechanism provides, essential to the cohesion of any social system or communal identity. Although not necessarily the only way, the unusual convenience of this method tells us something about the construct of the nation as it differs from other forms of social organization. Nations are modern entities, yet most identify as being in continuity with ancient predecessors. Images of defeat are able to resolve this apparent contradiction, rationalizing the notion necessary to the nationalist construction of history that current and ongoing national mobilization reflects continuity with a primordial but dormant ethnic solidarity, while at the same time resolving psychological ambivalence toward heroic symbols of the earlier, prenational cultures with which the modern nation identifies; symbols that serve simultaneously as ideals encapsulating the goals and values of the nation, and as obstacles to the modern, horizontal configuration of power necessary to a distinctly national form of social organization.

It is not my contention that a narrative of defeat is an essential element to nationalism or to the nation, insofar as there are many nations that do not place such symbols in a central role in their mythology and some that do not possess or commemorate them at all. However, it would be difficult, at this time, to discern any particular subset of nations most conducive to the phenomenon, as the elevation of symbols of defeat appears to occur across a vast diversity of nations at all points along the standard spectra of classification in the field. If a subset of nations conducive to the elevation of defeat had to be defined, it would conform to the "ideal-type" nation; those that are the most direct products of the very modernizing forces that ultimately served to transform the construct of the nation into the prevailing mode of sociopolitical organization on a global scale. It might therefore be more appropriate, at the conclusion of this work, to narrow the field by specifying subsets of nations that do *not* and would not be expected to significantly commemorate defeat because of their particular circumstances in relation to these modernizing forces.

For the purpose of this work, "defeat" will be defined narrowly to include only those myths or symbols that serve to commemorate a moment at which the nation, or a predecessor community with which the nation normatively identifies itself in continuity, suffered or is perceived to have suffered a military conquest represented as a historical turning point leading directly to a period of subjugation or domination, the effects of which are seen as enduring to at least some degree up to the present day. Note that it is *perception* that is key to the definition. As we will examine further, in many if not most cases, a valid historical argument could be made that the event in question was not in fact a pivotal defeat of long-term significance. The French were able to retake Paris only a few years after Joan of Arc's execution, and there remains an open debate among historians as to the actual outcome and immediate political significance of the Battle of Kosovo. What is important, however, is the pervasive if subjective impression threaded through the national tradition that these stand as symbolic moments of national weakness and subjugation. This would, however, still exclude images relating to lost battles or other military sacrifices viewed as part of a process culminating in victory. Hence, memories such as the Battle of Yorktown and the Alamo would not qualify, important though these are to American national mythology. Although such symbols may serve a similar functional purpose of commemorating and reinforcing national sacrifice or as images of violation, particularly for societies that do not commemorate defeat as such,[14] they

---

[14] See, for example, Roshwald 2006 (89–97) for discussion of the role of the Alamo as a pivotal image of sacrifice for Texan and American national mythologies.

nonetheless fall outside of the specific scope of this study. The same holds true for images relating to genocide and other instances of victimization not perceived as turning points in terms of their effect on the status of the community's self-determination, though again the function of such symbols within a national mythology as images of national sacrifice may be similar. The Holocaust and the Armenian genocide are not perceived as moments of transformation from a state of sovereignty to one of subjugation by their respective communities but serve rather to starkly reinforce a sense of ongoing, centuries-long defeat and subjugation. The terrorist attacks of September 11, 2001, though certainly commemorated in the United States as a day of national victimization, galvanizing sacrifice and solidarity, are not perceived as moments of defeat, at least not according to this definition.

Neither is this work part of a recent literature examining the "culture of defeat,"[15] which explores the mythology and culture that develops in a nation as a consequence of the immediate and current experience of defeat and subjugation, such as in Germany after World War I. Indeed, many, if not most, of the nations examined in this work stand in positions of regional power, their political autonomy and independence of action fiercely defended. All the more reason why the centrality of images of conquest and humiliation to their mythology and identity appears paradoxical. It is my view that such symbols, even when so narrowly defined, are sufficiently common in national mythologies (in contrast to other forms of social organization), and unusually so (in the sense that, where such symbols are central to a nation, they can be shown to have been elevated in importance during the process of nation building and their meanings altered considerably as the group has morphed from an ethnic community into a national identity wedded to a political program) that an examination of this particular category of symbols has the potential to offer unique insights into "the nation" as a general concept.

The first section of this work develops a theory of symbols of defeat, based on theoretical antecedents. Chapter 1 sets the groundwork from the existing literature on the theoretical study of nations and nationalism, primarily drawing from the discipline of political sociology. Chapter 2 explores the religious function that nations and their myths serve to fill in the context of modernity, developing a model to explain how symbols of defeat, in particular, contribute to resolving basic human dilemmas that enable the sort of social cohesion and mass mobilization the nation

---

[15] For example, Schivelbusch 2003.

requires in order to succeed. The second section of this work substantiates this theory with reference to textual analysis of the content of particular myths of defeat. Chapter 3 substantiates and elaborates on the foundational role that images of defeat play in the structure and ritual of modern nations, in particular through examination of monuments and commemorative days associated with such images. Chapter 4 deconstructs the standard narrative elements of the myth; first the salvific elements: the sacrificial victim, the activist hero, and the implied promise of a future redemption; and then the mechanisms for obscuring the community's need for sacrifice: the sacred executioner, the internal traitor, the ambiguous characterizations of the past "golden age" and the present state of incompleteness, and the boundaries substantiated through the myth between national insiders and outsiders. Chapter 5 offers suggestions as to the practical implications each element of the theory might have to the conduct of diplomacy and international relations; and Chapter 6 explores categories of nations that do not commemorate defeat in any significant way, offering explanations as to why this is so and demonstrating how the distinct nature of these exceptions ultimately serves to prove the rule.

Of course, even if a reliable methodology existed for quantifying myth, the confines of space would not allow for a comprehensive survey of all national mythologies in all of their variations to test for both the relative prominence of symbols of defeat as just defined, as well as the extent to which the commemoration of these symbols conforms to the model proposed. Hence, we are confronted with a choice between either concentrating in depth on a limited number of cases so as to clearly demonstrate the efficacy of the model, or sampling a broad cross section of national mythologies to demonstrate the widespread nature of the phenomenon. This work endeavors to balance these approaches, focusing in depth on a few key cases while presenting evidence indicating the existence of a wider body of further examples in support of each element of the argument. Although such a balance has the benefit of utilizing the strengths of both approaches, it also leaves us vulnerable to the weaknesses of both. Naturally, the cases examined in depth have been chosen as the most vivid examples around which the model has been developed, leaving open the possibility that this model might be effective for only these few cases, or for a broader type to which these few cases belong, with little insight to offer on nations and nationalism in general. Although reference to a wider body of examples will address this objection to some degree, the limitations of space do not allow me to offer any more than indications that these cases reflect a larger pattern. I hope to show, however, that enough evidence exists to at least indicate the frequent recurrence of a pattern supportive of the theory, thus indicating a possible direction for further research on the part of experts with greater familiarity with the mythologies of particular nations. At the very least, I show that this pattern represents a recurrent phenomenon in modern politics and nationalism often ignored by scholars, with particular relevance to understanding the behavior of nations in conflict situations.

Anthony Smith once described the study of the beliefs key to the continuity of nationalism and ethnic identity as "essential if we are to begin to understand, and so perhaps to ameliorate, the many social and political problems in this area." For in order to understand the nature and intensity of conflicts surrounding ethnic identity, we must be willing to examine not only the economic and political circumstances in which nationalism and ethnic conflict emerges but also take seriously each community's own understanding of its ethnic history, myths, and shared memories, and "most of all, we need to explore the continuing impact of ethnic myths, symbols and traditions in popular consciousness, and the way they continue to condition attitudes and behaviour to immigrants, minorities and outsiders, even in the most apparently rationalist and pragmatic societies."[16] It is only through such an approach that we will further our understanding of why nationalism continues to be such a compelling vehicle both for political legitimacy and individual human identity, how it can drive individuals to acts of both altruism and aggression, and therefore how its more negative tendencies can be contained and controlled.

---

[16] Smith 1999: 141; from a lecture delivered at the London School of Economics and Political Science on April 25, 1991, also quoted in *Ethnic and Racial Studies* 15(3), July 1992.

I

Theories of Nations and Nationalism

Modernism and Ernest Gellner

The earliest paradigm for understanding the nature of nations and nationalism is that of nationalism itself. Nationalist ideology typically represents the nation as, if not a natural, enduring, primordial entity, then at least an inevitable product of historical forces. At least in its "organic" form, nationalism is characterized by the following assumptions:

- that the world consists of natural nations and has always done so,
- that nations are the bedrock of history and the chief actors in the historical drama,
- that nations and their characters are organisms that can easily be ascertained by their cultural differentiae;
- however, members of nations may, and frequently have, lost their national self-consciousness along with their independence,
- and, therefore, that the duty of nationalists is to restore that self-consciousness and independence to the "reawakened" nation.[1]

These assumptions are evident in the genre of national histories that began to develop in the 19th century, carrying through to postcolonial literature into the present day; one that endeavored to trace the trajectory of "the nation" as a continuous protagonist across epochs of global civilization.[2] However, they had already come under critical scrutiny by the beginning

---

[1] From Smith 1998: 146.

[2] A selection of characteristic documents from anticolonial nationalist movements and leaders is presented in Kedourie 1971. Ozkirimli 2010: 51–2 provides a comparative analysis of key themes.

of the 20th century, when nationalism first developed as a distinct subject of academic inquiry. In the period between the First and Second World Wars, historians such as Hans Kohn, Carleton Hayes, Louis Snyder, Alfred Cobban, and E. H. Carr began to examine nationalism, as a mass movement for political unity or independence on behalf of a nation,[3] as a phenomenon related to modernity. But it is important to note that it was nationalism as an ideology, rather than the nation as a construct, that was problematized in this manner. Even those historians who were hostile to the idea of nationalism nonetheless took it as given that it was a reflection of a preexisting reality such as the nation or nationality, even if it was only enabled by the instruments of mass mobilization modernity provides.

It was Elie Kedourie who first proposed an argument suggesting that nationalism as an ideology was prior to the nation as a construct. In the opening line of his book, *Nationalism*, he states unequivocally that "nationalism is a doctrine invented in Europe at the beginning of the nineteenth century," going on to explain:

It pretends to supply a criterion for the determination of the unit of population proper to enjoy a government exclusively its own, for the legitimate exercise of power in the state, and for the right organisation of a society of states. Briefly, the doctrine holds that humanity is naturally divided into nations, that nations are known by certain characteristics which can be ascertained, and that the only legitimate type of government is national self-government.[4]

But what strikes Kedourie in particular is the manner in which this notion, bizarre in premodern times, came to be accepted as self-evident in modernity with no discernable event to mark the transition: "These ideas have become firmly naturalized in the political rhetoric of the West which has been taken over for the use of the whole world. But what now seems natural once was unfamiliar, needing argument, persuasion, evidence of many kinds; what seems simple and transparent is really obscure and contrived."[5]

Kedourie saw the origins of the doctrine in the Enlightenment notions of self-determination promulgated by Kant and Rousseau, converging with the organic notions of language and culture of the German Romantics, and invoked by 19th-century intellectuals frustrated by social immobility in order to effect social revolution. But although Kedourie's

---

[3] A definition paraphrased from Hayes 1931: 292–3, cited in Ozkirimli 2010: 31.
[4] Kedourie 1966: 9.
[5] Ibid.

approach has served as the starting point for the understanding of nations and nationalism as modern phenomena, critics contend that it tends toward intellectual determinism. Indeed, what is most striking about the nation is that unlike any other system of belief, it achieved its dominance and came to be taken for granted as the primary organizing principle of politics and identity without the need for any definable moment of origin, founding document, or great thinker.[6] To subsequent theorists such as Ernest Gellner, this suggested that the origins of the nation were to be found not so much in the convergence of ideas but in the underlying social forces that generated the context in which these ideas could germinate.

Gellner defined nationalism as "primarily a political principle, which holds that the political and national unit should be congruent,"[7] elaborating in a later work that this principle "maintains that similarity of culture is the basic social bond. Whatever principles of authority may exist between people depend for their legitimacy on the fact that the members of the group are of the same culture."[8] But far from being a natural or obvious notion, or, for that matter, an artificial and constructed one, Gellner asserted that the idea of common culture as the basis of political legitimacy became possible only in the context of modes of social organization unique to the modern era.

Dividing history into three distinct eras – tribal, agrarian, and modern–industrial – Gellner offered explanations as to why nations either could not or did not form in the two previous eras, at least not in the sense that we understand the term today. In hunter–gatherer societies, the rudimentary nature of political leadership and the lack of a codified culture meant that the problem of the relationship between polity and culture was never an issue. The idea that leadership positions must be held only by members of the same culture as the unit being governed is relevant only in a world in which governance by impersonal institutions is taken for granted. It was only in the agrarian age that the expanding size of populations necessitated a complex division of labor, leading to the need for political centralization and impersonal political institutions; that is, the state. Thus, the problem of the relationship between political power and culture did arise in some agrarian societies and, in such cases, the potential for nation formation existed. This was mitigated, however, by

---

[6] Gellner 1983: 123–4.

[7] Ibid.: 1.

[8] Gellner 1997: 3.

the structure of the majority of these societies, which were better served by systems of hierarchical organization placing a far greater emphasis on social standing.

According to Gellner, the pivotal distinction between agrarian societies and modern industrial ones was that the former were not concerned with the goal of increasing their overall output to the betterment of the whole collective. Rather, concern focused on who had control over the distribution of that output, or, as Gellner puts it, "who governed the store." In such societies, power led to wealth rather than wealth leading to power; social standing determined one's entitlement. Thus, each stratum in agrarian society jealously guarded its own standing, eager to differentiate itself from lower strata that would usurp its privilege given the chance. Differentiation of rank therefore had to be visible and felt. The less ambiguous such differences were, the less chance there could be for friction. An individual's station with its rights and duties was central to that individual's identity, and thereby an instrument of social discipline, a notion summarized in Plato's *Republic*, in which morality is defined as each element in the hierarchical social structure performing its assigned task and no other.

According to Gellner's model, then, the main function of culture in agrarian society was to reinforce and underwrite the hierarchical order. Culture was used to differentiate elites from the masses rather than as a force for unity; therefore, cultural difference rather than commonality was the basis of political legitimacy. Rulers were legitimate not because they were the same as those they ruled but because they were superior; hence, the gulf between the elite and the rest of the population had to be maintained by differing norms, values, even languages, and sometimes sanctified by differing myths of descent. The ruling classes tended to despise work and value "nobility," a term that varied in usage from the mere fact of membership in a status group to possession of the values and culture thought to characterize the group, primarily, concern for the responsibilities of station and the trappings of position.

Culture, as such, cannot perform this differentiating role while at the same time marking the boundaries of a polity. Therefore, in a society in which the organizing principle is status expressed through culture, and in which the social status of individuals is established and reinforced by cultural nuance, devoid of mobility, nationalism cannot operate. Without the principle of similarity of culture to establish political bonds and boundaries, organization in agrarian societies tended to be both larger and smaller than the limits of cultural difference. Local power was concentrated in economic units such as city-states, village communities, and clans that would coexist with multiethnic empires that expanded without reference to linguistic, religious, or cultural commonality. The most characteristic political formation of the era made use of both principles; a transethnic empire superimposed on subethnic communities, such as were the Ottoman and Habsburg Empires. Neither did conflict tend to make reference to cultural difference. Feuds would occur between clans within the same wider culture, while aristocrats would duel only with others of the same rank.[9]

According to Gellner, rapid change occurred because of the different modes of social organization required for production in an industrial economy. To begin with, a modern system must be, at least to some degree, meritocratic, maximizing growth by making optimal use of human resources. Given the limited qualifications necessary for leadership in agrarian society, positions could be filled in any random manner, and heredity was as good as any. But in a society geared toward growth rather than stability, one cannot fill the role of, say, a CEO the same way as one would that of a medieval baron. The value placed on growth in industrial society demanded the maximization of human resources, which in turn demanded social mobility. However, the relinquishing of old roles and occupations between, let alone within, generations was incompatible with the sacralizing of stations in the agrarian social order. Were the old social system to remain in place, the constant replacement of members of higher strata by members of lower ones would cause friction. Thus, a reevaluation of social mobility, predicated on a principle of baseline human equality, was a natural development.

In Gellner's model, this need for social mobility was key to the rise of nationalism, as it depended on all members of the society possessing the same basic set of skills, enabling context-free communication. This meant mass literacy according to shared language, symbols, and values transmitted through the mediation of a homogenizing high culture. This high culture had to be mastered by anyone who wished to operate effectively and enjoy social mobility within a given economy and society; therefore, the state took responsibility for codifying and providing it by means of a generic system of mass public education. This led to the notion that homogeneity of culture was the primary political bond and that mastery of a given high culture was a precondition to full political, economic, and social citizenship. One had to satisfy this condition, and only this

[9] Ibid: 14–21.

condition, rather than any ascriptive station important to the agrarian system, in order to enjoy the privileges of citizenship, or else one had to assimilate, migrate, or otherwise change. This was not a matter of ideology but a practical necessity, though one that prevails only under social conditions specific to the modern industrial era; it is neither inherent in our psyche nor a political invention at the service of other interests.

This was the balance that Gellner struck between the primordialist position of nationalism itself and radical constructivism. Nationalism is neither a historical accident nor an intentional fabrication but rather the necessary consequence of certain social conditions that happen to be widespread at this time. Its roots are deep, but this does not mean that they are universal to the human condition.

The Limits of Modernism

The position that nations are creatures of modern nationalism rather than nationalism being an expression of preexisting nations has since achieved widespread, though not uncontested, consensus in the field. Not only nationalism as an ideology but also the nation as a structure reflect fundamentally modern modes of social organization, requiring modern instrumentalities such as state bureaucracy, capitalism, secularism, mass literacy, and mass political participation to come into being. Numerous scholars have refined this thesis from various disciplinary perspectives, mostly over the question of the precise agency by which nations are formed and nationalism as an ideology promulgated. These can be broadly divided into two categories: constructivists, who focus on the underlying social forces that converge to make the nation possible; and instrumentalists, who concentrate on the role of human agency, usually elites intentionally manipulating national identity toward political ends.

To John Breuilly, nationalism must be seen as a form of politics, and politics is ultimately about power, which in the modern world comes down to the question of who may legitimately control the state. For him, then, nationalism refers to "political movements seeking or exercising state power and justifying such action with nationalist arguments," the latter being, the claim that a distinguishable nation exists, that its interests and values supersede all others, and that it must strive to be as independent as possible.[10] Such arguments have increasing salience in the modern world because of the increased distinction between the public

[10] Brueilly 1993: 2.

and private spheres, between the state and civil society. Where institutions such as churches and guilds had once monopolized economic, cultural, and political functions for all their members, now institutions such as parliaments, churches, private firms, and families serve discrete functions across multiple groups within society. This led to a greater emphasis on the individual as an autonomous modular unit possessed of multiple layers of identity. But under such conditions a new principle had to come into play to substantiate the connection between the individual and society so as to compel individuals to subordinate themselves to the state, making collective existence possible. This was provided by the political idea of citizenship and the cultural notion of society as possessing a collective character, which merged to produce an ideology capable both of legitimating state action and mobilizing the support of the masses.[11] But because, at least in the beginning, nationalism is almost invariably a movement of opposition to existing configurations of power, the product takes on a bewildering multiplicity of forms based on how these principles are merged and the character of the state that is opposed.

Coming from a Marxist perspective and examining nationalism in the context of a larger project on the history of modernity, Eric Hobsbawm coined the seemingly paradoxical term "the invention of tradition" to explain how ruling elites engineered nations and nationalism to counter the threat posed by the emergence of mass politics in the period between 1870 and 1914. The increased need to involve previously excluded categories of people as political subjects introduced the problem of how to maintain their loyalty and obedience. Invented traditions are "practices, normally governed by overtly or tacitly accepted rules and of a ritual or symbolic nature, which seek to inculcate certain values and norms of behaviour by repetition, which automatically implies continuity with the past,"[12] and innovations such as mass public education, public ceremonies, and the mass production of public monuments are singled out in this regard. Although nearly all forms of society "invent" tradition in the sense of adapting existing traditions and institutions to novel situations, during periods of rapid social change when the need to generate stability becomes desperate, traditions can be invited outright for entirely novel purposes. Despite their historical novelty, nations must nonetheless appeal to history to "legitimate action and cement group cohesion."[13] As

[11] Brueilly 1996: 163–6.
[12] Hobsbawm and Ranger 1983: 1.
[13] Ibid.: 12

another Marxist theorist, Tom Nairn, frames it, "the new middle-class intelligentsia of nationalism had to invite the masses into history; and the invitation-card had to be written in a language they understood."[14]

Nairn's position on the genesis of nations and nationalism focused on the uneven pattern of development that characterized global processes of industrialization in the era after the French Revolution. As industrialization spread, it was experienced by developing countries as domination on the part of the core countries and the imposition of foreign norms. Indigenous elites therefore had to find ways to merge popular expectations of material progress with local notions of sovereignty and distinctiveness. Thus, Nairn too sees all nationalisms as balancing inherently paradoxical features: "It is through nationalism that societies try to propel themselves forward to certain kinds of goal (industrialization, prosperity, equality with other peoples, etc.) *by a certain sort of regression* – by looking inwards, drawing more deeply upon their indigenous resources, resurrecting past folk heroes and myths about themselves and so on."[15] Michael Hechter has proposed a similar thesis, though instead of focusing on uneven relations between societies, he emphasized the importance of uneven relations between groups within societies. Adapting the notion of "internal colonialism," he argued that as relations between core and peripheral groups within a society intensify with the onset of industrialization, the core will dominate and exploit the periphery, leading to the stratification of groups characterized by economic inequality. Awareness of this inequality, in conjunction with palpable cultural differences between groups and means of in-group communication, will lead to group solidarity, and members of the disadvantaged group will assert the dignity and equality of their culture and seek autonomy on its behalf.[16]

Each of these models has been subject to numerous specific criticisms.[17] Indeed, with the exception of Gellner, none of these theorists claims to have devised a grand theory of the general origins of nations and nationalism so much as frameworks for understanding the context in which nations form. For our purposes, however, the most relevant criticism is that many of these theories, while purporting to locate the formation of nations in modern technologies and instrumentalities, nonetheless tacitly adopt cultural difference between groups as a necessary preexisting

---

[14] Nairn 1981: 340.
[15] Ibid.: 348.
[16] Hechter 1975: 9–10, 39–43.
[17] Many of which are summarized in Ozkirimli 2010: 120–37.

condition without much insight into just what manner of difference serves to satisfy this condition. Nairn, for example, makes this point explicitly: "As capitalism spread, and smashed the ancient social formations surrounding it, these always tended to fall apart along the fault-lines contained inside them. It is a matter of elementary truth that these lines of fissure were nearly always ones of nationality."[18] But can this simply be taken as "elementary truth" without further examination? Or, if these fissures of nationality indeed preexisted the social forces of modernity that drastically increased their salience, is it not still incumbent on us to seek their source and examine the question why certain "national" fissures proved more relevant than others? Even if, following Hobsbawm, we view the cultural content of modern nations as consisting largely of "invented traditions," we cannot automatically equate the creation of a symbol, ritual, or monument with its widespread popular acceptance. Some such inventions proved more resonant than others, and the logic behind this resonance must not simply be taken for granted. If, indeed, the masses had to be invited into history in a language they understood, whence does the language come and why is it so readily understood?

Therefore, the limitations of modernist theory, recognized to some extent by these theorists but more so by their critics, must be taken into account to prevent modernism from itself becoming a countermyth to nationalist primordialism; one that could engender a tendency to deemphasize the needs for continuity and meaning that nationalism must satisfy if it is to be successful. For even if the particular configuration of culture and organization that produced the nation is uniquely modern, most modernist theorists appear to tacitly recognize that both culture and organization are undeniably persistent and perennial forces throughout history. Cultures are transmitted over time, and though they can change rapidly, they have often proven continuous even over historical watersheds in which forms of social organization have shifted. Therefore, one cannot dismiss out of hand the nationalist endeavor to find evidence of the antiquity of the nation. Continuity of some sort and to some extent might well be authentic in many cases, even if it has occurred over shifts in both cultural norms and political structures.

Gellner himself recognized that even if loyalty to a culture, over and above loyalty to land or monarch, is a modern phenomenon, the culture itself commanding that loyalty is not necessarily something new. Rather, a preexisting culture provides the raw materials from which nationalism

---

[18] Nairn 1981: 353.

constructs the nation. However, while acknowledging that a nation can be in genuine continuity with a preexisting culture in some respects, he is insistent that this need not be the case and that such claims on the part of national ideologies should not be taken at face value.

It is nationalism which engenders nations, and not the other way round. Admittedly, nationalism uses the pre-existing, historically inherited proliferation of cultures or cultural wealth, though it uses them very selectively, and it most often transforms them radically. Dead languages can be revived, traditions invented, quite fictitious pristine purities restored ... the cultural shards and patches used by nationalism are often arbitrary historical inventions. Any old shard and patch would have served as well. But in no way does it follow that the principle of nationalism, as opposed to the avatars it happens to pick up for its incarnations, is itself in the least contingent and accidental ...

Nationalism is not what it seems, and above all it is not what it seems to itself. The cultures it claims to defend and revive are often its own inventions, or are modified out of all recognition.[19]

Consequently, according to Gellner, the high culture developed by nationalism can be seen as having been imposed on the masses to the same extent as was the allegedly foreign domination that nationalism sought to replace, even if the former does at least attempt to generate consent through links to local folk tradition.

But the idea that nationalism's use of preexisting cultural elements was entirely arbitrary, that "any shard or patch would serve as well," was unsatisfying to later theorists who picked up on Gellner's modernist approach. There had to be a reason why certain elements of an existing cultural heritage should be selected over others in the formation of a national tradition, and those studying the phenomenon of nationalism should not exempt themselves from exploring those reasons by appealing to the fact, however true, that the final construct is artificial. Clearly, there are some nations more united and able to mobilize greater loyalty and sacrifice than others, as well as cases in which constructed national identities and mythologies have failed to adequately mobilize populations. The modernist paradigm does not explain why one fabrication designed to suit the prevailing social order should differ in that respect from another. There is, rather, a genuine process of rediscovery at work in the nationalist appeal to the past, to which an alienated intelligentsia applies an existing cultural heritage associated with a living community to a political program. That cultural past provides vital memories, values, symbols,

---

[19] Gellner 1983: 55–6.

myths, and language without which the ideology of nationalism would have no teeth. These elements have popular resonance only because they are founded in living and continuous traditions authentic to at least part, if not all, of the community in question, which unites the group and differentiates it from outsiders. As Anthony Smith puts it:

> To see nations as composed largely of 'invented traditions' designed to organize and channel the energies of the newly politicized masses, places too much weight on artifice and assigns too large a role to the fabricators. The passion that the nation could evoke, especially in time of danger, the sacrifices it could command from the 'poor and unlettered' as well as the middle classes, cannot be convincingly explained by the propaganda of politicians and intellectuals or the ritual and pageantry of mass ceremonies – unless, that is, the public was already attuned to both propaganda and ceremonial... The 'inventions' of modern nationalists must resonate with large numbers of the designated 'co-nationals' otherwise the project will fail. If they are not perceived as 'authentic' in the sense of having meaning and resonance with 'the people' to whom they are addressed, they will fail to mobilize them for political action.[20]

The argument that follows is that although symbols may have very different meanings in the national context than they had to their prenational cultures, they would not have the power that they do if they did not have some authentic resonance to at least some element of those prenational cultures.

Ethnosymbolism and Anthony Smith

In proposing what has been termed the "ethnosymbolic" model, Anthony Smith defined the nation as "a named human population sharing an historic territory, common myths and historical memories, a mass public culture, a common economy and common legal rights and duties for all members."[21] This definition, by its construction, favors the modernist paradigm because only postindustrial and post–French Revolution groupings could meet the latter of these criteria. In the ancient world, humans were for the most part divided into fairly fluid ethnic categories, with some more durable ethnic communities such as the Persians, Egyptians, and Israelites, who possessed states run by and for members of the dominant ethnic community, even while members of other ethnic groups resided in their territory. But with diffuse and divisive power structures including

---

[20] Smith 1998: 130.
[21] Smith 1999: 11 (Introduction).

vast class divisions with different rights, duties, and entitlements (particularly to education), and with a localized economic life with no single division of labor, these communities could not be called nations in the modern sense. That is not to say that it is impossible for there to have been premodern cultural units that met many of the criteria that define a modern nation, but if indeed there were some that did, they could represent only isolated instances, the product of a local configuration of circumstances. Without a widely accepted and elaborated doctrine of nationalism, there was no framework whereby a cultural group could claim such a designation and no status or entitlements to be gained by doing so.[22]

But although the overall framework of the nation is a modern innovation, Smith recognizes that many of the elements that define the boundaries and content of nations predate modernity, suggesting that modern nations do have premodern precursors and form around recurrent antecedents. Hence, Smith distinguishes between the modern nation and the ethnic community, or *ethnie*, defined as a named human population with myths of common ancestry, shared historical memories, and one or more common elements of culture, including an association with (though not necessarily possession of) a homeland, and some degree of solidarity, at least among elites.[23] Fear of conflating earlier collective cultural identities with modern nations must not lead the researcher to downplay the role of ethnicity in premodern history, for even if nationalism as an ideology and, hence, the nation as an entity, is a modern occurrence, *ethnies* have existed throughout the history of human society. Acknowledging the possibility of linkage between modern nations and premodern *ethnies* is vital to an understanding of how, where, and why nations form, as well as why different nations and nationalisms, though alike in certain basic elements, also bear such distinctive features.

When one compares Smith's definitions of nation and *ethnie*, it is clear that the link occurs in the area of myth. Both nations and *ethnies* are named, have myths of ancestry, shared memory, association to land, and a sense of imagined community. But as important as it is to recognize this continuity, it is equally necessary to highlight the discontinuity between the two concepts, which occurs in the realm of social and economic institutions and instrumentalities. As Smith observes, *ethnies* and nations both emerge as a cluster of myths, symbols, memories, values, and traditions

---

[22] Ibid.: 106–8.
[23] Ibid.: 13 (Introduction).

drawn from the shared experience of several generations, including a myth of descent. But in premodern times, ethnicity was not the basis of polity formation except in rare instances when it was used to mobilize against a threat to a shared value or symbol such as religion. This would change in the modern world when developments such as industrialization, bureaucracy, and print literature brought culture to the fore as the basis for polity formation. "It is exactly those features of nations that *ethnies* lack – a clearly defined territory or 'homeland', a public culture, economic unity and legal rights and duties for everyone – that make nations ultimately different from *ethnies*, despite the fact that both possess such features as an identifying name, myths of common origins and shared historical memories."[24]

It is therefore incumbent on us to remain mindful of this distinction between the continuity of ethnic identity and the discontinuity in modes of ethnic mobilization connected with the rise of nationalism, as both factors are liable to affect the manner in which various ethnic and national myths and symbols are understood. Although it is possible, indeed likely, that the precise nature of an ethnic community's symbol system or hierarchy of values will change in the transition from the premodern to the modern, even where the mechanisms delineating the boundaries between "us" and "them" remain constant, there are also reasons why people within the group will respond to certain symbols and myths, whereas those outside the group do not. The ability to call on a well-documented ethnic history was to prove a major cultural resource for nationalists developing myths of ethnic origins, election, golden age, and sacred territory. Although acknowledging that national movements often have unique and distinctive features, Smith breaks down the ethnosymbolic system of the nation into six common elements:[25]

1. The *myth of temporal origins*, establishing the event or moment that caused the community to come into being, distinguishing itself from outsiders;
2. the *myth of location* or migration, establishing the legitimacy of a claim to land and resources, and to rule within given borders;
3. the *myth of ancestry*, establishing a symbolic kinship link between a common ancestor and the current members of the community through successive generations. This need not mean actual

---

[24] Smith 1998: 196.
[25] Discussed at length in Smith 1999: 62–8.

physical kinship but may focus on the transmission of certain values and shared memories within lines of descent, conferring a sense of special dignity and establishing a definitive bond over time as well as space, organizing the social world between kinsmen and outsiders;

4. the *myth of the heroic age*, producing an ideal image of a pristine past containing heroes who provide models for virtuous conduct and who speak in the community's authentic voice. The heroic age is represented as a time of liberation from outsider domination providing a platform for the group culture to realize its full potential in its purest form and therefore serves to represent the best of the community's traditions. This is where the community asserts its uniqueness, expressing what Weber would call its "irreplaceable cultural values." Preservation of heritage and autonomy is transformed into a sacred duty, not just toward themselves but also to the world.

5. the *myth of decline*, in which old virtues were forgotten, moral decay set in, pleasure and vice overcame discipline and self-sacrifice, and old systems dissolved; and finally,

6. the *myth of regeneration*, which transforms the symbol system from an explanatory myth to a prescription and rationale for mobilization, providing a quasi-messianic promise of ideal fulfillment alongside concrete and achievable goals such as attaining independence, growth, the building of institutions, cultural homogenization, social integration, and demarcating the boundaries of territory.

We may note at the outset that this system relies on a conception of time that is decidedly linear. No matter how ancient or primordial the nation is presumed to be, the need to firmly establish antiquity and ancestry requires the establishment of a sacred moment of birth, from which time stretches onward to a point of future redemption. But just because nationalist time is linear does not mean that it is unilinear in the sense of being evolutionary. With political mobilization as its underlying goal, nationalism must stress the reality of regression and regeneration and the role of human agency, with national consciousness being the key to rectifying the ills of past and present.

The nationalist, as a matter of principle, believes that it is inherent in human nature for people to want to be governed by those of their own culture. That this is the very definition of freedom is viewed within nationalist ideology as a universal and self-evident principle. However, this principle comes into conflict with the evident historical fact that ethnic solidarity invariably waxes and wanes throughout the history of an ethnic community, especially because nationalism, as an ideology that stresses such solidarity as the primary political value, did not really exist until recent times. As Gellner has observed, lack of nationalism in past eras is often explained by nationalists as reflecting a negative state of affairs, requiring a need for "awakening" to put history back in order. According to this model, the nation had to have been in existence all along as a persistent and primordial reality but was merely dormant because of an unfortunate set of historical circumstances that caused or were caused by a lack of political mobilization. The "dormition" of nationalism itself becomes a central symbol and myth of the national ideology, necessary to explain the historical absence of the nationalist principle according to a system in which the nation is natural, self-evident, and universal.[26]

Viewed in this light, we see how a myth or collective memory of defeat might serve a vital function in a national myth–symbol system, as it speaks to several key components of that system. It provides a ready explanation for the historical decline of the nation but in such a way as to focus attention as well on the qualities of the heroic age that were destroyed and on a prescription for mobilization and renewal. It also reinforces in-group–out-group boundaries by attributing the decline, or at least the circumstances leading to it, to the agencies of an enemy that can be externalized. In order for the golden age to be restored by means of a revived ethnic solidarity, it must be seen to have fallen, that solidarity destroyed. Highlighting the moment of fall therefore invites a sense of continuity with the current age of regeneration.

The Limits of Ethnosymbolism

But although the ethnosymbolic model can explain the place of images of defeat in a national myth–symbol system, it cannot, in itself, explain their centrality; neither does it explain the increased sense of urgency that accompanies conflicts over symbols and territories that relate specifically to such images. Ethnosymbolism provides a basis for more comprehensive understanding of the nation and national identity than does modernism alone. Tradition cannot be invented and then imposed arbitrarily on the masses, and without mass mobilization, the national mission will fail. The

[26] Gellner 1997: 7–9.

myths and symbols chosen and employed must resonate with at least some significant segment of the population if mobilization is to be successful. The weakness of this model, however, lies in its narrow definition of the conditions under which a given myth or symbol will have such resonance. The focus of Smith's model is authenticity: Symbols must be genuinely present in the heritage of the existing ethnic community or communities being forged into a nation.[27] But such ethnic authenticity – or, more accurately, perceived authenticity – is only one possible reason why a given signifier may have meaning to a national group.

Smith acknowledges but does not specifically examine the fact that nations, as they develop, will often define themselves in contrast or even in opposition to the *ethnies* from which they have developed, competing with the ethnic identity for allegiance: "Even when a rich vein of 'ethno-history' has been discovered and mined, the 'cultural wars' have only begun...in these processes new self-definitions of community are forged, often in the teeth of resistance by the guardians of the older ethno-religious self-definitions, so as to lay the basis for entry into the world of nations."[28] This would appear, on the surface, to compromise his thesis that continuity with an *ethnie* is the vital resource on which the nation draws. Yet he does not take it as such a challenge, nor should he, though the reasons why bear further exploration. In fact, discontinuity can prove to be as much of a resource to an aspiring nation, and this is evident in the content of national mythology. It is the exception rather than the rule for a modern nation to adopt unaltered the defining symbols and myths of the *ethnie* with which it identifies. It is more common for a nation to reinterpret, elevate, or even invent symbols and attribute them to the cultural inheritance of the nation where, in fact, they were not nearly as central to the preexisting *ethnie*.

If a nation is to compete, it must establish itself as different from and better than what has preceded it. Often the national ideology will do so by claiming a greater authenticity than the principles associated with the existing ethnic culture, identifying as a purifying manifestation of an

---

[27] In *Chosen Peoples* (2003: 37–40), Smith defines authenticity in the context of the nationalist framework as encompassing that which the nation considers to be unique, genuine and essential to its character, arguing that the authentic serves to secular nationalism what the sacred served to traditional religion: "...the authentic is the irreplaceable and fundamental, that which we cannot do without or think away. It is this necessity that separates 'us' from 'them', our nation from all others, and makes it and its culture unique and irreplaceable"(40).

[28] Smith 1991: 67–8.

earlier golden age that was subsequently corrupted. But this need not always be the case, and even where it does occur, it is generally only one strand of the nationalist discourse and not universally acknowledged or internalized. On the other hand, a national ideology will confront the nation's ethnic origins very differently to the extent that it identifies its foundation in a moment of revolution. A nation explicitly founded on the principle of strangling the last king with the entrails of the last priest (to paraphrase Diderot) does not have to negotiate a balance between modernity and continuity; or, at least, is confronted with the problem in a very different way.

Herein lies the flaw in the ethnosymbolic model. In practice, relationships between particular nations and any definable ethnic heritage are complex and varied; from those such as Germany or Israel normatively represented as being in continuity with a long and continuous cultural tradition, to those such as France where significant segments of the political culture see their nation as representing a radical rupture from said tradition, to those such as the United States and Canada that are explicitly defined as novel and innovative multicultural political projects yet are no less effective at engendering loyalty and social cohesion.

The observation that the terms "nation" and "nationalism" tend to be applied to constructs and ideologies so diverse as to appear to be different phenomena has led to the development of typologies distinguishing different forms of nationalism; the most popular being the distinction between the "civic" and the "ethnic." Indeed, this distinction can be traced to the modern origins of nationalism itself, when political disputes over sovereignty were framed according to different evolving conceptions of legitimacy. In the debate over the appropriate disposition of the territories of Alsace and Lorraine, Ernest Renan held that the voluntary commitment of the populations of these territories to the French state rendered them a legitimate part of France, arguing that the nation amounted to such a voluntary community, a "daily plebiscite" dependent on the continued civic commitment of its members. In response, Friedrich Meinecke argued for a more organic conception of nationality, following the German Romantics in claiming Alsace-Lorraine for Germany on the basis of commonality of culture. This dichotomy was systematized in scholarly studies of nationalism by Hans Kohn, who distinguished a "Western" political form of nationalism from an "Eastern" genealogical–organic one.[29]

---

[29] Zimmer 2003: 175.

However, there has since developed a general consensus among scholars employing such language that no single nation can be said to conform perfectly to either of these ideal types. Rather, every nation represents its own distinct and indeed fluid amalgamation of civic and ethnic elements. As Oliver Zimmer framed it in an influential article, nations are possessed of a body of symbolic resources, which can be selectively deployed as mechanisms for determining the boundaries of national identity in either a voluntaristic or organic manner at various points in time.[30] Thus, scholars with an affinity for ethnosymbolism's emphasis on the importance of ethnic continuity can find solace in the argument that the stability of even the most ostensibly civic of nations depends to some degree on ethnic elements; a dominant ethnicity that is the wellspring of a common civic culture possessed at least of shared language, values, and political principles. And although such nations may be more inclusive than those based around deterministic principles of common descent, mastery of this common culture with its roots in some authentic prenational ethnic tradition nonetheless becomes the litmus test for full national belonging.[31]

But is it indeed the case that a matrix of signifiers authentic to a preexisting ethnic tradition is the basis around which a modern nation forms and is maintained? This notion would appear to be disproven by the fact that authenticity, even when perceived, can often be shown to be fictive even in the case of a nation's most important defining and unifying symbols. There are many cases in which a symbol perceived without question as authentically ancient to a national–ethnic culture was in fact invented or at least resurrected from near-obscurity relatively recently in the course of the nation-building endeavor, and other (though admittedly rarer) instances in which this discontinuity is conscious and explicit, and a central, unifying national symbol is not even perceived as having any long-standing durability at all. This is true for nations from across the various spectra of classification – the lateral and the demotic, the civic and the organic – even those with the richest possible ethnocultural heritage.

This dynamic is particularly noticeable when one is examining symbols of defeat and the mythology of those nations in which such symbols are prominent. In most cases, these symbols can be shown to have been radically elevated, if not invented outright, in the process of nation building, even in situations in which the nation in question maintains a strong

---

[30] Ibid.: 177–81.
[31] An argument to this effect with regard to American national identity is made by Kauffmann 2002.

connection to an ethnic heritage rich with authentic cultural signifiers from which to draw. If Smith is correct, and it is the authenticity of a given symbol to an ethnic community that provides it with the resonance needed to mobilize a national identity, why would a symbol not deeply connected to the ethnic tradition be perceived as having such a connection specifically as a consequence of the nation-building process?

Symbols of Defeat: Authenticity and Modernity

A brief examination of the symbols of defeat that will be analyzed further in this work reveals that they conform more closely to Hobsbawm's notion of "invented tradition" than to ethnosymbolism's stress on the importance of ethnic continuity. Yet many are drawn from the mythologies of national traditions that conform to the ethnosymbolic model in most other respects. Zionism sought to develop a Jewish national identity out of a clearly defined ethnoreligious group with a long and continuous history full of powerful symbols and narratives suitable to almost any occasion. The only benefit the symbol of Masada had in its favor was the fact that it was a documented event in that history, recorded in the works of Josephus as the final battle fought by the Romans against the Judean revolt of 66–73 C.E. As a result, it was, for some time, tacitly assumed within the national tradition that this event had always held a central place in the Jewish construction of history, a notion famously expressed by Yigal Yadin, Israeli statesman and the archaeologist most associated with excavating the site, in a speech at Masada to new recruits of the Israeli Defence Forces Armoured Divisions when he stated that the sacrifice made by the Zealots "elevated Masada to an undying symbol which has stirred hearts throughout the last nineteen centuries."[32]

In fact, Masada goes virtually unnoticed in the source texts of Jewish tradition between the time of Josephus and the rise of Zionism at the turn of the 20th century. There is no mention of it in the Talmud, a text that often relates historical events in great detail, and it is mentioned only once in any other Jewish source: a medieval Hebrew literary text called the Book of Jossipon, essentially an overhauled Josephus presenting a less hostile account of Second Temple period Judaism than is evident in the original. This demonstrates that, although Masada was an authentic event in the Jewish past, it was virtually irrelevant to the Jewish construction of history and identity prior to the advent of Zionism. Medieval Jewish

[32] Quoted in Zerubavel 1995: 227; Alter 1973: 21–2.

scholars had access to Josephus; therefore, the events of Masada were not alien to them. It was simply not considered a significant episode; therefore, the story did not develop in Jewish collective memory until its entry into the Zionist construction of history.[33] Traditional Judaism focused more on the descent of the Jewish people from Abraham as a common ancestor, substantiating connection to the territory by means of the story of his migration from Ur to Canaan at God's command. The key foundation myth of the Jewish tradition, providing a notion of special dignity and divine election, was the memory of liberation from slavery, promulgation of divine law, and return to the land under Moses, leading directly to the "heroic age" that culminated in the reigns of David and Solomon.[34] These transitions were of far greater importance to the Jewish tradition than the transition from antiquity to exile marked by the Roman defeat of the Judean revolt. But even this latter transition was commemorated within traditional Judaism by means of very different symbols, with the end of Jewish independence marked not by the fall of Masada but by the destruction of the Second Temple, and the transition to Exile symbolized by the departure from Jerusalem of Rabbi Yohanan ben Zakkai and the founding of the religious academy at Yavneh, an event described in five different versions by the Talmud, which enabled the survival of Judaism as a religion through the years of diaspora.[35]

The first recorded mention of the Masada story as a unique case of Jewish heroism occurred during the debates between Mikha Berdyczewski and Ahad Ha'am in the early 1920s. Subsequent developments, from the first Hebrew translation of Josephus in 1923 to the publication of Yitzchak Lamdan's poem "Masada" in 1927, helped to transform this footnote in Jewish ethnohistory into a quasi-sacred image central to the civil religion.[36] Lamdan's poem, in particular, which employed the image of ascending Masada as an allegory for the Zionist project and included the iconic line "Never again shall Masada fall,"[37] was quickly adopted as a kind of secular liturgy, incorporated alongside the relevant sections of Josephus into ritual pilgrimages, first by Zionist youth movements during the pre-state period and then by elite military units who were regularly sworn in at the site.[38]

---

[33] Zerubavel 1995: 62; Ben-Yehuda 1995: 213.
[34] Smith 1999: 80.
[35] Shargel 1979: 359.
[36] Ben-Yehuda 1995: 288; 2002: 18, 48; Liebman and Don-Yehiya 1983: 41–3.
[37] Lamdan 1971: 215.
[38] Zerubavel 1995: 62, 116.

Yael Zerubavel has proposed that Masada was adopted as a counter-narrative suitable to the very different construction of history necessary to Zionist political goals. Zionism defined itself openly as a break from Jewish tradition, which was seen as having developed a culture of passivity in response to the conditions of exile. However, it nonetheless relied on this tradition for the symbolic framework that served to legitimate its claims, whether for territory, for the right to self-determination as a genuine ethnic community, or the right to speak in the name of the Jews and Jewish interests. It could not reject traditional Jewish symbols and their framework outright because it relied on the legitimating framework they provided and therefore had to make use of its resources in constructing its conception of history. But at the same time, it had to use these resources in a radically different manner than had the prenational ethnoreligious community in order to accentuate innovation. The success of Zionism, then, depended on its ability to apply a plausible new interpretation to an existing corpus of cultural and historical memory in order to harness the existing religious framework toward new secular ends.[39]

According to its secular nationalist outlook, issues of adherence to divine law were less important than was the question of the people's presence in and sovereignty over the land. Hence, the national past was divided into eras according to the level of sovereignty enjoyed, as understood in nationalist terms. The Zionist construction of history divided Jewish history into two broad periods – Antiquity and Exile – with the Zionist enterprise representing the onset of a third period, that of national regeneration. It was a point of agreement among the early Zionists that Exile was a period of lack, a uniformly dark time of suffering and persecution in contrast to the era of national fulfillment characterized by Antiquity.[40] This notion of a division between independence and Exile, marked by the end of the Second Temple period, already existed within the traditional Jewish framework; but to Zionism it was the central, if not the only, division of significance. It is for this reason that most of the images that made up Zionism's conception of the "heroic age" came from this period rather than from the Davidic monarchy that was the basis of this myth for traditional Judaism. With history broadly divided between Antiquity and Exile, it was natural for the Zionist historical narrative to take the last period that fell under the category of Antiquity, prior to the

---

[39] Ibid.: 25.
[40] Zerubavel discusses the basic construction of Zionist history in 1995: 31–2.

vast emptiness that characterized its perception of Exile, as the basis to
establish continuity.

The Second Commonwealth was the last period during which the Jews
had a temple, a political as well as religious center, and in which a major
revolt for political and territorial sovereignty took place. It contained
such figures as the Maccabees and Bar Kokhba, depicted as willing to fight
and die for national freedom even against impossible odds, unlike biblical
figures who lived with the certainty that God was on their side. This was a
significant point of contention between Zionism and traditional Judaism.
Reliance on God as savior stood in conflict to the value of national
self-determination. In traditional Judaism, God is the ultimate source
of authority; but to a national ideology, the ultimate font of authority
must be the cultural collectivity. The Second Temple period was the
last period in recorded Jewish history that offered models of national
mobilization in and for the land, as well as images of institutions that
represented national renewal.[41] With this moment of transition between
Antiquity and Exile so pivotal to the Zionist construction of history, it
became necessary to mark it with a historical moment that would enable
reinforcement through commemoration. Existing religious imagery was
inadequate to the needs of Zionist ideology. Yohanan ben Zakkai, in
particular, represented an unacceptable willingness to relinquish political
authority in the name of religious heritage. Consequently, a countermyth
was required. It had to come from the existing cultural matrix of Jewish
history, yet challenge the traditional paradigm. This was the role played
by the story of Masada.

The ethnosymbolic paradigm might find support in the claim that
it was precisely the inauthenticity of Masada to the preexisting Jewish
ethnic tradition that caused its role as a unifying symbol to ultimately be
usurped by a more authentic one: the Western Wall. And although this
may hold some truth in the sense that the latter symbol had genuine ties
to the existing religious tradition as well as to the ethnic history, in that
case, too, historical authenticity was largely fictive, and the perception of
such authenticity rose in direct conjunction with the Zionist movement.
As with Masada, the notion that this monument represented a symbol
of continuous significance to the Jewish ethnoreligious tradition from the
moment of exile up to the present day was tacitly and almost universally
accepted. This narrative is expressed, for example, in a chapter written
by a rabbi for a book on the Western Wall published by the Israeli

---

[41] Zerubavel 1995: 23; Liebman and Don-Yehiya 1983: 15–6.

Ministry of Defence, in which the source of the monument's sanctity is identified in part as stemming from the fact that "for more than one thousand five hundred years, Jews in all generations have watered the courses of the Wall with their tears and melted its stones with their kisses."[42] In fact, Judaism has traditionally shied away from cults of holy objects or places. External and tangible religious symbolism, though present in Jewish tradition, tended to be deemphasized further to the second commandment prohibition against idolatry. As with Masada, the site of the Western Wall has no formal standing in Torah or rabbinic law, and no reference to it appears in the source texts of Jewish tradition.[43]

The first documented use of this particular site as a place of prayer does not appear until the 15th century and was apparently due more to its convenient location as the closest approach to the Temple Mount from within the Jewish Quarter than to any inherent sanctity attributed to the site itself. However, a local folk tradition in relation to the site began to develop from this time onward. Jewish mysticism contributed the notion that the indestructible Divine Presence, the *shekhinah*, which was said to have once resided in the Temple, had relocated to the Western Wall after the Temple's destruction. As a result, stories began to proliferate of the Wall having miraculous properties or serving as a unique focal point for divine intercession in a manner highly unusual to normative Jewish ritual. This led to the practice of placing prayers and petitions in the form of letters between the stones, a custom maintained to this day. Thus, by about the 17th century, the Western Wall had at least become a part of the folklore and ritual of the local Jewish community of Jerusalem. But at this point, the symbol had only a limited appeal outside of the immediate environs of that community. Identification with it was never a defining element of Jewish identity. Indeed, medieval Hebrew art tended to depict Jerusalem and the Temple most often through images of the Dome of the Rock, until about the middle of the 18th century, when the first images of the Western Wall began to appear as pictorial symbols of the Temple.[44]

---

[42] Ha'Cohen 1983: 81–3.

[43] Although traditional scholars have tried to find hints of it in earlier writings, the closest we find are vague Talmudic references to a "Western Wall" as a prominent feature of the ruins at which Jews were permitted to mourn once a year during the period of Byzantine rule over Jerusalem. It is, however, more likely that these referred to a fragment of the Temple itself, though many of the legends relating to these ruins came later to be attributed to the western retaining wall sanctified today (see Noy 1983: 106, and Peters 1986: 127–8).

[44] Vilnay 1973: 20; Noy 1983: 108.

Whatever sanctity was afforded the Western Wall stemmed from its status as a fragment of the Temple that was itself the holy object rather than from its status in its own right as a symbol of the Temple's destruction.

The meaning of this symbol, however, would be altered radically through contact with the ideology of nationalism. This conceptual shift paralleled concern on the part of Jews to assert sovereignty over the site. In the 1860s, Sir Moses Montefiore made efforts to purchase or otherwise establish Jewish rights over the site as part of his efforts to advocate on behalf of Jews in the declining Ottoman Empire. As Christian communities within the Empire were asserting themselves through the patronage of foreign governments, there was a fear that the Jewish community would be left unprotected, and Montefiore sought to provide them with a patron to counteract this impression. A significant aspect of the patronage extended to Christian communities by foreign governments involved the protection of holy places, and it helped for Montefiore to have a Jewish holy place to sponsor as a concrete representation of his patronage.

The association of this site with notions of sovereignty evolved further as Ottoman passed on to British rule, and it became a flash point of conflict with Zionism's national "other." When Jews tried to introduce new elements into worship at the Wall, such as bringing candles, benches, and dividers to separate men and women as required by tradition, each innovation, however seemingly trivial, was opposed by Arab nationalists, with skirmishes turning political and sometimes even violent as they were interpreted as precedents that could lead to assertions of autonomy over the Temple Mount itself. As a result, and due as well to their association with the practices of a sovereign Jewish state in antiquity, religious rituals performed at the Wall were reinterpreted by Zionist youth movements as national or even military rites.[45] After the War of Independence in 1948, the Wall came under Jordanian sovereignty, along with the whole of Jerusalem's Old City; and though the armistice agreement of 1949 stipulated free access to all holy sites on both sides of the border, the ongoing state of hostilities prevented Israeli Jews from gaining access to it. There were several points from the Israeli side of the city where one could look at the area of the Old City in which the Wall was located, even if the Wall itself could not be seen. This served only to augment its appeal as a symbol. The desolation of the Wall and the implied violation of the ceasefire terms by Jordan were added to the narrative surrounding

---

[45] Friedland and Hecht 1991: 31–3; Liebman and Don-Yehiya 1983: 78–9; Wasserstein 2001: 326–7; Aner 1983: 132.

the site. And once it was captured by Israel in 1967, it became a powerful symbol of the reunification of Jerusalem, representing both the perceived injustice of the divided city and the euphoria of victory in the Six Day War.[46] It is only then, or at least over these decades, that the Wall could be said to have evolved into a symbolic focal point for the whole of the Jewish people.

Zerubavel identifies this need to break from tradition as unique to Zionism, in contrast to most national movements of the 19th century that relied on a sense of continuity with the existing ethnocultural community. In fact, it can be shown that, on the contrary, a significant number of other 19th-century nationalisms conform just as well to this pattern in representing a radical departure from previous norms aimed at filling a long-standing lack in the community. Kosovo, likewise, may have been an authentic event in the history of the Serbian ethnic community, but the advent of nationalism elevated it to a status it had never previously enjoyed. Just as Abraham and Moses, David and Solomon had been more important symbols to traditional Jewish history, prenational Serbian ethnic identity was based more on the figures of Stefan Nemanja, who united the Serb tribes establishing the Nemanjić dynasty, along with his brother Rastko, "Saint Sava," who founded the distinct religious tradition in the form of the Serbian Orthodox Church. The Serbian heroic age was represented by David-like conqueror Milutin and the Solomon-like lawgiver Stefan Dušan, who ruled the Serbian kingdom at the height of its power.[47]

Kosovo may already have been understood as the moment when this golden age was destroyed, and commemorated as such to some degree; but its elevation to the focal point of the Serbian construction of history can be traced directly to the events associated with the development of modern Serbian nationalism. Karadjordjević invoked the image of Kosovo during the Serbian uprising of 1804, for example, in a speech to insurgents in which he called on them to "throw off, in the name of God, the yoke which the Serbs carry from Kosovo to this day," comparing his commanders to the hero Miloš Obilić.[48] When Vuk Karadžić compiled and published his collections of Serbian folk poetry during the subsequent period of Serbian uprisings against the Ottomans, choosing the most authentic versions of particular songs as well as determining the priority

---

[46] Liebman and Don-Yehiya 1983: 151.
[47] Background on the basic elements of the Serbian national myth is taken from Velikonja 1998: 21–2 and Mojzes 1994: 16–8.
[48] Djordjevic 1991: 313.

in which they should be placed, the Battle of Kosovo emerged as the focal point of this epic landscape. Stories about the preceding feudal period, reflecting both the greatness and corruption of the medieval Serbian state, are seen in terms of the approaching disaster, and the events that follow tell of its results, or of efforts to ameliorate the results.[49] But it was Prince Bishop Petar Petrović Njegoš, ruler of Montenegro during the second quarter of the 19th century, who would transform the Kosovo legend into a battle cry for national liberation, primarily through his epic poem *Gorski Vijenac*, "The Mountain Wreath" (1847). Vidovdan developed into a national day of commemoration only in the late 19th century, officially adopted as such in 1903. Prior to that time, it had been observed mainly by the monastery of Ravanica as the day on which its saintly founder died.[50]

Similar examples of the invention, or at least convenient rediscovery, of tradition further to generating a constructed authenticity can be found in other nations that came to elevate images of defeat during formative periods of nation building. Joan of Arc may have always existed as a distinct figure in French history and collective memory, but her development into a national symbol of universal appeal (if contested meaning) can be seen as having evolved and matured alongside the concept of the nation itself. She was a popular figure in her day and hence left traces in contemporary writings and was continuously commemorated as a figure of local importance in Domrémy, her place of birth; in Orléans, the location of her greatest triumph; and, to a much lesser degree, in Rouen, where she was martyred. Although this served to generate a body of materials for the later production of the myth, as well as a plausible narrative of continuous commemoration, beyond these locales she was largely forgotten between the 16th and 18th centuries, an age that viewed the medieval period as a time of barbarism, preferring instead to identify with the ancients. The notion that she had heard divine voices was scoffed at by the *philosophes*, an attitude expressed in Voltaire's farcical *La Pucelle*.[51] Although Voltaire made ample use of her story for rhetorical purposes, he had little symbolic interest in *la pauvre idiote*, who had allowed herself to be used and then destroyed by absolutist ruling powers.

Still, Voltaire's work sparked renewed interest in the scholarly study of Joan of Arc, and the first histories of her life appeared subsequently, the

[49] Koljević 1991: 124–5; Djordjevic 1991: 311; Bakić-Hayden 2004: 28–31.
[50] Emmert 1990: 81.
[51] Winock 1998: 437, 443–9.

myth being thereby authenticated through an intellectually acceptable scientific historiography. Efforts to present Joan as a national symbol could be said to have begun during the Revolution, when she was often depicted as a historical precursor to the allegorical Marianne. But these were rarely more than half-hearted, as revolutionaries had little interest in a figure whose primary achievement was defense of monarchy out of loyalty to the Church. During the first *défense nationale*, there was even a debate as to whether to melt down the Joan of Arc statue at Orléans to make cannons, with the faction in favor arguing that Joan had been an arch-royalist, and opponents identifying it as a memorial to one who had defended the nation against an external enemy.[52] At the same time, the absolutist monarchy had no interest in perpetuating the notion that it owed its existence and survival to a heroine of "the people," nor did the Church wish to elevate a figure it had burned as a heretic.

The revolutionary–republican interpretation and appropriation of Joan of Arc came about only a generation after the Revolution, with the romantic–liberal historiography of the 1830s and 1840s, at which time the weak-willed tool and victim of Crown and Church became Jules Michelet's *fille du peuple*, and it was only in the aftermath of the French defeat to Germany in 1870–1871 that she developed into a figure contested by all elements of French political culture. It was during this same period that the *Song of Roland* came to prominence as well. Before the first translation of this epic text into modern French in 1870, few scholars even knew of its existence but, at that point, as one historian notes, it "was transformed within a few years from a minor part of the collective unconscious to a national myth."[53]

The place of the fall of Constantinople in the subsequent history of Greek cultural myth and memory is equally complex. Although the Church, as the only distinctly Greek political institution under Ottoman rule and custodian of collective memory, marked it as a significant historical moment signifying the fall of the Byzantine Empire, records contemporary to the period of Ottoman rule indicate that the resulting subjugation of Orthodox Christians to the Ottomans was taken to be God's will. The divine verdict rendered the Ottomans rightful rulers, with more animosity directed toward the Catholic Latins than the Muslim Turks, and the fall of Constantinople depicted as serving, on the one hand, as divine

---

[52] Schivelbusch 2003: 139–40; the compromise eventually struck was that the statue was melted down, but the cannon forged from the iron was named *Pucelle d'Orleans*.

[53] Christian Amalvi, quoted in Schivelbusch 2003: 142, see note 83.

punishment and on the other as divine intervention, delivering the faithful from the specter of union with the Catholic West, thus preserving their autonomy on a spiritual level.[54]

Early manifestations of Greek nationalism among the intellectuals of the 18th and early 19th centuries tended to claim continuity with the ancient Greeks alone, interpreting the Byzantine period as a time of foreign subjugation under Roman rule. According to this narrative, the moment of defeat that marked the rupture of Greek sovereignty was the Battle of Chaeronea in 338 B.C.E., after which the Greeks were ruled by a succession of conquerors, starting with the Macedonians and ending with the Turks, which included the Byzantines.[55] Although laments to the fall of Constantinople may nonetheless have persisted in popular culture, their relative lack of prominence was such that folklorists as late as the mid-18th century were unacquainted with them, with some even commenting that this event was hardly commemorated.[56] This would change radically by the end of the 19th century, and the rise of the "Great Idea," when folklorists – N.G. Politis the most prominent among them – would identify laments for the fall of Constantinople, the *Song of Hagia Sophia* in particular, as ubiquitous if not defining elements of Greek culture throughout the subsequent period of domination. It is only during this time that it became a popular literary motif as well.

While it may well be that a kind of protonational sentiment was at least partially evident in the motivations driving the Hussite Wars (1420–1434) and the revolt of the Bohemian Estates (1618–1620), the counter-reformation that followed the defeat of the latter at White Mountain was successful in suppressing and eradicating any assertive manifestation of Czech ethnic identity and comfortably incorporating the elites of the provinces of Bohemia and Moravia into the establishment of the Habsburg Empire. A Czech high culture was essentially nonexistent in the intervening centuries during which Czech was mainly a peasant dialect, and heroic figures more suitable to the Catholic and Habsburg reality were grafted onto Czech culture. As Derek Sayer puts it, "had there been no medieval Bohemian state, there might very possibly have been no modern Czech nation either. But this modern nation is not so much rooted in that medieval experience as retrospectively reconstructed out of it. *Bílá hora* fractured Czech history and identity; the links to the

---

[54] Anagnostopolou 2002: 83–4.
[55] Politis 1998: 1.
[56] Herzfeld 1982: 57.

past were severed."[57] The elevation of Jan Hus and the Battle of White Mountain to the center of the national construction of history was a prod-uct of the 19th-century National Revival, further to what Sayer describes as "the (re)invention of the 'imagined political community' of the modern nation."[58] Although it was the figure of Hus who took on the status of the Czech nation's most iconic martyr-hero, the White Mountain myth was a crucial corollary, substantiating the connection between the modern national movement and this earlier era of which Hus and St. Wenceslas had been a part. This enabled a sense of common identity between these figures and a later national movement operating under very different cir-cumstances and with a very different agenda, with the intervening time recast in national memory as "300 years of darkness."

A similar dynamic is evident in the elevation of the fall of Barcelona to the center of Catalan national memory, an even more recent inno-vation masking the relatively successful incorporation of Catalonia into successive Spanish state systems over the intervening centuries. Catalan cultural organization was effectively destroyed after the fall of Barcelona and, when it did reappear in the 1950s and 1960s in resistance to the Franco dictatorship, it had adopted very different social forms in relation to very different political ideologies. The notion of restoring a sense of distinct Catalan political identity developed largely in reaction to Franco's repression of the fledgling Catalan cultural revival, centered on recovery of the language. This made defense of the language into a political act, and language rights became an issue around which national democratic forces could converge.[59]

The first public celebration of the *Diada* in 1964 was also the first postwar Catalanist street demonstration. It thereafter became an annual occurrence, gradually incorporating participation from all social and political segments identified with Catalan national distinctiveness in reac-tion to the Francoist regime, culminating in the *Diada* of 1977, two years after Franco's death. A million people attended this gathering to demand a statute of autonomy for Catalonia. This was at the time hailed as the largest demonstration in postwar Europe. It was certainly the largest dur-ing the process of political transition, as well as the largest in Spain up to that date, causing the annual commemoration of September 11 and the Catalanist movement in general to be inexorably intertwined in popular

[57] Sayer 1998: 52.
[58] Ibid.: 13; see also Pynsent 1994: 201 and Roshwald 2006: 56.
[59] Conversi 1997: 137–9.

imagination with the struggle against dictatorship and the broader movement for democracy and decentralization. Thus, 1977 became as poignant
an element of the myth surrounding this date as 1714, with the two dates
presented in the national construction of history as bookends, bracketing
an aberrant period of national subjugation and quiescence. September 11
was legally declared the national day of Catalonia in 1980 as the first
public act of the restored Generalitat of Catalonia.[60]

Even in the case of the Yaa Asantewaa War, an event as recent as
the turn of the 20th century, it took the developments that led to the
incorporation of Asante into a modern Ghanaian national framework
before this memory, and the iconic figure of Yaa Asantewaa herself, could
be transformed into objects of commemoration. For much of the previous
century, little attention was paid to her. It is even reported that during
the early decades of colonial rule, derisive songs were sung about her,
emphasizing how she lost the war and fled.[61] The process of independence
and the liberation struggles of the 1960s saw her narrative rehabilitated
as that of an anti-colonial defender to some extent. But it wasn't until
the 1980s and 1990s that her symbolism evidenced widespread appeal,
in the context of reasonably successful efforts to transcend ethnic politics
and unify the state under a stable regime.[62]

These examples are consistent with the transition from a premodern
to a modern conception of identity. Previously, if a war was lost or a
rebellion put down, leading to the dissolution of a state, that was the
end of it. A group might continue to defend its religious or local autonomy against the assimilating or centralizing tendencies of the new political center, but the idea that a polity can persevere in spirit so long as its
members maintain faith in common cultural signifiers identified as distinct to it requires a uniquely modern, national sentiment. In this register,
defeat, if anything, is retrospectively perceived as strengthening the eternal nation by galvanizing its members to greater struggle in the interests
of resurrecting the state.

This does not entirely compromise the explanatory value of the ethnosymbolic model, insofar as this model recognizes that the nation is, in sum,
a modern construct, even if the discursive components from which it is
constructed are constrained to some degree by the demands of the existing
ethnic tradition. However, if these cases do indeed demonstrate that in

[60] Ibid.: 122, 142; Guibernau 2004: 63; Rovira 2006.
[61] Day 2000: 153.
[62] Brown 2000: 119–24.

many instances even the most pivotal and unifying myths of a nation – even those of nations clearly and explicitly associated with authentic premodern *ethnies* rich with an existing matrix of cultural myths and symbols – turn out in fact to be modern fabrications, this would at least call into question the conclusion that the link between modern nations and premodern *ethnies* lies in the realm of myth. At the very least, it demonstrates that the ethnosymbolic paradigm cannot, in itself, provide an adequate answer to the question of why certain myths or symbols might come to the center of a national mythology over and above others. If authenticity to a genuine and continuous ethnic tradition is not the condition that causes these symbols to be adopted, then what is? And why, for that matter, is a *myth* of authenticity regarding these symbols nonetheless so forcefully asserted and widely accepted? Clearly, the test that a symbol must pass in order to successfully generate mass emotional identification is not authenticity *per se*. Rather, authenticity, whether factual or not, comes to be perceived if the symbol passes another more subtle, hidden test, the precise nature of which we have yet to determine.

On the surface, this evidence would appear to favor a more thorough-going modernism. But I submit that more careful examination will rather reveal the nation to be a more complex and nuanced structure than either of these broad theoretical categories accurately reflect. Indeed, the elevation, reinterpretation, or invention of symbols of defeat in the process of nation building points to the role that these symbols in particular have further to the development of the nation as a construct organizing and rationalizing modern society. But Smith's insight into the conditions that favor certain symbols and therefore certain nations should not be discounted. He is correct in identifying an existing ethnic community with a predefined mythology as an important resource in the construction of the nation. But, in many if not most cases, the value of this resource lies as much in its ability to give the nation something to be *dis*continuous with, to define itself against, as it does in the need for continuity. Thus, we identify the nation as a system of identity burdened with an inherent contradiction.

One would think that the presence of such a contradiction would weaken rather than strengthen the nation as a system of meaning. But if this contradiction mirrored a dilemma inherent to the human condition, the opposite might be true. In which case we could further hypothesize that the success of a national discourse to mobilize its potential population would depend to a large degree on the effectiveness of the mechanisms it uses to resolve this dilemma. As Smith observes, the nation, in order to survive, must succeed on two levels: the sociopolitical and the cultural–psychological.[63] But what if the needs that must be satisfied on one level are opposed to those that must be satisfied on the other? On a cultural level, the nation, in order to provide a satisfying construct of identity, must distinguish insiders from outsiders, and the signifiers that reinforce such cultural distinctions are necessarily derived from the nation's perceived ethnic heritage. But ethnic distinctiveness is different from national distinctiveness. As modernists such as Gellner observe, in order to give ethnicity relevance in the modern world, the signifiers that determine ethnic communities must shift in the process of nation formation to account for modern institutions and instrumentalities. There is, therefore, a complex dialectic between preservation and invention in that process. The nation must be both preserved and invented insofar as, broadly speaking, it is the former that satisfies the cultural–psychological and the latter that addresses the sociopolitical.

The need for authenticity, although genuine, is only one side of the process of building a nation from an ethnic heritage. There also needs to be a perception of innovation, if not a radical inauthenticity. Hence, the word that best describes a nation's attitude and relationship to its ethnic heritage is *ambivalence*, and that carries us into an entirely different theoretical register.

The Nation as a Surrogate Religion

To complete our explanation, then, we must look beyond the political character of nationalism as an ideology defending the idea that nation and state should be congruent and examine the capacity of the nation to provide meaning and identity to the individuals that compose it. Benedict Anderson touches on this question in the course of his analysis of the nation as an "imagined" community, by which is meant that communion is perceived even though members will never know, meet, or even hear of most of their fellow-members.[64] This notion of imagined community places Anderson, to some extent, in another category of nationalism theorists, broadly labeled "postmodernist," concerned less with the question of when nations began so much as how and why they are continuously reproduced. Nationalism is approached as a discursive formation; a "way of speaking that shapes our consciousness,"[65] and a particular

[63] Smith 1991: 69–70.
[64] Anderson 1991: 6.
[65] Calhoun 1997: 3.

conceptual framework with a characteristic set of features that serves to shape an ideal–typical mode of collective identity and social solidarity. As such, it should not be reduced to a political ideology or doctrine but rather amounts to "a more basic way of talking, thinking and acting."[66] Eric Kauffmann has represented it metaphorically as an interpretive lens that colors and filters a body of otherwise diverse and unrelated referents into potential symbolic resources forming a coherent identity construct.[67] Michael Billig's notion of "banal nationalism" fits into this framework as well. Billig saw it as a mistake to equate nationalism with the sentiments and ideologies asserted aggressively in times of crisis. Rather, it is to be found in the routine language and symbols that serve as constant background reminders of national identity, establishing the boundaries and framework that render nationalism available and salient as a mobilizing force when crisis occurs. What matters is less the "flag which is being consciously waved with fervent passion: it is the flag hanging unnoticed on the public building."[68]

Anderson concurs with the perspective that "nationalism has to be understood by aligning it, not with self-consciously held political ideologies, but with the large cultural systems that preceded it, out of which – as well as against which – it came into being."[69] It should therefore not be placed in the same category as, for example, fascism or communism but rather viewed as a discrete category of human experience comparable to religion. However, he is careful to stress that the focus in his work on the imagined nature of national community should not be taken to suggest fabrication or falsity. Indeed, all communities larger than primordial villages are in the same sense "imagined." The originality of Anderson's thesis therefore lies not in the observation that the nation is an imagined community but rather in what sort of imagined community it is and what makes such imagining possible. The nation is a particular sort of community imagined as both limited and sovereign, and such an imagined construct becomes possible only in the context of modernity. "The nation is imagined as *limited* because even the largest of them . . . has finite, if elastic, boundaries, beyond which lie other nations. . . . It is imagined as *sovereign* because the concept was born in an age in which Enlightenment and Revolution were destroying the legitimacy of the divinely-ordained, hierarchical dynastic realm."[70]

[66] Ibid.: 11.
[67] Kauffmann 2008: 450–3.
[68] Billig 1995: 6–8.
[69] Anderson 1991: 12.
[70] Ibid.: 7 (emphasis in original).

Traditionally, religion has been the discourse concerned with the role of the self in the universe, answering ultimate issues not addressed by political ideologies. According to Anderson, this meant providing explanation and comfort in the face of suffering and especially death, incorporating human fatality and finiteness into a larger meaning-system of continuity and immortality. The 18th century marked a period in Europe when traditional religious thought was in decline, a process Anderson sees as having been influenced by extensive contact with other religions and the consequent relativization of religious traditions with hitherto universal meaning systems into territorial space. However, because the decline of religious belief did not bring with it a decline in the suffering that belief was meant to rationalize, a new meaning system was needed to provide a sense of continuity and make fatality seem less arbitrary, and it had to be one that could account for evident territorial divisions. According to Anderson, then, it was key to the success of nationalism as an alternative to traditional religion that it offered a sense of continuity to a community presented as limited, one that did not and was not intended to encompass all of humankind: "The most messianic nationalists do not dream of a day when all members of the human race will join their nation in the way that it was possible, in certain epochs, for, say, Christians to dream of a wholly Christian planet."[71] There were insiders and outsiders, and the presence and permanence of such boundaries was a necessary defining element to the national idea.

Of particular note in Anderson's model of nationalism is the manner in which the ideology stresses the sense of community as a value. "Regardless of the actual inequality and exploitation that may prevail in each, the nation is always conceived as a deep horizontal comradeship. Ultimately it is this fraternity that makes it possible, over the past two centuries, for so many millions of people, not so much to kill, as willingly to die for such limited imaginings."[72] For it is through this sense of being part of something greater than oneself that the nation provides a sense of continuity, placing personal sacrifice and suffering in the context of a higher principle. It is in the interest of "transforming fatality into continuity" that nations have been conceived as coming out of an immemorial past and promising a limitless future. The unusual preoccupation nationalist imagery seems to have with death is taken by Anderson as proof of this argument, demonstrated by the ubiquitous Tomb of the Unknown

[71] Ibid.
[72] Ibid.

Soldier, a distinctly national sort of shrine, glorifying and commemorating the sacrifices of a fellow group member distinguished by his very anonymity. In highlighting that nationalism is more than just a political ideology, Anderson points to the absurdity of the idea of a Tomb of the Unknown Marxist or a cenotaph to fallen liberals.[73]

But Anderson was not the only one to observe the capacity of the nation to function in a similar manner to religion, or even to theorize that the nation might serve the function left vacant by the decline of traditional religion in the modern secular world. Gellner already recognized the affinity between the nation and an explicitly Durkheimian conception of religion, particularly with regard to the symbolic resources nationalism uses to substantiate its discourse: "Durkheim taught that in religious worship society adores its own camouflaged image. In a nationalist age, societies worship themselves brazenly and openly, spurning the camouflage." He stressed, however, that this spurning of camouflage does not render the discourse of nationalism any less illusory in the final analysis than that of religion, with the presumed folk culture worshipped by the former being as much a construction assembled to suit the needs of the society as is the divine order worshipped by traditional religion. "A sociological self-deception, a vision of reality through a prism of illusion, still persists, but it is not the same as that which was analysed by Durkheim. Society no longer worships itself through religious symbols; a modern, streamlined, on-wheels high culture celebrates itself in song and dance, which it borrows (stylising it in the process) from a folk culture which it fondly believes itself to be perpetuating, defending, and reaffirming."[74]

Anthony Smith, as well, notes the capacity for the nation to take up the role left vacant by traditional religion and, like Anderson, identifies this role as being primarily to provide meaning in the face of mortality: "Perhaps the most important of its functions is to provide a satisfying answer to the problem of personal oblivion. Identification with the 'nation' in a secular era is the surest way to surmount the finality of death and ensure a measure of personal immortality."[75] He goes on to identify the nation's unique capacity in this regard as stemming from its claim to a distant past that, in turn, suggests a permanence promising a comparably glorious future to be realized by succeeding generations.

[73] Anderson 1991: 9–10.
[74] Gellner 1983: 56–8.
[75] Smith 1991: 160–1.

This insight provides yet another explanation for the importance of symbols of defeat in a national mythology, for an emphasis on the periods of hardship and victimization that the nation has endured places greater focus on that nation's durability or even immortality than does emphasis on periods of ascendance. But while Anderson, Gellner, and Smith all recognize the nation's unique ability to serve in this capacity, it remains to be explored exactly how and why the nation, as opposed to any other manner of identity, is uniquely suited to take on these characteristics and play this role. If, as they appear to acknowledge, many of the signifiers substantiating the nation's distant past must be reconstructed or even fabricated, then why couldn't any other construct (such as an ideology, party, or class) engage in such imagination or fabrication with comparable success, to portray itself as ancient and immemorial, horizontal and territorially limited?

Anderson locates the rise of the nation in the decline of Latin as the universal language of the intelligentsia in favor of the rise of local vernaculars resulting in the development of linguistic/literary territorial divisions. Although acknowledging the common attention paid to death by both religion and nationalism, he does not follow through on this thought and examine whether this very characteristic is what enabled the nation to fill the needs satisfied by traditional religion once the linguistic–literary developments effecting the latter's decline were at play. Smith suggests that the notion of kinship gives the nation better prospects than other identity signifiers, reinforcing the sense of participation in an immortal project through the idea that past, present, and future generations are related ancestrally if not genetically, and not just ideologically or spiritually. But does this apply to more civic-oriented nations, in which national bonds can be no less strong, yet in which any concept of blood kinship that might be expressed is consciously fictive and metaphorical?[76] I would argue that Smith addresses the issue more directly when, elaborating on the conceptual importance of these blood ties, he touches on the centrality of sacrifice to this notion:

The chief reason why the symbolic and ritual aspects of nationalism impinge so directly on the sense of individual identity today lies in its revival of ethnic ties and ethnic identification, and especially its commemoration of 'the forefathers' and

---

[76] For example, the use of the term "Founding Fathers" to describe figures pivotal to the inception of the United States may be suggestive of the conceptual importance of purported kinship ties, but no construction of American national identity takes this language as anything other than figurative (see Roshwald 2006: 271).

the fallen in each generation of the community. In this nationalism resembles those religious faiths that, like Shintoism, set great store in communion with the dead and worship of ancestors. Like those religions, nations and their remembrance ceremonies bring together all those families that have lost kinsmen in war and other national disasters, and all who look back to common forefathers, so as to draw from their example that strength of purpose and spirit of self-sacrifice that will inspire in them a similar heroism.[77]

But can we really say that this aspect of the nation is merely "symbolic and ritual"? If so, then why is the nation able to harness such symbols and rituals in a way that other forms of identity cannot? Why *isn't* there a Tomb of the Unknown Marxist or a cenotaph to fallen liberals, and why do we find such notions absurd whereas they are perfectly natural in the national framework?

It is not these symbols and rituals themselves that enable nationalism to serve a religious function. Rather, they are mere expressions and reflections of something basic to the construct of the nation that gives it a unique capacity to serve in modern industrial society the purpose that religion served in the premodern agrarian one. But before we can substantiate this claim, we must go back to first-principles to better establish just what that purpose entails.

[77] Smith 1991: 162–3.

2

Totem Sacrifice and National Identity

Anthony Smith has proposed that the key quality vital to the adoption of a given symbol or set of symbols as part of a national identity is that symbol's authentic resonance to a preexisting and enduring ethnic community. This explanation must not be taken lightly, if only because it is the explanation by which nationalist ideology itself most often justifies its use of symbols and is therefore indicative of both the ideal vision of the nation and the expectations of the mobilized population. At the same time, however, numerous cases have been seen in which the authenticity of symbols central to a national identity, though perceived, is clearly fictive, and an image presented and accepted as an enduring symbol of the community has, in fact, been invented or elevated through the nation-building process. Thus, although authenticity may significantly improve the capacity of a symbol to be adopted by a national ideology, clearly it is neither a sufficient nor necessary condition; and although the perception of authenticity may be a vital component to a symbol's widespread acceptance, that perception is dependent on something other than fact.

So while I would concur with Smith as to the importance of the perception of authenticity to the acceptance of a given symbol, as well as with his rejection of Gellner's conclusion that in the construction of a national mythology from ethnic–symbolic components "any shard or patch would serve as well," the question of the source of this perception of authenticity – of why it can or would be invented for certain symbols and not for others; of why one "shard or patch" might prove better than another – remains unanswered. Indeed, the fact that symbols of defeat, in particular, are frequently attributed with an invented authenticity in the process of nation building would suggest that this category of symbol has particular relevance toward understanding the change in meaning systems that accompanied and effected the rise of the nation. Something about these symbols makes them easy to accept as authentic national signifiers, and the extraordinary consensus within nations surrounding such symbols, as well as the otherwise inexplicable fanaticism that tends to accompany threats leveled against them, suggests that their purpose is not merely rhetorical but also incorporates a numinous quality demanding a deeper psychological explanation.

This chapter will develop a theoretical model to explain this dynamic. Starting from the hypothesis with which Chapter 1 concluded – that the nation serves the function in the modern world that religion served in premodern times – I will elaborate on what that function necessarily entails: the channeling and control of human violence through the reification and sacralization of social order embodied in the symbol of the "totem." From there, I will explore the importance of myths and rituals of violent sacrifice toward managing that function; and finally propose an explanation as to how symbols of defeat might perform the sacrificial function in a manner particularly suitable to the context of a modern national society. Although the model developed here is largely speculative, it is hoped that subsequent chapters examining the content of myths and rituals surrounding national symbols of defeat will indicate a body of empirical evidence supportive of the hypotheses and the assumptions on which it is based and for which my theory serves as a compelling explanation.

Totem Violence and Social Order

The notion that the function of religion is to effect and enforce reconciliation between individual drives and the constraints of society is best associated with Emile Durkheim, who noted the importance of myth, symbol, and ritual to the successful completion of this function through his examination of the concept of the totem. Starting from the assumption that without the constraints of social order the human individual will be motivated by unlimited desire, he viewed the first imperative of morality and society as the enforcement of discipline. Individuals must consent to limit their desires, to obey imperatives that both fix the objectives they may set themselves and indicate the means they may rightly use to achieve them, and this consent must be reinforced on an ongoing basis. He endeavored to substantiate this view by turning to the clan and the totem as what was deemed to be the earliest and simplest and therefore most elemental forms of human organization and religion.

The clan is a group with a sense of kinship beyond palpable and observable consanguinity; in short, an "imagined community." This identity, because it is not immediately observable, must be expressed and reinforced symbolically, through shared association with a common image, usually a plant or animal. This is the totem, which is the basis on which the universe is divided into the categories of sacred and profane, a division that Durkheim considered the essence of religion. The totem is the symbol of the clan, thereby serving as a means to differentiate the clan from outsiders, asserting the uniqueness of its society and culture. It, in turn, could be expressed symbolically with an emblem that transformed any person or object bearing it, transferring it into the realm of the sacred. Often, a myth would form attributing the clan's physical descent to the totem animal. It became simultaneously the symbol of the god and the flag of the clan, both of which individual members of the society saw as superior to themselves and on which they depended.[1]

Durkheim's insight, in contrast to the prevailing theories of his time, was to conclude that this ritual was not a reflection of mere delusion, nor were the symbols worshipped by primitive peoples personifications of the forces of nature that they sought to appease. Rather, these symbols and rituals were aimed at appeasing a force even more elemental to human existence, yet more difficult to point to and comprehend: the force of society itself, its abstract organization, and the omnipresent threat of its breakdown. Totemism was the clan's worship of its own society, and the quality of sacredness was attributed to that which symbolized the society itself, the group's agreement to be a group and the behaviors necessary to maintain these bonds.

Society demands that we subordinate our internal drives to its apparently external demands and rules of conduct, which are often opposed to our basic biological instincts and inclinations. It therefore requires that we sacrifice and submit to personal inconvenience, implicitly aware that social life would be impossible if we do not. Religion reflects the vague sense all socialized human beings experience that they are a part of something greater and more durable than their own mortal individuality and on which their individuality and sense of meaning depends. Each individual feels compelled to accept a certain code of behavior based on his or her communication with this superior, sacred principle. According

[1] Durkheim 1971: 206; see also Freud 1946: 147.

to Durkheim, then, the purpose of all myths and rites of religion is the same: to reinforce the norms and boundaries that engender the group by giving these fragile abstractions the appearance of objective facts of nature. The key point that must be understood for our purposes is that the sense of danger that religious systems are built to confront is not illusory but palpable and real, and that religious ritual is genuinely effective in neutralizing that danger. The durability and universality of religion as a human phenomenon stands at least as *prima facie* evidence that it could not be predicated solely on "vain fantasy."[2]

Naturally, this position leaves itself open to accusations of functionalist reductionism. Defining a construct strictly according to its function means that any construct that serves the same function must be considered a common phenomenon. According to Durkheim's definition of religion as any system of symbol and ritual that sacralizes the social order, the nation wouldn't just be similar or comparable to religion; it would actually *be* a form of religion. I am not prepared to go so far as to equate the nation with religion, for to do so would be to obscure significant differences between a system that sacralizes society with reference to a divine transcendent and one that does so by other means. Nonetheless, Durkheim's functionalist model remains of particular value to our inquiry because it is strictly the function of religion, not its form, that I argue the nation has taken on in the modern world. Whatever else religion is or does, and whatever other forces might go into shaping a religious tradition, this would not be expected to apply to a construct such as the nation that, even if serving a comparable function, does not do so within the framework of any relationship between the individual and a universal transcendent. Thus, I am prepared to adopt Durkheim's definition of religion, though with the added clarification, important to most other sociological definitions of the concept, that religion is generally distinguished from other discursive constructs (even those that might serve similar functions) as involving recognition of and some manner of communication between juxtaposed immanent and transcendent realms.[3]

But another criticism that could be leveled against Durkheim's model is that it is predicated on the questionable assumptions that clan totemism indeed reflects the simplest and therefore most fundamental form of

---

[2] See Durkheim 1971: 87; also Aron 1967: 35–46.

[3] The immanence/transcendence dichotomy is associated with the work of Niklas Luhmann. Talcott Parsons uses the dichotomy of natural/supernatural in a similar manner; Peter Berger, nomos/cosmos; and Roland Robertson, empirical/super-empirical. See Beyer 1994: 5.

religion, that the simplest forms of religion necessarily attach to the simplest forms of society, and that the conclusions drawn from examination of these simple forms can necessarily be generalized to more complex manifestations of related phenomena.[4] The notion that one can sort religious traditions along such a spectrum presumes a kind of teleological progress from the simplest and most primitive forms of social organization to the more complex and evolved, culminating in our own contemporary societies that bear only traces of these primitive elements as remnants and indicators of our origins. If we are to demonstrate the wider applicability of this insight in the absence of these assumptions, we must first connect this construct to a fundamental element of the human condition and, second, be willing to test for its presence in other forms of religion, and even in other constructs such as the nation not ordinarily labeled as religion but potentially serving an equivalent function.

It is not difficult to hypothesize the evolutionary roots of the religious impulse, defined in such terms. The success of the human species during the period of our existence as hunter–gatherers – a period amounting to 95%–99% of our history, during which our biological evolution was completed – depended on the realization that self-interest in terms of food and protection was best served by traveling and hunting in packs. Society set rules for human pack behavior, and those best suited to accepting those rules – those who, for whatever reason, were more capable of assimilating and adhering to the norms of social order – survived to pass on their genetic material.

Walter Burkert has proposed that the separation between sacred and profane pivotal to the Durkheimian conception of religion began with the need to ritualize and reinforce the institution of the primitive hunting party. This required mechanisms for the rechanneling of violence, such that it was forbidden within the pack and redirected to its exterior. Inhibitions the individual might experience toward inflicting violence had to be overcome for the sake of the hunt, but humans have no braking mechanism for intraspecific aggression. The existence of weapons therefore presented as much of a threat to the community as it did to its prey. Ritual preparation was used to reinforce behavioral codes that maintained a precarious psychological balance, mobilizing the community by elevating aggression while at the same time ensuring this aggression was kept under control according to strict rules that channeled it against the prey while deflecting it from the community. The key to these norms was sharp and

---

[4] Giddens 1986: 103.

uncompromising distinctions, primarily between good killing and bad: what may and may not be killed, eaten, or both; who may authorize violence and when; and rules separating spheres of life in which weapons were or were not permitted. Here we see the first demonstration of the ambivalence that stands at the core of social order: The same activity, violence, had to be portrayed as both good and bad in a manner that would appear arbitrary to the individual without the intervention of ritually reinforced social norms enforcing the distinction. The same act allowed and even praised in one realm would be condemned as murder in another. The communities that best survived and prospered were those best able to develop and reinforce these norms in place of natural instincts.[5]

The point that must be taken from this model is that ritualization of the social order was predicated on the ordering and channeling of violence. The sacred has long been understood as consisting of forces that humans cannot master. The insight we derive from the foregoing analysis is that human violence is primary among these forces; perceived as no less dangerous and palpable, and no less external a threat, than any tempest, flood, or plague, and one that is also no less endemic and unpredictable. It carries with it the threat of the collapse of the society on which the individual depends, not just for identity and meaning but also for survival. Violence therefore stands at the core of any religious system, and this must be recognized if one is to understand how religion serves its function as the legitimating basis of social order.

The distinctions between sacred and profane on which social existence depends are ultimately distinctions between good violence and bad. The basic survival needs of the community depended on its members being able to kill, yet to restrain the impulse to do so indiscriminately, and to appropriately distribute the rewards of the kill evenly to the group rather than claiming them. It was thus that killing and eating ceased to be merely instrumental acts of survival but rather became the focal point around which all patterns of social behavior were coordinated. Social survival and biological survival become intertwined and thus conflated. The prey was no longer merely food to be taken but rather the basis of complex social bonds on which the group relied for survival, causing it to be anthropomorphized into the very emblem of the group. Ritual, therefore, is a solution to a biosocial set of needs requiring adjudication for survival; beginning with need for food, leading to the need for social cooperation, engendering the need to project aggression outward, to the need for a

[5] Burkert 1983: 17–19.

myth–ritual system that enabled this shared projection to function as it should.

The functioning of such a system required the development of a capacity for abstract representational thinking. This is true both on a species-historical level – humans could not become social until our species acquired this ability – and an individual-psychological one – an infant is not fully incorporated into social order until he or she develops this ability. However, the development of abstract representational thinking was and is a fundamentally alienating experience. It is a transition from real, direct experience to experience mediated by available representations; from immediate fulfillment of desires to fulfillment structured and constrained by seemingly arbitrary norms.

The notion that the core of the human personality is formed largely according to how the individual negotiates this transition early in life tends to be associated in the modern world with Freud and his later followers and critics. Although, as Gellner points out in his critique of the psychoanalytic movement, the dualistic notion of the human as characterized by incessant conflict between body and mind, between animal impulses and a higher spiritual nature associated with the maintenance of social or moral order, could be seen as fundamental to Western religion, if not universal to religion itself, as well as being a preoccupation across the spectrum of philosophical thought.[6] What Freud contributed was simply a language useful for modeling this experience in scientific terms. Representing direct experience and immediate gratification of basic desire in the figure of the Mother, the Father, by contrast, represents the figure from whom the norms of social order are imparted and internalized. The child takes the Father as an ideal, wanting to be like him and play his role, yet at the same time recognizes that internalization of this ideal necessitates the acceptance of norms that constrain the full and immediate satisfaction of basic desire, represented by prohibition of the Mother.

René Girard elaborated on this model by detaching it from the assumption that desire for the Mother is an objective fact rather than itself being the product of the socialization process. According to Girard, the primary mechanism by which socialization is effected is imitation. Rather than being intrinsic in the relationship of the individual to the object, desire is in fact dependent on and rooted in the adoption of a model. Desire follows from imitation insofar as it is merely one of the aspects of

---

[6] Gellner 1985: 11–30, 220.

the model that the infant observes and mimics in its effort to discern the rules that will enable it to function as an autonomous personality in the social world. However, by adopting the Father's desires, the son inadvertently places himself in competition with the Father for those objects, creating a disruptive potential for rivalry unacceptable to the Father and ultimately to the son as well. Surprised to find himself engaged in such competition, the Father responds with the child's first experience of violence: the first "no" spoken to the child and backed with the potential of force.

Nothing in the initial impulse to imitate explains or prepares the individual for this equally sweeping contrary command that follows. The son, reaching for the object of his model's desire, is wholly innocent, merely following orders. He does not realize that he can become a competitor to his model any more than a worshipper sees his own desires as being in competition with those of his god. Thus, in the mind of the child who receives constant impulses to imitate his parents, this counterorder represents an act of expulsion, inexplicably forbidding the very imitation that has otherwise been encouraged and thus excommunicating the child from his only apparent font of identity. The infant's devotional and therefore unnuanced initial act of imitation is rewarded with an inexplicable rejection and disgrace that can only be regarded as a terrible condemnation, a judgment of the disciple's inherent unworthiness to imitate the model and participate in the superior level of existence the latter enjoys. This leads to bewilderment and terror, as the individual struggles to discern the rules that determine which command is to be obeyed and when.

Ambivalence, then, stems from the fact that the developing individual is inevitably confronted by two conflicting commands emanating from his models; it is the nexus between the desire or command to imitate the Father as the source of identity and law, and the awareness that the very system of law the Father provides commands that certain things are his sacred prerogative and must not be imitated. Such contradictory signals are thus endemic to the human condition because they are built into the very process of socialization. Humans cannot respond to the innate impulse to imitate without immediately encountering a corresponding counterorder not to imitate and, until order is internalized, these signals will appear contradictory and arbitrary. A normal, socialized mind is one that distinguishes the boundaries between these categories properly, according to the prevailing social order, and a successful social order is one that can facilitate this process by rationalizing this contradiction, thereby channelling and alleviating the confusion and despair it engenders.[7]

One must be careful not to take too literally what is itself a sort of scientific myth, more effective as an explanatory metaphor than a firm hypothesis. To begin with, the Father in this model should not be equated strictly with the individual's actual father. Indeed, the use of the term "Father" may only confuse the issue, as it is a role that in practice is filled by a complex network of influences, from parental figures and role models to the representational images themselves; myths, stories, symbols, and leaders imparted as exemplars of social norms. Adopting this model to the language of the emerging field of semiotics, Lacan found it more appropriate to refer to the "image of the Father," a term we could perhaps neutralize further by referring to the object of identification as the "symbolic ideal,"[8] a signifier representing order, albeit an order palpably different from the natural one the child experiences; an order that institutes society and communal responsibility; in other words, an order of law. Entering the symbolic register necessitates a loss, in the form of a prohibition of the Mother, a property that Lacan expressed in more abstract terms as a primordial "Real" – the impulse to immediate satisfaction of desire, complete fulfillment through direct experience – which is sublimated into representations and symbolizations expressed in a structure of rules and therefore of limits. What the child seeks is not simply, as Freud would have it, unrestrained sensual fulfillment as represented by the Mother but rather full autonomy of action he observes the Father/model enjoying. The Father is not simply father, but King, and

---

[7] Girard 1977: 146–7, 170–9. A salient objection at this stage would be to question whether the model, as described, can be applied evenly to both male and female. So long as we are interpreting terms like "Father" and "Mother" on a metaphorical level – as signifiers representing social order and unrestrained direct experience and fulfillment, respectively – we recognize that these are elemental forces that, broadly speaking, influence the development of male and female alike. Although questions surrounding the differences in the ways these forces have an impact on development depending on gender have spawned a rich body of post-Freudian literature, these nuances are not relevant to the current study.

[8] Stavrakakis 1999: 31–8. In *Group Psychology and the Analysis of the Ego*, Freud (1991) refers to the "ego ideal" a term that would later be transformed in his writings into "superego." I prefer to use different language to stress that I am speaking more of a concrete association or image that represents the object rather than an abstract faculty of the human psyche. Although it must also be noted that use of the term in the singular does not mean that this role is played only by a single image or association at a given time, as in a sort of archetype. The symbolic ideal is inevitably a composite of images, associations, myths, ideologies, figures, and so on of varying importance at various times, the sum of which forms a basis by which the principle of social structure and identity is understood.

in imitating the King, the infant learns to desire not just the Mother but also the Throne, only to have this desire rebuffed as soon as it becomes manifest insofar as it challenges the very system of social constraints that the child is trying to assimilate.

Thus, the dynamic of imitation becomes both the means by which we are incorporated into the system of norms and symbols that society embodies and, at the same time, the greatest palpable threat to the integrity of those norms and symbols on which we rely. The lack engendered by our entry into a sociosymbolic order results in our dependence on the structure it provides, as our striving toward the Real can be understood and expressed only in terms of language and symbols shared by the social system. Because it is through these symbolizations that we must strive for fulfillment, but also their constraints that are the evident obstacle to our attaining it, we both need and resent the social framework, sentiments we transpose onto whatever serves to represent it. The symbolic ideal is therefore, at the same time, both loved and hated; it simultaneously provides both the means by which desire can legitimately be fulfilled and the constraints that prevent its uninhibited exercise. It is the model from which the norms of social order are learned and internalized through imitation, yet also above the order that it imparts, possessed of special prerogatives that must not be imitated. The distinction between that which must be imitated and the special prerogatives to autonomy that must not be contains within it no externally evident logic. These prohibitions appear arbitrary to the newly forming personality.[9] It is these arbitrary, exceptional, and potentially dangerous prerogatives to autonomy that characterize the totem and thereby define the sacred.

It is here that individual psychology merges with the realm of politics. What Benedict Anderson would call an "imagined community" is created when a number of otherwise autonomous individuals place the same object in the role of their symbolic ideal, thereby identifying with one another through it and adopting in common the otherwise arbitrary system of order it personifies. Lacan refers to this common point of reference as a *point de capiton*, which gives construction and coherence to a system of symbols and metaphors. It is not the symbols and metaphors themselves but rather the structure built and fixed around such a nodal point – a signifier that is itself otherwise empty of meaning – that makes up an ideological discourse. Elements of the discourse acquire meaning in their relation to the *point de capiton*. One might consider "the nation" itself

---

[9] See Freud 1991: 134; Girard 1977: 146–7, 170–9.

to be such a signifier, a term that means nothing in and of itself except insofar as it organizes and articulates a large number of otherwise heterogeneous myths, symbols, and values. Anyone doubting this equation need only look to the reverence often afforded to national flags, pieces of cloth with an otherwise arbitrary collection of shapes and colors that are treated often as living beings and attributed a wealth of abstract meanings, associations, and imperatives.[10] We thereby recognize that what unites a mass of thousands or millions of people in imagined community is not a rational decision over a political or social vision but rather a libidinal investment on the part of each individual toward an image or notion that embodies the nodal point of the social system to which he or she has submitted. If the nodal point vanishes or is discredited, the mass disintegrates, as the illusory character of the collective identity is revealed.[11]

In *Totem and Taboo*, Freud proposed a hypothesis that carried this construct to the social–anthropological level. Adopting Durkheim's assumption that humanity's presocial, animal nature would be motivated toward unrestrained, individual fulfillment, he took as humanity's starting point the Darwinian model of the "primal horde," dominated by a violent and jealous male who kept the females to himself by brute force, driving away competitors, including his sons. The transition from this to the earliest forms of human society required a point in human development at which the sons were able to cooperate in their collective interest to kill the father, accomplishing together what they would have been unable to do individually. The goal was to be free of the restrictions his presence placed over their ability to satisfy their own desires without inhibition – in effect, to become like him. However, even after the murder was committed this was impossible, for any one of the brothers who took on this role could do so only at the expense of the others, thereby replacing the father and introducing the problem all over again. For the "brotherhood" of society to remain stable, they had to reintroduce the image of the father as the symbolic head of the clan, continuing to enforce his presence and will, effectively sanctioning the rules that allowed the community of equal brothers to maintain itself.[12]

It is in this way that the totem came to represent the community, and anything associated with it entered into the category of the sacred. It was forbidden for members of the clan to harm the totem animal, except in a

[10] This dynamic is examined in detail in the American context in Marvin and Ingle 1999.
[11] Freud 1991: 137, 147; Stavrakakis 1999: 78–80, 109.
[12] Freud 1946: 183; Freud 1991: 168.

ritual sacrifice in which the whole of the clan was required to participate, during which the animal was killed, often in an unusually cruel manner, and consumed. The ceremony involved rituals to expiate the clan from the guilt of the act, including rites in which the animal was solemnly mourned. After the ritual mourning came festivities, during which acts normally forbidden to the group were temporarily allowed.

Most theorists who have engaged Freud's hypothesis of the murder of the primal father have warned against taking it too literally.[13] The actual occurrence of such a murder is unverifiable, and the claim to have extrapolated a supposedly unique event in the distant past from relatively recent cultural documents is dubious at best. The totem ritual would not be meaningful if its only purpose was expiation of a crime thousands of years in the past of which the participants, having not read Freud, would be completely unaware. What it offers, rather, is a metaphorical language for modeling the transition from the asocial to the social; a transition from a herd whose rules are maintained by brute force, to a society maintained by voluntary submission to the group's collective capacity for brute force, through symbols that serve to represent and sublimate this capacity. More important than the literal truth of the model is the wider point it makes regarding the way we represent and resolve the tension stemming from the individual's socialization: the internalization of the requirement to suppress natural desires out of long-term self-interest and the interests of the community. Whether or not the murder of the primal father was a real primordial event, the passage from nonhuman to human, from instinctual to social, was and is a passage that must be rationalized through commemoration and ritualization in every society.

The universality and common features of totemic rites and prohibitions between otherwise diverse and independent cultures suggest that they trace back to some general cause; if not a single event in our common history, then a universal aspect of our common humanity. Ritual expiation of guilt is necessary only if it absolves an act that, in the same metaphorical sense, we still wish to commit and continue to commit on an ongoing basis. Society exists as the product of tacit, mutual agreement over and acceptance of the renunciation of individual autonomy of action even in absence of any brute force to compel it. On some level, we are aware that the social world we inhabit is and must remain different than the world that would be if our basic animal natures were left to

---

[13] See Girard 1977: 197–8; Burkert 1983: 74; Freud himself refers to it as a "just-so" story (1991: 154).

their own devices. The removal of the brute force of the primal father activates the need for every individual to surrender – sacrifice, one might say – the instinctual impulse to take his place. It is not that the primal father is killed that matters so much as that he is absent, however he is made absent, in that it is not his murder that presents a problem for the community but rather the state of affairs that attains once he has ceased to exist. Without the father, the brothers remain with no means of differentiation between them, no law by which to structure the division of spoils, a crisis that would lead to a reversion to unrestrained violence if left unchecked. The genesis of society, then, is found in the agreement of mutual renunciation reached by the brothers, the means and mechanisms the community employs to compensate and prevent the primal father from being replaced. Totem ritual, then, is not a reenactment of the murder of the primal father but rather the resolution of it; not a depiction of the cause of the communal crisis but rather its conclusion. As Durkheim observed, the fact that the myth or ritual festival always appears to begin with a period of normlessness and lawlessness and end with a restoration of order suggests that they are reenactments of the community's conception.

Violence is, on the one hand, the danger that religion exists to prevent, yet it is also the basis of any form of human social organization that successfully prevents it. It is the thing from which we wish to escape and, at the same time, that to which we must submit in order to enable social, *ergo* human existence. It is both primitive and the key to civilization. It is both loved and feared, depended on yet abject, and the same ambivalence is felt toward anything that represents it, which will, by definition, include the most pivotal defining symbols of society. It must be worshipped, while its true face is hidden from the worshipper, and a myth, symbol, or ritual will be successful to the extent that it achieves this conflicted purpose. The key ritual that achieves this purpose and therefore the core rite of religion itself to which all ritual points and from which all religions derive their social power, is sacrifice.

The Function of Sacrificial Ritual and Myth

Violence cannot be expelled permanently from society. It is inherent in the very mechanism of socialization and crucial to the means by which social order is maintained. We generally perceive our own societies and their development in terms of the elimination of violence. In fact, the process is one of transformation and substitution; turning disordered "reciprocal" violence that threatens the group and its norms with an endemic cycle of perpetual retaliation committed by individuals solely in their own interests into good, "generative" violence that is unanimous and therefore unifying, committed collectively by the community with the sanction of the totem. A community must neither embrace nor expel violence but rather limit it to as controlled a context as possible, eliminating it from ordinary daily life by restricting it to the sacred, so as to reap its benefits without being devoured by it. Rites of sacrifice function to channel aggression in such a way as to keep it from destroying the group that the group relies on, to generate unanimity from cycles of reciprocal violence. Elements of aggression and conflict scattered throughout the community are drawn together and directed against a social-ritual substitute that the community chooses from outside its ranks, and are eliminated, at least temporarily, with that substitute's destruction. This substitute is often called a "scapegoat," after Leviticus 16:20–22, though in his studies of the centrality of sacrificial ritual to religion, Girard preferred to adopt the term "surrogate victim."

It is not the outsider but rather the brother who is the true source of aggrieved feelings. The forces of nature, the threat of enemies, or the wrath of a vengeful god might all be perceived as mortal threats to the individual or group. But the most terrifying threat to the integrity of the society comes not from external violence but rather from the hostility that every group member feels toward the restrictions and restraints imposed by group membership. The violence of the community must be successfully discharged against sacrificial victims who, on the one hand, resemble the members of the community enough to satisfy this impulse, but on the other hand are clearly identifiable as outsiders such that they serve the function of drawing the violence outside of the community.

Because the surrogate victim must be both insider and outsider, the ritual will compensate to the extent that the victim is deficient in one respect or the other. Victims, whether human or animal, who are not members of the community will first undergo rituals to elevate their status and symbolically incorporate them; whereas victims who are insiders will be symbolically expelled or subject for a period of time to different norms of behavior. Ancient rituals of human sacrifice tended to draw their victims from the margins of society: slaves, prisoners of war, criminals, children who had not undergone rites of initiation; in general, those with no place in the community, who had no share in the social bonds that defined the community, who were, for whatever reasons, not integrated. However, at the opposite end of the spectrum, the king was often a sacrificial victim. His unique position at the center of the community rendered him particularly suited to stand in for the totem. He was, at the same time, the ultimate insider, yet different and isolated from all other community members as subject to entirely different rules and the bearer of radically different social bonds. He embodied, better than any surrogate, the ambivalent feelings that group members experienced toward the group. On the one hand, he was loved and depended on as the very thing that held the social order in place. Yet as symbolic custodian of sovereign violence, he possessed autonomy from the restrictions of the society he represented in a manner that engendered both envy and fear among those who remained bound by them.

Although the victim must sufficiently resemble the community such that violence against him or her is sufficient to satisfy the community's impulse to violence against itself, violence against the surrogate victim must not entail a risk of retaliation. The point of sacrificial violence is to put an end to reciprocal violence, providing an outlet that satisfies violent impulses without inviting new ones in the form of reprisals. Girard saw this as evident in the seemingly comical guilt and sorrow, along with apologies and pleas for forgiveness directed to sacrificial animals from which there was clearly no risk of vengeance or reprisal.[14] Hubert and Mauss describe these in comparing Hindu and ancient Greek rituals:

Excuses were made for the act that was about to be carried out, the death of the animal was lamented, one wept for it as one would weep for a relative. Its pardon was asked before it was struck down. The rest of the species to which it belonged were harangued, as if they were one vast family, entreated not to avenge the wrong about to be done them in the person of one of their number. Under the influence of these same ideas, the instigator of the slaughter must be punished by beating or exile. At Athens the priest at the sacrifice of the *Bouphonia* fled, casting his axe away. All those who had taken part in the sacrifice were called to the Prytaneion. They threw the blame upon each other. Finally the knife was condemned and cast into the sea. The purification which the sacrificer had to undergo after the sacrifice resembled moreover the expiation of a criminal.[15]

Freud maintained that such juxtaposition of opposites – the victim as both insider and outsider, simultaneous mourning and celebration, the temporary permission if not obligation of acts normally forbidden, and particularly the manner in which the sacrificial murder is both the ultimate crime and the ultimate act of piety – demonstrates the ambivalent feelings

[14] Girard 1977: 6–13.
[15] Hubert and Mauss 1964: 33.

that the clan had toward the sacrificial act, stemming from ambivalence toward the primal Father represented in the totem sacrifice, and ultimately to the social order to which these, in turn, refer. Loved and admired as the provider of the terms of the group's morality and common identity, the symbolic murder of the father by the group generates a genuine sense of remorse. Identification with him is symbolized by the act of totem consumption, a ritual requirement for members of the clan, whereby each member acquires an equal share of his strength. At the same time, he is hated, as the order he symbolizes is a necessary hindrance to the exercise of unlimited autonomy; hence, the celebration during which acts normally forbidden according to his imposed morality are temporarily allowed before order is once again restored.[16]

When sacrificial rituals are looked at from outside the community that relies on them, it is easy to view them as manifestations of gratuitous violence, characteristic of only the most rudimentary or dysfunctional of societies. But if sacrifice is indeed the key generative act of society, then all human social systems have been generated by manifestations of such violence. The violence is merely unrecognizable as such to those who are capable of seeing only its generative aspect. This is not to say that humans worship violence as such, nor does religion, whether primitive or modern, amount to a "cult of violence." On the contrary, these rituals, barbaric as they seem to outsiders, offer real protection to the community in that they genuinely unify the community over the organization and control of violence. As Girard puts it, "violence is venerated only insofar as it offers us what little peace we can expect. Non-violence appears as the gratuitous gift of violence; and there is some truth in this equation, for men are only capable of reconciling their differences at the expense of a third party. The best men can hope for in their quest for non-violence is the unanimity-minus-one of the surrogate victim."[17] Because violence can never be expelled completely from the group, it is far preferable to limit it by directing it unanimously against a single victim performed by the whole of the community, or at last someone clearly acting on its collective behalf, rather than allowing it to proliferate randomly and repeatedly against multiple victims throughout the community. Therefore, to view sacrificial rites as manifestations of a pathological morbidity in humanity is to miss the point. No matter how violent these rites may appear, their purpose is *always* the expulsion and abolition of violence.

[16] Freud 1946: 181–3.
[17] Girard 1977: 258–9; see also 103.

But to suggest that violence is at the core of religion is not to say therefore that all religion is equally violent. One could argue that the evolution of civilization lies in just how far the community is able to distance itself from the act of original violence, first through multiple mechanisms of substitution that channel its violence against increasingly innocuous targets, then by transposing the ritual onto the mythic–symbolic register. Myth serves as a recollection of the scapegoat process. Social prohibitions are highlighted through their violation by a mythic hero who brings about destruction in so doing. The image of his subsequent sacrifice, performed to counteract that destruction, becomes a ritual to be emulated during comparable times of crises. The murder of one mythic character by another generates a sacrificial divinity that embodies the source of all that makes one human, namely cultural order: sacred rites, familial regulations, and various prohibitions that make up the community's unique social compact. Although the violations of the hero and his ultimate demise are depicted as tragic, in fact, the community needs the surrogate victim to transgress and to die in order for the crisis of reciprocal violence to be resolved, for the community with its distinct social order to maintain its integrity or even to come into being. Unanimity is therefore of vital importance to the myth. The whole of the community must be complicit in the violence and validate the rationalizations that obscure this complicity if the ritual is to be successful. Only unanimity serves to interrupt the cycle of reciprocal violence that would otherwise continue to alternate between mythic protagonists.

Violent death can be found, in some form or another, at the core of nearly every society's foundation myth, and though there are multiple variations in terms of the mechanisms by which the true function of the myth is obscured, certain common elements point to a remarkably similar formula. The core of the myth, as with any sacrificial rite, is the experience of a symbolic death brought about by human violence and the identification of the community with the act, its victim, and, by indirect extension, its perpetrator as well. Founding ancestors or tutelary divinities are rarely shown accomplishing anything creative or positive; Oedipus is not credited with winning any battles, promulgating any distinct law code, or creating anything of lasting worth for Thebes. They exist only to sin, acting in violation of social norms, or even (such as in the case of Dionysus) not acting at all but being detrimental to social order simply through their unnatural presence. This justifies their violent removal by the unanimous collective or by a figure, often some form of outsider, who acts on its behalf. From this collective violence, and from nothing else, a new cult is born, a social system established, or a culture founded, and the victim's heroism or divinity is taken for granted simply from his having played this role. Having sacrificed himself to atone for his transgression, he thereby saves humanity and thus becomes a divinity as guardian and exemplar of the norms and prohibitions he violated. He is depicted as being in control; at the very least willing his own sacrifice so as to absolve the community of responsibility, if not as having planned and manipulated the entire crisis intentionally so as to dispense the gift of a new beginning to the community.[18]

In various studies of sacrificial myth and ritual, Hyam Maccoby has shown how this dynamic is evident in the mythology and ritual of Christianity. Christ must die in order for mankind to be saved. Therefore, on some level, the Christian wants Christ to be crucified. However, as Christ is also the symbolic ideal for the Christian community, this desire cannot be expressed openly, and hence the crucifixion is mourned and depicted as a tragedy, in a ritual dynamic comparable to that performed over the totem in which the sacrifice is reenacted, mourned, and then ritually consumed in equal portion by the whole of the community who thereby achieve unity with the symbolic ideal through their common identification with it.[19] "In Christianity, this conflict [between good and evil] is resolved not by a picture of unremitting struggle, in which good eventually wins, but by a story of the apparent sudden defeat of the good, which meekly surrenders to evil. But goodness thereby gains a greater victory since this very abnegation and defeat is what was needed to nullify evil."[20] It is therefore not enough to view the crucifixion as a salvation myth. It is, in fact, a foundation myth, the very moment that makes the identity category of "Christian" possible. Indeed, according to the Pauline tradition, identification with the suffering of Christ, acknowledgment that his sacrifice serves as atonement for one's own failure to live up to his ideal, and participation in the corresponding rituals is the very thing that distinguishes a Christian and thereby creates and defines the Christian community. Even in historical terms, there was no Christian community to speak of until the crucifixion transformed the followers of Jesus (the primal father) into a community of equals bound by a common link to Christ (the symbolic ideal).

[18] Girard 1987: 90–93.
[19] Maccoby 1982: 180.
[20] Maccoby 1992: 1.

But in noting that the sacrificial crisis can be resolved through myth, I do not mean to suggest a hierarchical or evolutionary model of societies, starting from primitive human to animal sacrifice, and then on to symbolic and then mythic sacrifice, with each stage replacing the previous and society becoming more civilized with each graduation. Although this may be how we wish to see the evolution of our societies, in fact, the surrogate victim operates simultaneously on multiple levels in most forms of society. Myth, symbol, and even actual violent ritual can work in tandem to channel the community's violence to its exterior, with myth serving to give coherence and meaning to ritual action. The true nature and purpose of these myths, symbols, and acts of violence must be hidden from us if they are to be effective; hence, what we easily recognize as violent and condemn as primitive and barbaric in ancient or even contemporary but foreign cultures will be taken for granted in our own societies. Although we may find it in the hypothetical murder of the primal father, the totem ritual, the tragedy of Oedipus, the cult of Dionysus, the sacrificial rituals of Leviticus, or the crucifixion drama, none of these incarnations stands as the unique origin point of the ritual from which later expressions derive. Although each might serve as a narrative model that later cultures, fashioning their own sacrificial myth, might adapt, they are each themselves an expression of something deeper if not inherent in the human condition.

But if sacrifice of the surrogate victim is the foundation not just of a particular culture or set of cultural forms but also of culture itself, both civilized and primitive, then surely it must be present as well in the mechanisms that hold our present-day societies together. It is in light of this insight that we must turn back to the question of defining the nature and function of the nation in the modern world.

Religion, Nation, and State

If the construct of the nation serves the function in the modern world that religion served to premodern times; if, *vide* Durkheim, that function is to sacralize and thereby substantiate the social order on which the group depends for survival; if this requires the ordering and channeling of violence to the benefit rather than the detriment of the group; and if the primary means by which this ordering is achieved is through the myth and ritual of unanimous violent sacrifice: Is the fundamental purpose of the nation in fact to serve as the ideological or discursive mechanism for the channeling and control of violence? And does it employ sacrificial myth and ritual toward this function?

Commenting on the French Revolution, Durkheim observed that "things purely secular in nature were transformed by public opinion into sacred things: these were the Fatherland, Liberty, Reason. A religion tended to become established which had its dogmas, symbols, altars and feasts."[21] This led him to theorize that nationalism had the capacity to serve as a surrogate religion, whereby the nation was substituted for the deity and the citizen body for the church. Rituals developed to reinforce the norms of the society culminating in a form of collective self-worship, a civic religion performing roughly the same function as its traditional counterpart though springing from secular, nontraditional sources: "What essential difference is there between an assembly of Christians celebrating the principal dates of the life of Christ, or of Jews remembering the exodus from Egypt or the promulgation of the Decalogue, and a reunion of citizens commemorating the promulgation of a new moral or legal system or some great event in the national life?"[22] But recognition of this commonality did not lead him to take the next logical step and explore the extent to which his general theories on the role of religion in society could therefore be applied to an understanding of the nation, presuming, rather, that the primitive impulses at the core of religion were transcended in the modern, rational age that the principle of nationalism represented.

This teleological assumption is also evident in the approach of Max Weber, whose contribution to the understanding of nationalism lay in his recognition of the importance of nation-states to the character of the modern West. In his *Freiburg Address* of 1895, Weber described the "national state" as "the temporal power-organization of the nation,"[23] in effect taking the nation as a preexisting starting point and viewing the nation-state as the entity that through its organization of violence along national lines best enabled the nation to achieve its true potential. Weber saw the nation as the highest and most rational principle on which governance of the state could be based. In the modern world, the state required the legitimation afforded by the nation, and the nation required the state to protect its integrity from the threat of outsiders.[24] However, on the question of just what this thing called "the nation" was in its essence, Weber was more ambiguous: "It certainly cannot be stated in

---

[21] Quoted in Smith 1998: 98.
[22] Durkheim 1971: 427.
[23] Quoted in Guibernau 1996: 34.
[24] Smith 1998: 13–14.

terms of empirical qualities common to those who count as members of the nation. In the sense of those using the term at a given time, the concept undoubtedly means above all, that one may exact from certain groups of men a specific sentiment of solidarity in the face of other groups. Thus the concept belongs in the sphere of values."[25]

Weber's position was that this sense of national solidarity was itself the nation, with the question of whether this would make the nation a natural or constructed entity left unaddressed. In denying that members of different nations could be distinguished by any clear set of categories such as language or race, he went as far as to deny that one could determine the basis of this sense of solidarity by any means or, indeed, that there was any reason why one would wish to do so. Consequently, he was able to support the nation as a political value – indeed, as a means to political salvation, best served by the strengthening of nation-states – absolved from having to answer the question of why and by what process such a "sentiment of solidarity" might form around a given set of signifiers. The nation-state existed to protect this vaguely defined commonality of sentiment that might be shared between members of either a language group, ethnicity, or territory, but Weber offers no explanation into the dynamic behind why any or all of these traits might be taken to define a nation. As an entirely subjective entity, the nation was impervious to such deconstruction.

In *Blood Sacrifice and the Nation*, Carolyn Marvin and David Ingle go so far as to suggest that in reifying the nation in such a manner – either by drawing sharp distinctions between primitive religion and rational modernity or between the "sentiment" of the nation and the crude instrumentalities of the state – early sociologists were themselves unconsciously respecting the "totem secret," observing the taboo by which the continued efficacy of a religious system can be maintained only so long as its true, violent function remains obscured. They observe that normative theory on the relationship between the state and nationalism relegates violence to the past and the primitive or, at worst, to deviant and dysfunctional societies, a reflection of the failure of social structure rather than an essential component of it. Some theorists go so far as to identify in the use of and appeal to violence a substitute for more stable means of generating group identity. The totem secret is thereby preserved when violence is recognized and deemed abject, but only in social systems unlike our own; those that are either palpably foreign or relegated to an

---

[25] Weber, *Essays in Sociology*; quoted in James 1996: 94.

earlier era. It cannot be recognized in systems we associate with our own time and place, or, if it is, it must be rationalized as a benign defensive response to the violence of others.[26]

But religion is not a mere relic of a particular era of the past or a quirk of a particular backward culture. It is a phenomenon that has been a factor throughout human existence, recognizable in every variety of human culture and every watershed of human evolution. The universality of religious phenomena demands an interpretation that bridges the realms of the cultural and biological. Some 40,000 years ago, the human species developed the capacity for representational thinking, which first created the gulf between represented and direct experience that was, in turn, the genesis of language, culture, religion, and art; factors that have been integral to human existence ever since.[27] To suggest that any of these elements has now been transcended would therefore be to suggest that our present age is not merely postmodern but posthuman.

On the surface, this resort to sociobiology might appear to compromise the overall modernist–constructivist framework of my argument, but it does not. For although modernism may stand as the best paradigm to explain the nation, it remains so only as long as one is mindful that, although what we call the nation may be a particularly modern form of social organization, it is still nothing *less than* a form of social organization. As such, it must share in all of the basic characteristics of this fundamental and primordial aspect of the human condition, even while it may have other characteristics specific to its modernity. Any theory of the nation must in some way account for the fact that whatever else the nation is and does, it is also a manifestation of the basic human tendency to form groups and must therefore serve whatever needs the basic behavior of group formation serves. Particularly if one is hypothesizing that the nation stands as a surrogate for religion, one is tapping into a symbol system both unique and universal to the human condition, albeit in modern form. Therefore, if sacrifice is indeed fundamental to religion in all its forms, then this must be no less true of the nation if we are to make the argument that the nation has taken on the function of religion in the modern world. If violent sacrifice as a mechanism for the ordering of violence is an inevitable by-product of our very capacity for social existence, it would take a momentous revolution indeed to justify the

---

[26] Marvin and Ingle 1999: 11–12.
[27] Burkert 1996: 1, see also 19.

claim that we have, only in the present day, found a way to maintain a functioning social order without it.

One must therefore remove the materialist assumptions and rationalist teleology from the conclusions of early social theorists if one is to effectively assess the structures of modernity according to their broader theoretical frameworks, the goal being a more properly Freudian, Durkheimian, or Weberian understanding of the nation than Freud, Durkheim, or Weber themselves provide; one that better conforms to their insights on related structures they examine such as religion and the state. Durkheim saw the true purpose of religion as being to provide sacred legitimation to the social order, to codify and reify the norms of society to protect it and to protect us from the fear of its collapse. Myth and ritual were the means by which the personality and unity of the society was reinforced. "It is by uttering the same cry, pronouncing the same word, or performing the same gesture in regard to some object that they [the people] become and feel themselves to be in unison."[28] He considered that adherence to a new national form of myth and ritual might replace traditional religion as the custodian of the community's social norms. However, the assumption that this represented a scientific and rational alternative to a primitive religious past prevented him from fully applying his theory of religion's totemic form and function to this modern, secular manifestation. Yet no explanation is offered as to how or why this model should apply any differently to premodern systems than to modern ones that serve the same essential function.

However, Durkheim's model remains valid, even if one removes this teleological construction and approaches it from the opposite assumption: that these human impulses and dilemmas remain no less relevant today than they were in primitive, classical, or biblical times; that all that has changed is the manner in which they are resolved. Modern society may indeed have killed its transcendent gods, instead openly worshipping what it deems to be best in itself. But the function of this worship is still the organization of violent authority, the sacralization of a social compact on the use of violence by which uncontrolled violence is expelled from the society. As such, it remains inherently totemic – a system for the control and ordering of violence through its sublimation to a symbol that represents communal unanimity.

According to Durkheim, human beings cannot become attached to higher aims and submit to a rule if they see nothing above them with

---

[28] Quoted in Guibernau 1996: 27.

which they can identify. With the removal of a transcendent father figure, it is the nation-state that ideally takes on the role of ultimate arbiter of violent authority, with traditional, transcendent religious systems acceptable only insofar as they are willing to relinquish such authority. The nation-state serves to absorb all forms of social activity, making society more than a mass of unorganized individuals, which would abandon them to a demoralizing *anomie*. It is for this reason that the individual submits to the state and the state, in turn, serves as an organ of moral discipline and social justice. The state gives dignity to the rights of individuals while at the same time imposing necessary restrictions and limitations on those rights.[29] If this is the case, we must therefore view nationalism, the legitimating ideology of the nation-state, as taking on the function of religion in the modern context, insofar as it adopts religion's ultimate sociological role. It is the civil religion that sets boundaries, determines who may kill, and constructs the framework upon which identity is defined.

It is here that Weber's insights into the character of the modern state become relevant. In a formulation that has come to be widely accepted, Weber defined the state as a human community that successfully claims a monopoly on the legitimate use of force within a given territory, going on to view it as a uniquely modern instrumentality providing a form of organization more rationally suited to the values of the nation than any that preceded it. However, applying the insights of the modernist approach to the nation, which holds that the ideology of nationalism precedes and therefore constructs the nation, one could just as easily turn the equation around, taking the state as the starting point and proposing that the construct of the nation serves as the unifying ideological basis necessary to the maintenance of such an instrumentality. If, then, the state is by definition a mechanism for the ordering of violence, how can the nation as its legitimating conceptual basis be absolved of this violent function?

Weber distinguished between state and nation by defining the state as an instrument of violence and the nation as an idea based on "sentiment," a benign attachment. But the only way the state as an instrumentality can function legitimately is if the nation as an ideological construct can successfully induce a voluntary, which is to say "sentimental," submission to its violent authority.[30] This is done by means of a complex system of myth, symbol, and ritual, the purpose of which is to establish boundaries

[29] Guibernau 1996: 24–25, 39.
[30] Marvin and Ingle 1999: 11.

between insiders and outsiders, transferring the community's capacity for violence to the state as the unanimously appointed arbiter of violence.

Theories of Nations and Nationalism Revisited

We have noted that the capacity for the nation to serve a religious function, and even the centrality of sacrifice to that function, is already widely recognized by theorists of nations and nationalism. Indeed, it stands as a curious point of agreement between theorists of otherwise diverse and conflicting perspectives, who recognize the primacy of sacrifice within the national discourse even as they proceed to locate the origins of the nation elsewhere entirely. Ernest Gellner noted that Durkheim's model of religion as society's camouflaged worship of itself applies just as well to the rituals of nationalism, minus the camouflage. He then locates the origins of the nation in the process of transition to modern industrial society, a model that has been observed to be particularly applicable to nations that formed in the wake of the collapse of empires in Central and Eastern Europe but less so in other contexts. Both Benedict Anderson and Anthony Smith recognized the capacity of the nation to fill the role of religion in terms of providing the individual with a sense of ultimate meaning and lasting purpose in the face of mortality. But then they too proceed to locate the genesis of the nation in other processes; for Anderson, the advent of print capitalism leading to the development of written vernaculars, whereas Smith focuses on the importance of durable preexisting ethnic traditions.

The primary explanation each theorist provides to explain the rise of nations proves to be far more applicable to some cases than to others. Yet each acknowledges the function that the nation fills as a surrogate for religion as a common secondary explanation, applicable to all of their divergent models. We must therefore explore the possibility that it is this common secondary explanation that in fact represents the key insight into the function of the nation in the modern world, with the differing primary explanations representing various processes by which different nations might develop further to this function. A harmonious synthesis of these varying models becomes possible only when we read them in light of the preceding insights as to what this religious function entails, given the centrality of violence and sacrifice to the very basis of culture and social order. Certain developments associated with modernity – among them secularization, industrialization, and the development of written vernaculars and the modern bureaucratic state – induced changes in the

social fabric that rendered traditional religious mechanisms for reinforcing the sacrifice and renunciation necessary to the maintenance of social
existence inoperative and obsolete. "The nation" is the label we give to
the discourse that filled the resulting vacuum, reconstituting the system
around ethnocultural signifiers that were (for reasons we have yet to
ascertain) more applicable to the modern context. Although authentic
preexisting signifiers were certainly preferable for this purpose, where
these were unavailable authenticity could be invented, for the true source
of the signifier's resonance and power was not in its authenticity but
rather in its ability to complete the ritual and hold social order in place.
This serves to explain the deep level of commitment and sacrifice that
could be engendered even by purely functional constructs.

Addressing the fear of death by providing a broader, more permanent
meaning to individual life is indeed a key defining element of religion and
the nation alike. But although it is easy to assume such fear to be a basic,
instinctual element of the human condition, one must be careful not to
take it as an independent variable, itself devoid of cause. Understanding
the root source of this fear, what it involves, and how it shapes and is
shaped by the individual personality can enable us to better understand
how it is that the nation performs this function better than any other
form of social organization, even those that successfully did so before
the advent of modernity. Going back to Durkheim, we recognize that
there is something the human individual fears more than his or her own
mortality; more than death or even oblivion. That is *anomie*: the collapse
and loss of the system of society that our species has evolved to rely on for
its continuity. Anderson is therefore correct that the nation serves to fill
the role of religion but not strictly in the sense of providing a belief system
to rationalize individual mortality. One must look closer at why such a
belief system is needed and how it fills this role. The nation has replaced
religion not just in terms of giving meaning to the individual but also
to rationalize society that reinforces this sense of meaning. It replaces
traditional religion in the role of arbiter of violence, the custodian of
killing authority to which the individual surrenders his or her own in
order to reap the benefits, both material and psychological, of being part
of a society.

Smith reaches closer to the mark with his references to sacrifice, in
terms of the social need the nation must fill in compelling individual sacrifice to the benefit of the collective, exemplified by the ultimate sacrifice
of dying for the nation in times of war. But rather than deconstructing
the psychological meaning of sacrifice itself, he views this condition as

satisfied by the perception of the nation as a permanent, primordial entity in contrast to the finiteness of individual existence; hence, the value to the national mythology of continuity with a palpable ethnic past.[31] Focused on the need for nations to have a reservoir of authentic ethnic myths and symbols to draw on, he gives relatively little attention to what in my view is his key insight into the true source of a national myth's or symbol's power.

This is not to dispute Smith's conclusion that the authentic presence of a myth or symbol in a nation's perceived ethnic past is important. His observations remain valid; ethnic authenticity, or at least the perception of it, is indeed vitally important but not because it is the true source of a symbol's power. Rather, because it is the most plausible means most nations have at their disposal to *distract* from the true source of a symbol's and, by extension, the society's power. That source is violence – sacrificial violence, to be precise; what Girard termed "generative violence" – which provides the means to channel and thereby control violence to the benefit rather than the detriment of the community. Ethnic authenticity, then, is an alibi; a Trojan horse that enables the society to allow a symbol into the center of its mythology long enough for it to effect its true functional purpose. The claim that the purpose of a symbol, and the mission of the nation it represents, is to preserve and defend an ancient culture of unique historical value serves to effectively hide the symbol's true purpose and the nation's true mission: to organize violence in the present. And the reason this alibi is so determinedly manufactured by national elites and effortlessly perceived by nationalized masses, even where it is wholly fictitious, is because it is needed to properly obscure this secret, a vital element of the sacrificial ritual that holds the society together.

It is only now that we are able to propose our own definition of this elusive entity known as the nation. Drawing from similar theoretical sources, Marvin and Ingle proposed that a nation is "the shared memory of blood sacrifice periodically renewed."[32] This definition is insightful insofar as it incorporates key elements hitherto neglected. Definitions that focus on the importance of language, ethnicity, territorial space, political principles, or institutional structures that are often but not always the basis for nation formation rarely explain exactly why the signifiers on

---

[31] See Smith 1998: in his critique of Gellner 45–46, and of Anderson 140–142; also 1991: 160–62.
[32] Marvin and Ingle 1999: 4.

which they focus are attributed such meaning in some contexts but not in others. Marvin and Ingle's formulation addresses the question of just what process it is that engenders a commonality of sentiment around any particular set of signifiers. But for this reason, this definition is in a sense too broad yet at the same time too narrow to be truly effective. Too narrow because "periodic renewal" is only one ritual means by which social order might be legitimated (albeit one particularly applicable to the case that they examine of the United States). Too broad because, as we have seen, the theoretical sources on which it is based indicate that blood sacrifice is, in fact, the essential element of *any* form of social order, not just the nation. By this definition, Christianity could be construed as a nation, but to view it as such would be to neglect the significant differences between premodern and modern systems of social order.

The only precise definition of the nation, then, would be one that combines Marvin and Ingle's insights with those of theorists of nationalism such as Gellner, who recognized the specifically modern character of the nation. If the basis of society is the organization of violence enabled by a shared memory of generative sacrifice, and nationalism is a principle that holds common culture to be the primary political bond, then a national society is a political community based on the principle of common culture, enabled by a foundational memory of generative sacrifice. A national discourse[33] would then be the system of myth, symbol, and ritual that serves to channel human violence so as to legitimate and enable social existence in the context of modernity. The sum total of social relationships established on such a basis and legitimated by such a discourse amounts to a nation.

Two aspects of this definition demand further elaboration before we continue: It is unashamedly both functionalist and modernist. As a functionalist definition, it is not meant to displace or supersede existing definitions of what the nation is in its substance. Definitions such as that of Anthony Smith, cited in Chapter 1, which delineate the component parts of the national discourse, remain vitally important toward an understanding of how the modern nation approaches its function. I will, however, make the bold contention that the functionalist definition is the only one capable of distinguishing the nation from all other social constructs in all cases. It applies to all constructs commonly understood to be nations and does not accurately apply to anything that is not. Any social system in which a network of signifiers – be they political or cultural, ethnic or

---

[33] A term that would encompass but not be limited to nationalism as an ideology.

civic, voluntaristic or organic – enables a group of people in a modern social context to agree to submit to a common authority over the use of violence within the group, projecting that violence to the group's exterior is understood to be a nation; and this definition, in turn, explains why this construct has come to be the dominant means of constructing identity in the modern world.

But because this condition of "modernity" is contained in the definition itself, obviously our definition begs modernist assumptions. This is necessary if it is to be analytically useful. The purpose of any term (even, and I would say especially, in an academic context) is to reflect shared meaning. Thus, to avoid begging a particular theoretical perspective, we must start and work backwards from the current and popular shared meaning of the term "nation" rather than imposing a set of criteria on it. Thus, although the debate as to whether or not there were nations in antiquity may preoccupy modernist, perennialist, and ethnosymbolist scholars of nationalism alike, it is ultimately uninteresting for the purposes of my argument, dependent more on how one chooses to define the nation and therefore what one is looking for than on any objective measure. The fact remains that the advent of modernity brought radical changes to the way that our societies are organized, and with these came changes in the shared meanings of the terms used to signify those societies. Any commonsense understanding of "nation" at present connotes elements at least some of which are intrinsically modern, such as a mass public culture, common economy, and common rights and duties for all members. And note that we are still speaking of the nation, and not the state, when invoking such elements, for these elements are as much a factor of social norms and relationships (the national society) and the discursive systems that legitimate them (the national discourse) as they are of the institutions and instrumentalities that actualize and enforce them (the nation-state). The idea that an imagined community encompasses some manner of common economy is distinct from the institutions that generate one; the ideal that members of the community must be homogeneous in terms of their rights and responsibilities can exist independently of the specific laws and enforcement mechanisms that enable this.

By "modernity," then, I do not refer to a particular time period but rather to a configuration of social norms and forms of organization uniquely associated with the present day that have evolved over the preceding centuries. I shall leave it to others to elaborate authoritatively on the essence of what this "modernity" consists of, when it came into being, and define and debate the relative significance of its component elements;

but consensus would appear to be that they include at least some degree of secularization, mass literacy, mass politics, and the bureaucratic, territorial state, and that defining moments include the Enlightenment, the revolutions of the late 18th century, and industrialization.[34]

"Culture" is another term contained in the definition that will remain intentionally undefined, again to avoid constraining the common-sense definition of the term under the assumptions of any prechosen theoretical perspective. What is key to nationalism is the principle that common culture is the primary political bond, however culture may be understood by the agents adhering to the principle. In varying contexts, this could mean anything from religion to myth to descent, language, political principles, or table manners. It is difficult to deny, for example, the salience of a common political culture even in avowedly multicultural nations such as the United States. On the other hand, a more "ethnic"-type nation such as Israel could appear identical to its predecessor *ethnie* in terms of myths, boundary mechanisms, and so forth. Nonetheless, the subtle shift in perception that leads its members to view their loyalty as owing primarily to their common culture rather than to a monarch, land, or divinity remains of pivotal significance to its status as a nation.

This is not to say that nations, or constructs so closely resembling them as to be effectively indistinguishable, could not have existed in premodern times. On the contrary, if modernity is defined according to a particular set of norms and structures, it is not out of the question that at least some of these elements might have been present in ancient societies and some might be absent in present-day ones. Hence, it is theoretically possible for a premodern or postmodern society to exist in the present day for whom violence is organized by something other than a national discourse; and it is similarly possible for elements associated with modernity to have existed in certain places and times in the more distant past, enabling the formation of something that resembled a nation in most significant ways. Indeed, if we have established that the modern nation must serve the same sociopsychological set of roles as premodern religious systems, surely there will be at least some examples of such premodern religious systems resembling modern nations more than they differ. If every society, even premodern society, requires myth and ritual in order to function, and if the distinctive set of myths and rituals of a given society can justly be called the core of its culture, it becomes impossible to argue that there was ever a time that culture did not have political salience in terms of

[34] For a related definition, see, for example, Giddens 1990: 1–6.

defining the boundaries of a political community and the basis of political legitimacy. Yet the distinction remains useful because it is this condition – modernity – that is intrinsically associated with the entity known as the nation. For whatever resemblance certain premodern societies might have had to modern nations, being a nation would have meant something very different in a global context devoid of a widely shared conception of it as the ideal unit of sociopolitical order. The watershed events of modernity did engender significant social change, and if "the nation" serves as a label that appropriately reflects our understanding of the nature of that change in terms of the way our social systems came to be organized and legitimized, then the label does us a service.

The efficacy of this definition is further demonstrated in the clarity it sheds on issues such as the ambiguous relationship between the nation and other social constructs such as religion and the state. The confusion in popular discourse between the terms "state" and "nation," and the need to carefully distinguish between these two distinct concepts, is a problem that has long preoccupied the field of nationalism studies.[35] Yet the fact of this confusion points to an obvious affinity between these two constructs, one that is easily explained in light of our functionalist definition. It is, as we have already observed, the distinction between the social norms and relationships themselves, the discourses that legitimate them, and the instruments and instrumentalities that enable them. Given Weber's definition of the state as the institution with the monopoly on the legitimate use of violence, any discursive or ideological system that successfully served to underwrite the modern state could rightly be called nationalism according to my definition. Conversely, it would be natural for the adherents of any ideological system that served to organize violence within a community to seek the institutions of a state. But although this is the most likely scenario in the modern context of an international system in which the state is the primary unit of power, it is also conceivable for such a discourse to forge a community of violence without a state or even without any aspirations for one, so long as the resultant community was able to find expression in other institutions.

Similarly, the relationship between the modern nation and the discourse and institutions of traditional, sectarian religion can also be better understood in light of this functionalist definition. The nation fills the role in the modern context that what we now call "religion" filled in the premodern one, but this does not mean that religion has ceased to

---

[35] See, for example, Connor 1978.

exist or lost its relevance. It is simply no longer the universal, ideal organizing principle for establishing social order. The symbols of traditional religion nonetheless may be among those "shards and patches" co-opted by nationalists to substantiate and solidify the national order and, where they are effective and dominant, the product is "religious nationalism" of a sort that favors as insiders to the community of violence members of the particular sectarian group with which those symbols are associated. However, symbols of premodern traditional religions need not be used as part of the national myth–symbol system for that system to effectively serve its religious function, and a nation will co-opt these symbols only if and when they remain effective in providing a sacrificial surrogate sufficiently representative of the emergent national community.

But of greatest significance for our purposes is the fact that this definition of the nation provides a key insight into the question of just what it is that makes a myth, symbol, or ritual meaningful or not within a national discourse. If the basis of religion is the social ordering of violence, and if the nation has taken on the role of religion since the nation-state came to serve as the sole legitimate arbiter of violence, then the nation amounts to the body of myth, symbol, and ritual that enables this function. A symbol therefore has meaning within the national mythology not based on its ethnic authenticity but rather based on how successful it is in articulating, ordering, rationalizing, and reinforcing the controlled violence that is the social order, the manner in which violence is organized to generate the social compact on which we rely for identity, meaning, and survival.

Enthusiasm for a sports team, sentiment toward a flag, and other practices that tend to fall under the heading of "banal nationalism" all occur and are effective to the extent that they have a role in structuring and channeling violence further to the social order on which humans rely; a social order that is, at present, secular, modular, and growth oriented. The authenticity of a symbol to the nation's perceived past improves its ability to so channel and structure violence, but only because the structure of modern society renders culture the primary principle for political organization, for functional reasons that Gellner has explained. For this reason, the perceived connection of a symbol to the culture comes to be valued, and the authenticity of this connection will be a factor in though not the root cause of a symbol's efficacy, insofar as it serves to hide the secret that must remain hidden if the symbol is to be effective: namely, the centrality of violence to that symbol's power, the fact that submission to a violent god is what this symbol truly represents and enforces, a need that is not merely functional but also deeply felt, much as it might be repressed. This explains both why the age of nationalism favors nations with authentic ethnic roots – the truth, after all, is the best alibi – but also why authenticity proves so easy to invent where this condition does not exist: because the perception of authenticity satisfies a deeply felt set of sociopsychological needs engendered by the structures of modernity.

The alibi that hides the totem secret is such a vitally important element of the discourse that it would not be an exaggeration to say that it is, in fact, the nation itself. After all, if my theory is correct and all societies are, at root, organizations of violence underpinned by a sacred rationalization, then what is particular about the nation, as opposed to other social formations, is the manner in which it obscures this true purpose of its existence, a particular form of rationalization uniquely suited to modernity. Hence, it is entirely justified to say that a national society is more likely to form around an existing ethnic core than not, insofar as such a core is the most convenient means to provide the alibi on which the social system relies for its very maintenance. Indeed, rather than challenging the ethnosymbolic model, my theory offers a further, functional explanation as to why Smith's observations on the importance of preexisting ethnicity are correct, while at the same time explaining the numerous exceptions to the rule: namely, that although a ready-made ethnic culture is the simplest and therefore most popular means of hiding the totem secret, there are others that can be adopted when circumstances demand such as, for example, defense of a unique political principle or historical mission.

Symbols of Defeat and National Totem Sacrifice

My argument thus far can be summarized as follows: The nation fills the function of religion in the context of modernity. Religion is, at root, the symbolic worship by society of itself, and society ultimately depends on the suppression and control of individual violence and its channeling to the benefit of the group. The means by which religion and, by extension, the nation achieves this purpose is through the mechanism of generative sacrifice, by which the violence of the community is unanimously directed against a surrogate victim. Therefore, the efficacy of the national discourse and its component myths, symbols, and rituals depends on its capacity to serve this purpose, in particular by reflecting and maintaining this system of generative sacrifice.

One need not start from the theories of Freud, Durkheim, or Weber, Girard or Burkert to support this model. Their theories merely provide a language for comprehending what can be empirically observed in the myth–symbol systems of modern nations. Indeed, it is my view that examination of the myths, symbols, and rituals of the modern nation and, in particular, symbols of defeat serves to substantiate their theories better than their examinations of primitive ritual or classical myth ever could, thus proving that what they observed was not a contingent phenomenon but indeed an elemental aspect of the human condition, as much today as throughout history. Although many of these thinkers were affected to some degree by a teleological view that saw modern society as having transcended these primordial, violent impulses, with perhaps only a few remnants left as indicators of where we came from, in fact what they saw in classical drama, tribal ritual, and biblical text is exemplified *a fortiori* in the mechanisms of our modern national societies. And nowhere is this dynamic more evident than in myths and symbols of defeat and in the elevation of these myths and symbols in the process of nation building.

If the mechanism of the surrogate victim is indeed a foundational element of all forms of human society, then we should be able to recognize the dynamics of the totem sacrifice in the myths and rituals of modern nations. Indeed, one could argue that the problem is even more acute in the context of modernity than in the agrarian past. As we have noted, one point around which Durkheim's theory of religion has been criticized is his assumption that the forms of religion functional to rudimentary homogeneous societies will necessarily apply to complex hierarchical ones. He thereby neglects the ideological function of religion, stressed by Weber and particularly by Marx, in legitimating social hierarchy and discrete group interests.[36] But even if Durkheim's theory cannot be generalized to all forms of religion in all forms of society, it could nonetheless apply to constructs that serve the function of religion in societies collectively imagined as homogeneous in form. The nation is a construct that fits such a description.

The ideal nation, by its very nature, lacks the physical presence of the overbearing father figure to whom the otherwise identical brothers can surrender their sovereignty. This renders the sacrificial crisis created by their sameness more acute in a socially mobile environment in which difference is increasingly obscured rather than reinforced, leading to competition, violence, and the blurring of boundaries. A nation, to effectively function as a nation, must generate unanimity out of this

[36] Giddens 1986: 103–4.

uniformity, commemorating sacrifice at the core of its mythology so as to justify ongoing acts and rituals of renunciation in its national life. The question, then, is this: Why and how is the nation able to perform this function in a modern context in a way that religious systems that did so successfully in the past no longer can? If society is indeed, at root, a sacrificial system, then it can be dissolved and replaced only if its participants come to adhere to another sacrificial system with greater commitment. Therefore, the quality of the means by which a given social system – such as nationalism in general, or a particular nation – commemorates sacrifice, in relation to the broader social reality with which the individual and group is confronted, will tell us a lot about the reasons for that social system's success or failure.

We have already, in the course of examining existing theories of nations and nationalism, explored three partial explanations for the prominence of symbols of defeat in national mythologies: (1) They serve to substantiate a connection between the modern nation and a primordial past, explaining as well the "dormition" of the nation in the intervening time; (2) they provide a sense of historical injustice or grievance around which a community can mobilize; and (3) they reinforce the sense of the nation as a durable if not indestructible entity in ways that images of victory and contentment never could. But although each of these explanations might locate a role for symbols of defeat in the mythology of any society, none of them sufficiently explains the phenomenon whereby such symbols can be elevated specifically in the course of modern nation building, often to a place of centrality.

A fourth explanation provides such insight. It is my view that the elevation of an image of defeat to a central role in the national construction of history and memory furthers the nation's ultimate purpose of organizing and channeling violence through submission to a violent authority by the manner in which it serves to reconstruct and reenact the sacrificial ritual. Although not the only possible means by which a nation might complete this ritual, it is a particularly convenient means for reasons that can be understood only through closer examination of the distinctly modern norms and structures that the national discourse in particular exists to rationalize. Modernist theorists of nationalism such as Gellner and Anderson have already elaborated on what these norms and structures are. Industrial society must be meritocratic, in principle allowing wide space for social and economic mobility enabled, in turn, by a common means of communication – common language, symbols, and values – transmitted via mass education. It necessitates an ideology of baseline equality of all members, common rights and responsibilities, homogeneity of culture, and a horizontal rather than hierarchical structure of authority. It recognizes societies as limited, enclosed by finite boundaries, within which the community is entitled to sovereignty and outside of which are other communities similarly entitled.

It is important to note, then, the conceptual similarity between the transition Freud describes from the "father horde" to the "brother clan" and the transition described by Gellner from the agrarian hierarchical to the modern industrial society. Both the primal horde and the agrarian society are characterized by a vertical structure of authority in which levels are distinguished by the endowment of differential entitlements and codes of behavior – that is, different cultures – in contrast to the totem clan and the modern nation that can both be characterized as horizontal in structure based on theoretical equality. With the pretensions to universality characteristic of traditional religion removed, nationalism, like totemism, provides a structure (and a symbol representative of that structure) meaningful only to members of the group.

This parallel is not offered merely as a basis for metaphorical comparison. I would argue that there is a direct continuity between the rituals of primitive religion and the myth–symbol system of the modern nation as pertains to the resolution of this tension. The nation, to give structure and meaning to its symbol system, collectively chooses totemic symbols in the form of images from its cultural heritage, and this totem, in encapsulating and representing the unique cultural values of the nation, is sanctified and worshipped by the group. However – and here is my key point – the totem must also be seen to die if the nation, as a horizontally structured brotherhood of equals, is to come into being. This necessary ambivalence, addressed in totemic society through rites of sacrifice, is resolved by the myths, symbols, and political rituals of the modern nation.

It is difficult to make an empirical case, beyond the broadest speculative model, as to how an individual resolves the ambivalences inherent in the process of socialization because many of these mechanisms will be beyond direct observation. Freud, for example, referred to dreams as the *via regia* to the unconscious, but we do not have direct access to the content of dreams beyond what the dreamer is able and willing to recall and report. This problem is less acute when operating on a societal level, because such mechanisms, in order to exist, must be discernible in some manner of communication between group members. It has been proposed, for example, that myths function for a society in much the same way as dreams do for the individual. In addition to transmitting and reinforcing the values of a community, they can also serve a cathartic function, expressing in disguised form ambivalences, contradictions, and dilemmas that the society cannot confront directly.

It is in these dilemmas, and the mechanisms for resolving them, that we come to the root of what is often termed the "Janus-faced" nature of nationalism, an ideology that looks to both the past and the future, that can provoke acts of both extreme altruism and extreme hostility. The double-faced god of peaceful and warlike countenance is only the most obvious mythic manifestation of the fact that every divinity that stands as a symbolic representative of the sovereign violence of the community has within it a dual nature, both gentle and terrible. The "divinities" of the secular national myth are no different. These figures are both feared and needed, conflicting impulses, both of which must be satisfied in order for society to function. In the case of the nation, there are two levels of ambivalence that must be addressed. The first is an ambivalence not unique to the nation but rather intrinsic to all forms of social order: that which is felt toward the society itself – loved and depended on for the order it provides, yet resented for the restrictions it imposes to provide it – and ritually transposed on to the surrogate victim who symbolizes the community's sovereign violence and against whom unanimous violence is ultimately directed by the community as a means of channeling this resentment to productive, generative ends. But the second, related conflict is particular to the specific mechanisms according to which the nation resolves the first. It is an ambivalence that the nation feels toward its perceived ethnic past that must be revered without being restored.

This adds a new dimension to the role of symbols of defeat in a national mythology. It is my contention that it is possible, indeed frequent, for the defeat myth to become the axial element of a national mythology. Where the symbolic ideal must be destroyed in order for the horizontal form of social organization that distinguishes the modern from the traditional, the nation from the *ethnie*, to come into being, the myth of defeat serves, in effect, as the foundation myth of the nation.

It may seem counterintuitive to propose that a nation's defeat and its foundation could occur in the same symbolic moment, but such is the nature of ambivalence and the mechanisms for resolving it. Several theorists of nationalism have identified the myth of descent – the notion, however tenuous, that the nation is an extended family, the product of a common lineage – as the key, defining element of ethnicity and, therefore, by extension the foundation myth of those nations that extend from such a preexisting ethnic community.[37] Although consistent with the ethnosymbolic emphasis on the importance of preexisting ethnic ties, this view is empirically contradicted, as we have seen, by the fact that not all social constructs considered to be nations are derived from or even associated with ethnic communities of descent, and even among those that are, not all of them build on myths and symbols authentically resonant to those preexisting communities.

Descent may be the key element of a nation, but not descent in literal terms of common lineage, even on a mythic or figurative level. Rather, the myth of descent is one of descent from a common sacrificial moment, an element that can be located in some form or another in the mythologies of all nations. The two may coincide; the surrogate victim in whom the sacrifice is embodied may also be a mythic common ancestor. This may well enhance the efficacy of the myth but is hardly necessary in order for the myth to be foundational, whereas the condition of generative sacrifice is. "Blood" therefore is important not in terms of consanguinity but rather in terms of common identification with the same blood sacrifice. A community may or may not perceive itself as descending from common ancestors, but even if it does, perception of distant familial ties alone does not translate into national community unless it is accompanied with a sense that those common ancestors suffered and sacrificed to maintain the group as a group. In which case, the perception of common ancestry exists merely to obscure the true locus of the communal bond, and commemoration of sacrifice and common ordeal becomes even more important where mythic blood ties, whether fictive or authentic, are relatively absent.

To suggest that a moment of defeat serves as a nation's foundation myth is not to say that the nation in question came into existence at the moment of this purported defeat. Neither national myths themselves nor any reasonable scholarly interpretation would support such a contention. National mythologies are more likely to represent the nation's birth point in their myths of common descent, migration, or the founding of a dynasty, whereas modernist theories of nationalism generally view the genesis of nations as the product of circumstances that in most cases prevailed only some centuries after the mythical moment of defeat. But a

---

[37] See Connor 1994, Chaps. 2 and 8; Smith 1991: 160; 1999: Chap. 2. Smith alternatively suggests in *Chosen Peoples* (2003: 172–4) that it is the myth of the Golden Age that "stands at the heart of a community's ethno-history, (and) forms one of the key foundations of national identity." His eventual position seems to be that the entire interlinking network of myths is necessary, but with an emphasis on origins or ancestry and the "high points" of communal golden age or ages.

nation's foundation myth need not be congruent with the *ethnie*'s actual
or mythical moment of birth. In these cases, the application of the modern ideology of nationalism to a distinct cultural community becomes
possible only because the memory of the defeat was available to give
that community a sense of cohesion and meaning according to a structure amenable to a national form of social organization. Identification
with the myth of defeat thereby becomes the key litmus test of belonging,
to determine identification with the ideal that had been defeated, with
the suffering of those who held to its memory, and with the hope of its
eventual restoration.

An *ethnie* might well preserve images of decline or defeat in its myth–
symbol system to commemorate a collective trauma, to reinforce values
by warning against certain behaviors, or even as a means to encourage
cultural mobilization. These images, however, are unlikely to serve as the
nodal point that essentializes the community's foundation. Beccause the
ethnie is not required to rationalize any particular form of social organization, it is more likely to take as its reference point a myth of temporal
origins, of ancestry, of location–migration, or of the heroic age when
the values of the culture achieved full expression. Identification with a
moment of origin, with a common ancestor, or with a territory is a more
appropriate means of distinction between insiders and outsiders in a premodern ethnosymbolic system. But a nation must be more than just a
distinct cultural community. It is a community with a common political
purpose, one that relates legitimacy of governance to a horizontal form
of social organization requiring the theoretical equality of all community
members. The myth of the heroic age provides a nation with the raw
materials it requires to construct a symbolic ideal, in the form of heroes
or other concrete representations that embody the values of the society,
assert its uniqueness, and speak in the community's authentic voice. However, this heroic age will inevitably refer to a period that was prior to the
national idea and the forms of social organization associated with it.

The people of a nation must come to terms with the evident and
explicit fact that they no longer live in the heroic age, as well as the
implicit and hidden fact that, deep down, they no longer wish to; or,
more to the point, that the destruction of these norms and structures,
either as a consequence of the historical moment of defeat or on an
ongoing symbolic level in the present day, was and is a vital element to
the development of the modern national society in which they do live
and wish to continue to live. Therefore, just as the social structure of
the modern nation is comparable to that of the totem clan, the attitude

of the nation toward the symbols of the heroic age is comparable in its ambivalence to the attitude of the clan toward the totem. It is loved for the fact that it provides the symbolic framework that serves to structure the nation, offering the promise of a return to a lost state of harmony, unity, fullness. However, it is also secretly despised because the symbolic framework it provides is also the barrier to fulfillment, and the promise of fullness in the future age is therefore not only fictional but impossible.

This ambivalence is evident from even a cursory look at national myths and symbols of defeat in contrast to the mainstream political cultures of the nations that revere them. Israelis might commemorate the destruction of the Temple through their unanimous identification with the ruins of the Western Wall, while at the same time maintaining an avowedly secular society with no desire to rebuild that Temple and live in the sort of theocratic state it represented. Similarly, Serbs who mourn the defeat at Kosovo have no wish to reconstruct the feudal monarchy that was defeated there. Ghanian admiration of Yaa Asantewaa does not reflect a will to restore sovereignty to the Asante confederacy any more than modern Greek attachment to Constantinople reflects a desire to resurrect the institutions of the Byzantine Empire or to relocate the capital of the nation-state to present-day Istanbul. French Canadian reference to the Battle of the Plains of Abraham or Catalan commemoration of the fall of Barcelona may or may not point to a desire for greater political autonomy, but it certainly does not reflect nostalgia for the French crown and incorporation into its colonial empire, nor glorification of the Habsburg claimant to the throne of Aragon, respectively. Anyone who reads such intentions, even unconscious ones, into the reverence that these modern national groups have for these symbols grossly misinterprets the political reality. When in the process of nation building, the common culture attempts to usurp the role of traditional religion in encapsulating unanimous violence, the actual god or gods of the religion or *ethnie* with which the culture identifies become rivals. Serbs do not wish to restore a Prince Lazar to the throne. They, as a community, want to collectively take his place – to be what he is – and they must destroy him first in order to do so. Similarly, Israelis do not wish to rebuild the Temple. They wish to embody the sovereignty it represents, so it too must be destroyed in order for that sovereignty to be truly realized. In all cases, the destruction of these polities is as vital an element to the modern nation's existence as is their authentic presence as part of the nation's remembered past.

Hence, the images chosen to represent continuity with a premodern society are images that can also serve, in a manner consistent with the protocols of ritual sacrifice of a surrogate victim, to viscerally represent the dismantling of that premodern society; a process that is necessary for a new, national society to take its place. But it is an event that must nonetheless be mourned and, if possible, blamed on the agencies of an outsider because the fact that the sacrifice is in reality demanded and desired by the community itself must be repressed. For although nationalists cannot but revere these champions and paragons of their distinct culture as heroes, the notion that they and the institutions they represent should still be ruling over the people is unthinkable.

It is for this reason that the actual restoration of the heroic age is rarely more than a vague messianic goal in national ideologies. If any real effort is made to reinstitute the political structures that characterized that age, it takes place on the margins of the movement and is seen as extremist, sometimes as a more abject threat than the nation's external enemies. Those who do explicitly adopt such goals are viewed by the majority of nationalists as objects of shame, ostensibly because they threaten to exacerbate conflict but, in fact, because their very presence on the political landscape threatens to expose the totem secret: the need for the mainstream national mythology to destroy what it ostensibly idealizes. Serbs want Lazar to die and his army to be defeated; Israelis want the Temple to be destroyed and Masada to fall. The aim of nationalism is not the final fulfillment of the national ideal but rather the ongoing mobilization of the nation toward that unreachable goal. Since no symbol system can completely express the fulfillment of direct, unmediated experience, were the ideal to be achieved, the heroic age restored, the illusory nature of its promise of fulfillment would become evident, and the effect would be the same as if the totem had been removed or discredited in any other way – the symbol system would lose its framework and collapse back into a set of heterogeneous signifiers. The nation would, in effect, cease to exist.

Thus, the defeat of the totem becomes necessary to rationalize a form of social organization very much at variance with the one it represented; to forge the "brother clan" from out of the "father horde." Myths of defeat are about the expulsion of violence from the community, the very act that generates the community itself. They represent the national society's channeling its violence unanimously against the totemic symbols of its own origin; against the premodern myths on which they depend and which they must destroy in order to be a distinct and modern nation. The nation must be forged in fire; in an event, whether mourned or celebrated, that destroys whatever came before, while providing an archetypal image of sacrifice to serve as a model for the individual member of the society who surrenders his own capacity for violence to the will of the group. Although the *ethnie* may come into existence by its birth, the nation comes into being only through sacrifice, and where that sacrifice is embodied in a myth of defeat, identification with the totem in its moment of defeat is transformed into the key distinction between national insiders and outsiders. Just as the whole of the clan was required to participate in the ritual sacrifice and consumption of the totem, just as Christians are defined by their identification with and ritual consumption of Christ, the whole of the nation must identify vicariously with the moment in which the totem is defeated and thereby take on their share of the guilty fruits of this sacred crime, which is both the dignity of their association with the totem (and through it with each other) as well as the social mobility enabled by its absence.

3

Symbols of Defeat in National Monument and Ritual

The preceding chapter identified four distinct but related explanations as to why a nation might elevate an image of defeat to the center of its mythology:

1. Such symbols substantiate the connection between the modern nation and a primordial past, at the same time providing a ready explanation for the nation's "dormition" in the intervening time.

2. They offer a conception of the nation as durable if not indestructible, able to persevere through even the worst of disasters.

3. Focus on a moment of historical injustice makes rectification of that injustice a motive to justify national mobilization.

4. Myths and symbols of defeat also serve a ritual function, resolving an ambivalence that members of the nation feel first toward the constraints imposed by social order itself and then toward their own ethnic heritage, which is relied on for the society's symbolic content but represents a form of order that must be rejected and transcended in the modern world.

To substantiate this argument empirically, we should be able to locate and recognize these functions in varying expressions of national myth, as well as in the norms and ritual affirmations of the nation. However, it is important to note that operating within the register of Freudian theory demands caution in avoiding certain standard Freudian pitfalls. Any attempt to empirically verify a theory that employs concepts such as ambivalence and repression runs the risk of falling into circular reasoning. Simply put, repression amounts to the need to hide something from oneself. On the level of a society, a collective dynamic of repression will occur when the structure of the social order compels those who submit to it to repress the same thing in the interests of maintaining that order. In other words, we are, by definition, looking for contradictory evidence. We are seeking that which is hidden from view and the mechanisms employed to hide it. In which case it becomes all too easy to dismiss behaviors or texts that do not appear to manifest the theorized dynamic as examples of mechanisms by which the dynamic is repressed from consciousness.

This is a danger to which my theory is vulnerable, for I am not simply arguing that the nation employs repression. It would be more accurate to say that the nation *is* repression. My theory holds that repression of the core violent function of society will be compelled in some manner by every form of society, but that it is the eccentricities that define the mode and character of each distinct society that will determine exactly what it is that needs to be repressed and how this is done. It is my position that the nation amounts to the sum total of myth and ritual used to enable and then repress the violent function at the core of modern society. Demonstrating the efficacy of this model must involve more than just sifting the available evidence into two clear categories: that which serves to enable, and that which serves to repress.

But it does not automatically follow from the theory that a secret must be hidden from the consciousness of an individual or group that this secret is therefore entirely indiscernible. For although a measure of Freudian jargon may be employed to articulate my model, it clearly rejects many of the assumptions on which orthodox Freudian methodology is predicated; in particular, the understanding of the unconscious as an infinitely devious faculty of the human psyche in terms of its ability to hide its secrets from the conscious mind, one that can be accessed only by means of a defined therapeutic technique.[1] In fact, the unconscious is a notoriously poor conspirator: It leaves incriminating documents lying around; it breaks down under cross examination, unable to reconcile the contradictions in its cover story; and it fails to adequately convince certain co-conspirators to varying degrees, leaving them to squeal to the authorities. This is particularly true when one is dealing with a collective unconscious, especially when one is looking in as an outsider to the collectivities in question.

"Collective unconscious" does not refer here to any deep, primordial element of the psyche as may be posited by the Jungian tradition but simply to those elements of the individual unconscious that are held in

---

[1] See Gellner 1985: 208–9.

common with others by virtue of their having been socialized into the same group identity. If, as proposed, the core of the human personality is formed by the manner in which the individual reconciles his or her biological drives with the requirements of socialization, it stands to reason that elements of personality must fall into three categories: those that are universal to the normal human experience of socialization, those that are specific to the manner in which the individual negotiates that experience, and those that are particular to the group(s) into which the individual is socialized. Naturally, this is a typology; elements cannot be sifted neatly into categories because even elements that are group specific will not be experienced by each member of the group in the same way but rather will be subject to the eccentricities of the individual experience. Nonetheless, it is exclusively this third category of personality elements that is of interest to this study. Such group-specific elements are empirically accessible by their nature as they must of necessity exist in some manner of communication among group members.

In which case, it is indeed possible to assemble a body of evidence against which my theory can be tested as an explanation. Specifically, we should be able to find elements of the sacrificial ritual and surrogate victim as described in the previous chapter built into the mythologies and rituals of modern nations, including the following:

1. Personification of the community in the form of a symbolic ideal who becomes the surrogate victim.
2. Mechanisms for the projection of guilt and responsibility for the act away from the community and onto outsiders.
3. The requirement of unanimity. Only the whole of the community can participate in an act of totem violation forbidden to any single member. Anyone depicted as unable or unwilling to participate cannot be considered a part of the community, whatever other characteristics of membership he or she might share.
4. The temporary violation of norms and juxtaposition of opposites such as those described by anthropologists as inherent to the dynamics of the totem ritual.

It is this fourth element that may provide us with the most direct evidence. We are looking for flagrant contradictions that nonetheless appear to comfortably coexist within the fabric of the mythical narrative; elements that appear illogical in tandem unless explained by the conflicting psychological impulses they serve to satisfy. These contradictions will reflect those of the totem ritual such as the ambiguous status of the surrogate victim as a boundary crosser, simultaneously both insider and outsider; the juxtaposition of mourning and celebration of the sacrificial act; and the temporary permission, if not obligation, of acts normally seen as violations of social norms. These contradictions all point to the manner in which the sacrificial murder, normatively regarded as a crime – indeed, elevated in its criminal status by the excess of reverence afforded to its victim – is transmuted into an act of piety.

Although the particular ways in which these elements manifest will vary widely from nation to nation, the need to repress the violent core of society is basic to any social order, and the need to repress ambivalence toward signifiers associated with the premodern ethnic past is basic to the particular form of society known as the nation. It is for this reason that the ritual tends to follow a predictable script, even across highly varied societies and cultures. A figure (or figures) who (1) symbolically represents the nation, (2) willingly and with foreknowledge chooses martyrdom and defeat, but nonetheless (3) fights and struggles valiantly and (4) must be betrayed by a close member or members of his or her (or their) own community in order to be (5) vanquished and ultimately killed by an outside force that personifies the community's most significant "other," (6) who is himself or herself (or themselves) subsequently killed or conquered, either by divine providence or through the activism of other members of the community who sacrifice toward that end. The story concludes with (7) some indication of the indestructibility or continuity of the hero/savior/nation in spirit, pointing to the promise of a future redemption.

There are multiple ways that these narrative elements can be expressed, and these will vary from nation to nation. But the presence of these elements is remarkably consistent. They may be expressed either in the form of specific allegorical figures or symbolic events; in characterizations attributed to entire groups, ethnicities, or social classes featured in historical representations; or through more subtle narrative devices that serve the same purpose and convey the same message. Obviously, given the confines of space, the defeat myths of every nation cannot be examined for their correspondence to the narrative described. Even for those nations I do examine, it is a practical impossibility to thoroughly assess every possible manifestation of the national myth in order to establish universally and beyond doubt both its centrality to national identity and its conformity to the script described here. The best I can do is to offer some striking correlations to this narrative across various national cultures, especially pronounced during intense periods of nation-building activity, all of which manifest similar contradictions pointing to the ambivalence that the myth is structured to resolve.

This brings us to the question of sources. How does one go about determining with confidence the content of a nation's mythology, collective memory or construction of history as an object of examination? A national myth cannot be tested against a set of externally verifiable data, such as historical documents, for a group's collective construction of the past is different than its actual history. One can offer a far more objective argument by examining historical documents in order to draw factual conclusions about the past than one can by reading the minds of a given population at a given moment in time in order to discern how they perceive their past. National myth does not exist in any concrete or canonical format against which various expressions and understandings can be tested. It is resistant to such codification because it is not monolithic, and any literary expression of a myth can reflect only a certain interpretation relevant to a particular time, place, and sectional set of interests. Although there may be signifiers common enough to be deemed universal to the nation and particular enough to be deemed characteristic, even these will involve multiple conflicting narratives, stresses, and understandings driven by varying class, regional, and political–ideological differences.

This introduces difficulties for works such as this that endeavor to draw conclusions about a group's identity based on its understanding of the past. A group's collective memory cannot be fully understood through historical records or literary texts because memory is not a literary phenomenon. Maccoby notes that, on the contrary, once myth is fixed to literary form, it tends to lose much of its power, though certain media such as religious texts and epic songs consciously endeavor to preserve the mythic aura in that they do not serve merely to tell stories but rather as literary enactments of ritual.[2] A myth exists independently of any particular documenting or telling of it and is therefore not written but understood.

We would be better advised then to view myth not as an expression of group history but rather as a form of language, which more than the sum total of words and rules of grammar listed in a dictionary ultimately exists in the realm of shared meaning. Written records can only be a reflection of that shared meaning but, as well, they provide us with vital clues as to how people at various periods constructed and reached such

[2] Maccoby 1992: 4.

understanding. To reconstruct a myth, then, we will be required to examine the process by which the social construction of the myth took place. In other words, even if one cannot make a definitive statement as to what a group's myth-symbol system or collective construction of the past *is* at a given moment in time, one can at least offer a plausible extrapolation drawn from observation of what it *does*, in terms of how the myth has manifested in constructions of history, expressions of culture, and political discourse. We can reconstruct the fundamentals of the national myth through the writings, statements, and actions of those socialized into a particular construction as they pertain to mythic images or past events and whose works have in turn influenced the manner in which subsequent generations were socialized.

Such sources can be placed on a continuum from those bound by the principles of scholarly empiricism to those more openly engaged in creative endeavor. At the scholarly end of the scale, we have national historians such as the Czech František Palacký, Konstantinos Paparrigopoulos of Greece, Israel's Yigal Yadin, or Ghana's A. Adu Boahen. Although such historians are dependent on their sources to present a picture that can be objectively defended as factual, these sources are inevitably weighed and interpreted in light of contemporary assumptions and modes of understanding and presented in light of contemporary needs. Empiricism is only one of these; the nation, with its sense of *longue durée* and distinct character, is another. But far from being opposing forces, these two principles actually complement each other. The use of historical documents and relics authentic to the distant past in the construction of the national conception of history enhances the nation's claim to longevity in a manner that can be presented as objectively defensible even to outsiders. It is for this reason that such histories, although they can be said to operate on an elite level, also have a broad social impact. The constructions of the past provided by scholars and elevated with the imprint of scholarly objectivity are adopted as canonical, influencing the history codified in textbooks and disseminated through mass public education, thereby contributing toward the shaping of popular understandings.

The question of what *really* happened at Kosovo, Masada, White Mountain, or Constantinople, interesting though it may be, is of only peripheral concern to this work. The details are of interest to us only to the extent that the mythical narratives at any given time may be at variance with those historical sources from which the myth would have been at least partially constructed, or with earlier understandings pointing to a change that, if not justified by the discovery of new sources, could be hypothesized as indicating a shift in ideological assumptions. As we have seen, and shall examine further, such shifts in perceptions and interpretations can indeed be correlated with the social changes inherent to the processes of nation building.

But the historical record is not the only or even the primary source according to which group identity is constructed. A child's socialization into a collective memory precedes the formal study of history and can therefore have a greater effect on identity and subsequent behavior. Children in nursery schools learn about major historical figures and events from stories, poems, plays, and songs that blend fact with fiction, history with legend, in a way that renders them more appealing to the very young but also forms sentiments and ideas about the past that will persist.[3] It is these sentiments and ideas, more than the factual events of the history itself and more than any particular restatement, fictional or historical of those events, that are pivotal to understanding the nature of the group's identity.

Historical records collected by national historians are therefore only one of the forces that go into shaping the collective construction of history, and rarely are the most broadly influential. Consequently, efforts to examine the ways in which a nation conceptualizes its history require using not only credible historical documents but also records relating to education, oral traditions, family socialization, religious codes, and messages imparted by religious professionals, as well as various canonical and noncanonical texts, including epics, chronicles, hymns, law codes, songs, stories, and literature, all of which compete with scholarly appraisals to crystallize memory and myth in the construction of an image of the past. Some of these sources may predate the modern nation, but what is of relevance to our study is the way in which they are packaged and presented to serve the modern nation's needs.

Folklorists such as N.G. Politis of Greece and Vuk Karadžić of Serbia, famous for collecting such sources relevant to their respective national traditions, were bound by a principle of empiricism similar to that of the national historians. But rather than seeking what was historically factual, their goal was the more nebulous category of the culturally authentic, understanding of which is more openly subjective. The texts they collected and published, though not necessarily treated as literally true, were nonetheless considered part of the unique cultural heritage of the nation. Therefore, judgments of the folklorists as to which texts were of

---

[3] Zerubavel 1995: 6.

greatest priority and which versions most authentic could not help but have been informed by contemporary concerns and assumptions as to the character of the nations to which they belonged, however scrupulously the rules of scholarly accuracy were maintained.

But just as we are not seeking the true history behind the national myth, neither are we seeking to distill the most authentic form of the myth in the sense of determining its earliest or most popular incarnation stripped of deviations that might have been the result of later additions or redactions. As Levi-Strauss often stressed, there is no "most authentic" in the study of myth. All variations of a myth must be taken into account because it is the sum of these variant versions that forms a totality, and necessary elements omitted by one version will often be supplied by another. What may appear as a late, inauthentic addition can add an essential element to the myth at the point in time in which it was added, significantly affecting the manner in which the story shapes identity and meaning. As Maccoby, for example, points out, Judas could not have both hanged himself and burst open in a field, yet the need to express both overwhelming guilt and divine retribution necessitated that both accounts be preserved in the gospels.[4]

Thus, if the content of a myth appears to change at a certain point in time, one must examine the circumstances that may have precipitated the change. And, if different, even contradictory versions of a myth coexist at any given time – indeed, if, as occurs in some cases, contradictory events or interpretations are contained even within the same text – one must explore the questions of what interests are served by each of the divergent accounts and why these interests were more important than internal consistency. As with the historians, the folklorists are as much the objects of our study as they are sources of data, insofar as their efforts to determine the most authentic form of their national myth tell us more about their own motivations, dependent on the social contexts in which they were operating, than about that of their subjects.

Finally, we have works of literature, which cannot be tested against historical facts or documents because they openly reflect a creative vision, even while they may use historical events as their raw materials. Certain authors straddle the divide between art and folklore, such as Andrejs Pumpurs, who wrote the Latvian epic poem *Lāčplēsis* based on a collection of Latvian folk tales, but more openly engaged in an act of creation to generate a product suitable to the nation's contemporary needs; an

---

[4] Maccoby 1992: 59, 102, cf. Matt. 27:5; Acts 1:18.

endeavor whose success can be measured only by the widespread popularity this epic achieved relative to previous similar efforts. Others straddle the divide between literature and history, such as the Czech Alois Jirasek, whose works endeavored to evocatively portray historical events of national importance within the broad confines of historical accuracy. Other authors, such as Alexandros Papadiamantis of Greece, used historical events and periods as the settings for their fictional works, while Petar Petrović-Njegoš of Serbia and Israel's Yitzchak Lamdan evoked the relevant events as allegories.

It is important to note that even elements of a myth consciously understood by national elites and masses alike as fictional can often have relevance; particular relevance, in fact, for if they are considered ahistorical there must be some other explanation, beyond the preservation of an authentic past, as to why they are retained as integral elements of the story. Nationalists are often acutely aware that the historical accuracy of their myths is far from their most important feature, and it is often in works of literature, unbounded by the constraints of empiricism, that the centrality of such elements becomes evident.

It must, however, be reiterated that all of the preceding sources, even taken together, can be considered only as elite reflections of the deeper national myth rather than as the documented myth itself. In assessing the popular resonance of the constructs reflected in these written sources, we can only offer speculation grounded not just in the popularity of these works but also in the level of popular mobilization that appears to have called on these constructs and their appearance in political discourse.

Focal Points in National History

Significant historical changes are usually the result of a process over a span of time rather than a single event. Yael Zerubavel notes, however, that collective memory tends to appoint particular events as symbolic markers of change. This serves to give a sense of coherence to a collective construction of history, as well as offering a better opportunity for ritualized remembrance than does a gradual process of transition, as the year of the event becomes an emblem (1066, 1453), the date a locus of cyclical ritual (Vidovdan, *La Diada*), the number of intervening years a slogan ("300 years of darkness"), and the location a monument (Masada, Kosovo Polje). Such events are presented as turning points that changed the course of the group's development and are therefore elevated beyond their immediate historical context into symbolic moments that serve as paradigms for understanding the group's history as a whole.

However, the flip-side of this process is equally important: As some elements of the past are elevated, others are minimized or even forgotten. Hence, the separation of the master historical narrative into periods, with certain pivotal events serving as turning points, is a process fraught with political implications. Ideological principles will inevitably inform the covering-up of certain events or elements, whereas others are transformed into political myths that serve as a lens through which the group interprets the past, understands the present, and prepares for the future.[5] If we apply Anthony Smith's ethnosymbolic model to this principle, we can conclude that because the purpose of a commemorative narrative is to highlight the group's distinct identity, the most important symbolic moments will tend be those that distinguish the group from others, asserting its distinct traits such as ancestry, land, or unique values, thereby dispelling any denial of the group's legitimacy as a distinct and independent entity.

The following chapters examine the mythical perception of events that are understood within the historical narratives of their respective societies as turning points marking the transition from a period of autonomy and prosperity to a period of subjugation and decline; moments in which history turned against the nation. Further, I explore how commemoration of these moments through the mythical narrative serves, paradoxically per-haps, to reinforce the solidarity, legitimacy, and sense of distinctiveness of the group.

In nearly all of the examined cases, the notion that a "golden age" of autonomy was abruptly ended by the specific moment of defeat is a fictional product of the mythical narrative, to the point where, in many cases, the selection of a particular event as the pivotal moment of tran-sition between independence and subjugation appears almost arbitrary. The Serbian mythical narrative would identify defeat at the Battle of Kosovo as the decisive turning point between independence and national servitude, in which the renaissance brought to fruition during the reign of Stefan Dušan was rudely interrupted by the conquest of Serbia by the Ottoman Empire. According to the myth, the defeat of Serbian forces under Lazar Hrebeljanović at the hands of the Ottomans destroyed the medieval Serbian state, resulting in the Serbs' subjugation under Turkish rule. In fact, the Empire had already begun to disintegrate shortly after the death of Dušan in 1355. By the late 1370s, it had already been divided

5 Zerubavel 1995: 8–9.

into a patchwork of autonomous principalities, the largest of which was ruled by Lazar out of the town of Kruševac.[6] On the other hand, Serbian independence was able to survive to some degree for another 70 years after the battle with only minimal Ottoman interference. Despite formal vassal status, autonomy was maintained under the reign of Lazar's son, Stefan Lazarević, and Serbia even enjoyed a period of economic recovery and cultural renaissance as large numbers of Christian refugees from other areas of the Balkans – priests, monks, writers, architects, and artists from Bulgarian, Greek, and southern Serbian regions subject to the Ottomans – migrated to his principality. Serbia did not formally lose its independence until 1459.[7]

Even more intriguing is the fact that many contemporary records hail the battle as a glorious Serbian victory. King Tvrtko of Bosnia, who was not himself at the battle but sent a contingent, describes it unambiguously as such in letters to the senates of Florence and the Dalmatian city of Trogir. The same impression is given a few years later in a book by a French author, Philippe de Mézières, and in the first reactions of Byzantine writers who declared the battle a humiliation for the Turks.[8] At the time, the death of the sultan at the battle would have been the only detail significant to most of these writers, and the immediate withdrawal of the Turks to Anatolia to deal with the matter of succession would have given the impression that they had been successfully repelled. But there are even early Serbian sources that suggest a Serbian victory, though most are religious texts in the form of eulogies designed to encourage a cult of sainthood around Lazar as martyr, and it is therefore difficult to discern whether victory is meant in the spiritual or political sense.[9] As one such verse goes:

> When the pagan horde lunged at you . . .
> You, holy new David opposed them
> And defeated that Goliath
> With his multitude of heathen
> And as a martyr because of blood
> You are crowned with the victor's wreath.[10]

Some secular Serbian accounts, such as the chronicle of Peć, give descriptions of the battle that offer no clear sense of who won or lost, preferring

---

[6] Malcolm 1998: 58–9.
[7] Emmert 1990: 2–3, 32.
[8] Ibid.: 44–6.
[9] Mihailovich 1991: 142.
[10] *Sluzba knezu lazaru*, quoted in Emmert 1990: 70–1.

instead to focus on the deaths of Murad and Lazar.[11] There is, however, evidence that the battle came to be regarded as a defeat within a few generations. The Bulgarian writer Konstantin in the court of Stefan Lazarević in 1411 described the battle as a Turkish victory.[12] Regardless, it is clear that in the decades immediately following the event, there were competing interpretations even within the Serbian cultural milieu as to the outcome of the battle and its meaning. Why then did the vision of defeat ultimately win popular appeal? The answer, at this stage, is probably more political than psychological. As time went on and Ottoman domination of the region became a reality, people searched for an explanation for their state of subjugation. They found it in the records and songs of a battle that had been built up extensively by both the church and the remaining state institutions through the promotion of the cult of Lazar, which enhanced the prestige and legitimacy of Lazar's son and, by extension, the church that continued to rely on his patronage.[13]

Although the defeat of the Judean revolt against the Romans in 70 C.E. might be less ambiguous, the appointment of this event in general, and the fall of Masada in particular, by the Zionist construction of history as the moment when the last vestige of Jewish independence fell, justifying the subsequent rise of Zionism as a long-delayed new beginning, is also largely a fiction. The collapse of Jewish autonomy at the end of the Second Temple period, like the collapse of Serbian autonomy at the hands of the Ottoman Empire, was the result of a gradual process that began long before Masada, was not significantly affected by this particular event, and was only fully completed several decades afterwards.

The autonomy enabled by the dissolution of the Seleucid Empire in the second century B.C.E. began to dissolve shortly after the successful Maccabean revolt as Roman power in the region became a reality. The short-lived independence of the Judean polity can be said to have been ended already when Pompey marched into Jerusalem in 63 B.C.E.[14] Ironically, the last period during which the territory could be said to have enjoyed any vestige of independence from foreign power was during the reign of Herod, who, by maintaining a level of cooperation with the powers in Rome, was able to rule the territory with relative autonomy during which time he rebuilt the Second Temple as well as the fortress

---

[11] Emmert 1990: 72–4.
[12] Malcolm 1998: 76.
[13] Emmert 1990: 75.
[14] Shargel 1979: 361.

at Masada. It was only after his death that the region formally became a province of the Empire, ruled directly by governors appointed from Rome. But despite its penchant for radical reinterpretation, the Zionist historical narrative could hardly transform Herod from a figure vilified by the Jewish tradition into an inspirational symbol of self-sacrifice in defense of the continued freedom and independence of Judea, when the record makes it very clear that he died of old age while doing everything in his power to defend his own authority. Instead, the mythical narrative plays up his dependence on Rome and his questionable Jewish ancestry, identifying him as an outsider and an example of foreign domination.[15]

More than 1,800 years later, it was a similar gradual process that led to the incorporation of Asante into the Gold Coast Colony under British rule. But, as Adu Boahen notes, the Yaa Asantewaa war made a greater impact on memory than any of the previous campaigns of 1807, 1824, 1826, 1873–1874, and 1896 between the British and Asante, some of which were of greater strategic consequence.[16] The defeat of the Asante in 1874 was considerably more decisive than the 1900–1901 revolt of only a fraction of Asante provinces led by Yaa Asantewaa. But at that time, Britain was not interested in exercising direct rule, resulting in an uneasy period during which a defeated and unstable Asante polity continued to exist at the sufferance of the British. This attitude changed with the specter of French and German competition for territory and Asante allegiance, and direct rule was imposed in 1896. But this was the result of a bloodless coup in which Asantehene Prempe I, along with several of his key lieutenants, were arrested and exiled. This was another moment of greater significance to the loss of Asante independence; however, the lack of violent resistance made it a poor symbolic focal point for commemoration. In short, the lost war took place in 1874 but was not accompanied by a loss of independence; the loss of independence occurred in 1896 but was not the consequence of a lost war. The Asante revolt of 1900–1901 provided a better symbolic focal point, partly because it resulted in the "Ashanti Order in Council" of September 29, 1901, formally

[15] An example of this can be found in the book on Masada written under Yigael Yadin's name for young readers: "Herod was a foreign king who ruled over the Jews. (He died about the time Jesus was born.) The Romans had put Herod on his throne, and he was able to remain there only because the power of Rome was behind him. The Romans called Herod a client-king. In return for supporting him on the throne of Judea they received from him much wealth – which Herod took from his subjects and paid to his Roman masters" (Yadin and Gottlieb 1969: 7–8).

[16] Boahen 2003: 27.

declaring Asante to be *de facto* British territory by right of military conquest, but also because this moment, unlike previous, more decisive campaigns, incorporated both sacrifice and defeat according to a narrative
appropriate to British, Asante, and later Ghanaian interests, containing
an adequate wealth of culturally suitable images on which to draw.[17]

Similarly, the Czech national myth would identify the Battle of White
Mountain as the moment of the Bohemian Kingdom's final collapse,
when, in fact, it would better be described as the end of a Protestant
aristocratic revolt against what was already a Catholic Habsburg status
quo. Loss of autonomy and incorporation into the Habsburg Empire was,
in this case as well, a gradual process that can be said to have started as
early as the end of the Hussite wars, when the Bohemian crown passed
from a native Czech to a Polish dynasty, thereafter to be transferred to the
Habsburgs who immediately initiated a process of consolidating power
against the claims of the traditional nobility.[18] The pivotal significance
of White Mountain even in the national construction of history was not
uncontested. Palacký ends his *History of the Czechs* with the Battle of
Mohács (1526), arguably a more historically tenable end point to the
autonomy of the Kingdom of Bohemia. According to Robert Pynsent, it
was the Revivalists and subsequent nationalist intellectuals who tended
to focus on the Battle of White Mountain as the moment of disaster,
despite the effective decline of Czech culture and political power during
the period between these events, largely because of their construction of
modern Czech identity around the principle of language. Having adopted
the Veleslavin dialect as the model for a revived literary Czech, the greatest
achievement of which was the Kralice Bible (1579–1588), their ideology
dictated that Czech literary culture could have entered into its period of
degeneracy only after White Mountain.[19]

"Axis natio"

Mircea Eliade frequently noted in his various studies of comparative religion that such focal points serve as more than just convenient loci for
commemoration. These myths, monuments, and commemorations serve
a vital ontological purpose. Human beings cannot function in entirely
homogeneous or continuous space and time. They require reference points
that serve to define the sacred; qualitatively distinct interruptions in

[17] Akyeampong 2000: 5; Wilks 2000: 13–15.
[18] Sayer 1998: 42.
[19] Pynsent 1994: 173.

space and time that enable communication between the temporal and the eternal, the ephemeral and the absolute. And the possibility of such points of contact implies the potential for one greater than all others – the *axis mundi* – variously identified as the center of the world, the spot where creation began, the place where the distance between the planes of heaven, hell, and earth is shortest and thus where communication with both the divine absolute and the world of the dead is most achievable.

Because the *axis mundi* serves as the locus where cosmic regions intersect, where all dimensions of the universe are accessible, it is a place sacred above all others. It defines reality, for as the place where one is closest to the Supreme Being, it is the place where being is most fully manifest. For this reason, it is experienced in a state of ecstasy. It allows access to transcendent states of being that cannot be articulated in mundane terms and is thus a place where ordinary social norms are suspended. It is a place of active passage and transition, of border crossings where beings of radically different nature come together and merge with one another; where opposites coexist as contradictions are resolved in the process toward a more whole, spiritual existence. The *axis mundi* is frequently expressed through the image of a sacred mountain, a place deemed to be the highest point in the universe and thus the closest terrestrial contact point to the heavens. But it can also be replicated by human effort and take the form of a sacred pillar, statue, emblem, building, or the precincts of a sacred city. Replication spreads the capacity for contact with the transcendent reality to anything touched by the emblem.[20]

But, as with most theorists we have examined, Eliade too posits a radical distinction in this respect between primitive religious and modern nonreligious man, with the latter better able to accept homogeneity and continuity and thus experiencing little need for reference points to the sacred. But while respecting that the difference between premodern and modern norms might cause such reference points to assume a radically different character, even to the point where they are unrecognizable as the same phenomenon, I propose that this element that Eliade has identified as universal even among widely differing forms of religious practice is not merely primitive but rather primordial, as basic to the human condition in modern times as it has been in the traditions that he compares. Modern man is no less in need of reference points that transcend the homogeneity of space and time, but the ultimate reality to which these points refer is very different than in the case of religious man. National man is not

---

[20] Eliade 1959: 20–2, 36–8, 68; Sullivan 1987: 712–13.

concerned with the whole of creation but merely with a certain bounded section of it; it is not the heavens with which he must communicate but rather the "imagined community," all of its members over space and time, the vast majority of whom he can never know but with whom he must nonetheless identify in order to place his own mortality in the context of something enduring. A symbol serving such a function in this context could be called an "axis natio."

Religious man can live in only a sacred world because it is only in such a world that he participates in being. By extension, modern man can exist only in the nation. His existence is predicated on connection with the transtemporal national reality, a connection that must be substantiated with a concrete point of contact. This point of contact can take many symbolic forms, but these all share the common characteristic of linking all members of the nation, and only those members of the particular nation, not just over contemporary space but also through the *longue durée* of the distant ethnic past and the indeterminate future.

It might be supposed that the adoption of Masada as a national symbol by the early Zionists unconsciously called on the impulse to locate the axis point in a mountain, an instinct expressed in traditional Judaism with the construction of the Temple on Mount Moriah in the heart of Jerusalem. But it is more likely the association of the site with a moment of mass national sacrifice, along with its status as both a natural and archeological landmark, that made it an appropriate focal point for a specifically national mythology. The permanence of the mountain as a part of the landscape associates the symbol with the territory while providing it with a convincing claim to authenticity that could nonetheless weather social and ideological change. By incorporating the mountain into the national communion, the connection of the nation to an immemorial past and its longevity in an indefinite future is assured, however the twists and turns of history might alter the nation and its circumstances in the details. The site offers a sense of continuity with *something*, while the fact that artifacts are brought to light in support of a particular interpretation of what that something is lends power to the interpretation, providing a tangible link not just to a vague sense of the past but also to an actual story, albeit one capable of change along with political circumstances and the needs of the nation. The presence of the same sacred place (where any number of rituals could be conducted), the same ancient story (subject to various embellishments), and the same archaeological artifacts (from which one could pick and choose) preserves a sense of continuity even through radical shifts in the ideological messages communicated through the symbol.

The fact that the Masada story was anchored to a geographical location also provided a locus for commemorative ritual. In her study of Israeli collective memory, Zerubavel emphasizes the role of pilgrimage in the development of the Masada myth. In the early days of the Yishuv, the trek to the site was viewed by Zionist youth movements as an initiation rite, involving activities at the top of the mountain that developed all of the essential elements of a ritual that at times consciously parodied traditional Jewish liturgy. Hikers referred to the journey to the top of Masada as *aliyah b'regel*, the same biblical term used for the ancient pilgrimage to the Temple during pilgrimage holidays. In this way, secular national symbols were consciously substituted for traditional religious ones. The change in site was also accompanied by a change in time. Rather than the traditional pilgrimage days of Passover, Shavuot, and Sukkot, the most popular time of year for this *aliyah b'regel* was Hanukkah; a relatively minor holiday in the traditional Jewish calendar but one that was associated with a struggle for national liberation.[21]

The climb up the mountain would be timed so that arrival at the summit would coincide with sunrise, followed by a reading of Yitzchak Lamdan's poem, "Masada," or recitation of the story as told by Josephus, in particular the speeches attributed to the commander of the Masada defenders, Elazar Ben Yair. This served to transform the listeners into symbolic actors, vicariously playing the roles of their ancient predecessors who once listened to that same speech. Drawing on the Jewish tradition of reading sacred texts in a sacred space, this was a secularization of religious ritual and sanctification of secular ritual, transforming the national symbol into a quasi-religious one. In this context, a poem such as "Masada" became liturgy and an ancient account like Josephus a sacred text on par with the Bible. Groups would light fire inscriptions made of canvas shaped into letters that would burn at night, most often of Lamdan's verse "never again shall Masada fall."[22]

This line from Lamdan's poem became a national motto that, as such, outlived the popularity of the poem itself. Although the line might appear to express optimism and hope, the poem as a whole was not an optimistic work but rather was pervaded throughout with a sense of loss and despair, reflecting Lamdan's own experience immigrating to Palestine in

---

[21] Zerubavel 1995: 64, 124–6; Passover tended to be a second choice for trips to Masada for similar reasons. For example, in 1963, a group of Israeli commando officers decided to hold a Seder on Masada to celebrate "the feast of liberation on the spot which has come to symbolize the struggle for Israel's freedom."

[22] Zerubavel 1995: 128.

the aftermath of World War I. In the poem, the protagonist returns to Zion exhausted and near death, disappointed by the failure of all other avenues of redemption. Masada "sits on the brink of chaos" but it is there that he will raise the "banner of the last rebellion." Along the way, he is confronted and tempted by personifications of the many alternative solutions chosen by Jewish youth who remained in Europe – revenge, fatalism, a socialist activist stance, and so on – all of whom insist to him that Masada (which is to say, Zionism) is "a lie" or "a fiction," "a new snare laid by Fate in its scorn for the last remnant," or "invented by the despairing and confused who have no strength to hold the oars" of world revolution. But as these alternative routes fail one by one, Masada comes through as the only viable option for the future.[23] The work is more about the journey than the destination; the question of whether the Zionist enterprise will ultimately succeed is left open. The trek up the mountain is described as difficult, demanding determination against doubt, mental distress, and physical fatigue, and thus the poem is characterized by radical shifts of mood, from despair and longing for the past to a frenzied optimism. In context, then, the declaration that Masada shall not fall again is less a confident affirmation than a cry of desperation, where the protagonist is reenacting the defenders' last stand against the Romans through his own last stand against the nightmare world around him.[24]

The use of Masada as a reference to Zion elevated the symbol to the level of a historical turning point, representing the return to Masada as the cure for a historical rupture. Symbols of continuity are central to Lamdan's poem, which contains numerous metaphors such as the rekindling of fire and adding a new link to the chain of history. In that sense, the return to Masada represents more than the ongoing struggle of the Jews against their numerous enemies throughout history but also a revolt against the verdict of history itself[25]:

Against the hostile Fate of generations, an antagonistic breast is bared with a roar:

Enough! You or I! Here will the battle decide the final judgement![26]

If the age-old Fate derides: "In vain!" we will pluck out Its inciting tongue! And in spite of itself, the derisive negation, defeated, shall nod its head: "Indeed, indeed. Amen!"[27]

[23] Lamdan 1971: 200–2; see Zerubavel 1995: 118; Shargel 1979: 361.
[24] Alter 1973: 22.
[25] Zerubavel 1995: 115–7.
[26] Lamdan 1971: 199.
[27] Ibid.: 215.

Fate comes through in the poem as a manifestation of God, who is explicitly removed from his place of primacy in the Jewish construction of history. "Finished, finished and completed, though not 'finished and completed with praise to God, creator of the world.' We have no praise for God, creator of the world – As from now, a new book of Genesis is opened on the wall." Lamdan turns traditional symbols and liturgical formulas on their head, and the final line, "Be strong, be strong, and we shall be strengthened!,"[28] is addressed to the people, who replace God as the focal point of this new liturgy.

But although these symbols of continuity juxtaposed against a radical rejection of traditional Jewish alternatives were retained in the adaptation of this poem to the national mythology, the ambivalence – the image of Zionism as a desperate last resort, less a refuge than a last stand – disappears into what is presented as a proud, heroic narrative. Pessimistic expressions of loneliness and loss dissolve in favor of the hopeful aspects of the account, culminating in the verse: "Ascend the chain of the dance! Never again shall Masada fall!"[29] Stripped of its context, this line was turned into the essence of the Masada lesson. The use of the word "again" reinforced the sense of continuity pivotal to the Zionist construction of history and was the first explicit identification between the final holdout of the Jews against Roman domination and the new Jewish settlement in Palestine, wherein "Rome" served as a metaphor for the hostile European world.[30] But the poem went beyond the parallel between Masada as the last fortress to fall in the revolt and modern Zionism as the last resort of the Jewish people following events in Europe. At the same time, the fall of Masada, although it is not described directly, is depicted in contrast to Zionism as the first outpost of Jewish renewal. "The son of Yair shall again appear. He is not dead, not dead!"[31]

This sense of identification was taken up by the youth movements, as expressed in a Hebrew guidebook, *Do You Know the Land?*, written by Joseph Braslawski in 1950: ["The youth] come to draw from Masada strength for future struggles for our national life that is renewing itself in the land. Those who ascend Masada proclaim that the last defenders of the Great Rebellion did not die in vain; [they fell] for the sanctification of political and spiritual sovereignty. [Today] their labors reap rewards, for

[28] Ibid.: 233–4.
[29] Ibid.: 215.
[30] Ben-Yehuda 1995: 221–3; Zerubavel 1994: 77–8; Shargel 1979: 362.
[31] Lamdan 1971: 215.

their sons have returned to their borders."[32] The trip, in its association with a turning point in national history, came to be viewed as a turning point in individual development as well, a transition from youth to adulthood or from immigrant to "new Hebrew," and the effective erasure of the 2,000 years that separated the renewal of national life from the defeat at Masada. It was a form of national sacrifice, leading to a sense of national salvation as arrival at the summit was meant to demonstrate that difficult though the effort toward national fulfilllment might be, it was not unachievable.

At the time, there was no access by road and no cable car to the summit, and reaching the site through either the Judean desert or along the Dead Sea shore was a complex and often perilous undertaking. Field trips could last for a week or longer, under difficult conditions that involved threatening situations such as dehydration, treacherous climbs, searches for tracks and routes, or encounters with hostile Bedouin and the British police. Thus, the trip had a sense of adventure that contributed to its ritualistic element. It was not something that could be done by just anyone, not even by just any Jew. Completing the trip placed one among a select elite with the ability and willingness to succeed in an effort that served as a symbolic parallel to that required for achieving a Jewish homeland. It demanded a high degree of physical fitness, willpower, and daredevil mentality; the same qualities of the "new Hebrew" deemed essential to the success of the Zionist endeavor as a whole. Furthermore, it would only be undertaken by those willing to identify with a process that, through Lamdan's poem, had come to symbolize the quest for national fulfillment, as well as with the sacrifice of Masada's ancient defenders.

A genre of personal narratives developed that related heroic youthful adventures in unfamiliar or enemy territory in which the protagonists overcame obstacles and survived through their resourcefulness and daring. After several fatal accidents, school groups were forbidden from formally undertaking the trip, but trips continued regardless, arranged independently by youth groups, often in defiance of their elders' advice or authority. These new threats and obstacles only enhanced the appeal of the pilgrimage, as the purpose was to confront challenges, and the deaths sanctified the bond between the "new Hebrews" and this symbolic center. Defiance of authority, in this case the British, represented defiance of the forces of history spoken of in Lamdan's poem, and triumph over such obstacles represented the revival of a national spirit suppressed by those

---

[32] Quoted in Zerubavel 1995: 128.

forces. Social solidarity was stressed as a higher value than obedience to authority in the schools and youth movements, and field trips in general were used as mechanisms for reinforcement of group solidarity. Defiance of law and order also served as a means of distinction against the Exile Jewish mentality.[33]

After the founding of the state of Israel, armored divisions of the Israel Defence Forces (IDF) were frequently sworn in at the top of Masada. There was no organized decision to this effect, but rather it was carried over from the fact that many of the commanders of the IDF had come from the Palmah, where Masada had played an important symbolic role. It was a common symbol whose meaning was understood by anyone with a history in the prestate youth or defense movements, and everyone had associations and memories connected to it; of treks, ritual readings of Josephus and Lamdan, and so on. As Shaul Bevar, one of the commanders credited with starting the ritual, commented:

It was important to have a challenge, and the site had to have a historic meaning. In the eyes of the Palmah's members, the most natural thing was that this challenge and historical meaning would be suggested on top of Masada. There were many Palmah members in the armored units. Everyone you said 'Masada' to remembered a ceremony from his days in the youth movement – the guy with the flute and Lamdan's poem... Personal experiences are immediately brought to memory... Masada is the real thing. In Masada you walk in history.[34]

In effect, the state co-opted the youth tradition of pilgrimage. The official character of the ceremony transformed what had once been a spontaneously developed expression against authority into a formal contract between solider and state.[35] As time went on, a standard structure evolved for the swearing-in ceremony, based to a large extent on the rituals that had been conducted by the prestate youth movements. In his book, *The Masada Myth*, Israeli sociologist Nachman Ben-Yehuda distinguishes the basic ingredients as follows: (1) the trek to Masada and climb; (2) a parade in formation at the top of the mountain; (3) a loud reading of sections of Ben Yair's speech in Josephus, and sometimes passages of Lamdan's poem; (4) fire inscriptions, usually stating "Masada shall not fall again";

---

[33] Zerubavel 1995: 121–4.
[34] Ben-Yehuda 1995: 151; Ben-Yehuda noted from his interviews that none of the commanders who were attributed with having initiated the idea claimed that it was a new practice when they took command, instead perceiving the tradition to have gone back to the Palmah.
[35] Zerubavel 1995: 130–1.

(5) the swearing in; (6) a speech by both the commander and usually a chief military rabbi; and (7) receipt of personal arms.[36] The overriding message was continuity, identifying the values of the modern IDF with those supposedly held by the ancient defenders of Masada: love of country, love of independence, and readiness to sacrifice. The swearing-in was meant to be the mirror image of Masada's fall; the new heroic age was to begin at the place where the last one ended. It was an act of historical defiance, asserting that the Roman army, in the end, did not win; that the Jewish nation was not beaten; that "we are here again." The oath would begin with the words, "Because of the bravery of the Masada fighters, we stand here today," and end with Lamdan's line "Masada shall not fall again."[37]

When large-scale excavations of the site began in 1963 under the direction of Yigal Yadin, widespread participation of the public both in the financing of the project and as volunteer workers elevated the endeavor to the level of a national ritual. The excavations were depicted in the press as heroic efforts, a story in their own right, and a symbolic resurrection of the event itself in a manner that preserved the notion of continuity.[38] Such imagery was used quite openly by Yadin, for example, when he stated on Israeli radio that the decision to open the dig to volunteers would not have occurred to him "if Masada hasn't been of such enormous significance. It is inconceivable that if we dig at Masada, people would not volunteer to take a part in this excavation, even for a short period only."[39] In 1964, a fundraising campaign was launched in which thousands of children from schools and youth movements went door to door selling donation units of 5 Israeli liras each. The goal was to collect a total of 1.5 million liras. The campaign received official backing from the president of Israel, who called on Israelis to donate, and the Israeli army provided both manpower and resources for the dig itself. According to Yadin, army headquarters considered the excavation to be an "educational enterprise." Of the average 200 people on Masada at any given time during the period of the excavation, 50 to 80 were volunteers (both from Israel and abroad), 30 were military personnel, 40 to 50 were Israeli children, and the rest were staff. Because the volunteers would change every two weeks or so, ultimately thousands were able to

---

[36] Ben-Yehuda 1995: 152–3.
[37] Ibid.: 147–8; Shargel 1979: 363.
[38] Zerubavel 1994: 84.
[39] Quoted in Zerubavel 1995: 65.

participate in the experience, in addition to the hundreds of thousands who gave their symbolic financial support.[40]

Masada might appear at first glance to be a dubious axis symbol, given the lack of significance attributed to the site over most of Jewish history and the fact that it has since been eclipsed by other sites of more durable significance. But it is precisely this unique history that makes it such a valuable test case. Here is a symbol that was elevated from obscurity by the conscious intent of national elites, for a nation that was in no way suffering from any shortage of authentic ethnic symbols. It was embraced spontaneously and enthusiastically by the mass national movement. Then, in just a few decades, it declined just as rapidly as it had risen in the face of social change, to the point where it has already been picked apart by psychologists and sociologists from within the culture. This is a dynamic that demands explanation, as well as provides us an opportunity to examine a symbol of defeat throughout its (admittedly accelerated) lifespan as a national axis point.

Clearly, the choice of Masada was far from arbitrary. Not just any mountain would do, it had to be a mountain that could plausibly be presented as a concrete manifestation of the transition point between an earlier period of sovereignty and the intervening period of domination, such that the connection between the modern national movement and that earlier period could be established. The fact that this transition point was marked by a violent sacrifice in the form of the mass suicide of the defenders made ritual commemoration of the moment by means of this monument all the more poignant. As we shall see when we examine more closely the stereotypical national defeat narrative, Zionist historiography tended to obscure the motif of suicide, transforming what could be interpreted as a defeatist posture by subsuming it into a broader, heroic category of "fighting to the end." The notion that the last defenders of Jewish sovereignty gave their last full measure in its futile defense provided motivation to those who portrayed themselves as the pioneers and later the new defenders of a sovereignty restored.

This sense of continuity was demonstrated when the bones of approximately 25 people were discovered during the excavations of Masada. Evidence as to the identity of these remains was weak,[41] but when Yadin

---

[40] Ben-Yehuda 2002: 74–6.
[41] It in fact appears most likely that the remains were of Romans. The three bodies found in the Northern Palace were apparently buried with ceremonial armor, a practice common among Romans but not among Jews. The bodies were found along with the bones of

declared these to be the remains of at least some of the defenders, specu-
lating as to whether one of them could even be the last defender spoken
of in Josephus,[42] a call was raised in the Knesset, primarily from the religious parties, that the remains be buried as soon as possible according to
Jewish tradition. In July 1969, a formal military burial ceremony was held
on a hill near the site that was dubbed the "Hill of the Defenders." The
event attracted an impressive group of dignitaries, including Menachem
Begin and chief military Rabbi Shlomo Goren who conducted the ceremony. IDF soldiers raised their weapons in salute, and the graves were
marked with stones identical to those used in IDF military cemeteries.
This was a dramatic expression of continuity, whereby modern Israelis
identified with the ancient defenders of Masada by bringing them into
the same moral system of rights and obligations as contemporary soldiers
and citizens. The deaths at Masada were reframed as a sacrifice to the
modern state in a manner that served to blur the line between antiquity
and modern nationalism, through a ceremony comparable in spirit to
commemorations of the Unknown Soldier.[43]

Masada is an example of a national axis point embodied primarily in
a geographical location. Its association with a natural landmark such as
a mountain, and with the ancient relics excavated from an archeological
site, contributed to its power by providing it with an aura of authenticity

---

several animals, possibly grave sacrifices, including pigs – again, unheard of in Jewish
burial practice. Yadin concluded from the presence of pig bones, as well as the haphazard
manner in which the bones were arrayed, that "they were flung here irreverently by the
Roman troops when they cleared the bodies after their victory"(Yadin 1966: 194), but
there is some evidence, in fact, that the bodies had originally been buried in an orderly
manner and that the grave was later disturbed by hyenas. Nor do Yadin's speculations
explain why only 25 bodies were so discarded. The remains of the other 935 alleged
suicides have yet to be located (Ben-Yehuda 2002: 115–34).

[42] (*Wars*, VII:9:1): "... They then chose ten men by lot out of them to slay all the rest;
every one of whom laid himself down by his wife and children on the ground, and
threw his arms about them, and they offered their necks to the stroke of those who by
lot executed that melancholy office; and when these ten had, without fear, slain them
all, they made the same rule for casting lots for themselves, that he whose lot it was
should first kill the other nine, and after all should kill himself. Accordingly, all these
had courage sufficient to be no way behind one another in doing or suffering; so, for a
conclusion, the nine offered their necks to the executioner, and he who was the last of
all took a view of all the other bodies, lest perchance some or other among so many that
were slain should want his assistance to be quite dispatched, and when he perceived that
they were all slain, he set fire to the palace, and with the great force of his hand ran his
sword entirely through himself, and fell down dead near to his own relations"; cf. Yadin
1966: 194.

[43] Ben-Yehuda 1995: 241–3; 2002: 134–7; Zerubavel 1994: 85; 1995: 129–30.

independent of any particular political context and therefore flexible to interpretation. The mountain had been there to witness whatever had taken place; therefore, incorporating the mountain as a person into the national communion served to connect the modern nation across the barriers of time to these totemic events, providing as well a locus for ritual that served to commemorate and reinforce this continuity. But it must be noted that such a natural and authentic monument, though certainly helpful, is not a necessity, for it is not the object itself that is the *axis mundi*, or even the *axis natio*. Rather, the object stands as surrogate to the myth that it signifies. Hence, it is not necessary for the object to be natural or even ancient in order for it to have the aura of the sacred; all it must do is successfully embody the myth.

The *axis mundi* of traditional religious systems could also be embodied in an emblem that rendered sacred anything it touched, which is how even objects of recent human fabrication such as an idol, a temple, or a city could be made to fill this role. This remains true for the nation, as evidenced by the immediate reverence and centrality to national myth and ritual attributed to manmade statues erected in commemoration of totemic figures. By evoking the image of the mythic sacrificial figure in concrete form, the statue immediately generates a site of memory that evokes an aura of the timeless and sacred almost as soon as it is erected. Indeed, by the act of placing the statue, the modern nation serves to connect its own contemporary authority across time to various points and personalities in the national history. Such was the case with the placement of the memorial to Jan Hus on Staromestske Square, the location of the execution of the 27 Czech lords after the defeat at White Mountain. This served to connect multiple associations of time and place, linking the martyr hero of the height of the Bohemian Kingdom to the moment of its fall to the contemporary national revival.

In a similar manner, as soon as a statue to Joan of Arc was erected in 1875 on the Place des Pyramides in Paris, it became a gathering point for political demonstrations by republicans, Catholics, and nationalists alike, all of whom attempted to portray her, through the presence of her statue, as associated with their cause. When the centenary of Voltaire's death in 1878 coincided with the anniversary of the execution of Joan of Arc, demands were made by anticlerical republicans for a demonstration on May 30 at the newly erected statue, in which activists were urged to deposit wreaths at its base with the inscription, "To Jeanne la Lorraine. To the French heroine. To the victim of clericalism." This resulted in open scuffles between Catholic and republican activists and the authorities who ultimately banned demonstrations by either party.[44] Depositing a wreath of mourning at the foot of the statue came to be understood as a symbol of identification with Joan of Arc, and May 30 – the date of her execution, over and above the date of any other accomplishment or milestone in her life – came to be adopted as the most auspicious symbolic point in time at which to demonstrate such identification. Similar struggles for the right of various political factions to lay wreaths at the foot of the statue occurred in subsequent decades, such as an effort by Freemasons to place a wreath on May 30, 1894, that said, "To Joan of Arc, abandoned by the monarchy and the priests, victim of the clergy." In May 1909, the Action Française celebrated Joan's feast-day at her statue in what Robert Gildea describes as "an obvious bid to appropriate her patronage for the extreme Right."[45] One of the benefits of a statue, or of any concrete manifestation of the *axis natio* for that matter, is that it has no say in whether or not it wishes to join a demonstration. All one needs to do is stand next to it and appear plausible, and one has thereby incorporated it, and thus the nation itself, into one's political cause.

A century later, the development of ritual commemorations for the Catalan national day provides a remarkably similar example of this dynamic. Popular commemorations of the fall of Barcelona have also come to revolve around a ritual floral offering, in this case to the statue of Rafael Casanova, located on the spot where he was wounded in 1714 at the old gate of Sant Pere and the current crossroads of Ronda de Sant Pere and Ali-Bei Street. In contrast to the Joan of Arc myth, where May 30 came to be adopted as a convenient date for commemorations that focused on the monument, in the case of Catalan national myth, it was the date, September 11, that came first, whereas the statue of Casanova, a figure who is not significantly stressed in the mythical narrative itself, served to fill the need for a concrete focal point for commemoration. Although this ritual appears to have begun spontaneously, it soon came to be institutionalized, with diverse organizations with varying relationships to the nation, such as trade unions, cultural and professional associations, and football teams each in turn making their own floral offering in a ceremony that lasts until midday. The ceremony echoes the totem ritual, with each element of the nation individually but unanimously indicating their identification with and submission to the symbol standing in for the totem.

---

[44] Gildea 1994: 156–7; Winock 1998: 451.
[45] Gildea 1994: 159.

As with the commemoration of Joan of Arc, this has not proven unproblematic to efforts to deploy the symbol in the interests of national unity. Officially, all political parties are welcome to participate in the floral offering ritual, and for a time all Catalan parties did, including the conservative, state-centralist Popular Party (PP). However, more recently, PP representatives have declined because they were previously targets of shouted abuse, and sometimes eggs, from radical Catalanists. The inability of a group or interest to ritually identify with the totem places that group or interest outside of the national communion. Therefore, in an effort to promote unity, the Catalan government tried to institutionalize an alternative event at Ciutadella Park that could incorporate representation from across the political spectrum. But this too has proven controversial whenever singers invited to perform at the event sing in Spanish, perceived by radical Catalanists as an affront on the day marking the defeat that led to the outlawing of the Catalan language.

As a result, alternative and competing sites of memory have arisen as an outlet for more radical national interests during the *Diada* celebrations. Along the Ronda de Sant Pere, stalls are set up by various Catalanist organizations and parties where people can buy activist material with various emblems and symbols. In the evening, a demonstration is held whose attendants regularly number in the thousands. A hundred meters away, behind the Church of Santa Maria del Mar, stands the *Fossar de les Moreres*, marking the spot where those who fought in the battle of 1714 were buried. The inscription on the commemorative monument is taken from a poem by Frederic Soler: "*Al fossar de les Moreres no s'hi enterra cap traïdor, fins perdent nostres banderes serà la urna d'honor*" [in the Fossar de les Moreres not a traitor is buried; even if we lose our emblems it will be the urn of honor]. It is here – at a monument to a more anonymous collective sacrifice, comparable in that respect to that of the defenders of Masada – that the most radical groups of left-wing Catalanists meet during the morning of September 11. By the end of the day, the site is covered with stalls distributing symbolic emblems, t-shirts, and pamphlets.[46]

As with the *axis mundi*, once the *axis natio* has come to be embodied in a manmade emblem, this emblem will proliferate beyond the ritual center, spreading its numenous power and incorporating into the nation everything it touches. The spread of the Joan of Arc cult in the late 19th century serves as a paradigmatic example. Once Frémiet's statue

[46] Rovira 2006.

had been erected on the Place des Pyramides, new images of Joan were commissioned by all departments. Further, as Pierre Marot writes, "the Maid's popularity was expressed in the most varied and surprising ways":

She became involved in businesses of all sorts. Shops, restaurants, and hotels availed themselves of the heroine's name. The most diverse objects bore her stamp: utensils, beauty aids, candy, exotic foods, liqueurs, beers, soaps and even cement! It was almost beyond belief. School notebooks were decorated with her banner, and children's games were placed under her patronage: games of "snakes and ladders" featured episodes of her life, and "construction games" included her house in Domremy and the Place du Vieux-Marche.[47]

It is also possible for an axis point to anchor itself in time as well as in space, by means of a commemorative day. Commemorating a foundational moment of sacrifice as one's national day not only institutionalizes cyclical ritual remembrance of that sacrifice but also associates current members of the nation with all of those, living and dead, depicted as having participated in the same ritual act of remembrance and renewal over the intervening years. Typically, in both national and religious rituals, once such a commemorative day has been established through its association with a key foundational moment, the sacred quality associated with it causes numerous events of supplementary importance to either be retrospectively attributed to or arranged to coincide with it. It is natural for events of sacred significance to manifest on the day when the boundary between the sacred and profane is at its most narrow.

We have already seen how May 30 came to be understood as an important symbolic date in which to enlist the patronage of Joan of Arc. Also characteristic of this pattern is Vidovdan, St. Vitus Day, on which the Battle of Kosovo occurred, which was transformed from a minor religious commemoration into the Serbian national day over the course of Serbia's wars of independence in the 19th century and formally recognized as such in 1903. At each commemoration, priests and politicians would exhort the people to avenge Kosovo by unifying the divided territory of Serbia and, beginning with the declaration of war on June 28, 1876, a habit emerged of selecting that day to initiate momentous events. It would, for example, be an understatement to suggest that it was an unfortunate choice of timing for a state visit of Austrian Archduke Franz Ferdinand to Sarajevo in 1914 because his assassination on that day by a Serbian nationalist was the flash point that began World War I. It was the date of the signing of the constitution of

---

[47] Quoted in Winock 1998: 442.

Yugoslavia in 1921, of the 1928 assassination of Croat political leader Stjepan Radić, of the official announcement of the split between Tito and Stalin in 1948, and of the 1989 pledge by Slobodan Milošević to "liberate" the Serbs of Kosovo by any means necessary.[48]

A similar dynamic occurred when September 11 was adopted as the Catalan national day, making it, as well, a natural rallying point for political action in the name of Catalan autonomy and therefore a day in which numerous other events relevant to autonomy and the struggle against dictatorship took place. In the same way that interests as divergent as republicans and Catholics could all associate themselves with the statue of Joan of Arc, the *Diada* provided an ideological bridge whereby sociopolitical interests as diverse as the church and the far-left could converge on common issues such as the integration of immigrants and Catalan language rights.[49] Some of the most dramatic and unifying events of protest against the Franco dictatorship resulted from the attraction of this day as an expression of Catalan cultural unity and were subsequently added to the narrative, enhancing the sacred quality of this moment in time. A recent political demonstration that received widespread press attention was the *Un País, Una Bandera* [one country, one flag] campaign, which demanded that on the day of September 11, town councils in Catalonia should fly only the Catalan flag, without the Spanish flag alongside, contrary to Spanish regulations for public buildings. According to the campaign's statistics, in 2001 at least 846 town hall buildings, nearly 90% of the total, complied.[50]

The point here is not to suggest that the activities that take place during the *Diada* indicate a more widespread enthusiasm for Catalan independence than has been hitherto assumed. On the contrary, it is during the totem festival that impulses the society collectively wishes to repress are temporarily allowed, enabling what one might call a "ritual radicalization" that provides an outlet for sentiments that might upset the sociopolitical order outside of this safe and confined space. The 1977 protests forged a link between the state–federal and national–regional causes by conceptually associating individual autonomy embodied in democracy and the struggle against dictatorship with a Catalan national–cultural autonomy lost with the fall of Barcelona. And while it might be easy to interpret a campaign such as *Un País, Una Bandera* as a nationalist

[48] Majstorovic 2000: 173; Perica 2002: 8.
[49] Conversi 1997: 131.
[50] Rovira 2006; http://www.estil.net/pais/index.html.

provocation, it could also be taken as a ritual form of reconciliation. Catalonia could be symbolically independent on its totemic national day, a tribute to the sacrifice of those in 1714 who died in a failed effort to maintain its sovereignty, thus enabling it to remain comfortably incorporated into the Spanish state system for the other, ordinary 364 days of the year when the spirits of those martyrs weren't paying quite so close attention.

It is interesting to note, by way of contrast, that as much as the Israeli national mythology elevates memories of defeat in the form of monuments, commemoration of these moments of defeat are conspicuously absent from the national calendar. Defeat is commemorated in place, not in time, a point rendered all the more curious by the fact that the Jewish religion did have a day for the commemoration of defeat on its traditional calendar: Tisha B'Av, which, like the national festivals just described, served within the tradition as a lightning rod for the commemoration of numerous catastrophes in Jewish history that occurred on, were attributed to, or arranged to coincide with that date. As the date given for the destruction of both the First and Second Temples, it became a symbol of persecution and misfortune, the loss of independence and the sufferings of Exile. The Talmud cites it as the day on which the Children of Israel, after the Exodus, were told that they would not be allowed to enter the Promised Land. It is also considered to be the day that Betar, the last stronghold of the Bar Kokhba revolt, fell to the Romans and the day on which the expulsion from Spain was decreed in 1492. Commemoration involves the observance of mourning rites comparable to those performed over the death of a close family member, with prohibitions on food or drink, bathing, sexual intercourse, any form of work, and even the study of Torah with the exception of passages relating to mourning and lamentation.[51]

Although Tisha B'Av was never the most important Jewish holiday, it would nonetheless appear to have been ripe for elevation and exploitation on the part of a national movement seeking to highlight its historical moments of defeat. This was not done, and though it remains in the Jewish liturgical calendar, it passes virtually unnoticed from the point of view of Israeli civil religion, which prefers to commemorate martyrdom through secular–national holidays of recent innovation such as a remembrance day for fallen soldiers and Holocaust memorial day. One could speculate that Tisha B'Av was perhaps too closely associated with the norms of

[51] Encyclopedia Judaica 1972: 935–7.

passive acceptance of transcendent authority associated with the existing religious tradition to have any traction for the activist, national one. The transition from *ethnie* to nation required palpable change in the manner in which the commemoration of defeat was approached.

Negotiating the Transition from the Universal to the National

Israel: The Temple and the Western Wall

The best way to illustrate both the similarities and the differences between the premodern *axis mundi* and the modern *axis natio* is through an examination of processes by which a symbol serving the latter function to a nation has come to replace a symbol serving the former to its associated or constituent ethnic community. In particular, we can note the utility of placing a memory of defeat in this role in terms of its capacity to negotiate the transition. A good place to start would be with what might be considered the paradigmatic *axis mundi* of the Western, monotheistic world – the Temple Mount of Jerusalem – and the process by which its sacred power was transferred within the Jewish national narrative to the Western Wall.

The city of Jerusalem, the location of the Temple, and in particular the rock on which the "Holy of Holies" was built served as the *axis mundi* of traditional Jewish religious mythology, the bridge between the immanent and transcendent realms and thus the focal point for the most formative moments, ideals, and symbolic figures in the Jewish construction of history. Although the rock of the Temple was not the highest mountain in the vicinity, it was depicted as the largest, described in Jewish mystical theology as reaching deep into the *tehom*, the primordial waters that preceded Creation. It was thus both a barrier and an access point to this preformed realm of chaos and *anomie*.[52] It has been variously identified by different streams of Jewish tradition as the center of the earth, the point where the creation of the universe began, the place where Adam was first created, where Cain and Abel built their altars, and where Noah performed a sacrifice upon emerging from the ark.[53] In the Jewish ethnic foundation myth, it came to be identified as the place where Abraham built the altar on which to sacrifice his son Isaac at God's command, only to be ordered at the last minute to replace him with an animal sacrifice (Gen. 22:1–4), thus relating the location to the sacrificial cult. Alternatively, it has been

---

[52] Eliade 1959: 41–4.
[53] Midrash Tehillim, 92:6; cf. Vilnay 1973: 69–70; Ha'Cohen 1983: 83.

identified as the spot where Jacob wrestled with the angel after which he was given the name of Israel, as well as the rock from which the tablets on which Moses received the covenant were hewn,[54] all of these being key moments in the Jewish conception of common descent and identity. This sacred status came to be adopted to some degree by both Islam and Christianity. Medieval Christian maps of the world placed Jerusalem at its center, and the site of the Temple of Jerusalem was identified in the Qur'an as the necessary stopover point enabling Mohammed's journey to heaven (Sura 17:1) leading to the construction of the Dome of the Rock on the site in the seventh century and the designation of the precinct as the *Haram al-Sharif* [the Noble Sanctuary].[55]

As we have noted, the Western Wall began its career as a sacred site simply due to its convenient proximity to this original holy place. Even when it began to develop a sacred status in its own right, it was inherited only on a provisional basis from the Temple that had been destroyed. This status was, at first, soundly rejected by the earliest proponents of Zionism, who viewed the Wall not only as a monument to a destruction and degradation that the Zionist movement was meant to correct but also as a relic of a superstitious faith that the movement desired to transcend. However, the writings of the few early Zionists who did identify and engage with this symbol point to its transformation from a mere reference to the *axis mundi* of the Temple Mount into a sacred object of the national religion on its own merits. At the end of the 19th century, Mordechai ben Hillel Ha-Kohen, who would go on to become an important figure in the Zionist movement, described a visit to the Western Wall that bears quoting at length, given the acute sense it exhibits of the importance of concrete symbols to the identity of an imagined community:

I started to organize my stay in the city, but I soon realized that I did not have the strength to withstand the desire – nay! The urgent need – to hurry to the Western Wall. I remember nothing of the way I went; my legs bore me, and I went blindly like an animal following its herder. My eyes were lifted aloft all the time staining to catch the first glimpse of the Wall. 'This is the Western Wall', murmured my guide in a holy whisper; but I would have known anyway . . . I do not remember how my shoes left my feet, how I fell full length on the ground, how I started kissing the flagstones under me or how I began weeping such copious tears that became torrents. My heart was in turmoil. I did not attempt to control myself or stop the flow of tears which I wept like a small infant without sense or words. The

---

[54] Bereishit Rabba 55:8; 69:6; Midrash Tihillim 91:7, Sifri Devarim 354, Zohar 231b, cited in Vilnay 1973: 10–11, 71–2.
[55] Friedland and Hecht 1991: 22.

attendant did not approve and interrupted me, handing me a Psalter and showing me the verses which were to be recited at the Wall. Idiot! Did he not realize that at that moment I had no need of any verses, of any prayerbook, or of any liturgy.

I departed the Wall grievously heartbroken. In such a spirit had I left the cemetery in Homel, my home of the previous summer, when I buried my only beloved daughter. I left the Wall and the cemetery and I knew that I was leaving a great part of my life, a whole piece of my heart. Oh! that there should be no such moments in the life of any man! For such moments can bring a man down suddenly or, at least, lead him to madness. I remember and I am distraught! Dread is all around me!

It was not what my eyes saw or the desolation at the Wall that so struck me but rather my inner soul-feeling. For in its appearance there is nothing in this Wall to so disturb the strings of a man's heart and to incite such a storm inside a Jew. There is not even 'destruction' there. The stones have been burned with fire, the Wall is not destroyed, the rows of its stones do not cast the shadow of death and, generally, surely the terrible destruction deserves a more fitting memorial than that given by this Wall?! After having said all this, I still must say that what this Wall does is truly awesome; for so great is the holy trepidation that falls on the Jew in this place that for the sake of the Wall and for its sake alone every Jew should make the pilgrimage to Jerusalem. The cities of Judah and the streets of Jerusalem are filled with memorials, by their thousands, dear to every Jew and with each step he will hear the echoes of pleasant memories and see memorials which silently will tell him what was ours in days long past. But even if they all did not exist, even if they were all rolled together and stored out of sight, and only the Wall still remained; even then it would be worthwhile for the Jew to take all the trouble in the world to come and see it with his own eyes. There are scholars who cast doubt on the verity of the traditions about this Wall. They have no heart and they lack understanding! They cannot believe that the tradition speaks the truth, that a wall can stand for two thousand years, and that truly there still exists in the world a survivor from that 'universal house of prayer'. A survivor of all the trials and tribulations which have not ceased to visit this wonderful country from the day that Judah was exiled from it and strangers swallowed it. Let the scholars wonder at it as they will – for us it is no wonder! We know that we are a people of legends. Who knows! Perhaps the whole Jewish people is a legend! But in that legend, there bursts forth a spring of life of exalted strength, and that legend can laugh at the facts of real life! Why do I need to know which of the Wall's stones are from the walls of the Temple Mount and which were added to it later? I know that there is no nation and no people in the world which comes to prostrate itself and pour out its heart in front of this Wall; but our brethren come from all the lands of their exile to tell their sins before these holy stones. Only Israel – in all its families – cries there! That is the proof that there we stand behind our Wall. The Wall is ours and let no man dare to try to touch it![56]

---

[56] Quoted in Naor 1983a: 73.

Here we see many of the themes that would come through as pivotal in subsequent accounts relating to the Western Wall. The Wall is anthropomorphized into a living being; Ha-Kohen relates it to his deceased daughter. His experience of it is described in mystical terms, an experience of religious ecstasy and dread, in which ordinary norms are suspended and words fail to articulate an experience that transcends mundane modes of communication. But this is not the mysticism of traditional religion. On the contrary, the structures and symbols of traditional religion are explicitly rejected, as symbolized by his rejection of the offered prayerbook. There is no reference in this account to the traditional interpretations of the Wall's significance; no reference to the presence of the *Shekhinah*, or even to the religious importance of the Temple itself. The specific reasons why the Wall might be considered holy are immaterial. It is holy because it is recognized as holy by the Jews, all the Jews, and only the Jews. That is reason enough. "Perhaps the whole Jewish people is a legend," he says, even going so far as to openly recognize that the historical authenticity of this symbol is irrelevant to its power to the imagined community. Scholars can debate the facts – the symbol nonetheless is, was, and will remain the focal point of the collective identity, no less powerful for its having been deconstructed.

Another account, written by A. S. Hirshberg in 1901, poignantly illustrates how an image of defeat is particularly suited to such a transformation from a universal to a national axis symbol:

Here I was, standing before the Wall, this silent witness to Israel's glory of ancient times and against it I saw all those places and all those times of suffering and torture throughout the whole world and all history! The inquisitions and the pogroms that have been visited on our pitiful nation passed before my eyes – and those stones do not move. . . . Tears blind me and the letters in the prayerbook dance before my eyes. My nerves jangle and my innermost emotions are totally shaken and sweep over me so that I almost faint. . . . I turned to escape like a fugitive from this Wall without finishing the prayer I had started, but the beadle held me and gave me a wick to kindle in the small, inferior oil lamp that stood at the end of the Wall. For me it was as though he had given me a memorial candle to kindle for the soul of our people dying there in exile.[57]

While recognizing prayer as the appropriate behavior in the presence of the Wall, Hirshberg, like Ha-Kohen, appears to take pride in his religious naïveté. However, he nonetheless has what could only be described as a mystical experience. Both experiences express the sense of overwhelming

[57] Naor 1983a: 77–8.

emotion of the totem ritual, in which all social norms and categories are broken down and the Real is experienced without barrier. The transcendent ineffable reality that is experienced in these accounts is that of the nation, Israel, and the Wall is the concrete symbol that holds the whole of the nation together across both space and time; an axis not between heaven and earth but rather connecting all members of the imagined community in all periods of its history, a reality greater than any one individual part of that totality can express. It is a symbol that merges the glory of Antiquity and the pain of Exile, reconciling the two in the individual Jewish identity. By marking the end of glorious Antiquity, it gives meaning to the intervening period of "suffering and torture," fitting this otherwise formless period into a coherent historical narrative.

The transition in the elevation and meaning of the Western Wall as a national symbol that may have begun with these vaguely expressed sentiments in the 19th and early 20th centuries can be said to have come to fruition in the moment that the object itself was physically and conceptually claimed by the nation, when Jerusalem was captured in 1967 during the Six Day War. Many of these same themes appear in accounts of the event, in which the capture of the Wall takes on a ritual character comparable to the totem feast. It is imagined as a communion of the whole of the nation, present and past, as ancestors both ancient and immediate are invoked and the Wall itself anthropomorphized into an active participant in the drama. Social norms are temporarily turned upside-down: The avowedly secular turn religious for a day, soldiers steeped in a culture of machismo speak proudly of weeping like children, the leaders of the nation stand speechless, and the rabbi enters a virtual ecstatic trance of prayer. Descriptions of the scene reflect a sense of chaos and unreality, as the most articulate commentator finds that words fail, and even the authors of the accounts themselves cannot be contained within conventional rules of grammar, expressing their sentiments through disjointed sentence fragments. But most interesting is the fact that although the Temple Mount and the Western Wall were captured in the same moment, both the participants at the time and the accounts after the fact seem to explicitly ignore the former site, concentrating all of their attention on the latter. One paratrooper, Moshe Amirav, described his experience:

We ran there, a group of panting soldiers, lost on the plaza of the Temple Mount, searching for a giant stone wall. We did not stop to look at the Mosque of Omar even though this was the first time we had seen it close up. Forward! Forward! Hurriedly, we pushed our way through the Magreb Gate and suddenly we stopped, thunderstruck. There it was before our eyes! Grey and massive, silent and restrained. The Western Wall!... Slowly, slowly I began to approach the Wall in fear and trembling like a pious cantor going to the lectern to lead the prayers. I approached it as the messenger of my father and my grandfather, of my great-grandfather and of all the generations in all the exiles who had never merited seeing it and so they had sent me to represent them.[58]

The event appears as a sacramental moment in which the secular–nationalist ideology represented by the soldiers claims the symbol from the tradition, embodied in either their own grandparents or mythical ancestors who are invoked or depicted as being spiritually present at a moment and a place that connect all members of the nation across space and time. The book *The Lions' Gate*, which tells the story of the fighting in Jerusalem, describes the scene as follows:

(Colonel) Motta (Gur) was leaning against one of the walls feeling as though he had come home, to the goal of all his aspirations. Names out of history jumbled together in his mind. The Temple Mount, Mount Moriah, Abraham and Isaac, the Temple, the Maccabees, Bar Kokhba, Romans, Greeks. We are on the Temple Mount. The Temple Mount is ours!...

The deputy commander's force reached the Western Wall. An Israeli flag is flying above it. Embraces, kisses, Le-Hayyim!

Paratroopers are pouring down the narrow steps. Their feet take them down but their eyes are lifted on high. Paratroopers are weeping.[59]

Motta Gur himself (who would go on to become a general and chief of staff) offered his perspective in the book, *The Temple Mount Is In Our Hands*:

To the right and above – the Western Wall. Large, gray, bare, silent stones. Only the small hyssop bushes in the Wall, for all the world like piercing eyes, give it life. We stop for a moment on the winding steps. Khaki dominates the area: the soldiers are praying, swaying back and forth devoutly. A curtain has been spread on the Wall – for the moment it is a military synagogue. Rabbi Goren is standing there, reciting a prayer out loud, pouring out his soul. He is already hoarse. He has not stopped praying there for two hours. After our emotional encounter on the plateau, he and his aides went straight to the Wall...

Rabbi Goren, Major-General Narkiss and the Deputy Chief-of-Staff, Major-General Bar-Lev embraced each other publicly. Narkiss just said, 'This is extraordinary, indescribable,' and Rabbi Goren once again recited the Kaddish 'in memory of those who fell for the liberation of Jerusalem, the Temple Mount and the Western Wall'.... The sounds of weeping joined with the words of prayer... and,

[58] Quoted in Naor 1983b: 146.
[59] Naor 1983b: 146.

toward its end, overcame them. The unity of the dead and the living hovered over the Wall and the worshippers there. . . .

I remembered our family visits to the Wall, twenty-five years earlier, walking through the narrow alleys and the markets. I cannot remember details; I was only a child then. But I do remember the impression the worshippers at the Wall made on me, or am I remembering a picture from a later, older date? White-bearded Jews dressed in caftans and wearing shtreimels, the round fur hat they brought with them from Eastern Europe. For me, they and the Wall formed one unit.

I returned to reality. Rabbi Goren, in battle-dress, is reciting a prayer and behind him the soldiers are praying.[60]

A ritual commemoration of a sacred moment does not merely recall that moment – it invokes it, collapsing the ordinary progression of time and carrying past moments and future expectations into the ongoing present. A sense of continuity with the past, cemented by this moment and place, was expressed by the writer Yehuda Ha-Ezrahi: "I saw the sacred stones and, wondrously, it was as though I had already been there only the other day. They are so familiar. No, not the other day. But generations ago! They are so old; breathing in the touches and kisses and the weeping and the dirges and the supplications and the prayers of generation after generation."[61] Another soldier, Abraham Duvdevani, wrote:

We went through a gate and down some steps. I looked to the right and stopped dead. There was the Wall in all its grandeur and glory! I had never seen it before but it was an old friend, impossible to mistake. Then I thought that I should not be there because the Wall belongs in the world of dreams and legends and I am real. Reality and legend, dream and deed, all unite here. I went down and approached the Wall and stretched out my hand towards the huge, hewn stones. But my hand was afraid to touch and of itself returned to me. I closed my eyes, took a small, hesitant step forward, and brought my lips to the Wall. The touch of my lips opened the gates of my emotions and the tears burst forth. A Jewish soldier in the State of Israel is kissing history with his lips.

Past, present and future all in one kiss. There will be no more destruction and the Wall will never again be deserted. It was taken with young Jewish blood and the worth of that blood is eternity. The body is coupled to the rows of stones, the face is pushed into the spaces between them and the hands try to reach its heart. A soldier near me mumbles in disbelief, 'We are at the Wall, at the Wall.'[62]

These accounts also contain some of the only exceptions to the dominant national narrative of the Six Day War and the conquests that resulted from

---

[60] Ibid.: 148–50.
[61] Ibid.: 154–5.
[62] Ibid.: 153.

it. The war is normatively depicted as wholly defensive in nature, fought solely against the specter of national annihilation. Yet several accounts indicate that the conquest of the Wall was, in itself, a legitimate rationale for the war. As "Jonathan," an intelligence officer with the battalion that liberated the Old City, explained, "'The Wall' was a concept everybody understood. There, we began to listen to the radio again and to discover what was happening on the other fronts of the war. Only here did we begin to understand that what we had done in Jerusalem was the heart of the matter, the heart of all the things that had been done in those June days."[63] Raphael Amir, broadcaster for Israel Broadcasting Services, accompanying the commanders to the Wall, reported from the scene: "I'm not religious and never have been, but this is the Wall and I am touching the stones of the Western Wall." In a book written after the war, Joseph Hermoni described the effect of hearing Amir's broadcast:

I do not know that broadcaster's name, but he deserves the thanks of all of us because he succeeded in suddenly making clear how stupid is the devious controversy over 'Who is a Jew?'

He succeeded because he stood before us naked, vulnerable, after he had lost all his armour of professionalism. He did not talk with the newspaperman's objectivity, he wasn't articulate, he couldn't even control the recording machine he was carrying. That's why we all felt how history was beating its wings.[64]

Here we have a clear demonstration of the foundational nature of the symbol. Suddenly, the question of "who is a Jew" (and, by implication, a fully credentialed insider to the Jewish nation) was no longer a matter of religious law. A Jew is anyone who experiences that moment as part of the nation, who identifies with the symbol that was claimed.

It is interesting to note that remarkably similar themes can be found in Serbian accounts of the conquest of Kosovo during the First Balkan War: the temporary breakdown of social norms and categories, the inexpressible nature of the experience, and the sense of continuity with the whole of the imagined community, whereby the soldiers of the present claim the symbol from ancestors representing the cultural tradition. The declaration of war in October 1912 mentioned Kosovo as a priority among its war aims, referring to the region as " . . . the glorious and saddened mother of our Kingdom where lies the historical kernel of the old Serbian

---

[63] Naor 1983b: 141.
[64] *Si'ah Lohamim* [fighters talk], quoted in Naor 1983b: 156–7.

state, [its] kings and emperors . . . and the glorious capitals of the Neman-jici: Ras of Novi Pazar, Priština, Skoplije, and Prizren."[65] This gave the conflict the character of a holy war. Soldiers are said to have removed their shoes when crossing the battleground and to have taken bits of soil with them as relics to commemorate the event.[66] Czech statesman Thomas Masaryk, who was witness to the battle, reported that Serb soldiers wept and removed their caps "as if by command," and one Serbian soldier described the scene and his reactions as follows:

The single sound of that word – Kosovo – caused an indescribable excitement. This one word pointed to the black past – five centuries. In it exists the whole of our sad past – the tragedy of Prince Lazar and the entire Serbian people.

Each of us created for himself a picture of Kosovo while we were still in the cradle. Our mothers lulled us to sleep with the songs of Kosovo, and in our schools our teachers never ceased in their stories of Lazar and Miloš . . .

My God what awaited us! To see a liberated Kosovo. The words of the commander were like music to us and soothed our souls like the miraculous balsam.

When we arrived on Kosovo and the battalions were placed in order, our commander spoke: 'Brothers, my children, my sons!' His voice breaks. 'This place on which we stand is the graveyard of our glory. We bow to the shadows of fallen ancestors and pray God for the salvation of their souls.' His voice gives out and tears flow in streams down his cheeks and grey beard and fall to the ground. He actually shakes from some kind of inner pain and excitement.

The spirits of Lazar, Miloš, and all the Kosovo martyrs gaze on us. We feel strong and proud, for we are the generation which will realize the centuries-old dream of the whole nation: that we with the sword will regain the freedom that was lost with the sword.[67]

The unification of Jerusalem activated a quasi-messianic strain in some quarters of Zionist thought and, since 1967, a small triumphalist faction of religious Zionists have tried to affirm Jewish rights over the Temple Mount, led by no less a figure than Ashkenazi Chief Rabbi Shlomo Goren who was present at the capture of Jerusalem in his capacity as the army's chief rabbi.[68] On several occasions, Rabbi Goren attempted to organize prayer services on the platform of the Temple Mount and engage in

---

[65] Djordjevic 1991: 320.

[66] Cohen 2001: 7.

[67] Emmert 1989: 19–20.

[68] According to one apocryphal account, when the Israeli Army captured the Temple Mount, Rabbi Goren asked Army Chief of Staff Uzi Narkiss to immediately destroy the Dome of the Rock with explosives and claim the site. Narkiss expressed shock at the suggestion, telling Goren that if he persisted in these requests he would take him to jail. (Gorenberg 2000: 100).

archaeological investigations further to establishing the precise location of the Temple in order to determine where on the platform traditional Jews could or could not go.

But more interesting than this movement to assert Jewish rights over the Temple Mount is the fact that it has always remained on the margins of Israeli political culture. As soon as Jerusalem was taken, as houses were being razed to complete the plaza in front of the Western Wall, Defense Minister Moshe Dayan ordered Israeli flags removed and paratroopers withdrawn from the Haram. Security for the site was immediately restored to its Muslim guards and the keys to eight of the nine gates of the compound (the one exception being the Maghrebi Gate adjacent to the Western Wall) were returned to Muslim authorities, with the Israeli presence reduced to a small police post.[69] Dayan pressured Goren to desist in his efforts to pray and investigate at the site, explicitly telling him that "when Jews who wish to pray appear at the entrance of the Temple Mount, they will be diverted by the security forces to the Western Wall," a policy that continued even when the government came under the control of Menachem Begin's Herut party with its roots in Revisionist Zionism.

Although the Law for the Protection of the Holy Places granted the theoretical right of Jews to pray on the Temple Mount, the granting of complete control to the Muslim Council allowed them to deny access to Jews and to set their own rules of conduct on the site, amounting to the effective surrender of traditional Judaism's *axis mundi*.[70] These decisions could, of course, be rationalized as political compromises necessary to accommodate the sensibilities of the state's Muslim inhabitants and neighbors. But it must be noted that outside of a narrow religious–nationalist constituency, there was no outcry against this decision to surrender Judaism's holiest spot to foreign or even enemy sovereignty, a decision that engenders little resentment in the mainstream of Israeli political culture to this day. It is a point of contention only for religious–nationalist groups such as Gush Emunim, as well as a small group called the "Temple Mount Faithful" who have made several flamboyant efforts to pray at the Temple Mount, sometimes sparking violence. The state, however, has consistently defended the status quo against Jewish extremists and has faced little in the way of mass opposition from the general public for this position.

[69] Wasserstein 2001: 328.
[70] Friedland and Hecht 1991: 39–45.

The conspicuous lack of interest to the point of distaste shown by the political mainstream toward any assertion of claim to the Temple Mount, in sharp contrast to the intense emotions engendered by the ruins on its periphery, is indicative of the decisive shift in focus from the *axis mundi* to the *axis natio*. This does not mean that the Temple Mount has been rendered irrelevant to the national ideology. On the contrary, the fact that the state and the society has shunned asserting or even advocating for the rights of Jews over the spot considered by Judaism to be the holiest point on earth – even the right to pray there, which can easily be expressed in terms of the secular democratic principle of freedom of religion – indicates a recognition that this symbol is downright dangerous to the nation. The danger does not relate to Israel's relations with its neighbors, which are clearly not an obstacle when core national values such as the Western Wall are at issue. Assertion of sovereignty over the site would fundamentally alter Zionism by bringing a political and religious institution into competition with the common culture as the center of the belief system and the focal point of community loyalty. Far better for the national ideology to revere a symbol that, while on the one hand glorifying the ideal, on the other hand also serves as a tangible reminder that the ideal is no longer in their midst and that its realization remains a distant prospect. As much as nationalism might look to the memory of that ideal as the height of cultural achievement, and as much as the reconstruction of a national polity resembling that ideal might be the end goal of nationalism, nationalism is nonetheless defined as loyalty to a culture. Should primary loyalty shift to anything other than the common culture, it would no longer be nationalism. In other words, if Israel were ever to rebuild the Temple – even conceptually, in the sense of making this the goal of the mainstream national ideology, the focal point of the community's loyalty – there would, in effect, be no more Jewish nation. Hence, the reminder that this ideal remains distant is as important to the national mythology as its centrality.

This is why the Western Wall acquired its pivotal importance at the expense of the Temple as the totem symbol of the Jewish nation: because of its ability to reconcile opposites, contradictions that are present both in Jewish nationalism in particular and in the nation as a construct in general. It is a reminder of the Second Temple, a structure pivotal to Jewish national history, yet one that the nation has no desire to see rebuilt and restored to its position at the center of the social order. As a symbol that can at the same time embody both fulfillment and lack, it serves to resolve the ambivalence of those who do not adhere to either radical secularism, religious anti-Zionism, or a religious–nationalist ideology but rather are required to reconcile the varied traditional–religious and secular–nationalist elements of their individual identities in more subtle and complex ways.

Secular anti-Zionists have little use for either the religious or national-ist implications of the symbol, religious anti-Zionists consider it an inap-propriate merging of these two incompatible ideologies,[71] and religious nationalists like Shlomo Goren or the Temple Mount faithful consider it a mere shadow relative to the true locus of importance: the Temple itself. These, however, are all ideologies that fall outside of the national mainstream. The vast majority of Jews and Israelis might recognize the Temple as a unifying symbol of ancient glory pivotal to the notion of con-tinuity on which the national ideology relies, but the last thing they want is to live in the sort of Temple-centered political culture that characterized that age and would supposedly characterize its restoration. It is for this majority that the Wall effectively maintains a sense of continuity with the Temple, yet serves as a unifying symbol far more suitable to a modern national context than this original *axis mundi* ever could, satisfying the need to link the individual not to the divine transcendent but rather to all other members of the nation over space and time who have signified their membership through their identification with it.

Clearly, then, the factor of defeat is a large part of what enabled the Western Wall to both signify the Temple while at the same time usurp its status, paralleling the need for the nation to establish itself both in continuity with and as a replacement of the preceding ethnic culture. The ability of this symbol to both vicariously depict the Temple and at the same time viscerally reenact its destruction is cathartic to a community that requires this destruction in order to maintain itself as a nation but must obscure this guilty need from consciousness in order to perceive continuity. However, to demonstrate that the use of defeat as a mechanism to effect such a transition is not unique to Zionism, we turn for comparison to another, unrelated ethnic and national tradition that can demonstrate the efficacy of a symbol of defeat in enabling transition from an axis symbol suitable to the structure of a premodern past to one suitable to a current national reality.

---

[71] For example, Moshe Hirsh, spokesperson for the ultra-Orthodox anti-Zionist sect Neturai-Karta, has described the Western Wall as the "Golden Calf" of Zionism, leading a generation toward a false religion (Friedland and Hecht 1991: 37).

Ghana: The Golden Stool and Yaa Asantewaa

The *axis mundi* of traditional Asante society was the Golden Stool, an object that connected transcendence to sociopolitical sovereignty in a classically Durkheimian manner. Simply put, the Golden Stool was the throne of the *Asantehene*, the paramount chief of Asante. But the object held a sacred totemic status beyond this functional symbolic purpose. It embodied political authority and sovereign violence, serving as a focal point symbolically connecting all living members of the social order with both the transcendent and with their ancestors. This comes through clearly in the myths associated with the object's origin, described, for example, in a Ghanaian textbook on Asante history, as follows:

> On the appointed day the chiefs met, each waiting to be the paramount chief elect. The atmosphere looked calm. Okomfo Anokye appeared amidst drumming and dancing. After some magical dances, he paused a little, jumped here and there and began to call something from the sky. Drumming started again and the priest conjured. The sky became tense and a deafening noise was heard. Then a stool studded with gold descended on the laps of Nana Osei Tutu. It therefore meant that he had been chosen by the ancestors and the gods as the unquestionable king of the kings of the Asante Nation.

> Finger nails and a small collection of hair from each chief were collected, all burnt and the ashes, some smeared on the stool and the rest mixed in palm wine for all to drink.

> Okomfo Anokye told them that the stool contained the spirit of the Asante Nation. The potion they drank meant that they had sworn to the gods, which meant that they had taken an oath to unite and forget their past individual histories. Osei Tutu took the oath of allegiance to the stool and the chiefs, and each chief in turn took an oath of allegiance to Nana Osei Tutu and an oath never to raise arms against the Golden Stool. That was the beginning of the Asante Kingdom.[72]

The arrival of the Golden Stool marks the foundation of Asante as a society and political order, the agreement of the group to be a group united under the Kumasi-based leadership, and to adhere to rules of conduct regarding in-group violence. Its arrival is a moment of ritual power, during which the normally vast distance between heaven, earth, and the ancestors is bridged, and sacred parts of the physical bodies of the ancestors present at that moment are incorporated into the object. The Golden Stool is not a possession of the *Asantehene*. On the contrary, it embodies the office he serves and represents the continuity of that office irrespective of the office holder. The society could endure periods

[72] Kwadwo 2004: 7.

during which the office of *Asantehene* remained vacant, but numerous testimonies stress the popular perception that were the Golden Stool itself to be lost, the society could not survive. Therefore, the object came to be adopted into the society as a living member, more diligently protected than even the king himself, and subject to special rules of conduct. Special rituals, for example, associated with the Stool's replacement when its wood began to rot testify to the object's numenous power as the totem symbol of sovereign violence. It was connected to the body of the society; to desecrate it was to damage oneself as well as the society.[73]

One of the key differences between the Yaa Asantewaa war and previous, arguably more politically decisive defeats of the Asante at the hands of the British was the pivotal role of the Golden Stool itself in the drama. This may be a large part of what rendered this revolt more suitable as a commemorative moment than other events of greater political significance, providing it with a wealth of culturally appropriate imagery for later exploitation by a national movement. Historical accounts all concur that whatever the underlying grievances, the immediate *casus belli* from the point of view of the rebels, and of Yaa Asantewaa in particular, was an arrogant speech made to the Asante chiefs by the British governor of the Gold Coast, Sir Frederick Hodgson, in January 1900, in which he demanded the Golden Stool in recognition of his status as the official representative of sovereign authority over Asante.[74] Although most of the Asante leadership was, at the time, willing to come to some accommodation with the effective authority of Britain, this formal claim to what both sides recognized as the ritual center of Asante sovereignty was unacceptable. Colonial Resident Captain Donald Stewart observed that even Asante chiefs and kings who remained loyal to British authority throughout the rebellion nonetheless would grow bitter at any mention of British interest in the Golden Stool and neglected to assist in efforts to acquire it.[75]

One of the specific roles of the *ohemma* or "queenmother"[76] in Asante political culture was that of guardian of the royal lineage, assisting in the

---

[73] Akyeampong 2000: 6–7; McKaskie 2000: 94–5; Asirifi-Danquah 2002: 18–19.
[74] Boahen 2003: 37–8.
[75] McKaskie 2000: 84.
[76] A distinct office in the Akan political heirarchy, not to be confused with simply being mother of the king, the *ohemma* was a kind of elder advisor, represented as the personification of wisdom, symbolic of peace, order, stability, and biological continuity, and a secondary point of refuge from the judgment of the court who could publicly admonish the ruler. In fact, in the interests of maintaining a balance of power, it was unusual for mother and son to simultaneously occupy what amounted to the highest male and female stools. Violation of the guideline was one of the factors precipitating the civil

selection of successors to the Stool they served by ensuring that the candidate was of legitimate descent from the appropriate founding ancestors. The assertion of claim to the Golden Stool on the part of someone lacking such credentials would therefore have been a particular affront to Yaa Asantewaa, as the protocols of Asante kingship violated were her special prerogative as the queenmother present who was closest in the hierarchy to the Golden Stool.[77] Thus, it was sensible for her to take on the role of symbolic head of the revolt. According to eyewitness accounts, she took this role seriously, actively instigating resistance at that moment and challenging the manhood of those chiefs who declined to follow her example:

When the men began to argue and discuss the issue, Yaa Asantewaa stood up and declared: "How can a proud and brave people like the Asante sit back and look while white men took away their king and chiefs, and humiliate them with demand for the Golden Stool. The Golden Stool only means money to the white man; they searched and dug everywhere for it. I shall not pay one *predwan* to the Governor. If you, the chiefs of Asante, are going to behave like cowards and not fight, you should exchange your loincloths for my undergarments."[78]

The lead-up to hostilities comes through in the narrative as a sequence of attempts by the British to find the Golden Stool and of the Asante to conceal it, and (as we shall later examine) the willingness of individual figures to assist either side in this endeavor came to be represented as the key litmus test of loyalty.

But although the Golden Stool was and remains a powerful symbol of a distinctly Asante ethnic continuity and sovereign authority, it was not and could not be elevated into a Ghanaian or pan-African emblem. As a symbol specific to Asante, it held power for only a distinct subset of Ghanaian nationals, and the relationships of sovereign violence it represented were at odds with the needs of an inclusive modern nation-state. Ghanaian national leaders like Kwame Nkrumah or Jerry Rawlings could assert no more legitimate a claim over the Golden Stool than Sir Frederick Hodgson. Even if they could, the leaders of modern Ghana did not wish to construct the sort of society that the claim of such prerogatives would imply. They could, however, associate themselves with

---

    war of the 1870s, when *Asantehemma* Yaa Kyaa supported the claims of her own son, Prempeh I, against those of an older claimant (Brempong 2000: 106–8).

[77] Brempong 2000: 106–7; Obeng 2000: 142–3.
[78] Boahen 2003: 118.

Yaa Asantewaa, a figure whose principal achievement was to fight in defense of the Golden Stool, and thereby claim a measure of her legacy in a manner suitable to a diverse national context. Rawlings in particular made overt personal efforts to embrace the Yaa Asantewaa legacy, though he was himself neither Asante nor even of the wider Akan majority ethnicity of which Asante was a part but rather was a member of the Ewe minority dominant in the southeast. He nonetheless referred to her frequently in his own rhetoric in which he sought to distance himself from the succession of corrupt civilian and military governments that had come to power in Ghana since independence. By naming his own daughter after Yaa Asantewaa, he symbolically claimed her as part his own family ancestry, extracting her from her particularly Asante ethnic context.[79]

The national historical narrative, as reflected by Adu Boahen, is quite open in identifying peace and stability as one of the long-term effects of the war:

> Never again did the Asante and the British face each other on the battlefield, nor did the Asante ever confront any other Ghanaian state. This atmosphere of peace and stability enabled the Asante to channel their spirit of adventure, dynamism and entrepreneurship into more constructive channels. This surely accounts for the phenomenal social and economic developments, especially in the area of cocoa production and the promotion of Western education, which took place in Asante in the two or three decades following the War.[80]

But if defeat is depicted as ultimately having been in the best interests of the Asante, how can it be seen as better than not having fought in the first place? What must be understood is that the modern Ghanaian state is not successor to the Asante confederacy, either in terms of its boundaries, its constituent communities, or its forms of institutional order but rather to the British colonial state that defeated and subsumed it. The key outcome of the Yaa Asantewaa war was the permanent subordination of Asante. It was not only the last time the Asante and the British clashed on the battlefield but, crucially, also the last time that the Asante revolted militarily against their incorporation into *any* Ghanaian state. Thus, although defeat at the hands of the British *per se* must be commemorated primarily as a tragedy, the subordination of the Golden Stool to the British colonial state was nonetheless a vital stage toward its eventual subordination to the Ghanaian national state; a state of affairs that must continue

---

[79] Day 2000: 157.
[80] Boahen 2003: 176.

and that is subtly perpetuated by the elevation of the memory of this event.

The Golden Stool represents an alternative and potentially competing locus of political sovereignty, one that therefore could not be claimed or elevated by a modern Ghanaian nation. The adoption of Yaa Asantewaa and the Yaa Asantewaa War into the Ghanaian national narrative was a far better means for incorporating that sovereignty into Ghanaian national identity, glorifying it as a golden age while simultaneously commemorating its defeat and subordination. By elevating the last defender of this alternative locus, the national culture thereby viscerally reenacts its defeat, mourning it as a tragedy blamed on an external force, enabling the modern national movement to depict itself as a reversal of that defeat while at the same time maintaining continuity of the defeat's beneficial effects.

These ambiguities, and the mechanisms for resolving them, are evident in sociologist Linda Day's first-hand account of the planning and celebration of events associated with the centenary of the Yaa Asantewaa War. According to Day, both national and regional leaders were at first noticeably ambivalent at the prospect of celebrating and associating themselves with Yaa Asantewaa's legacy. From the perspective of the ruling National Democratic Congress (NDC) party, there was concern that focus on the heroism and sacrifice of Yaa Asantewaa could stoke Asante nationalism, given that the NDC party under Rawlings had won little support from the region during the democratization process and the elections of 1992 and 1996:

> To many people of the region, there was a clear contradiction in celebrating a woman who resisted British rule, since to many of them, and perhaps to the country at large, the national government is the successor to British colonial authority. From this perspective, Yaa Asantewaa could be seen as an oppositional force to the authority imposed by any government from Accra, from the south, from the coast.... What if massively promoting and honoring a fighting Asante queenmother fired Asante nationalism and rekindled its dormant fighting spirit?[81]

A similar concern was experienced by Asante leaders, given that most of them did not trace their own lines of succession back to those chiefs who had fought with Yaa Asantewaa but rather to those who did not. In particular, Day notes that the sitting Edwesohene[82] had been noticeably cool

---

[81] Day 2000: 156–7.
[82] Chief of Edweso, Yaa Asantewaa's home province.

toward the Yaa Asantewaa legacy over the years prior to the centenary and reluctant to support projects in her name.

However, leaders on both the national and regional levels, all of whom were concerned with downplaying tensions between the region and the central government, swiftly discovered that associating themselves in common with the legacy of Yaa Asantewaa had a greater potential for generating unity than divisiveness. "Casting Yaa Asantewaa as a national heroine, one given unqualified support by the government, could potentially tie the Asante more closely to the grand narrative of Ghanaian national purpose and patriotism."[83] In the lead-up to the event, the Edwesohene filled Yaa Asantewaa's former position, the long-vacant stool of Edwesohemma, with one of her descendants. He also agreed to head the centenary coordinating committee along with the government-appointed (NDC) Ashanti regional minister, actively backing related infrastructural improvements such as the construction of a tourist village. He participated as "chief mourner" in the most ambitious event of the centenary, the funeral and reinterment of Yaa Asantewaa's remains, thereby casting himself in the role of a blood relative, the closest possible affiliation to her life and legacy, above even her own descendants.[84]

Other events included an international conference, a football match, the opening of the Yaa Asantewaa museum, a mass rally of women, an interdenominational church service, a tour of craft villages in the region, a concert, a play, a beauty pageant, a gala dinner dance, and a book launch, as well as a reenactment of the battle for the Kumasi Fort. Ghana's first lady, Nana Konadu Rawlings, herself of Asante background, who had previously visited the Seychelles to collect artifacts from the period of Yaa Asantewaa's exile there, was placed at the center of the commemorations. Along with two of her daughters, including the one named Yaa Asantewaa, she presided over the opening of the museum and the unveiling of a bust of Yaa Asantewaa in front of it.

The second annual Asante congress was held simultaneously with the centenary celebrations. The theme of that year's congress was "Celebrating the Vision and Heroism of Yaa Asantewaa." Concern had been expressed that failure to combine these events would lead to conflict, but in fact the message expressed by the congress was essentially the same as that which was evident at the centenary. Yaa Asantewaa was hailed as a great pan-Africanist, the leader of a cultural war, a "symbol of hope" for

[83] Day 2000: 157.
[84] Ibid.: 160–2.

the dispossessed of Africa and the diaspora. The events surrounding the centenary proved that the legacy of Yaa Asantewaa could be appropriated both by the proponents of Asante ethnic identity and representatives of the prevailing political order without any apparent conflict. The various constituencies represented at the centenary celebration – the Ghanaian state, the NDC, the Tourist Board, women's groups, and the Asante – each infused her legacy with various meanings. The event enabled the ruling party to demonstrate good faith toward the Asante, transforming an ethnic celebration into a national one.[85]

Another illustration of the manner in which Yaa Asantewaa served to symbolically bridge the uncomfortable relationship between tradition and modernity within the national construction of identity lay in her appropriation as a symbol of female emancipation. In her historical context, she was fighting in defense of the traditional norms and structures of Asante society against the political and social challenges posed by British domination. She took on this role in conformity to the traditional responsibilities of her station within that society and was recognized as leader by her Asante contemporaries rather than being vilified for transcending her traditional role. Nonetheless, her image as a female leader and activist defies the stereotype of a traditional Asante woman, making her ripe for adoption by a movement for social change she likely would not have supported during her own lifetime. Often in the developing world, struggles for female emancipation are depicted by opponents of social change as traitorous, insofar as they represent a revolt against the norms of traditional culture with which the nation identifies and are construed as serving the interests of the cultural imperialism of Western values. Yaa Asantewaa serves as a potent symbol precisely because she confounds that logic; her role of leadership and status as icon can be seen to have been sanctioned both by traditional Asante and modern feminist–nationalist norms.[86]

Day sees this incorporation of the myth into the modern Ghanaian narrative as epitomized by the reenactment of the battle at Kumasi Fort that took place as part of the centenary celebrations:

Though some may have been afraid that the event would stoke the embers of Asante nationalism, the omnipresent role played by the regular Ghanaian army, led by a northern general, made this a government-sponsored event, a national event. The government's goal of women's empowerment, as commonly articulated

---

[85] Ibid.: 155–9.
[86] Donkoh 2001: 2–3.

by the First Lady, was central to the program. The very public coverage of the afternoon's events, with the many national and regional dignitaries, and GTV video cameras guaranteeing a national television audience, lifted the Asantes' war against the British out of the realm of local legend and into the ranks of national myth. The staging of the mock battle ensured that a broad spectrum of Ghanaian society could be self-reflectively proud of its history.

To begin with, the mock battle was a fascinating and effective presentation of history as entertainment. The beating of the war drums quickened the pulse of the hundreds of observers and heightened our anticipation of the battle to come. The loud crackle and rattle of the muskets and the deafening sound of the cannons alternately startled, frightened, and amused the crowd. The sight of the "warriors" dressed in their smocks with their faced painted, their ancient but very fierce-looking guns charging the fort with no visible means of defense against the booming cannons being fired from within elicited our admiration and sympathy. Furthermore, the re-creation informed us, with no need for narration, why, at least on military grounds, a frontal assault on the fort was a heroic but ultimately losing venture. The numerous "wounded" men being carried off the field of battle after every cannon blast dramatized the losses the Asante people suffered for the dream of maintaining their independence.[87]

Many of these "Asante warriors" were portrayed by members of the Yaa Asantewaa Girls' High School Drill team, further emphasizing the theme of female empowerment. In the re-creation, Yaa Asantewaa (played by an 18-year-old student) was clearly and ahistorically depicted as personally leading the troops into battle.[88]

As with the Western Wall, we have in Yaa Asantewaa a symbol that points to and derives its power from its association with an earlier *axis mundi* even while it surpasses and usurps it in power and appeal, more suitable as it is to needs of the modern nation in no small part because it represents the necessary defeat of the premodern order represented by that earlier symbol. Just as modern Israelis want the Temple to be destroyed, those who identify as Ghanaian, Asante and non-Asante alike, want the Golden Stool to be superseded and stripped of its power; the sovereign violence it represented transferred to the authority of the modern national state. But because this desire cannot be expressed, it must be reenacted in cathartic myth and ritual. Yaa Asantewaa enables this, for her defeat justifies this transition, while the fact that it is her valiant struggle in the face of defeat that is celebrated serves to hide this need and shift the blame for this transition on to external forces.

[87] Day 2000: 163–4.
[88] Ibid.: 164–5.

Unity, Diversity, and Contestation

Over the course of the preceding chapters, several different terms have been employed to signify the same essential concept as seen from diverse theoretical perspectives: *axis mundi (axis natio)*, totem, surrogate victim, symbolic ideal. These terms all refer to a concrete focal point – a monument that can be seen and touched, a mythic character who can be named and whose deeds described, a moment on a calendar that can be experienced in real time – signifying the group's agreement to be a group. Identification with it represents one's identification with the group, one's agreement to follow the group's rules, to refrain from in-group violence, to sacrifice one's own capacity for violence to this concrete manifestation of the group's collective capacity for violence. What must be understood is that in the national context, symbols that come to serve in this capacity must, of necessity, belong to the whole of the nation – all of its members, equally – and not just to some social or political section of it. The symbol must be shared by all, irrespective of class or political orientation, because anyone who, for whatever reason, cannot or will not identify with it and signify his or her submission to it effectively ceases to be a part of the national communion, regardless of what other characteristics associated with the distinct national character such as language, religion, or descent the individual might share. This causes these symbols to appear paradoxically as both necessary forces for the forging of political unity as well as, at the same time, occasions for intense political contestation within the nation.

We have seen evidence of this dynamic in the Joan of Arc myth and the various ways it has been invoked in a French political culture bitterly divided among traditional Catholic, secular republican, and nationalist streams. Michel Winock identifies three distinct images of Joan of Arc parallel to these streams: the Catholic saint, the incarnation of the patriotic people of France, and the patron of exclusive nationalism.[89] Although noting that these images sometimes coexisted, it would be more accurate to say that they are three ideal types that can be detected in the myth, which in fact produced a complex number of hybrids suitable to all of the many political ideologies that have manifested in France since the Revolution, themselves the products of various converging ideological and social forces. The elevation of Joan of Arc to totemic status was

---

[89] Winock 1998: 449.

not the product of any one of these streams but rather the result of an attempted synthesis between them in the mid-19th century, epitomized by Michelet's depiction of her further to his effort to portray republican France, not as the radical break from tradition as it had hitherto been represented but rather as consistent and continuous with an eternal set of values found throughout French history.

The publication of Michelet's *Histoire de France* was a pivotal event in the development of the Joan of Arc myth, transforming her from the champion of the monarchy heeding supernatural voices, and therefore an unlikely representative of the anticlerical republic, to a model of heroism, popular common sense, and the founder of French nationalist sentiment.[90] Michelet introduced her as a woman of the people, embodying the democratic spirit of France, as well as a pious Catholic nonetheless betrayed by church and monarchy who turned her over to the English. In response, French Catholics adapted their perception of Joan as a national rather than a universal religious saint because of the contemporary accommodation of the Republic to Catholicism and vice versa, portraying her as fighting for the church, of which France was the "eldest daughter." Socialist writers claimed her as well, noting that Joan was born into the poorest class of society, defended her peasant brothers, and that she "never forgot that she was a woman of the people." She was betrayed by everyone other than the people: the king, the aristocracy, the moderates, the church, and the theologians of the Inquisition: "She does not belong to the monarchy, which allowed her to burn, or to the court, which ordered her to be burned, or to the clergy, which burned the poor, ignorant girl." Only the people continued to believe in her, and hence she belonged to the people: "Joan is one of ours, she belongs to us. And we do not want anyone to interfere with her."[91]

After the military defeat of 1871, her memory was fought over even more fiercely, claimed by monarchists and republicans, the church and anticlericals. It was during this time that efforts intensified to create a day of commemoration in her honor, an effort that on the one hand reflected efforts on the part of various parties to claim exclusive title to her memory and on the other to unify a fractured nation by means of a symbol of universal patriotism and resistance during a time of invasion. The leaders of the Third Republic considered that such a commemorative day had the potential for serving as a unifying "festival of patriotism,"

[90] Ibid.: 455.
[91] Lucien Herr, *Notre Jeanne D'Arc*, quoted in Winock 1998: 458–9.

acceptable as such to all elements of the French political spectrum, unlike Bastille Day, which was formally adopted as the national holiday in 1880. The bill to that effect introduced in 1884 articulated these goals explicitly: "on this day all the French could unite in a healthy communion of enthusiasm. Joan does not belong to any one party. She belongs to France."[92] But despite widespread support for the motion, fear that the clergy would somehow monopolize the occasion caused the bill's defeat. The ideological conflict between Catholics and republicans remained too profound to effect such a reconciliation, and soon the Dreyfus affair would wipe away any hope of national unanimity.[93]

Use of the image of Joan of Arc to both unite and divide continued into the 20th century. During World War I, she was invoked as an image of defense of an invaded fatherland, and the victory of 1918 therefore led to the realization of the goal of creating a national holiday in her honor, which was recognized on June 24, 1920, just one month after her canonization by Pope Benedict XV. As the deputy for Paris and president of the *Ligue des Patriotes* explained:

There is not a single person in France, regardless of his or her religious, political or philosophical opinion, whose deepest need for veneration is not satisfied by Joan of Arc. Any of us can find our ideal personified in her. Are you Catholic? She is a martyr and a saint, whom the Church has just placed on its altars. Are you a royalist? She is the heroine who made it possible for the son of Saint Louis to be consecrated according to the Gallican sacrament at Reims. Do you reject the supernatural? Never was anyone more realistic than this mystic; she was practical, disciplined, and sly, as soldiers are in every period. . . . For republicans she is a child of the people, more magnificent than any of the acknowledged great. . . . Finally, socialists cannot forget that she said, "I have been sent to console the poor and unfortunate." Thus all parties can lay claim to Joan of Arc. But she transcends them all. No one can confiscate her. Around her banner the miracle of national reconciliation can be accomplished today, just as it was accomplished five centuries ago.[94]

But although reconciliation between church and state, and therefore between the various streams of French identity in the face of foreign threat, may have been the overwhelming interpretation of Joan's legacy in official commemorations during the interwar period, she continued to be claimed by groups on both the left and the right challenging the bourgeois republic, by monarchists, and even by communists who represented

[92] Quoted in Winock 1998: 460.
[93] Winock 1998: 460–1.
[94] Quoted in Winock 1998: 467–8.

her as a member of the proletariat betrayed by the ruling classes. During the Second World War, she was claimed by both de Gaulle's resistance and by the Vichy Regime. In more recent times, Jean-Marie LePen's Front National evoked her campaign to expel foreign invaders as legitimation for its anti-immigrant agenda. Conflict over the memory of Joan of Arc was not confined to the manner in which all branches of French political culture have tried to identify with her but is also reflected in the way they have tried to exclude their opponents from being able to do so. As we have seen, Catholic activists have always sought to stress her loyalty and piety in contrast to the revolutionary secularism of republicans, epitomized by Voltaire's satirical abuse of her memory. Republicans, meanwhile, consistently identified their monarchist and clerical opposition with those who betrayed and executed her.

In the book *Nations as Zones of Conflict*, John Hutchinson criticizes Robert Gildea's conclusion that these intense struggles over the interpretation of the symbol of Joan of Arc throughout recent French history indicate a lack of any common symbolic framework or set of values around which a unifying national consensus could be built. On the contrary, Hutchinson argues, such conflict only reinforces the status of the symbol as a common reference point, indicating the imperative for all entrants to the political process to in some way define themselves in relation to it. These symbols are part of the shared language by which political discourse is expressed, and appealing to them as legitimating devices implies a larger encompassing framework – the nation – in which all parties participate and to whose overarching power they all submit.[95] Indeed, all parties must submit to this larger framework and must demonstrate their eagerness to submit to it. Conflict within the nation over the meaning of the nation's universal symbols, reflecting all of the political variations within the body of the nation itself, is therefore not only possible but also inevitable; even, to some degree, sought after by political actors.

We could go so far as to say that the more intense such conflict appears, the more central and unifying the symbol around which it takes place must be. If a symbol has been elevated to the status of a national axis point, then all constituent members of the nation must, of necessity, relate their own political orientations to that symbol, however divergent or conflicting these orientations might be. The reason such contests are so acrimonious is precisely because the stakes are so high; because identification with the national symbol has become a boundary marker, a litmus test of national

---

[95] Hutchinson 2005: 103–4.

belonging. If one is unable or unwilling to interpret a national axis symbol in a manner suitable to one's social or political affiliation, the result is the effective expulsion of that social or political group from the national communion. Conversely, then, if one can successfully portray one's political enemies as unqualified to claim association to the national totem, as being fundamentally opposed to its values and ideals, this amounts to the ultimate political victory, the absolute negation of their political legitimacy. For this reason, all social groups that are or seek to be constituent in the nation will, whatever their differences, seek to identify with the totem symbol and participate in its accompanying rituals. Indeed, the emotional intensity experienced in such conflicts itself becomes a mark of the national insider, insofar as those outside of the national tradition could not be expected to place any such value on the symbol in question.

We have seen examples of the simultaneously divisive and unifying potential of this dynamic. On the one hand, political actors attempt to disqualify their opponents from the ability to identify with Joan of Arc, thereby expelling them from the French nation. Yet, at the same time, even a nation bitterly divided to the point of civil war, such as France was in the aftermath of World War II, can be restored to a measure of unity by the evident fact that all parties to the conflict made reference to the same symbol as a common unifying principle, claiming to be the custodian of principles embodied in the same foundation myth. Similarly, we have seen how the inability of the state-centralist Catalan political party to plausibly participate in certain rituals related to the *Diada* celebrations threaten their effective expulsion from the Catalan nation, however Catalan their members might otherwise be in language, citizenship, and descent. However, at the same time, efforts by state, local, and regional authorities to develop more inclusive events that place a greater emphasis on September 11 as simply the Catalan national day, with less emphasis on what specifically the day commemorates, provide an easy means to generate a sense of national unity inclusive of all political orientations.

In Greece we see another case in which, as with France, the elevation of the defeat symbol was the product not of any one branch of a divided national culture but rather of an attempted synthesis into a unified and unifying national narrative, comparable to and, indeed, nearly contemporary with Michelet's efforts to portray republicanism in continuity with French tradition. Unlike many of our other cases, it is difficult to portray the fall of Constantinople as an arbitrarily selected commemorative moment, as it would have been universally recognized, both at the time as well as today, as symbolically and strategically pivotal to the fall of the Byzantine Empire. Nonetheless, the earliest manifestations of Greek nationalism did not place great emphasis on this moment in their constructions of history and identity.

The Greek national movement that developed among expatriate elites such as Korais in the late 18th century, through a merging of French Revolutionary principles with a sense of the glories of the ancient Hellenic past, viewed Byzantium and the Orthodox Christian civilization it engendered as regressive, representing a foreign occupation of the true Hellenic spirit. It thus could not identify the moment of Byzantium's fall as a Greek tragedy. The preexisting ethnoreligious tradition, on the other hand, although it may have preserved memories of the tragedy in popular discourse, had a largely passive attitude toward Ottoman domination and hence an ambiguous approach to the moment of Byzantium's fall. Nationalist historiography would later presume the Orthodox Church to have always been at the vanguard of the national struggle because it was the custodian of traits such as language, Orthodox identity, cultural idioms, and historical myths that would later be mobilized to define the national culture. But, in fact, the Orthodox clergy initially opposed the values and ideology of nationalism, recognizing that their authority over a universal community of Orthodox faithful, regardless of ethnicity and ruled from Constantinople, depended on their submission to Ottoman authority. Thus, the fall of Byzantium to the Ottomans, although perceived as a tragic loss of sovereignty on the one hand, was represented according to the terms of traditional theodicy: It was the will of God that Christendom should suffer for its sins through subjugation to the Turks. Nationalist goals were therefore portrayed as a revolt against the pious acceptance of God's will, much as traditional Judaism would later view Zionism. The conquest was even, at times, represented as a blessing in disguise, enabling the reunification of Orthodox peoples under a single authority in defense against the threat of Latin encroachment.[96]

The elevation of the fall of Constantinople to the axis point of Greek national–historical consciousness was a development that coincided with the rise of the "Great Idea" [Μεγάλη Ιδέα]. Simply put, this was a movement to (re)establish Greek hegemony over the widest territorial expanse that Greek culture had ever achieved, encompassing all ethnic Greeks (though the precise definition of this, and the nature of the state that would result, may have been open to various interpretations). But it is important to view this movement as more than just territorial irredentism,

---

[96] Herzfeld 1982: 128.

which, as such, would have had a lifespan only from about the 1840s until the "catastrophe" of 1922 and the resulting population exchange with Turkey that put an end to any further territorial ambitions. The effort to achieve these concrete political goals required a parallel movement to integrate those heterogeneous communities over which the movement laid claim into a unified national body.

As Paschalis Kitromilides puts it, "Greek nationalism, as expressed in the Great Idea, was motivated by concerns about social and ideological cohesion at least as much as, if not to a considerably greater degree than, by aspirations of territorial aggrandisement," with the effort to unify nation and church being among its key aims.[97] As a result, nationalists of the second half of the 19th century tended to play up the role of Byzantium rather than presenting the Enlightenment in contradiction to the Byzantine/Orthodox tradition, thereby bringing Orthodoxy into the definition of Hellenism by means of a more continuous presentation of history. Although 1922 might represent the collapse of the Great Idea as a political program, it could nonetheless be said that the social and ideological successes of the movement survived its political failure to become incorporated permanently into the emergent national consensus, forging and remaining the dominant conception of Greek identity.

Once Greece had achieved independence, the Byzantine period became important not only because it provided an essential historical link between the modern present and the ancient Hellenic past but also because the territorial reach of the Byzantine Empire provided an historical precedent necessary to justify the territorial ambitions inherent to the notion of redeeming ethnic Greeks from Ottoman rule.[98] From about the mid-19th century, historians began arguing for a central place for Byzantium in Greco-Roman continuity, a development best associated with Konstantinos Paparrigopoulos, and, indeed, evident in the evolution of his own work over time. At first, Paparrigopoulos echoed the Enlightenment view of Byzantium as a period of regressive domination, but this view was clearly reversed in his monumental work, *The History of the Greek Nation*, which carried Byzantium into the fold of "Romantic Hellenism," describing Byzantine history extensively and adopting it as an integral part of the history of the collective agent, the Greek nation, that was the central protagonist of his work.

[97] Kitromilides 1989: 185–6.
[98] Huxley 1998: 16.

Paparrigopoulos' overriding concern was to locate the Greek nation continuously through world history, depicting its survival and evolution through successive stages of sovereignty and domination, characterized by radically different political formations called by different names, but nonetheless indicative of the continuous development of an immutable and timeless entity. Byzantium was thus merely the character that this entity took during the Middle Ages, a historical high point of a continuous "Hellenic-Christian" civilization alongside classical antiquity and the modern Greek nation-state, in contrast to the "black periods" of Muslim conquest and Ottoman rule, represented historically by the conquest and loss of Constantinople. Kitromilides makes particular note of the way Paparrigopoulos spoke of Byzantium in personal tones, referring to "our medieval empire," "our emperors," and so forth. The reader was meant to be enthusiastic and proud of the Empire's achievements, noting in particular the role played by the Byzantine state in the preservation of "our language, our religion and more generally of our nationality" and to share the grief and despair over its decline and destruction. The year 1453 becomes a source of mourning and "the fall of Constantinople is felt as a personal loss, an open wound, an irreconcilable sorrow." The enthusiastic reception of Paparrigopoulos' history demonstrated that it "responded to profound needs and cravings in Greek society and collective consciousness,"[99] reflected in the noticeable impact that the model it developed had on contemporary poetry, literature, and on the growing field of folklore studies.

It was folklore studies, a field for which the term *laografia* was coined during this time, that set out to provide the empirical evidence to support Paparrigopoulos' historical model of Greek cultural continuity from ancient through to Byzantine up to modern times. The development of this discipline in Greece was not dissimilar to developments elsewhere in Europe, where folklorists were driven by the belief that their nation's original essence was best reflected in the diverse eccentricities of local myths, traditions, and dialects that had survived in isolation from the corrupting effects of foreign domination and influence. They viewed their vocation as being to collect and preserve as many of these elements as possible, as they now stood threatened by the homogenizing impulses of modernity, in particular, urbanization and mass public education. This view reflected the duality inherent in the nation-building process at this stage: The essence of the pure nation had to be defended from the very

---

[99] Kitromilides 1998: 27–30.

forces that were forging the modern national idea. Hence, although the folklore movement concerned itself with preserving local traditions, its wider purpose served the interests of asserting the principles of unity and continuity, for it was in these local traditions that the relics of the essential Greek culture, relevant to the whole of the nation across space and time, were presumed to be found. This is reflected in the fact that material contained in these anthologies tended to be organized thematically, rather than by region. The very act of collecting and preserving these local customs was thereby transformed into an effort to obliterate regional difference, as these elements were claimed by a unified tradition deemed to be the common heritage of the whole of the nation.[100]

Although the process was ostensibly one of preservation, the decisions made by the folklorists as to what was worth preserving, which versions were most authentic, how they should be organized, and what should be emphasized could not help but reflect contemporary concerns and assumptions as to what was essential to the national character and heritage.[101] Thus, it is interesting to note that images of defeat, and of the fall of Constantinople in particular, came to play an increasingly pivotal role in folklore anthologies around this time. Nikolaos Politis' *Selections from Songs of the Greek People* begins with a section on "historical" songs, almost all of which surround memories of defeat, beginning with the sack of Adrianople, highlighted by the fall of Constantinople, with the latest event commemorated being the failure of Greece to wrest Epirus from Turkey under the Treaty of Berlin in 1881. In contrast, songs commemorating internal struggles found little place in this collection, at least not in the section on history.[102]

Particular prominence was given to the *Song of Hagia Sophia*, commemorating the fall of Constantinople. As with Lamdan's *Masada*, a line from this poem, translated and interpreted as a declaration that the city would someday be "ours once more," was transformed by scholars and politicians into a national slogan expressing the ultimate aim of the Great Idea to recapture Constantinople and resume the liturgy in the Hagia Sophia.[103] Politis claimed that this song could be found "wherever Greek was spoken" and therefore stood as evidence of a deep-rooted common identity. The fact that people could be shown, through their preservation

[100] Peckham 2001: 69–71.
[101] Herzfeld 1982: 8.
[102] Ibid.: 117–8.
[103] Ibid.: 129–30.

of this song, to have identified in common with the fall of Constantinople proved that despite differences in dialect, self-descriptive terminology, or culture, a common nationhood nonetheless existed in the form of a shared sense of destiny. The argument was taken to the point at which possession of this song was identified as itself a boundary marker of Greek national belonging, one that could even transcend cultural, historical, and linguistic boundaries, such that when Politis noted that the song was found "even among the Vlach-speaking people of Macedonia," they were thereby brought into the framework of Greek national consciousness as a consequence. According to Politis, the song "explains the endurance of the race in the face of national calamities and the ineradicable optimism with which the enslaved nation envisages its liberation and reorganization."[104]

While accepting that a nation requires unifying symbols and alluding specifically to symbols of sacrifice in that regard, John Hutchinson, in *Nations as Zones of Conflict*, challenges the view that the nation, in order to be a nation, requires a hegemonic interpretation of its unifying symbols, or even that these symbols must reflect a long-term process toward cultural homogenization.[105] These differences, far from threatening the nation, are systemic, allowing for diversity within the nation as well as flexibility to social and political impacts. One might go so far as to claim that national belonging is defined by ideological competition over common signifiers, for only an insider to the nation would find those signifiers worth fighting over. Persistent differences within a nation help to maintain the social balance, for example between classes and ideologies; thus, one must view the nation not so much as a given set of myths and symbols but rather as a framework incorporating a diversity of myths, symbols, and values flexible to various ideological rankings of the various layers and to the perturbations of history. Nationalism is not a quest for homogeneity but rather a strategy for coping with diversity; thus, national symbols are not forces for homogenization but rather anchors around which diversity can safely revolve.

As we have seen, the elevation of Joan of Arc to the status of a French national axis point was neither preordained in the fabric of traditional Catholic French culture nor the product of the Enlightenment and Revolution. Rather, it began and progressed alongside the effort to merge these necessary but contradictory discourses of French identity. The very

---

[104] Quoted in Herzfeld 1982: 133.
[105] Hutchinson 2005: 108–12.

ambiguities that made her a poor representative of either the traditional Catholic cultural nation or the revolutionary republican political one – as a figure who on the one hand fought for the traditional religious culture but on the other is clearly depicted as having been betrayed and destroyed by the institutions of that same traditional religious culture – are what made her an ideal national symbol. It was precisely due to her eventual defeat and martyrdom that she could be portrayed as representing a principle deemed inherent to the nation, yet suppressed by the forces of history, even while the precise details as to the nature of that principle and the identity of the agents of its suppression could remain open to interpretation, therefore flexible to political diversity and social change.

A similar and near-contemporary story can be told about Greece. Although the preexisting cultural tradition, embodied in the institutional church, may have preserved the image of the fall of Constantinople as a folk memory to serve a particular narrow function – thus providing the later national movement with a plausible basis to claim continuous commemoration – the church itself could not elevate it to the status of a unifying axis point, in that it had come to terms with Ottoman domination for its effect of uniting Orthodox peoples under its sole political authority. Hence, it depicted this moment ambiguously, as a loss on the one hand but on the other as a liberation from the threat of Latin domination. At the same time, the revolutionary nationalist tradition, influenced by the European enlightenment and by the revolutionary ideas of France, identified with Hellenic antiquity. It had little use for Byzantium and therefore could not view its defeat as a tragedy. It was efforts to synthesize these streams in the mid to late 19th century that brought this myth to the forefront of the national narrative, insofar as the adoption of the fall of Constantinople as an axis point helped to reconcile these ideological and class divisions, providing a common reference point that allowed the modern national movement to lay claim to the myths, symbols, and cultural traits that had been preserved by the church. Although the disasters of 1922 may have put an end to the "Great Idea" that was the product of this synthesis, at least on a political–territorial level, the narrative that resulted nonetheless persisted as the symbolic framework defining a common Greek identity.

Ghana was confronted with the problem of reconciling an anticolonial national ideology that claimed continuity with precolonial indigenous culture with the fact that the modern national polity was successor to the colonial state, relying no less on the continued subordination of a diversity of indigenous societies. The authenticity of Asante tradition could be celebrated while at the same time reinforcing its ultimate subjugation and incorporation into what came to be the modern Ghanaian nation-state by glorifying not the symbols of Asante sovereignty itself but rather the figure of Yaa Asantewaa as the last leader of a violent but failed struggle in defense of those symbols of sovereignty and the cultural norms they represented. And as with the French and Greek cases, the elevation of the defeat myth was the sole product neither of the Asante ethnic tradition nor of the revolutionary anti-colonial nationalism of the independence period but rather of a later period when ethnic and civic narratives were successfully merging toward a cohesive Ghanaian political identity.

Israel's national mythology originally appointed Masada as its axis symbol, in part because of the symbol's ability to connect the modern national endeavor with a palpable monument whose origins and significance were associated with the end of an earlier period of state sovereignty. The Western Wall ultimately proved to have greater popular resonance, insofar as it was capable not only of connecting present with past but also of merging the traditional and national. Although the elevation of the symbol to a point of national and religious centrality may have been an innovation of modern nationalism, it is a symbol that, more than Masada, could plausibly be associated with the norms of the preexisting religious tradition on which the modern nation relied for its sense of continuity. As a symbol of the Temple, it stood, on the one hand, for continuity with the national and religious glory of ancient times, the current success of the nationalist endeavor in reestablishing sovereignty over this unifying symbol, and the expectation of the continued strength and efficacy of the nation. Yet, at the same time, as a symbol of the Temple's destruction, it represented the defeats of the past, the humiliations and deprivations of Exile, the continuing incompleteness of the present, evoking a hope for a restored future the precise character of which is left open. It would be inaccurate to say that the symbol holds one connotation for some and another for others. On the contrary, it serves to reconcile these conflicting impulses, all of which are integral to the national mythology, for those individuals who identify with it. It allows them to reap the psychological benefits of sovereignty over a unifying symbol, while leaving full realization of the ideal it represents to the indefinite future.

In France, Greece, Israel, and Ghana, we have seen four cases in which the elevation of a symbol of defeat to the center of the collective memory was neither embedded in the preexisting cultural tradition nor the radical innovation of a modern national one but rather the product, at a particular time and under particular circumstances, of efforts to merge these conflicting impulses into a coherent and unifying national narrative. The divisive and unifying functions of these myths, far from being opposing forces, are merely two sides of the same coin; necessary elements in the effort to forge a unifying myth out of a diverse and conflicted sociopolitical reality. The nation invariably contains a variety of cultural, social, and political subgroups generating counternarratives that will inevitably come into conflict. Maintenance of unity requires that this conflict be subsumed within a common framework, and the contested interpretation of symbols held in common to be universal is indicative of this framework.

Achieving and maintaining a flexible balance between the reality of diversity and contestation within the nation and the ideal of its unity is an inherent function of the national axis symbol. We have already begun to explore why images of defeat are particularly suited to such an ambivalent function. But to further examine this function in action, we must look more closely at the typical narrative structure of the defeat myth, with all of its contradictions and ambiguities, within the construction of national myth and memory.

4

The Defeat Narrative in National Myth and Symbol

In *Black Lamb and Grey Falcon*, Rebecca West describes her travels through the Balkans in the 1930s. During a visit to Kosovo, referred to in the book as "Old Serbia," her Serbian guide proceeds to translate a passage from an epic song, "The Downfall of the Serbian Empire." But first he explains, "it is not like any other poem, it is peculiar to us":

> There flies a gray bird, a falcon,
> From Jerusalem the holy,
> And in his beak he bears a swallow,
> That is no falcon, no gray bird,
> But it is the Saint Elijah.
> He carries no swallow,
> But a book from the Mother of God.
> He comes to the Tsar at Kossovo,
> He lays the book on the Tsar's knees.
> This book without like told the Tsar:
> 'Tsar Lazar, of honorable stock,
> Of what kind will you have your kingdom?
> Do you want a heavenly kingdom?
> Do you want an earthly kingdom?
> If you want an earthly kingdom,
> Saddle your horses, tighten your horses' girths,
> Gird on your swords,
> Then put an end to the Turkish attacks!
> And drive out every Turkish soldier.
> But if you want a heavenly kingdom
> Build you a church on Kossovo;
> Build it not with a floor of marble
> But lay down silk and scarlet on the ground,
> Give the Eucharist and battle orders to your soldiers,

For all your soldiers shall be destroyed,
And you, prince, you shall be destroyed with them.'
When the Tsar read the words,
The Tsar pondered, and he pondered thus:
'Dear God, where are these things, and how are they!
What kingdom shall I choose?
Shall I choose a heavenly kingdom?
Shall I choose an earthly kingdom?
If I choose an earthly kingdom,
An earthly kingdom lasts only a little time,
But a heavenly kingdom will last for eternity and its centuries.'
The Tsar chose a heavenly kingdom,
And not an earthly kingdom,
He built a church on Kossovo.
He built it not with floor of marble
But laid down silk and scarlet on the ground.
There he summoned the Serbian Patriarch
And twelve great bishops.
Then he gave his soldiers the Eucharist and their battle orders.
In the same hour as the Prince gave orders to his soldiers
The Turks attacked Kossovo.[1]

West's response to this passage demonstrates how myth is more than a set of stories. It is, rather, a symbol system, much like a language, that is only fully comprehensible to someone who speaks the language. West speaks a part of the language; that is, she speaks another language in the same broader language family of "nationalism." Considering herself a liberal nationalist (before World War II when such a notion was still plausible and common), she takes it as given that self-determination for a culture is an unquestionable good, domination by a foreign culture an obvious evil, and that this idea would have been self-evident even in Lazar's time and hence would have informed his resistance to Ottoman conquest. Thus, she takes a negative view of Lazar's choice of a "heavenly kingdom" over victory on the battlefield:

"Lazar was wrong," I said to myself. "He saved his soul and there followed five hundred years when no man on these plains, nor anywhere else in Europe for hundreds of miles in any direction, was allowed to keep his soul. He should have chosen damnation for their sake.... I do not believe in the thesis of this poem. I do not believe that any man can procure his own salvation by refusing to save millions of people from miserable slavery...."[2]

---

[1] West 1982: 910–11.
[2] Ibid.

She goes on to qualify this condemnation, chastising herself for putting the rights of the collective over those of the individual. But one can only wonder what her poor Serbian guide might have thought of these ponderings. For in the context of Serbian national mythology, what she is suggesting about Lazar the martyr is nothing short of blasphemy, of a sort that can be understood only if one imagines asking a devout Christian why Christ didn't just smack Judas upside the head, call a thunderbolt down on the Romans, and conquer Sin and Death on his own two feet. What must be understood is that in this poem, Lazar does not make his choice for himself as an individual, deciding to go to heaven rather than rule on earth. Rather, he chooses on behalf of the whole of the Serbian people, in his capacity as their leader and symbolic representative. What's more, he makes the best and most honorable choice possible in the name of their collective interests and well-being. This is a concept that is naturally incomprehensible to anyone who views the history from a nationalist perspective but is outside of the distinctly Serbian myth–symbol system.

The question that this chapter will explore is exactly what did Lazar do for the nation that was later to adopt him as its hero and symbol? Why is the fact that he did something of such vital importance taken for granted by the national narrative, as is the case with many national narratives that depict heroic figures whose only role is to willfully seek death and defeat, leading to their people's subjugation, as performing an invaluable service to the nation in so doing? This represents the first apparent contradiction pointing to the ambivalence that the sacrificial ritual reenacted in these myths resolves, and the power of this ritual is such that its logic is rarely examined critically, even by scholars.

The Kosovo Covenant

Of the Battle of Kosovo Polje itself, the following can be said with certainty: There was a confrontation on June 28, 1389, between forces led by Prince Lazar Hrebeljanović of Serbia and Ottoman forces led by Sultan Murad I. Heavy losses were sustained by both sides. When it was over, the Ottomans were left in possession of the field and both leaders were dead. Murad was succeeded by his son, Bayezit, who immediately returned his forces to the capital at Edirne in order to secure his succession. Lazar was succeeded by his young son Stefan Lazarević who, under the guidance of his mother Milica, agreed to become an Ottoman vassal shortly thereafter.[3] All of the otherwise conflicting contemporary sources

---

[3] Malcolm 1998: 61; Emmert 1990: 42.

agree on these points, and they are also reflected in the mythical narrative as expressed in subsequent epics, songs, and literature.

Although the elevation of Kosovo to the status of a foundation myth may have been the product of modern nationalism, this process was facilitated by the fact that authentic materials from which such a myth could be constructed were already available within the Serbian Orthodox cultural matrix. These were provided by the cult of Lazar that had already begun to develop in the years immediately following his death in battle. There was already a strong tradition in the Serbian Church of royal sainthood, though not yet one of royal martyrdom. Consequently, religious texts at the time were more concerned with reciting Lazar's achievements, of which killing Murad was the last, rather than with depicting his death as part of the framework of Serbian national destiny. However, reflecting the sense of despair that must have been prevalent following Lazar's death and the surrender of Milica to the Ottomans the following year, these accounts were the first to interpret Lazar's death as martyrdom sought and accepted willingly for the faith and for his people. Written within three years of the battle by Patriarch Danilo III, *A Narrative about Prince Lazar* included a speech allegedly delivered by Lazar to his troops that depicts him encouraging his men to eagerly pursue martyrdom as a clear choice so that they might serve as a symbol of piety for future generations. Speaking in what Danilo calls a "martyr's voice," Lazar describes the praise that will await those who sacrifice themselves in struggle for the faith:

You, O comrades and brother, lords and nobles, soldiers and vojvodas – great and small. You yourselves are witness and observers of that great goodness God has given us in this life... But if the sword, if wounds, or if the darkness of death comes to us, we accept it sweetly for Christ and for the godliness of our homeland. It is better to die in battle than to live in shame. Better it is for us to accept death from the sword in battle than to offer our shoulders to the enemy. We have lived a long time for the world; in the end we seek to accept the martyr's struggle and to live forever in heaven. We call ourselves Christian soldiers, martyrs for godliness to be recorded in the book of life. We do not spare our bodies in fighting in order that we may accept the holy wreathes from that One who judges all accomplishments. Sufferings beget glory and labors lead to peace.

The soldiers respond:

We do not spare ourselves because we know that after all this we must depart and become one with the dust. We die so that we may live forever. We bring ourselves before God as a living sacrifice – not as earlier with delusive feasting for our own enjoyment but in the good fight with our own blood. We give our lives freely so that after this we will be a vivid example to others. We do not fear the horror which has come to us nor the rage of those cursed enemies who lunge at us. Indeed, if we would think of fear and deprivation, we would not be worthy of good.

Following the response, Lazar, weeping like Jeremiah, calls for God's help:

O most merciful and gentle Emperor, free me from this life and from the tears of this present existence. With my own blood let me die fighting the good fight for you, Christ the Lord. May I be worthy to accept your praise through the martyr's wreath of suffering.[4]

The association with the mythology of the crucifixion is evident and intentional. Like Christ, Lazar is depicted as being in complete control, perishing knowingly for the faith. Martyrdom is not the result of his actions but rather the very goal. The anonymous *Eulogistic Narrative on Prince Lazar* goes even further, making the ultimate comparison equating Lazar's sacrifice with that of Christ himself:

You are the good shepherd who offered his soul for us. How shall we praise you? With which language is it worthy to celebrate you? O praiseworthy martyr, Lazar, come unseen to us and stand in our midst. Show us the songs of praise so that we will not be like sheep who have no shepherd. You are our shepherd; you cared for your flock which Christ the Lord gave to you. Do not surrender us to a shepherd whom we do not know. Do not scatter your flock which you gathered and for whose sake you shed your holy blood.[5]

This text implies that having sought martyrdom for the faith, Lazar's sacrifice enabled him to remain eternally among them as the "good shepherd" to intercede with God in order to keep his people united. One might even be tempted to say as a symbolic ideal rather than as a ruler exerting actual political power.

After the Ottoman conquest, Serbian tradition was preserved in the mountain villages, encouraged by the Serbian Church that incorporated the memory of the independent Serbian state into its ritual cycles, romanticizing the Nemanjić legacy and removing any negative connotations that feudalism might have had. Over time, the cult of Lazar was added to the cult of St. Sava as another vehicle by which Serbs identified as a united and distinct religious unit. Lazar's death at Kosovo was represented as vicarious atonement for Serbia's sins, which had called the wrath of God upon

---

[4] Emmert 1990: 63–5.
[5] Quoted in Emmert 1990: 66.

them and caused them to lose their state. The epic tradition developed during this time, drawn from the seeds of the early Lazar cult, through the recorded church and court histories, with the addition of new visions, experiences, and literary conventions.[6]

But although the culture could already accept the notion of martyrdom for the faith, and even the notion of someone who sought martyrdom in order to better serve as an intermediary between his people and God, a crucial element had to be added before this could be transformed into a national ideology. For one could certainly ask at this stage just what the nation, as such, had to gain from Lazar's decision to seek the "heavenly kingdom," as the only immediate results for the Serbian people in the earthly realm, even as the mythic narrative understands it, were the loss of the battle, the loss of their leaders, and eventual foreign domination. Indeed, several of the verses written in the decades immediately after the battle, although praising Lazar's sacrifice and asking his intercession, seem to subtly echo Rebecca West's suggestion that he got the better deal in his "heavenly kingdom" than his people got on earth.

To become a national ideology, the concept of martyrdom for the faith had to undergo a transformation, one that was informed by the experience of Serbs living under a more difficult Ottoman domination during the 18th and 19th centuries. *Pieces from Various Kosovo Poems*, one of the key songs in the Kosovo cycle collected by Vuk Karadžić in the early 19th century, casts the circumstances of Lazar's choice in a different light. In *The Downfall of the Serbian Empire*, Lazar is presented with the options of a heavenly or earthly kingdom by a divine intermediary. In *Pieces*, the decision is made after Lazar receives a message from Murad, who makes his choice clear:

> We cannot both of us be ruler,
> Send every key to me and every tax,
> The keys of gold that unlock the cities,
> And the taxes on heads for seven years,
> And if you will not send these things to me,
> Then come down to Kosovo meadow,
> We shall divide up this land with our swords![7]

According to this interpretation, Lazar is not given the option of victory or martyrdom. Rather, he is offered the choice to either surrender or to fight against impossible odds, a context that casts the more theological

[6] Emmert 1990: 121.
[7] Cited in Koljević 1991: 129.

interpretation of the *Downfall of the Serbian Empire* in a different light. As one prominent Serbian historian put it: "The Kosovo covenant – the choice of freedom in the celestial empire instead of humiliation and slavery in the temporal world – . . . is still the one permanent connective tissue that imbues the Serbs with the feeling of national entity."[8] The equation here is clear: The celestial empire is a metaphor for freedom, the earthly kingdom represents dishonorable vassalage. Thus, Lazar's decision to fight is no longer seen as a means to earthly victory, nor solely as a means to martyrdom for the faith, but rather as a way of dying in a state of freedom (which is to say nonsubjugation) and thus serving as an example of the ideal that places the value of remaining free above all other worldly concerns.

According to this value system, it would indeed seem that Lazar's choice was for his own honor over and above that of his people, but only if one fails to take into account his status as symbolic representative of the Serbian people, making the choice on their behalf. By dying in freedom rather than living in subjugation, as a symbol of the Serbian people's spirit, he ensures that they will remain free in spirit regardless of what might be happening to them in the earthly realm. Through his choice, Lazar becomes a model who provides a new set of values and a new framework resulting in a prescription for national survival and renewal. According to another Serbian historian, "the common people accept the interpretation originated and promoted by churchmen that the Serb nobles perished at Kosovo as a result of Lazar choosing the heavenly kingdom, because only in doing so may they expect redemption and regain their lost freedom in the future."[9] Lazar's action shows that despite the defeat, the nucleus of national, religious, and cultural consciousness was preserved, if dormant, in the collective folk memory; through songs, stories, and the like, and especially through the preservation of their distinct Christian, that is to say, Serbian Orthodox, identity and institutions. Therefore, the defeat is not final. Through the Church, the myth was developed that Serbs were transformed at Kosovo from an "earthly kingdom" ruled by an aristocracy to a heavenly, chosen people, destined for humiliation and martyrdom, but with the story still open for a triumphant ending.[10] That is, from an autonomous polity to an "imagined community"; a cultural community bound not by the instruments of state but by a common tie to

---

[8] Bataković, D., *The Kosovo Chronicles*, quoted in Malcolm 1998: 80.
[9] Radovan Samardžić, quoted in Bogert 1991: 181.
[10] Velikonja 1998: 24, 27.

a symbolic ideal expressed in religious, "heavenly" terms. To make such a transformation, however, requires a sacrifice; the sacrifice of the rulers and nobles who, until that time, had exercised "earthly" power over the Serbian polity. As Ralph Bogert puts it, "the Kosovo covenant conditions the life of a leaderless or 'decapitated' nation"[11]:

If the 'old testament' of the nation began with Rastko Nemanjic opting for eternal life and his subsequent founding of Serbian Orthodoxy, then at Kosovo a revolutionary quality was introduced into the nation's spiritual tradition with the invention of a new contract between God and Lazar. . . . What happened in terms of story rather than history was that the Serbian nation underwent a dramatic transposition, one in which the space of political power was closed and cultural space opened.[12]

The myth of the Kosovo Covenant not only serves to explain the state of subjugation by the Turks in a way that maintains the dignity of Serbia's heroes; it also serves as a basis to legitimize the mobilization of Serbs as a cultural unit by diffusing legitimacy away from the feudal aristocracy to the nation, symbolized by the consensual self-sacrifice of the presumed head of that aristocracy. The covenant is, in essence, an agreement before God by which the sacrifice of the elites is exchanged for the survival of the people. But the people have a stake in this agreement as well, which is to survive; to maintain the tie that binds them together through this mythic moment by continuing the struggle that the elites began according to the example they provided. Thus, the leader willfully participates in his own martyrdom and is thereby transformed into a model, a saint–fighter. Lazar, through his choice, removes himself from a position of political authority and transforms himself into a symbolic ideal, thereby transforming the "father horde" into the "brother clan," which he continues to govern not in person but in spirit.

The Savior

This is the key to every foundational national defeat myth: the symbolic destruction, through the defeat of a surrogate victim, of a sociopolitical order revered as a cultural highpoint, yet that must be destroyed in order for a national society to take its place. The character of the surrogate victim is vital to the success of the ritual. He is both insider and outsider; one of the group, yet one who stands apart, possessed of and symbolizing

[11] Bogert 1991: 181–2.
[12] Ibid.: 177–8.

the autonomy of violence that other group members might envy but are required to sacrifice in order to be a community. He must legitimately represent the apex of the sociopolitical order, yet in a manner that stresses identification with the masses. His role is that of boundary crosser; a group member who is to be expelled to its borders. And, most important, he must go willingly; he must voluntarily remove himself and the socio-political order he represents from history, so as to take the gravity of the crime and the threat of retribution off the conscience of the community. As Girard observed in *Violence and the Sacred*, a ritual sacrificial act assumes two opposing aspects, "appearing at times as a sacred obligation to be neglected at grave peril, at other times as a sort of criminal activity, entailing perils of equal gravity."[13] The sacred character of the victim stems from this contradiction; he is sacred because he is to be killed, yet killing him is a crime because he is sacred.

The tension created by the need to conform to this ritual narrative is evident in most defeat myths, for while historical axis points might be adopted in part because of their conformity to the necessary narrative, it is nonetheless difficult to find a historical figure fully capable of embodying both opposing aspects of the surrogate victim; both insider and outsider, regal yet humble. To the extent that a historical figure is one, the mythical narrative will be embellished to stress the other as well. If the symbol is a common person, some legitimate connection to the norms of leadership, and thus the right to stand in for the community as a whole, must be established. If the symbol is a leader, he or she is shown as well to be one of the people, of humble origins – rugged, rustic; honest and straightforward – sharing whatever plight the people confront and loved universally by the people, even chosen by them as their ruler or savior by means of some cryptodemocratic process.

The Kosovo narrative as expressed in the epic tradition tended to take for granted Lazar's status as successor to the Nemanjić tradition and therefore his legitimacy as ruler and symbolic representative of the Serbs, despite his not being descended from the Nemanjić dynasty whose Empire, which had reached its height under Dušan, had already disin-tegrated (Lazar ruled less than a quarter of this territory as a regional prince). The materials for such an elevation, however, had already been provided through efforts made by the Serbian Church to rationalize Lazar's claim to the Nemanjić legacy, given that Lazar and his successors had been the Church's primary sponsors at the time. Patriarch Danilo III's

[13] Girard 1977: 1.

account shortly after the Battle of Kosovo tells a story of Lazar being recognized by Dušan as divinely destined for the throne, even before the accession of Dušan's son Uroš, by means of a presumed bond between Dušan and Lazar's father that made them brothers in spirit if not in blood. Other accounts find different means to assert Lazar's legitimacy, often by marriage, but all stress a clear and peaceful transfer of authority between the death of Uroš and the leadership of Lazar, with legitimacy deriving directly from God.[14]

A similar concern is evident in Ghanaian national historiography of the Yaa Asantewaa War, to justify how a figure who officially held a secondary position within a provincial hierarchy could be represented as legitimate leader of what was depicted as an all-Asante rebellion and, by extension, symbolic figurehead of Asante sovereignty. This legitimacy is established in three ways. First, on a dynastic level, precedent is cited to show that although it may have been unusual for a woman to take on a role of political and military leadership in traditional Asante society, it was not unheard of for one of appropriate lineage to do so under the circumstances. In the absence of the king, the queenmother was expected to serve as effective regent so as to maintain continuity of political office and, because military positions were determinant of political positions, a woman who occupied a male stool took on the military responsibilities of the position along with the political and ritual ones. The sitting *Edwesohene*, Yaa Asantewaa's grandson, had been exiled to Sierra Leone along with Asantehene Prempe I. As *Edwesohemma*, Yaa Asantewaa would have been responsible for his duties in his absence; and as the *Edwesohene* had been one of the key supporters of Prempe I during the civil war and was consequently elevated to the status of a paramount chief and one of Prempe's key lieutenants, one of those responsibilities might well have been to serve as acting ruler of Asante as well.[15]

But although this narrative justifies Yaa Asantewaa's leadership as ascribed according to traditional communal standards, equally significant is the explanation that identifies it as an achieved position, satisfying modern individualistic values, whereby, as the one who successfully urged resistance on the reluctant chiefs, she is thereafter freely chosen by them to lead the movement. These events are generally attributed to a meeting in the home of another significant figure in the rebellion, Gyaasewahene Opoku Mensa, in the moments after Governor Hodgson's arrogant

---

[14] Emmert 1990: 34–6, 67.
[15] Boahen 2003: 147–9; Brempong 2000: 109; Obeng 2000: 143–4.

speech to the remaining Asante leadership, in which he declared that the Asantehene would never be restored, insisted on payment of a tax, and, most significantly, demanded that they deliver the Golden Stool.[16]

These two explanations balance the norms of the traditional society that is praised with those of the modern society that is served by the myth. But a third explanation that could be described as "totemic" is added to fortify Yaa Asantewaa's claim to legitimate symbolic authority: the notion that the Golden Stool, the symbol of Asante sovereignty over which the war was fought, was hidden in Edweso for much of the war and was thus effectively in Yaa Asantewaa's possession, within the borders of her personal sovereign territory. This notion appears frequently in oral traditions and is thus implicitly accepted as plausible if not factual by national historians, despite more reliable evidence that the Stool was hidden by Opoku Mensa and guarded by the Gyaasewa people far from Edweso between 1896 and when it was finally revealed upon the return of the Asantehene in 1920.[17]

But even while such efforts are made to associate Yaa Asantewaa with the norms of legitimate leadership, her humility and identity with the popular masses are also underscored. Popular accounts of the Yaa Asantewaa story tend to stress her continued commitment to her role and responsibilities as a mother, householder, and farmer; roles shared by any comparable group member. Also stressed is her fairness as a ruler, particularly her interest in helping and protecting the weak and vulnerable – women, children, and the poor – balanced against her desire to maintain traditional norms and defend traditional prerogatives. One popular history describes her as follows:

As an intelligent politician, a stateswoman and a nationalist, her reign as queen and king was marked with objectivity. She never discriminated against the poor nor the rich in her judgment of any issue which came before her. She endeared herself to her subjects by being outspoken and forthright especially when the poor were cheated by those in influential positions.... As a hard working wife, Nana Yaa Asantewaa worked deep into the evening, either sitting in her court as judge or working on her farm.[18]

In his study of Czech and Slovak national identity, Robert Pynsent observed that the martyr-leaders of Czech national mythology, such as

---

[16] Akyeampong 2000: 8; Boahen 2003: 37–38. Boahen emphasizes the language used by Major Nathan in a dispatch to Chamberlain that Yaa Asantewaa was "elected to command Ashanti forces" (118).

[17] Boahen 2003: 149, 174; Obeng 2000: 149–150; Akyeampong 2000: 4.

[18] Asirifi-Danquah 2002: 13.

St. Wenceslas, tended to be eulogized as cult figures specifically for their humble origins, noting how this tendency inserted a paradoxically democratic ethos into the Czech leadership cult. At the same time, however, he observes that although Czech nationalist historians have tended to associate this tendency with the Czech character, it is actually a common feature of national mythologies. The Hungarian St. Stephen's crown fell from heaven on to his head while he was having lunch by his plough, and the Polish Piast foundation myth also involved its founder being called from his plough. All of these legends of a call to leadership from humble origins can be said to call to mind archetypes from ancient Rome, such as Cincinnatus.[19] A similar dynamic is evident in the Kosovo myth, in which, on the one hand, the epics frequently refer to Lazar with the title "tsar" yet seem to depict him less as the leader of a medieval nobility than in the humbler character of a tribal chieftain more reminiscent of the patriarchal society in which the epics developed.[20] According to the myth, the autocratic leader is allowed to remain an autocratic leader only so long as he is seen to characterize and symbolize the will and condition, as well as the values and sentiments of the modern, horizontal, national society.

Perhaps the clearest illustration of this is to be found in Joan of Arc, whose youth, simplicity, and humble origins are precisely what enable her to represent the French masses enlisted to willingly serve and sacrifice for the state, thus enabling her mission and death to be retroactively designated as the foundation moment of French national sentiment. This notion comes through clearly in the closing lines of Michelet's history:

For the first time she [France] was loved as a person. And she became a person on the day she was loved.

Until then there was only a collection of provinces, a vast chaos of fiefs, a vague idea of a great country. But on that day, through the force of one heart, she became a nation [*patrie*].

Lovely mystery! Touching, sublime! How the immense, pure love of a young heart set a whole world on fire and gave it new life, the true life that love alone can give.

As a child she loved everything, say witnesses of her time. She even loved animals. Birds trusted her to the point of eating out of her hand. She loved her friends, her parents, but above all the poor. And the poorest of the poor, the most wretched of all, the most worthy of pity at the time was France.

---

[19] Pynsent 1994: 193.
[20] Gorup 1991: 166; Koljević 1991: 128–9.

She loved France so much!. . . and France, touched, began to love herself.

One saw this on the day she first appeared before Orléans. All the people forgot their peril. Seen for the first time, this ravishing image of the fatherland gripped them and filled them with enthusiasm. The people boldly sallied forth from behind their walls, they flew their banner, and they passed beneath the eyes of the English, who did not dare venture out of their fortresses.

Frenchmen, let us always remember that our fatherland was born from a woman's heart, from her tenderness, and the blood she gave for us.[21]

This passage, and the last sentence in particular, firmly identifies Joan of Arc as the foundation of the nation as a direct consequence of her blood sacrifice, not in the sense that she is considered in any way the founder of the French polity but rather the founder of a national sentiment that would germinate and come to fruition centuries later. Again, we see this expressed in the language of a mystical experience, yet one whose agent and goal is not the divine but rather "the people," of which Joan of Arc is deemed an incarnation because of her youth, her simplicity, her equal love for all, and the manner in which she herself was universally loved, thus transforming France "for the first time" from a heterogeneous "collection of provinces" into "a person" united by allegiance to a common principle.

Yet even Joan of Arc could not escape the ambivalence reflected in the need to tie even the most humble of surrogate victims to the norms of legitimate sovereignty, and there were instances of legends concocted attributing her with royal descent. For example, Pierre Caze's *La Mort de Jeanne d'Arc* of 1802 portrayed her as the child of an adulterous affair between Louis d'Orléans and Isabeau of Bavaria.[22] Winock dismisses these as fantastic and obviously fabricated legends, but the fact that they were fabricated makes them all the more interesting for our purposes of understanding the shifting social circumstances under which the myth developed. They provide Joan of Arc with a status that reconciles her humble origins with the need to represent her as a heroic icon of French sovereignty, a symbol of continuity between the traditional monarchical past and the genesis of national sentiment she is to represent. And, as Winock points out, these interpolations were the product of a rationalistic age that needed to legitimate Joan of Arc's role in a way that obviated the need for divine intervention.

---

[21] Quoted in Winock 1998: 455–6.
[22] Winock 1998: 449.

The fact that her actions had been motivated by divine visions was embarrassing to the rationalist, republican element of the national tradition that identified with Joan of Arc. Yet it is interesting to note that although the reality of these visions was often denied, this element was never simply dropped from the myth, or even downplayed, indicating that it continued to serve an important if subtle function in the collective memory. For although surrogate victims must belong to the community, they must also bear marks of difference, placing them at the margins of the community, possessed of the exceptional prerogatives of violent action enjoyed only by the totem that make them awe-inspiring on the one hand yet perverse and abject on the other. This marginality and exceptionality prefigures their roles as eventual boundary crossers, ultimately destined to be expelled unto death, whose sacrifice will eliminate the danger to the community that they symbolize.

Joan of Arc, a virgin called to martyrdom by God, could be said to represent the classic sacrificial archetype. But the opposite end of the spectrum works just as well. Yaa Asantewaa may not have been a virgin, but as a senior woman past menopause, she could circumvent the impurity Akan religion attributed to menstrual blood, thus allowing her to take on an exceptional androgynous role. She could organize, lead, and symbolize both male and female elements of wartime society, thus serving as a unique sacrifice embodying the community in crisis in its totality. She could cross borders, at the same time representing both defense of tradition and radical social change to the role of women and to notions of sovereignty.[23]

This ambivalence is evident in the contradictory views within the oral traditions as to whether Yaa Asantewaa ever fought at the front and fired a weapon herself or whether she directed the battle entirely from home and hearth in Edweso. This is essentially a conflict over whether the gender roles of the traditional Asante society being defended were respected or whether they were transcended in her willingness to engage in self-sacrifice alongside the soldiers she led. Establishing her active participation in the battle appears as a vital concern to national historiography, and a commonly accepted compromise concludes that she visited the battlefront to stand with and encourage the troops but did not fight herself. Accounts of her visits to the front include suggestions that while there she was impervious to cannons or bullets. As with Joan of Arc's visions, this supernatural detail is rejected by national historians as nonfactual yet

[23] Obeng 2000: 149.

cannot be simply dismissed from the historical narrative on those grounds. Rather, it enters the narrative through a back door, when historians note the frequency of this legend in oral accounts.[24]

Perhaps, then, the clearest expression of the archetype can be found in the myth least bound to the norms of rationalism and historical empiricism; the overtly legendary hero of the Latvian epic tradition, Lāčplēsis. According to the original legends, Lāčplēsis was the progeny of a union between a human and a bear, leaving him with a distinctive feature: the ears of a bear. Such a blurring of lines between the human and the animal is common in ancient myth, characteristic of the mythic god or king, with such marks understood as representing exceptional physical prowess and moral authority stemming from the generative violence that results from the dangerous merging of the civilized and primitive.[25] Such was the case with the Lāčplēsis myth, in which the conscious adoption of a legendary figure allowed free rein for the myth to openly express unconscious impulses that a more rationalist historicist national mythology would more studiously repress. The hero, although on the one hand the ultimate insider – the very representative of the nation and paragon of national values – is also marked as a partial outsider, not only non-member but nonhuman, possessed of an animal nature that represents his placement above and beyond the norms that govern the society he represents, thus prefiguring the sacrificial nature of his mission. Asocial like an animal, he possesses the violent autonomy characteristic of the true totem father and is thus, as well, the surrogate victim who must be destroyed if a fully human society is to emerge. This mark that places him outside of society is also, like Samson's hair, depicted as the source of the extraordinary strength that enables him to so serve the society. The Black Knight succeeds in defeating Lāčplēsis at the end of the epic only by first cutting off his bear ears in an act of symbolic castration.

As with the mystical elements of the Joan of Arc and Yaa Asantewaa stories, Lāčplēsis' part-animal nature was a source of some embarrassment to 19th-century Latvian nationalists, but again it was an element of the myth that could not simply be forgotten and discarded. Although a mythical demigod could be depicted as half-man and half-bear, this was problematic for a figure adopted as a paragon of a modern national resistance movement. Yet despite the fact that Pumpurs' epic altered the narrative of the hero's origins to say that he was simply raised by bears,

[24] Boahen 2003: 120–5, 133–5.
[25] Girard 1977: 253.

and even changed his name, which was originally "Lacasusis" (or "bear ear") to Lāčplēsis (literally "bear tearer" or "bear slayer"), there appears to have remained a sense that this element had to be represented somehow. In the freedom monument in Riga, the problem is circumvented with Lāčplēsis depicted as having long hair that conceals his ears. Other artists detach the bear ears from his head and pin them to his helmet as a kind of emblem or token. In his book on the Baltic independence movements of the 1990s, Anatol Lieven notes with some irony that by depicting Lāčplēsis in this way, the modern Latvian national movement was in effect symbolically castrating him just as did the Black Knight in the epic.[26] But perhaps there is no irony at all. Such castration is precisely what the national movement requires of its emblematic hero, and this is indeed the very function, albeit unconscious, of such depictions.

The embarrassment engendered by these marks of exceptionality, juxtaposed against the evident need to continue attributing these marks to national icons in some manner, is indicative of the core ambivalence the myth exists to address. For these symbols are such that they mark the surrogate victim not just as exceptional but also as an outsider to the norms of the modern, secular nation; as figures derived from a previous age predicated on a more primitive and superstitious framework of legitimation, a framework that is symbolically destroyed when they are killed or defeated. These elements are retained precisely because the nation wants to perceive its heroes in this way, so that when these surrogate victims cross the boundaries into death, they will take these elements with them. Joan of Arc's "voices" were consumed with her in the pyre of Rouen, much as Lāčplēsis' bear ears, and Yaa Asantewaa's invincibility to bullets. These supernatural, transcendent elements of the premodern ethnoculture are attributed to the surrogate victim in much the same way as sin was attributed to the biblical scapegoat and thereby expelled along with this stigma from the core of the community, subtly discredited by the defeat and symbolically destroyed in the sacrifice.

But the key mark of exceptionality in any surrogate victim is the way that he or she is made to appear to actively will his or her own sacrifice; at the very least, to gladly confront near-certain death and defeat in the face of impossible odds, if not to actively seek martyrdom and defeat as a desirable end in itself. Such intention is attributed to Lazar in the epics and folk songs in which he is depicted in advance of the battle declaring, as in *Tomorrow Is a Beautiful St. Vitus Day*, "Tomorrow I think to perish

[26] Lieven 1993: 123.

at Kosovo for the Christian faith"; or in *Tsar Lazar and Tsaritsa Militsa*, "For the honorable cross my blood to spill and to die for my faith . . . and for the faith to die with my brothers."[27] This willingness is expressed even more clearly in Israel's Masada myth: The Zealots defending Masada die by their own hand. The surrogate victim is invariably depicted as knowing he is going to die, accepting it, even seeking it eagerly, despite the immediate implications this has to the defeat and conquest of the group. That this is nonetheless a generative act is accepted implicitly by the group to which the myth belongs.

This is indicative of the reality that must remain hidden from the community that venerates the myth; the "totem secret" that it is the community itself that desires and demands the death as a means of renewal in order for that community to be formed and maintained. As Carolyn Marvin and David Ingle observe in *Blood Sacrifice and the Nation*, "The selection of the sacrificial hero, the insider who agrees to become an outsider, is a key episode in the totem myth, since a willing sacrifice keeps the totem secret . . . the lonely hero volunteers to bear sacrificial burdens for the group." The savior–leader embodies the sentiments that the group demands of its members and thus his willingness makes him a hero and embodiment of the group, but it also marks him as sacred, apart from the group. "The willing sacrifice is unnatural, a social exception. This makes him god as well as man."[28]

The Prince's Supper

But if Lazar's decision to seek martyrdom and defeat was made consciously according to the will of God and in the interests of his nation, why is it then necessary to go through the exercise of a bloody battle, let alone the drama of betrayal and intrigue that would come to characterize the Kosovo mythical narrative? Indeed, the notion of the Kosovo Covenant, Lazar's conscious choice to accept death and defeat, is only one of the themes that came to dominate the myth. There are three other characters whose roles in the drama are as vital to the efficacy of the ritual: the outsider, Murad, who acts as Sacred Executioner; the avenging Hero, Miloš Obilić, who stands as a model for national activism; and the countermodel, the Traitor, Vuk Branković. Their stories offer contradictory explanations for the defeat at the battle of Kosovo.

[27] Both as quoted in Markovic 1983: 115.
[28] Marvin and Ingle 1999: 74–5.

There are two very different approaches that any given Kosovo account can take toward the lead-up to the battle. The first, already discussed, presents Lazar as confronted with a choice: between a heavenly or earthly kingdom as in *the Downfall of the Serbian Empire*, or between honorable death and dishonorable surrender, as in *Pieces from Various Kosovo Poems*. This approach depicts Lazar making a Christ-like choice in the face of temptation, to sacrifice himself on behalf of the faith and his people. But another approach, no less christological, depicts Lazar giving a magnificent banquet on the eve of the battle. The idea of such a meal before a battle was well within Byzantine tradition, but in the mythical narrative, it is clearly worked into the framework of the biblical Last Supper, with Lazar in the role of Christ. The Kosovo narrative, however, inserts an unusual twist. Like Christ, Lazar knows that he will be betrayed by one of those closest to him. But while Christ at the Last Supper knew full well that the traitor was Judas, Lazar accuses the wrong guy.

In *The Prince's Supper*, also from Karadžić's collection, Lazar suspects his most faithful knight, Miloš Obilić, forcing him to stand away from the table during the banquet. Then, in an ironic display of Christ-like generosity, Lazar proposes a toast to Miloš, forgiving his presumed sin in advance in terms that make his suspicion clear:

> To thy health, oh Milosh, friend and traitor!
> Friend at first, but at the last a traitor.
> When the battle rages fierce tomorrow
> Thou wilt then betray me on Kosovo,
> And wilt join the Turkish Sultan Murad!
> Drink with me, and pledge me deep, oh Milosh,
> Drain the cup, I give thee in token!

With no sign of bitterness (for Miloš' loyalty is such that he cannot betray the higher ideal that Lazar represents), Miloš accepts the cup with which the toast was presented. Then he points to Vuk Branković as the real traitor, and pledges that his own faith will be proven in battle, promising that he will kill Murad:

> Never, Tsar Lazar, was I unfaithful,
> Never have I been, and never will be,
> And tomorrow I go to Kosovo
> For the Christian faith to fight and perish
> At thy very knees there sits the traitor!
> Covered by thy robes he drains the wine-cup,
> 'Tis Vuk Brankovitch, th'accursed traitor!
> And when dawns the pleasant day tomorrow

> We shall see upon the field, Kosovo
> Who to thee is faithful, and who faithless.
> And I call Almighty God to witness
> I will go tomorrow to Kosovo,
> I will slay the Turkish Sultan, Murad.[29]

Contemporary records and early cult sources, though they contain many of the themes that would later shape the Kosovo tradition, have little to say about the exact cause of the death of Murad. It appears that the letter from King Tvrtko to the senate of Florence in October 1389 made mention of a daring attack by "twelve loyal lords" during the battle, though historians consider many of the details of this account, particularly the choice of the symbolic number 12, to be fanciful. Another account, from an anonymous Catalan author in 1402, attributes the death of Murad to a powerful Hungarian knight, possibly one of Lazar's allies through marriage who would have sent a contingent to the battle. Ottoman documents speak vaguely about a solitary Christian solider who killed the sultan either by luck or trickery, and the later Serbian epic tradition may well have picked up on these accounts, but the surprising lack of detail over an issue that would have been of great significance to the Ottomans suggests that they really did not know what happened, and their accounts were probably influenced by other sources.[30]

The Serbian mythical narrative holds that the deed was carried out before the battle. Stung by Lazar's reproach, Miloš resolves to prove his loyalty by riding out on the morning of the battle to the Sultan's tent, where he declares that he had decided to join the Turkish side. The Sultan asks him to perform the ritual obeisance of kissing his foot, and, in the words of the earliest recorded song:

> Before the Sultan Miloš bowed,
> And he leaned o'er to kiss his knee,
> His golden dagger drew, and struck
> And underfoot he trampled him.[31]

The Hero

The heroic tradition that focused on Miloš Obilić appears to have come to the fore of the mythical narrative as the cult of Lazar was declining in the

[29] Tomashevich 1991: 209; see also Koljević 1991: 131.
[30] Malcolm 1998: 69–72.
[31] Quoted in Malcolm 1998: 68–9.

wake of the short-lived Lazarević dynasty that collapsed shortly after the death of Stefan. The Kosovo songs continued to develop in the mountain villages and came to reflect the values and conventions of the patriarchal society rather than the very different values of the feudal society in which the events they depicted took place. The ethos of the village during the period of Ottoman domination was a refusal to accept the right of any man to rule over another; therefore, the epic tended to glorify the image of the hero, identified as those brave men who fought against tyranny, with Miloš Obilić representing such an ideal, willing to sacrifice himself in such a struggle.[32]

The Kosovo myth provides a case in which the savior–leader and the hero–model are embodied in two separate and distinct figures. But as Anthony Smith notes in *Chosen Peoples*, the boundaries between these roles can often be blurred, and it is possible for both roles to be represented in the same symbolic figure or device. Their functions, however, are sufficiently distinguishable that they can be examined separately.[33] The savior stands apart from the group, exemplar of abstract national virtue in its purest form; a god-figure subject to worship, he acts in a way that only he can or should, possessed of prerogatives that are by definition denied to group members. The hero, in contrast, is a part of the group, its exemplar. He is a model for emulation by group members, and the example he provides is one of complete submission to the totem, symbolizing unconditional loyalty to the group as one who bows before its killing authority. But this model takes on a share of divinity when his submission becomes ultimate, to the point of the death of the individual body, and he becomes a symbol of the principle of submission itself.

Although a model for imitation, the hero is also a source of guilt, insofar as the imitation can never be complete unless the disciple himself becomes a sacrifice and is in turn transformed into a model that the living group cannot fully imitate. It is guilt that motivates continuing sacrifice in cycle. "The surrogate victim, the savior, is the son we expel into death ... with the death of enough sons, the group finds relief from internecine tensions. These will build again because the savior son becomes in death the demanding totem father who calls for more blood and more sons. The group will need more willing sacrifices on whom to vent its anger. New victims will be expelled along with the burden of group violence they carry. If not, the group will perish, a casualty of

---

[32] Gorup 1991: 116; Emmert 1990: 122–3.
[33] Smith 2003: 40–1.

internal disunity."[34] The discourse of the national myth often encourages this guilt intentionally in the face of recollections of sacrifice, rhetorically pondering what the nation would be if all members could properly emulate the spirit of the hero, intimating that failure to do so amounts to betrayal of the sacrifice, behind which lurks the threat of the death of the group through the dissolution of its social ties.[35]

The heroic element of the myth does not always find expression in a single figure. Indeed, because it represents a mode of sacrifice accessible to and demanded of the group as a whole, it is often far easier to portray this element through the depiction of heroic common and collective sacrifice. Unanimous consent and submission to the totem is the value that is stressed by this device; hence, the relative anonymity, the blending of iconic figures into the collective, is stressed at these pivotal moments. We have seen that Czech national history contains several iconic figures of individual martyrs, yet at the moment depicted as the turning point from independence to domination, the Battle of White Mountain, heroic individuals take a secondary role against the collective blood sacrifice of the 27 Czech lords executed in Staromestske Square. Israel's sense of national history also contains individual martyr-figures, both ancient and modern, but at the key moment of transition from Antiquity to Exile, it is the mass sacrifice of the collective that is stressed. The garrison at Masada had its commander, Elazar Ben-Yair; but it is the collective and unanimous nature of the mass suicide that is stressed at this moment. The commander serves as little more than a narrative device in order to articulate the sentiments of the collective. Even in the Kosovo myth, Miloš Obilić is understood quite differently from Lazar, as an exemplar of the mass of people who sacrificed in the same manner; not the symbol of the group's killing authority itself but rather a model of the group member who bows before it.

Masada provides us with perhaps the clearest test case of the national construction of a heroic myth. Although most of the defeat narratives examined in this work could draw selectively on a variety of conflicting yet equally authentic historical and literary sources in order to construct a suitable myth without sacrificing empirical validity, there was only one historical source that recounted the events of Masada: Flavius Josephus' *War of the Jews*. Put bluntly, without Josephus, there would be no Masada because the event would have gone unrecorded and been lost

[34] Marvin and Ingle 1999: 78–9.
[35] Ibid.: 13–14.

from historical memory.[36] Thus, deviations from the historical record are easier to spot; one need only search for discrepancies between expressions of the mythical narrative and the details of Josephus' account in order to determine how the mythical narrative was affected by contemporary concerns.

In his book, *The Masada Myth* (1995), Israeli sociologist Nachman Ben-Yehuda deconstructs the basic elements of the mythical narrative through an examination of extensive sources including newspapers and other media, school textbooks, literature and art, tourist guides, and the organs of various youth and political organizations, as well as personal interviews; both those that reflected, and those that contributed to the popular perception of the event throughout the history of the Zionist movement and the Israeli state. He offers two paradigmatic examples of passages that summarize the key elements of the typical Masada narrative. The first is the short paragraph from the Ministry of Foreign Affairs "Facts About Israel" pamphlet, cited in the introduction of this book. This passage is interesting in that coming from an organ of the state designed for consumption by outsiders, it offers insight into how the state wishes the event to be perceived. The second is an excerpt from Yigal Yadin's 1966 book on the Masada excavations, summarizing the events surrounding the fortress's fall:

At the beginning of the 66AD rebellion, a group of Jewish zealots had destroyed the Roman garrison at Masada and held it throughout the war. They were now – after the fall of Jerusalem – joined by a few surviving patriots from the Jewish capital who had evaded capture and made the long arduous trek across the Judean wilderness determined to continue their battle for freedom. With Masada as their base for raiding operations, they harried the Romans for two years. In 72 AD Flavius Silva, the Roman Governor, resolved to crush this outpost of resistance. He marched on Masada with his Tenth Legion, its auxiliary troops and thousands of prisoners of war carrying water, timber and provisions across the stretch of

[36] Notwithstanding mention of the event in the Book of Jossipon, a text clearly derivative of Josephus but with the addition of one crucial detail: In Jossipon, the men at Masada do not kill themselves after killing their families but rather proceed to meet their death in battle against the Romans. This highlights the ambivalence of traditional Judaism toward the very focal point of the story, the mass suicide, an ambivalence that would be evident in Zionist historiography as well. But even given these changes to the story, Jossipon could not be said to have had a significant effect on the development of the mythical narrative. The text did not have a dramatic impact on the medieval Jewish construction of history, and it is largely for this reason that even modern Israeli commemoration of Masada tends to refer to Josephus, whereas the text of Jossipon has largely been ignored despite the fact that it better corresponds to the mythical narrative (Zerubavel 1995: 62, 208; Ben-Yehuda 1995: 213).

barren plateau. The Jews at the top of the rock, commanded by Elazar Ben-Yair, prepared themselves for defense, making use of the natural and man-made fortifications, and rationing their supplies in the storehouses and cisterns.

Silva's men prepared for a long siege. They established camps at the base of the rock, built a circumvallation round the fortress, and on a rocky site near the western approach to Masada they constructed a ramp of beaten earth and large stones. On this they threw up a siege tower and under covering fire from its top they moved a battering ram up the ramp and directed it against the fortress wall. They finally succeeded in making a breach. This was the beginning of the end. That night, at the top of Masada, Elazar Ben-Yair reviewed the fateful position. The defensive wall was now consumed by fire. The Romans would overrun them on the morrow. There was no hope of relief, and none of escape. Only two alternatives were open: surrender or death. He resolved 'that a death of glory was preferable to a life of infamy, and that the most magnanimous resolution would be to disdain the idea of surviving the loss of their liberty.' Rather than become slaves to their conquerors, the defenders – 960 men, women and children – thereupon ended their lives at their own hands. When the Romans reached the height next morning, they were met with silence. And thus says Josephus at the end of his description:

And so met [the Romans] with the multitude of the slain, but could take no pleasure in the fact, though it were done to their enemies. Nor could they do other than wonder at the courage of their resolution, and at the immovable contempt of death which so great a number of them had shown, when they went through with such an action as that was.[37]

This passage is particularly informative, in that it was written by someone who made the study of Masada a significant part of his life's work, and who would therefore be expected to have an intimate familiarity with Josephus' account as well as the prevalent myth. Yadin is more careful than the Ministry of Foreign Affairs document not to say anything that is blatantly untrue or that could be easily contradicted by a reading of Josephus. However, through a carefully worded description that highlights certain elements of the story, omits others, and introduces new elements through informed speculation, he is able to make his account conform to the mythical narrative and thereby reinforce it. Among the discrepancies between Josephus' account and the mythical narrative, Ben-Yehuda makes note of the following points in particular:

1. Josephus makes it clear that the defenders of Masada were all from a distinct group called the Sicarii, best known for their use of political assassinations, primarily not against Romans but rather against

---

[37] Yadin 1966: 11–13; cf. Josephus; *War* VII:9:2.

other Jews who did not share their extremist political views.[38] Expressions of the mythical narrative obscure this element, and the defenders are rarely referred to as Sicarii. They are designated either vaguely as Jewish fighters or freedom fighters, such as in the Ministry of Foreign Affairs (MFA) paragraph or, more frequently, "Zealots," as Yadin does in his account and, indeed, in the very title of his book on the archaeological excavations of Masada. The index of his book does not even contain an entry for "Sicarii."

2. As with most expressions of the mythical narrative, the MFA passage states, and Yadin's account implies, that the "Zealots" came to Masada as the surviving defenders of Jerusalem, only after Jerusalem fell and the Temple was destroyed. In contrast, Josephus makes it clear that the Sicarii fled to Masada well before Jerusalem came under siege, driven away not by the Romans but by fellow Jews who disapproved of their terror tactics (*War* II:17:9). According to Josephus' account, they did not participate in the defense of Jerusalem or in any other significant confrontation of the revolt.

3. The question of how the defenders of Masada sustained themselves during the years between their arrival and the fall of the fortress is rarely dealt with in the mythical narrative, save for the mention that they had abundant supplies. An episode that is inevitably ignored, though Josephus relates it in great detail, is an attack perpetrated on Passover by the Sicarii against the Jewish village of Ein Gedi, some 15 miles away: " . . . they came down by night, without being discovered by those that could have prevented them, and overran a certain small city called Engaddi. . . . They also dispersed them, and cast them out of the city. As for such as could not run away, being women and children, they slew of them above seven hundred. Afterward, when they had carried every thing out of their houses, and had seized upon all the fruits that were in a flourishing condition, they brought them into Masada. And indeed these men laid all the villages that were about the fortress waste, and made the

[38] Josephus, *War* VII:8:1 specifies that the defenders of Masada were Sicarii, who are described in II:13:3 as follows: " . . . there sprang up another sort of robbers in Jerusalem, which were called Sicarii, who slew men in the day time, and in the midst of the city; this they did chiefly at the festivals, when they mingled themselves among the multitude, and concealed daggers under their garments, with which they stabbed those that were their enemies; and when any fell down dead, the murderers became a part of those that had indignation against them; by which means they appeared persons of such reputation, that they could by no means be discovered."

whole country desolate; while there came to them every day, from all parts, not a few men as corrupt as themselves" (*War* IV:7:2).

4. The mythical narrative generally presumes that the siege of Masada lasted from the fall of Jerusalem until it ended at the moment of the mass suicide, a total of three years. Again, this is said explicitly in the MFA account and implied in Yadin's. In fact, Josephus makes it clear that the Romans under Flavius Silva only got around to besieging Masada as a final clean-up action after the rest of Judea had been subdued (*War* VII:8:1). The siege could not have lasted longer than seven to eight months and could well have been as short as seven weeks.[39]

5. The mythical narrative generally portrays Masada as the site of numerous fierce battles with the Romans, up to the point at which the Zealots deemed their situation to be hopeless and committed suicide only as a last resort. Again, the MFA pamphlet states this explicitly, whereas Yadin invites the reader to the assumption. In fact, Josephus' narrative does not describe any battles between the defenders and the Romans, save for a brief skirmish the day before the suicide when the outer wall was first breached (*War* VII:8:5). Indeed, Josephus seems to suggest that the Sicarii were none too eager to confront the Romans. They avoided any manner of participation in the revolt itself by remaining at Masada, and one could easily interpret the suicide, in this light, as a means of avoiding confrontation.[40]

6. Restatements of the mythical narrative will often include excerpts from the speech that the commander of the Zealots, Elazar Ben-Yair, gave to the defenders exhorting them to choose an honorable death by suicide over the life of slavery to the Romans that would

---

[39] According to recent archeological research, cited in Ben-Yehuda 2002: 99.

[40] A children's book about Masada coauthored by Yadin deals with this problem in a creative way. After providing a detailed account of the fierce battle at the siege of Jotapata described by Josephus (who, in this case, was there), it proceeds to apologize for the fact that Josephus does not provide similar details about Masada but insists that such battles must have occurred since this siege lasted so much longer, providing a fanciful description of what those battles must have been like. "During that long time ... Zealot warriors must have made countless raids on the enemy, darting out from the walls to burn and destroy what they could of the Roman siege works or artillery. Many a fierce and bloody battle must have been fought on the slowly advancing ramp. And even after the ramp had crept to the summit, there must have been acts of heroism such as that of the brave Jewish patriot who, when the Roman battering ram was pounding the wall of Jotapata, stood up in plain sight of the enemy and hurled down a great boulder that broke off the iron head of the ram ... " (Yadin and Gottlieb 1969: 107–26).

result from their being captured. Often ceremonies and commemorations at Masada quote from these speeches. However, it is rarely
noted that Ben-Yair had to make two such speeches before the
group would acquiesce to the mass suicide. Although Josephus
makes his own admiration for Ben-Yair's words very plain (in contrast to the negative opinion he seems to have of the Sicarii in
general), he also makes it clear that a major persuasive effort had
to be invested to make them kill each other (and murder noncom-
batant women and children) in preference to being captured (*War*
VII:8:7).

7. Restatements of the mythical narrative will only occasionally
   include the detail, mentioned by Josephus, that there were seven
   survivors of the mass suicide: two women and five children (*War*
   VII:9:1). Most accounts ignore the issue, like the MFA paragraph
   and, like Yadin, concentrate on the passages in Josephus that
   describe the silence met by the Romans when they finally breached
   the fortress.

Ben-Yehuda contends that it was in the interest of transforming the complex episode described by Josephus into a simple heroic narrative that
certain elements of the story were omitted, others exaggerated, and still
others added. The narrative depicting the struggle of the last Jewish rebels
had to provide suitable surrogates with whom the nation could identify,
enabling a sense of common identity and continuity that could serve to
give the national ideology legitimacy. It also had to provide a model
offering a message of heroism, sacrifice, and resolution as a counter to
the image of passivity associated with Exile, so as to resolve the Zionist ambivalence toward symbols of the Jewish past. Thus, the principal
theme of the Masada narrative became the notion of the heroic fight
to the end, with the model image that of the Jewish warrior, willing to
die for his land. The myth also provided a tangible, physical link to the
past, representing a clear statement that the forefathers of Zionism lived,
worked, fought, and died in the land.

The narrative had to be assimilated to this expectation of heroism,
just as the Kosovo narrative had to be brought into a salvation framework. One does not expect heroes to perform acts of terrorism, to be
shamefully driven away from the site of the revolt by their own people,
to commit atrocities such as the Ein Gedi massacre, to shy away from
battle, or to hesitate at the decisive moment.[41] Hence, these elements

---

[41] Ben-Yehuda 1995: 266.

are quietly forgotten, and the narrative chooses instead to focus on the courage of the defenders in sustaining their resistance to the Romans for the three years after the fall of Jerusalem and their readiness to die for freedom. It must therefore elaborate where Josephus is silent. In doing so, it also obscures Josephus' elaborate description of the suicide. Between the fictitious descriptions of battle and the quiet acceptance of its conclusion, the problematic issue of mass suicide is suppressed by its being subsumed under the broader category of "patriotic death" or "fight to the end," with the precise means of death relegated to a marginal detail. This avoids the image of the suicide as an escapist solution.[42]

In a later work, *Sacrificing Truth: Archaeology and the Myth of Masada*, Ben-Yehuda concludes that Yadin was engaged in intentional deception in the twisting of his conclusions and of Josephus' narrative to suit the national myth. In light of the evidence he presents that Yadin both concealed archaeological evidence and presented speculation as fact to serve the mythical narrative, this is not a difficult conclusion to reach.[43] But one could counter that Ben-Yehuda gives insufficient credit to the human capacity for self-deception. An alternative explanation is that there are certain possibilities that one who has internalized a particular mythology may be psychologically incapable of entertaining and equating symbols of the national character with evil or cowardly deeds is one of them. Yadin was very much a part of a collective memory and, as Zerubavel points out, collective memory is as much about forgetting as it is about commemorating.[44] Hence, one could speculate that Yadin was as intent on deceiving himself as on deceiving the nation. He might well have memorized Josephus without giving the slightest consideration to those passages hostile to the Sicarii, dismissing them to the historian's pro-Roman bias even while citing him as an authority in other matters.[45] His omission of certain embarrassing finds can be explained by his refusal to recognize these details as important, and his assertion of speculation as fact by the possibility that he was simply unable to entertain alternative interpretations.

The equation between the defenders of Masada and the modern nation of Israel was not the product of Yadin's efforts. His work merely served to

---

[42] Zerubavel 1994: 76.
[43] Ben-Yehuda 2002: 208–9, 251–2.
[44] Zerubavel 1995: 5–9.
[45] In *The Masada Myth*, Ben-Yehuda notes that the perception of Josephus as a questionable character often gave psychological legitimacy to the effort to correct, which is to say, falsify his account where it contradicted the ideologically preferred narrative (Ben-Yehuda 1995: 266–7).

make this equation more plausible and palatable, psychologically bringing the symbol into line with the national ideal. The defenders of Masada
were not transformed into heroes in order to provide the Zionist national
myth with ideals of heroism. If ideals of heroism were all that were needed,
there would be plenty of authentic ones to choose from that would not
require the historiographical acrobatics evident in the creation of the
Masada mythical narrative. The dynamic, rather, works the other way:
The defenders of Masada *had* to be heroes because they are *us*, and *we're*
heroes. The symbolic identification and incorporation of the defenders
of Masada into the modern system of national rights and responsibilities
came first, in part because of the symbolic significance of the last battle of
the Judean revolt as a marker of the important boundary between Antiquity and Exile and in part because of the dramatic nature of the suicide as
a symbol of national commitment and sacrifice. It was only then that the
mythical narrative came into play to reshape the defenders of Masada to
suit the image of the national ideology that had adopted them.

But all of these changes point, as well, to another subtle shift that we
observe in the popular perception of the suicide at Masada that enabled
it to enter into the national mythology, comparable to the change that
occurred in the Kosovo narrative whereby Lazar's choice of defeat over
victory was transformed into a choice on behalf of the nation of honorable death over dishonorable subjugation. Namely, the meaning of the
concept of freedom was transformed by its application to the values of
nationalism. Ben-Yair, in his speeches to the defenders of Masada, makes
clear the fate he wishes them to avoid by their mass suicide.

And let us not at this time bring a reproach upon ourselves for self-contradiction,
while we formerly would not undergo slavery, though it were then without danger, but must now, together with slavery, choose such punishments also as are
intolerable; I mean this, upon the supposition that the Romans once reduce us
under their power while we are alive... Let our wives die before they are abused,
and our children before they have tasted of slavery; and after we have slain them,
let us bestow that glorious benefit upon one another mutually, and preserve ourselves in freedom.

But for abuses, and slavery, and the sight of our wives led away after an igno-
minious manner, with their children, these are not such evils as are natural and
necessary among men; although such as do not prefer death before those miseries,
when it is in their power so to do, must undergo even them, on account of their
own cowardice. We revolted from the Romans with great pretensions to courage;
and when, at the very last, they invited us to preserve ourselves, we would not
comply with them. Who will not, therefore, believe that they will certainly be in
a rage at us, in case they can take us alive? Miserable will then be the young men

who will be strong enough in their bodies to sustain many torments! Miserable also will be those of elder years, who will not be able to bear those calamities which young men might sustain! One man will be obliged to hear the voice of his son implore help of his father, when his hands are bound. But certainly our hands are still at liberty, and have a sword in them; let them then be subservient to us in our glorious design; let us die before we become slaves under our enemies, and let us go out of the world, together with our children and our wives, in a state of freedom (*War* VII:8:6–7).

Ben-Yair calls on the defenders of Masada to sacrifice themselves so that they might die in a state of freedom. But it is clear that he means freedom in a very literal, individual sense; the sense of not being a slave, of not being subjected to humiliations upon capture; a notion that would have been counted as honorable according to Roman values but that was not considered justification for suicide according to Jewish ones. Even when Ben-Yair speaks of the motivations of the revolt against the Romans, he appears to be speaking about violations against Jewish religious freedom rather than commitment to an abstract notion of national self-determination. Thus, we observe that the motives for the suicide came to be subtly transformed along with the meanings of the terms "freedom" and "slavery" in light of the ideology of nationalism. Now, the mass suicide was interpreted as having been motivated by a preference for death not just to slavery or to religious violations but also to the fact of foreign domination itself.

In short, before Masada could be transformed into a national myth, the Sicarii had to be converted to secular Zionists. The socialist and nationalist youth and defense movements that developed the myth in prestate Israel dealt with the ambivalence inherent in the fact that they shared neither the goals nor the values nor the tactics of the objects of their reverence by essentially glossing over the story as told in the only available source. As Ben-Yehuda observed:

There is an abyss separating the members of Hagana/Palmah and the Zealots, ideologically and pragmatically.... On the one hand, we have a religiously fanatic Jewish sect that committed some very questionable acts, did not participate in the defence of Jerusalem against the main Roman siege on the city, and witnessed (and contributed to) the loss of the partial national sovereignty they had possessed. On the other hand, we have mostly secular Jews returning after thousands of years in the Diaspora to participate in a renewed struggle for national statehood, in the middle of a terrible world war, after having indirectly witnessed the extermination of six million Jews.[46]

---

[46] Ben-Yehuda 1995: 146.

Or, as he puts it another way, "the irony lies in the fact that these very same secular Zionist Jews who rejected, by and large, the Orthodox yoke found themselves creating a secular ritual of admiration for people whom they would have rejected had they been contemporaries."[47] For the perception of continuity to be firmly established, the defenders of Masada had to be remade in the image of the Zionist ideal. Thus, the myth had to be transformed into a symbol of a fearless "fight to the end," socializing the values of personal sacrifice and commitment to the idea of a national state. Through their voluntary deaths, a group of fanatical religious terrorists are removed from history, transformed in the process into abstract symbols of devotion to secular national sovereignty.

The National Eschatology

It is in the very act of demonstrating and symbolizing this devotion that an event marking a military and political defeat comes to be transformed within the national myth as a spiritual and moral victory. Often this transformation is so complete that the event is depicted as a victory, and members of the nation have difficulty seeing it as anything else despite the clear and acknowledged historical ramifications of subjugation that ensued. The myth invariably contains subtle yet clear indications that the defeat ultimately served only to prove, once and for all, the durability and indestructibility of the nation, which is why the actions of the savior and hero in bringing the defeat about come to be seen as doing the nation an ultimate service. The defeat serves to demonstrate to future generations that the nation can withstand even the worst of historical catastrophes, from which it logically follows that an eventual resurrection is inevitable so long as the spirit of sacrifice exemplified by the heroes is maintained.

The Kosovo myth expresses this notion through a bizarre denouement to the battle described in a song from Karadzić's collection called *The Miracle of Prince Lazar's Head*. In this story, which takes place 40 years after the battle, the son of a Turk by an enslaved Serbian girl finds the head of Lazar in a well, which proceeds to move, by itself, to reunite with its body. Metaphorically, the head represents the spirit of the nation; thus, the historical beheading of Lazar represents the attempted destruction of an entire people. The message of the story is that the nation, despite its humiliation and subjugation, cannot or will not be destroyed; the "beheading" of the political body does not affect the survival of the

[47] Ibid.: 186.

national spirit. The first miracle, that the head and body do not decay for 40 years, expresses the resilience of the people demonstrated through their continued commitment and obedience; while the second miracle, the returning of the head to the body, offers a messianic promise of eventual renewal and rebirth as a reward for this continued commitment.[48] The message is that because of Lazar's sacrifice, reflecting a state of commitment to the nation that all can emulate, the disaster of Kosovo will eventually be undone.

Similar myths and legends associated with the fall of Constantinople appear in the corpus of Greek folklore collected by Politis, some of which employ a similar allegory-of-the-impossible device, such as the image of the fish that jumped half-fried out of a pan when the Turks arrived and would jump back into the pan when the city reverted back to Christendom. Other myths played on the mysterious disappearance of the emperor's body, the most popular alleging that he was temporarily transformed into a marble statue and would return someday, sword in hand, to chase the invaders away.[49] Durability and the hope of resurrection could be said to be the unifying theme of the text that Politis identified as the centerpiece of his collection, the *Song of Hagia Sophia*, which generated what became the national motto of the "Great Idea":

> God sounds forth, the earth sounds forth, the heavens too sound forth,
> and the great church of Hagia Sophia sounds forth also,
> with its four hundred sounding boards, sixty-two bells,
> where for every bell there's a priest, for every priest a deacon.
> The king sings to the left, to the right the patriarch,
> and the very columns shook from the sound of so much psalmody.
> As they began the mass and the king came out
> a voice came to them from heaven, from the mouth of an archangel:
> "cease the mass, bring down the saints' [icons],
> priests – take the holy objects; you, O candles, snuff out your light,
> for it is the will of God that the City should turn Turk.
> Only send word to the West that three ships should come -
> one to take the crucifix, the next to take the Gospel,
> and the third and last to take our holy altar
> that these dogs may not seize them from us and desecrate them."
> The Holy Virgin was seized with trembling, and the icon wept tears.
> "Be silent, Lady and Mistress, do not weep so much:
> again in years and times to come, all will be yours again."[50]

---

[48] Gorup 1991: 116; Popovich 1991: 247; Bakić-Hayden 2004: 37–40.
[49] Herzfeld 1982: 129.
[50] Politis, *Selections from the Songs of the Greek People*; quoted in Herzfeld 1982: 130–1.

In his study of the Greek folklore movement, Michael Herzfeld notes that the second-to-last word quoted that appears in the original vernacular text as "yours" came to be translated into modern Greek by Politis and other national folklorists as "ours." It was thus that the last line entered into popular political discourse as "ours once more." Herzfeld considers this a rare lapse on the part of Politis, who was generally one of the more conscientious of his contemporaries, whom he often castigated for their tendency to alter popular songs to suit their ideological judgments. However, this lapse is a subtle indication of an even more subtle process, evident in many national myths: the reinterpretation of a traditional, religious eschatology into national form.

It was not fraud or even simple carelessness that caused Politis to alter this word, any more than it was that which caused Yadin to transform Josephus' account of Masada. Rather, it was the changed social context that led to the preconceived notion that the text they were reading had to be interpreted as national in content, according to the normative framework of modern nationalism. The word "yours," addressed to the Virgin Mary, reflected an expectation of the eventual return of the city to Christianity or, perhaps, rendered another way, an assurance that the city is and remains eternally Christian in spirit, regardless of temporal rulership. But such a disavowal of the significance of territorial sovereignty would be unimaginable to someone operating in the context of a national ideology. Redemption had to be reinterpreted as addressed specifically to the Greek *ethnos* rather than to Christendom. The phrase "ours once more" makes no sense in the mouth of an archangel, addressed to the Virgin Mary, but made perfect sense to the many Greeks who proceeded to quote this line in patriotic speeches, literature, and scholarship as the quintessential motto of nationalist sentiment. The "ours once more" motif appeared throughout the 19th and early 20th centuries, and not always necessarily in direct reference to Constantinople but to any prospect of patriotic victory.[51]

This song, not just through its content but by its very existence, was interpreted as evidence of durability, identified as a trait innate and specific to the nation. Because of its prevalence, Politis denied that the Greeks had ever lost their hope or desire for independence after the fall of Constantinople, dismissing such an attitude as characteristic of an "oriental fatalism" that naturally could not affect them. He identified the maintenance of optimism in the future and struggle against insurmountable

[51] Herzfeld 1982: 133–5.

odds as typical of a Hellenic national character that thrived best during times of adversity:

Among the numerous laments for the sack of Constantinople which were composed right after that disaster, the folksongs have pride of place because, with profound simplicity, they express a feeling of perseverance throughout the great national travails and the enslaved people's certain hope of being restored to its freedom and to its rightful position. It is indeed a matter for wonder that these were generated at a time when the nation seemed to have lost all, with the Fall of Constantinople [just past] and not a glimmer of hope anywhere in sight. But the nation's great disaster comes exactly midway between fear and hope, desperation and encouragement. For before this disaster the prophecies of the future were pessimistic and predicted calamities and disasters, whereas after the sack [of Constantinople] they spread a completely different message, one which indicated a change in the national attitude. For a long time before the sack of the state capital, oracles predicted the imminent disaster, but immediately after the sack positive hopes for the nation's future destiny were born, and the conviction took root among the Greek people that it would inevitably regain by the sword the paternal heritage which the enemy had [likewise] seized by the sword... [52]

Politis' notion that this song defined the perseverance and continuity of the Greek nation might not be so fanciful. He may only have reversed cause and effect. His view was that the song was a reflection of a primordial national spirit that maintained its cohesion through hope in the face of disaster. But although the evidence might not support this notion of unbroken continuity, there is cause to conclude that the elevation of songs such as this by the national movement, and their identification by scholars such as Politis as definitive of a distinct national character, may have been significant to reinforcing a sense of common identity and shared destiny. Kitromelides, for example, notes that the specific efforts of the Greek state and its institutions aimed at homogenization of the Greek language and spread of Greek identity throughout the newly formed Greek state and the *irredenta* between 1830 and 1922 were largely ineffectual. He attributes the fact that the diverse Orthodox populations of these territories nonetheless came to define themselves ultimately as Greeks as being due more to the fact that this identity "articulated a primordial feeling of protest against oppression and their hope for redemption," noting only in a footnote the possibility that "it is precisely this symbolism that provided Greek irredentism with its psychological dynamism and which can account for its success in converting large numbers of people." [53] In

---

[52] Ibid.: n.50.
[53] Kitromelides 1989: 177, 190, n.90.

other words, the presence of a defeat myth that was ripe for elevation, as embodied in this song, enhanced the appeal of Greek identity as a catalyst for mass mobilization and revolt.

In the *Song of Hagia Sophia*, the durability of the nation or faith in the face of subjugation is represented by the holy objects being rescued from the conquest. A similar symbolism prevails in Ghanaian accounts of the Yaa Asantewaa War, where even though political continuity may have been broken by the defeat and exile of Yaa Asantewaa, symbolic, spiritual continuity is represented in the fact that the Golden Stool remained hidden and protected throughout the war and the subsequent period of effective British rule. The success in keeping the Stool hidden is metaphorically connected, in both popular and scholarly accounts, to the continuous maintenance of a spirit of resistance even in the face of impossible odds, leading to the war's outcome being represented as a long-term victory. Boahen claims in the conclusion to his history of the Yaa Asantewaa War that "the first and most important crucial effect was the preservation of the Golden Stool and ipso facto the survival of the concept and philosophy of the Asante nation and a united federal state. Had Yaa Asantewaa not raised the standard of revolt, there is no doubt the British would have seized the Golden Stool and with its disappearance would have vanished the soul, unity, vitality and all the myths and centripetal forces underpinning the Asante nation." Instead, because the Stool remained hidden, Prempeh could be restored upon his return from exile, and "Asante as a nation and a centralized state was revived and has remained strong, united and dynamic ever since,"[54] albeit as part of an incorporated Ghanaian state. Similar sentiments are reflected in popular history: "Although militarily Yaa Asantewaa lost the war, psychologically her resistance against the British attempt to dispossess Asante of the precious Golden Stool symbolizes a resounding victory for Yaa Asantewaa and the Asante kingdom."[55]

The same theme of ongoing durability and ultimate redemption in the face of subjugation and humiliation is threaded through narrative accounts of the Western Wall, although here we again see the subtle transformation of the myth from a traditional religious conception of durability and redemption into a modern national one. The conflicting themes of durability and degradation, subjugation, and redemption were already prevalent in early, prenational pilgrim accounts of the Western

[54] Boahen 2003: 174–5.
[55] Asirifi-Danquah 2002: xii.

Wall. These would tend to place great emphasis on the size and antiquity of the stones as a testament both to ancient glory – associated in particular with the height of the heroic age according to the traditional construction of history, the reign of Solomon who built the First Temple – and to the permanence of God's covenant with Israel.[56] The 17th-century rabbi, Moses Hagiz, related the durability of the Wall to God's enduring faithfulness to his people:

> For this wall has never been destroyed because it is built on the foundation that David laid, which no enemy hand ever touched. They [the enemies] used to say, 'Destroy it! Destroy it! Even to its base' (Psalms 137:7) but they only succeeded as far as the base but could not touch the base itself. Why? Because God swore to David that that would never be destroyed. And our eyes can see, for it stands today as though it had only now been finished by that divine craftsman who sunk those pillars to last for centuries not in a natural way but by a miracle.[57]

But the other theme that appears as a counterpoint to the notion of strength and durability in writings of the time is the notion of the Wall as a symbol of the people's defeat and degradation. Rabbi Hagiz's account goes on to record that until the time of Suleiman, Muslims would pile garbage against the wall as though to do so were a religious precept. He claimed that this was done as a symbolic act of destruction, as there was no other way of obliterating this last remnant.[58]

It was this combined dynamic of strength and durability in contrast to degradation and humiliation that made this symbol ripe for nationalist reinterpretation, although a subtle shift in the purpose and meaning of such narratives is evident. Durability was no longer said to reflect the glory of Solomon or the force of God's promise to the Jews of a future redemption but rather the strength of will and continuity of the Jewish people. Degradation was no longer God's just punishment for Israel's sin but rather a state of affairs that Zionism existed to transcend. Much attention continued to be paid to the period when the site was under Muslim sovereignty, during which Arabs, aware of the site's significance to Jews, harassed worshippers, scattering glass in the alleyways and dumping garbage and sewage against it. This only served to reinforce the site's national sanctity, as a symbol of the degradation of Jews by

[56] See, for example, Naor 1983a: 68–9.
[57] Ha'Cohen 1983: 89; Schaffer 1975: 138.
[58] Schaffer 1975: 141; for another example of the durability and degradation themes juxtaposed, see the excerpt from *Sha'alu Shlom Yerushalayim* by Gedaliah of Semyatitch (1699), quoted in Naor 1983a: 69–70 and Peters 1986: 129.

their enemies. For example, as the *History of the Haganah* reports, "the Jews' status regarding their most holy place – from the point of view of both religion and nationalism – was wretched. Hooligans from the nearby Magreb Quarter used to molest worshippers, throw stones at them and even beat them. The Arab police showed no concern."[59] The humiliations suffered by Jews attempting to pray at the Wall were interpreted differently between the traditional and Zionist narratives. Judaism incorporated these humiliations into the traditional theodicy, as an element of the state of degradation that was the punishment for the people's sin, whereas the Zionist narrative would attribute them to the nation's lack of ownership and possession of the site, an unacceptable by-product of the state of Exile that had to be overcome and therefore a pretext for the assertion of sovereignty.[60]

All of these symbols and metaphors of durability and ultimate resurrection in the face of defeat point to the same basic message: that the act of sacrifice, willingly accepted even when confronted with impossible odds, proves the resilience of the nation and will ensure the nation's survival so long as there are those willing to identify with and emulate such acts. Thus, there are some cases in which the only concluding metaphor of durability and eschatology lies in relating how word of the salvific act spread to all of the members of the nation, revivifying the otherwise moribund national consciousness. The only equivalent to *The Miracle of Prince Lazar's Head* to be found in the Masada mythical narrative lies in a concocted claim that the act of mass suicide was what provided inspiration for the nation to survive this moment of crisis and to eventually renew itself in the form of the Zionist enterprise. A children's book titled *The Glory of Masada* makes this notion explicit in its conclusion to the story:

This was the end of Masada, the fortress of supreme heroism. But this was not the end of the revolt. There is an end which is in essence a beginning. Such was the glorified end of Masada. Because at the very moment that the last Jew fell on his sword at Masada and the fierce battle reached its end, the Jewish people began to live again. How could it be?

The author then goes on to provide an entirely ahistorical description of how Josephus' account of Masada "spread all over the country and beyond and revived the rest of the Jewish nation, even though others believed that this nation was doomed forever."[61] This idea has been

[59] Quoted in Aner 1983: 128.
[60] Liebman and Don-Yehiya 1983: 159.
[61] Quoted in Zerubavel 1995: 226–7.

echoed by Yadin on numerous occasions. In a famous speech to the new recruits of the IDF Armoured Divisions sworn in at Masada, he declared:

We will not exaggerate by saying that, thanks to the heroism of the Masada fighters, like other links in our nation's chain of heroism, we stand here today, the soldiers of a young-ancient people, surrounded by the ruins of the camps of those who destroyed us. We stand here, no longer helpless in the face of our enemy's strength, no longer fighting a desperate war, but solid and confident, knowing that now our fate is in our hands.... We, the descendents of these heroes, stand here today and rebuild the ruins of our people.[62]

He went on to state that the Zealots "elevated Masada to an undying symbol which has stirred hearts throughout the last nineteen centuries." But as rhetorically satisfying as this may be, the complete absence of references to Masada in the source texts of Jewish tradition makes it doubtful that it stirred much of anything until about the 1920s.[63]

Similar rhetoric in relation to Kosovo can be found in Serbian national discourse. At a commemorative session of the Serbian Royal Academy of Arts and Sciences in Belgrade on June 11, 1889, Serbia's minister of Foreign Affairs, Cedomil Mijatović, praised the heroes of Kosovo in terms similar to Yigal Yadin's praise of the defenders of Masada as unifying symbols of national inspiration:

An inexhaustible source of national pride was discovered on Kosovo. More important than language and stronger than the Church, this pride unites all Serbs in a single nation.... The glory of the Kosovo heroes shone like a radiant star in that dark night of almost five hundred years.... Our people continued the battle in the sixteenth, seventeenth and eighteenth centuries when they tried to recover their freedom through countless uprisings. There was never a war for freedom – and when was there no war? – in which the spirit of the Kosovo heroes did not participate. The new history of Serbia begins with Kosovo – a history of valiant efforts, long suffering, endless wars, and unquenchable glory.... We bless Kosovo because the memory of the Kosovo heroes upheld us, encouraged us, taught us, and guided us.[64]

The reasoning, in both cases, is circular. The death of our heroes is inspirational not because it accomplished anything or even because it was intended to accomplish anything. It is inspirational simply because they died in order to serve as an inspiration. The *prima facie* illogic of this notion has been the basis of criticism within Israeli society of the "Masada

---

[62] Zerubavel 1995: 227.
[63] Alter 1973: 21–2.
[64] Quoted in Emmert 1989: 15.

myth" or the "Masada complex." As Israeli historian Benjamin Keder put it in an influential article:

> The rock on the shore of the Dead Sea is a dead end, a cul-de-sac, a dramatic curtain-fall. He who tells the soldiers of the armored corps at the swearing-in ceremony on the heights of Masada 'that it is owing to the heroism of the fighters of Masada that we are here today', is both deluding himself and deluding others. If Judaism has survived, if the Jewish people has survived, it is due not to Masada but to Jabneh, not to Ben-Yair but to Ben-Zakkai.[65]

Indeed, in practical terms, it is hard to see how the mass suicide at Masada contributed to the future survival of the Jews or even to the eventual rise and success of Zionism, just as it is difficult to see what Prince Lazar's defeat at Kosovo did to serve the freedom and independence of the Serbian people. But paradoxical though it might seem in strictly logical–historical terms, on a mytho–symbolic level, the otherwise senseless death and failure of the savior and hero figure or figures do indeed serve a vital purpose toward enabling the future survival and cohesion of the nation. To understand this, one must take into account that to be an imagined community, all individuals in the group must bind themselves to a common signifier, the same symbolic ideal. Leaders like Lazar and sects like the Sicarii can better serve their nations in such a role than they can as reigning despots or fanatical terror squads. In the mythical narrative, therefore, they perform two services to their nations: removing themselves from history and, at the pivotal moment of destruction that legitimates a later moment of renewal, transforming into suprahistorical images of inspiration.

This is not a historical interpretation but rather a mystical one. It asserts that death is not final but rather serves as a necessary phase to national rebirth, one that provides the key moment of inspiration and common identification necessary to reinforce continuity between antiquity and the present. Death serves as the ultimate form of atonement, legitimizing the acts of those who die. It is not a final defeat because it becomes a source of legitimation for those who identify with the fallen. The living succeed the dead and death, in turn, legitimizes the enterprise of the living. Regardless of whom the sacrificial surrogates might be, their readiness to die is rewarded within the larger context of national history insofar as their death guarantees the nation's survival, the seed of a future national revival. And the living generation, through

---

[65] Kedar 1982: 59.

identification with the heroes of the myth, are the ones entrusted with the solemn responsibility of turning defeat and death into victory and life.[66] Thus, the idea of inspirational sacrifice is not a tautology but a covenant, a contract with the past. Just as religious sacrifice mediates between man and God, national sacrifice mediates between the citizen and the nation, generating unity and continuity by means of the totemic ideal it creates, binding both the imagined national community over space and the historical cultural community over time to generate a single multidimensional collective. And this is a more ideologically satisfying conclusion to the defeat narratives than the ones that history alone generally provides.

The Sacred Executioner

The nation wants its hero, its savior, to willingly remove himself from history, leaving a conceptual opening for the foundation of a more authentically national society. However, this need that drives the sacrificial ritual also generates guilt on the part of the society performing it and a consequent desire to assign or shift the blame. This is demonstrated through the ritual mourning undertaken in primitive societies for the totem sacrifice. Disavowal by the community of responsibility for the very crime needed to create or reinforce the community is a necessary element to any sacrificial cult. In examining various national mythologies, one can discern two distinct ways that this is achieved. The first is to depict the symbolic ideal as voluntarily and altruistically accepting self-sacrifice so that the community can be formed or restructured to its benefit. The second is to blame the destruction on the agency of an external force, obscuring the ritual nature of the sacrifice by attributing it to a wicked deed performed by a murderer who is subsequently punished. As any myth–symbol system is a composite of multiple stories and images in which internal consistency is not a necessary element, most cultures developing a sacrificial myth will reinforce the point by opting for both methods concurrently. Put more simply, if Christ voluntarily chose to be crucified for the salvation of mankind, why is Judas blamed for his participation in the event? The answer is that this device separates the community from what is, in essence, a "necessary crime."

Sacrificial designates go willingly. But although it is the totem that sends them to die, it cannot be depicted as their visible executioner. That

---

[66] This notion of national sacrifice and national covenant is addressed to some extent in Liebman and Don-Yehiya 1983: 42, and Zerubavel 1994: 82.

role is reserved for an enemy, an outsider to the community. That it is the society's own regenerative center that demands the death of its children is the secret that must remain hidden at the risk of social breakdown. For this reason, violence is projected outward, onto an enemy-outsider figure that serves as a mirror image to reflect the society's self-directed hostility. This figure will embody all of the traits, particularly those traits related to the capacity for violence, that the group wishes to purge from itself via projection onto the Other. And it will, in so doing, serve as a convenient target against which the community's self-directed rage can be externalized and thereby expelled.

This is not to suggest that the enemy figures depicted in national myths were not real, the threats that they represented to the community at the time not credible. For again we find that truth is the best alibi. The more credible the external threat, the more effectively it serves to hide the true motive of sacrifice, the more blood can therefore be plausibly demanded, and the more unifying and satisfying the ritual will be. The totem secret demands that we pose as unwilling killers; it must be the outsider that forces the sacrifice, not us, and violence must be depicted as characteristic of that Other, not of us.[67] However, in taking on the blame for the death, the murderer performs a service to the society, absolving it of guilt for an act for which it is responsible and over which its members all benefit. As Haim Maccoby notes, "the community wants the sacrifice to occur, because otherwise there will be no salvation, but it shifts the responsibility to some evil figure. The death of the victim is mourned with every appearance of heartfelt grief, for the deeper the grief the more complete the dissociation of the community from the death which they desired."[68]

It is important, then, to consider this "sacred executioner" not as the opposite of the savior but rather as his mirror image, a "monstrous double"[69] who may appear in the narrative to serve a distinct and opposing function but in fact serves the same one: that of surrogate victim, a focus for the expression of the violent energy that the community must direct outward in order to survive, one who carries the traits of the community inimical to appropriate community formation beyond the boundaries of that community. The only difference being that where the surrogate victim is an outsider, that energy can be expended openly,

---

[67] Marvin and Ingle 1999: 78–80, also 90–1.
[68] Maccoby 1992: 11.
[69] See Girard 1977: chap. 6, 143–68.

devoid of the camouflage that must be employed when it is directed against an insider figure more explicitly representative of the society's symbolic center. The function of the myth is to divide the group's hostility appropriately between the figures of savior and scapegoat. We blame and, therefore, set out to kill the scapegoat, but in reality it is the death or transformation of the savior, the symbolic representative of the community, that makes the ritual effective. The scapegoat merely hides the need that demands the act. He does to the savior what we need him to do and we, in turn, enthusiastically do to the scapegoat what we secretly desire to do to the savior. "Though we set out to kill the scapegoat, the enemy beyond the border, only the savior's death makes the ritual work. . . . The ritual victim, the scapegoat, makes our anger and killing acceptable and disguises its real target. Our rage at the scapegoat provides a pretext to kill the savior."[70]

This serves to provide a further insight into why a relatively unimportant battle such as the Battle of Kosovo, which had few significant or immediate strategic or political results, came to occupy such a pivotal role in the Serbian construction of history. We have already noted the wealth of cultural imagery produced by the event but this wealth, in turn, must be attributed to the historical detail that the leaders of both sides were killed in the battle. Lazar's death allowed for the development of a myth of salvation through martyrdom and sacrifice, whereas Murad's spawned a heroic myth of struggle against tyranny. But in the context of the mythic structure, it is necessary to view Lazar and Murad as two sides of the same coin: the White and the Black Christ, so to speak, both of whom must be destroyed in order for salvation to be fulfilled.

Lazar, in the role of the righteous tyrant, sacrifices himself, whereas Murad, the evil tyrant, must be destroyed by a hero. But the upshot of both acts is that tyranny is destroyed, and the political forces dominating the Serbian cultural community are symbolically dismantled. Because Lazar is the symbolic ideal, the embodiment of the community, who performs a salvific act by his self-sacrifice, he cannot simultaneously be the target of open hostility by those who take the myth as a message to struggle against domination. Hence, these energies must be sublimated against another image, an outsider, an anti-Lazar whose role is played by the image of Murad. Thus, the murder of the surrogate victim is accomplished in a dual sense: both as self-sacrifice performed by the symbolic ideal in the person of Lazar, and as a heroic act against an enemy outsider

---

[70] Marvin and Ingle 1999: 79; see also Girard 1977: 250–1.

performed by a hero in the person of Miloš Obilić who acts as a model for further, ongoing struggle in the name of the same value. The former can be mourned and the latter celebrated so that both elements of the totem ritual are respected. It is Lazar's death, not Murad's, that the Serbian national community demands. The convenience of the Kosovo myth lies in the coincidence between these two deaths, providing both a sacrificial surrogate and a suitable alibi against which hostility can be redirected.

But although the psychological function of the sacred executioner might be parallel to that of the savior and hero, drawing to himself responsibility for an act the community secretly desires to commit itself, on a sociological level he continues to serve the perpendicular function of establishing and reinforcing distinctions and boundaries between insiders and outsiders. For if the savior is exemplar and the hero is model, the executioner is the negative principle, an antimodel, an embodiment of all that the nation is not and should not be. As Michael Billig puts it in *Banal Nationalism*, if "nationalism is an ideology of the first person plural, which tells 'us' who 'we' are, then it is also an ideology of the third person. There can be no 'us' without 'them.'"[71] This serves to neutralize the threat of in-group diversity, reinforcing a sense of homogeneity through common vicarious participation in unanimous communal violence. As Eric Hobsbawm puts it, "there is no more effective way of bonding together the disparate sections of restless peoples than to unite them against outsiders."[72]

Again, it is in the most overtly legendary defeat myth that we find the most direct and unmediated example of this dynamic. For one of the significant innovations that Pumpurs added to the body of Latvian folk tales in transforming them into the national epic of Lāčplēsis was to give the hero a clearly defined enemy; or, more accurately, to give his existing mythical enemy, the Black Knight, a clearly defined out-group identity and placement in historical time. He was identified with the Teutonic knights, singling out the Germans as the instruments in the defeat of an entirely fictional Golden Age of Latvian independence. To further support this equation, real historical figures of the late 12th and early 13th centuries were inserted into the narrative.[73]

But although distinguishing the executioner as a specifically defined outsider in ethnonational terms, it is also in this epic that we see the

[71] Billig 1995: 78.
[72] Hobsbawm 1992: 91.
[73] Lieven 1993: 122.

clearest metaphorical merging of the savior–hero and the sacred executioner in their common and unified function as surrogate victim at the moment of sacrifice. The climatic final battle scene of the epic concludes with Lāčplēsis and the Black Knight bringing each other down, simultaneously killing each other and being killed such that the blurring of their roles and the merging of their identities is complete. One is free to mourn the savior and despise the enemy executioner simultaneously without constraint, focusing these energies on the same conceptual axis point. The myth even provides for an immediate metaphor of durability and eschatology, expressed in the fact that the narrative does not explicitly depict the actual death of either figure. Instead, it concludes with an ambiguous suggestion that Lāčplēsis did not die but rather that his fight with the Black Knight continues out of sight and in perpetuity to this day, a metaphor for the unremitting struggle of the Latvian people to persevere in the face of threat and domination, followed by a suggestion that he might someday prevail and return to lead his people to a future and more complete state of redemption.

It was the Germans, as well, who came to be understood in national terms as the perpetual Other in the succession of events pivotal to Czech national history that, in their context, had more the flavor of dynastic and religious conflicts than national ones. Palacky's *History of the Czech Nation in Bohemia and Moravia* portrays Czech history as a constant battle of Czechs struggling for survival against German oppression. As Pynsent notes, "achieving the status of hero in the Czech national myth normally involves killing a large number of Germans . . . unless that hero is a 'heroic martyr', in which case he or she will often be killed by Germans."[74] But the identity of the enemy Other need not be fixed according to whatever ethnic identity may plausibly be attributed to the opposing force in the pivotal defeat. In cases in which the historical enemy no longer stands as a threat, the Other may be openly depicted within the national myth as a metaphor for a negative principle against which the nation continues to struggle, one that has come to be embodied in more contemporary enemies. Israel, after all, no longer has reason to fear Roman hegemony, yet hostility to Jewish national self-determination can clearly be found in other quarters. The Ottoman Empire no longer stands as a threat to Serbian national sovereignty, yet the label of "Turks" has come to be attributed to the perceived internal threat of Kosovar Albanians and Slavic Muslims, and political rhetoric frequently attributes any

[74] Pynsent 1994: 170–1.

external force seeking to dictate terms to Serbia as morally equivalent to the Ottomans.

Just as the question of what Joan of Arc was fighting for was a matter of intense dispute throughout the most formative periods of French national development, so too was the question of whom or what she was fighting against, to say nothing of who or what destroyed her. Were her enemies those of the French polity and Catholic faith, or were they the institutions of church and monarchy that ultimately betrayed and defeated her? Did she oppose the English as such or simply as any foreign force that would presume to dominate the French people? The flexible character of the Other is demonstrated by the manner in which the imagery of Joan of Arc was employed by French anti-Semites, from the anti-Dreyfusards to the Vichy regime. Although the notion was occasionally floated that Bishop Cauchon, the inquisitor in charge of Joan's conviction and execution, was of Jewish racial origins, no one seriously believed that Joan had historically been the victim of Jews. Nonetheless, it appeared natural for anti-Semites to cast the Jews as the enemy in the wider Joan of Arc drama insofar as Joan embodied France and the Jew, lacking peasant and Catholic roots, was seen to embody, by contrast, anti-France. Winock points out that the juxtaposition of "long live Joan of Arc" with "down with the Jews" as slogans in nationalist demonstrations and speeches indicates that these were two sides of a single coin, the necessary negative in order to enable articulation of the positive; naming the disease in order to justify the need for the cure, embodied in and symbolized by the national saint.

Within this register, Joan was glorified not for any specific achievement in her lifetime but, by the circular logic of the salvation myth, simply for the manner in which she embodied the French essence, in contrast to the foreign forces that conspired against the nation whether from without or within. In typical expressions of standard anti-Semitic dichotomies, Joan was contrasted as agrarian rather than urban, spiritual as opposed to material, rooted rather than nomadic, a laborer as opposed to an intellectual. She fought for unity rather than the dissolution of society; for the territorial nation as opposed to universal, world-conquering ideologies.[75] The effect was an effort to expel the Dreyfusards from the nation by excluding them from communion with the symbol of Joan. Edouard Drumont, France's most famous anti-Semite during the Dreyfus controversy, wrote in a letter that was read at a protest organized

[75] Winock 1998: 463–5.

by the Action Française to protest "against Joan of Arc's detractors" (specifically, a teacher at the Lycée Condorcet who delivered a lecture questioning the supernatural aspects of the story):

> you know what name we ascribe to the Enemy who has taken the place of the invading English of the fifteenth century and who is attempting to subjugate us through the corrupting power of gold, just as England sought to subjugate us through the brutal force of iron. That enemy we call the Jew and the Freemason. Today, however, do I not want to insist on this point, I merely want to shout with you: *Vive la France! Glorie a Jeanne d'Arc!*[76]

During World War I, Maurice Barrès speculated that the next mission of Joan, after the English had been expelled from France, would have been to ally with them in defense of Christianity and civilization against barbarian and pagan Germany. However, when the Vichy regime took power after France's defeat in World War II, its propaganda was able to utilize Joan of Arc despite the regime's reliance on that defeat and on collaboration with Germany, first by portraying Joan as having a particular animosity to the English rather than to foreign occupation in general[77] but also by reviving the anti-Semitic rhetoric that depicted her as the enemy of more abstract negative principles. Her humble roots as a peasant appealed to Vichy's "return to the earth" doctrine and was placed in contrast to the corrupt traits attributed to intellectuals and Jews. "Joan has nothing to do with money, with ideologues, with the false defenders of a rotten civilization, since she is associated with eternal youth and creative vitality."[78] "Like today's Gaullists, the intellectuals of her day, those of the University of Paris, expected great things from England."[79] At the same time, however, her image was being used by Free France and the Resistance as a symbol of resisting foreign occupation without the need to name specific enemies. Similarly, during the war in Algeria, both sides were able to invoke Joan on different levels: as defender of the glory and integrity of France on the one hand, or as the universal champion of national liberation and enemy of colonialism on the other. In more recent times, Jean-Marie Le Pen has invoked Joan of Arc, even reviving the prewar practice of marching past Fremiet's statue. In his

---

[76] Quoted in Winock 1998: 465.
[77] Gildea 1994: 161, 163; Winock 1998: 471.
[78] Robert Brasillach, quoted in Winock 1998: 471.
[79] Maurice Pujo, quoted in Winock 1998: 472.

rhetoric, Joan was invoked to save France from yet another category of "invaders": migrant workers.[80]

Thus, we see that the appointment of an enemy Other does not merely serve to set boundaries in terms of the traits deemed to define and distinguish the nation, such as language, culture, descent, or political–territorial citizenship. Although the Sacred Executioner must be seen as an outsider according to such terms, he also stands as an abstract principle, applicable to any time period, of all traits that the community wishes to disavow, all that threatens the cohesion of the community. The exaggerated brutality of the Other makes the in-group that much more noble by contrast and further ennobles their sacrifice in defeat. For if *we* represent culture, civilization, order, *they*, by contrast, are the very epitome of the uncivilized, acultured, normless. This serves to provide the myth of defeat with both a particularistic and universalistic element. On the one hand, it is a moment of trauma specific to the nation, a loss of sovereignty that must be corrected for the nation's own sake. But, on the other, it casts the nation as a collectivity in a providential role in world history, as the front-line defender of civilization against barbarism, an elect community that has suffered and sacrificed so that civilization, however defined, might flourish. This notion is particularly prevalent in certain European national mythologies – such as the Greek, Czech, Polish, and Serb – that the nation was arrested in its cultural development only because of geographic circumstances that compelled it to serve the role of defending civilization against the barbarian hordes, be they Ottoman, Germanic, or Asiatic. Defeat myths serve to substantiate this notion by providing a concrete moment to symbolize this blood sacrifice in defense of civilization; a moment of covenant during which the nation collectively demonstrates its willingness to take up this responsibility to civilization and suffer in a state of subjugation so that other nations farther behind this purported front line might flourish in a state of fulfillment.

In a nationalist framework within which sovereignty for the group is seen as the ultimate value, sacrifice of sovereignty must be retroactively understood as the ultimate sacrifice. For if *we* are exemplars of civilization, *they* the epitome of normlessness, then the period during which the group was dominated by the Other could be understood only as a uniform period of lack. Many nations will attribute a label to the period of domination that began with the defeat at the hands of the Other. Jewish nationalism has its Exile, Greek its *Tourkokrita*, Czech its "300 Years of

---

[80] Winock 1998: 473–5.

Darkness." Invariably, these concepts serve to obscure the cultural peaks and valleys that in fact characterized the historical periods in question. Focus is placed on the violence of the conquest and on the brutalities of the period of imperial decline that coincided with the later rise of nationalism, glossing over periods of relative stability and prosperity in between, even where these might have included noted cultural revivals that provided much of the raw material for future national movements.[81]

The claim suggested by these labels, then, is not that the community ceased to exist during this period, for in fact a distinct ethnic community – whether distinguished by nuances of language, culture, or religion – survived and, at times, even flourished. Rather, it serves to explain the lack of specifically national mobilization; the historically evident failure to associate this enduring community with notions of political sovereignty, even despite the presence of a tradition of state sovereignty within that community's collective memory and construction of history. The Other provides the appropriate alibi, and the more hyperbolic the depiction of brutality and slavery perpetrated by this Other, the more plausible the claim that an enduring aspiration for sovereignty among the community was only absent from this period due to its having been brutally suppressed. Within the mythic register, the Sacred Executioner, by virtue of performing his task with exceptional brutality, does the nation a service by giving plausibility to the narrative of national continuity.

The National Theodicy and the Not-So-Golden Age

Although the final destruction of the symbols representing the society's sovereignty might be attributed to the agencies of an external force personified by a named enemy outsider, the decline that made such destruction possible, if not inevitable, almost never is. It is most often attributed to flaws in the social order itself, flaws that are depicted as having been built into the society from its very inception.

An intrinsic link between the myth of defeat and its apparent opposite, the myth of the Golden Age, has already been theorized, in that it provides a narrative connection between this imagined high point, through an era of decline, to the incomplete present demanding national mobilization as a corrective. Anthony Smith examines this concept at length in *Chosen Peoples*: "Appeals to golden ages enable the community to realize its true

---

[81] See Zerubavel 1995: Chap. 1 for discussion of this concept in relation to the Israeli case; Millas 2004: 54–8 for the Greek; Pynsent 1994: 176 for the Czech.

and pure self, before the age of decline and humiliation. They also issue a challenge and a summons to emulate the golden past, or rather to recapture its spirit and thereby realise the nation's destiny."[82] The myth serves multiple purposes, providing a sense of continuity, a sense of distinctiveness and dignity in the face of either internal or external opposition or a present state of domination or weakness, establishing roots in territory, and, most important, giving expression and sanction to the quest for authenticity:

Nowhere does the cult of authenticity come into sharper focus than in the selection, and description, of golden ages. For they provide models of the nation's 'true self', uncontaminated by later accretions and unimpaired by corruption and decline. Golden ages represent, for nationalists, the pure and pristine nature of the nation, its essential goodness, as it was and as it should be, though presently obscured and disfigured beneath 'irrelevant' class, regional, and religious divisions. The tasks of the nationalist are, first, to rediscover the nation's natural goodness, and, second, to mobilize its members to 'realize themselves' by discovering and emulating the virtues of the nation. In this process of self-authentication, golden ages provide essential blueprints for realizing the national self and for encouraging the process of collective regeneration. This is what nationalists have in mind when they use the familiar metaphors of 'national awakening', 'rebirth', and 'regeneration'.[83]

But although this description of the form and function of the Golden Age in national mythology is insightful, it is not the whole picture. Smith claims that "there is no gulf between the golden ages of Jews, Romans and Persians at the end of the ancient world and those of modern nationalisms."[84] But this categorical statement could be called into question. Ambiguity is rarely present in premodern visions of the Golden Age. The Homeric Age, Ram-raja, the David monarchy were idyllic, a paragon if not of virtue then certainly of heroism, cultural achievement, or divine order. The purpose of a Golden Age predicated on the notion of a universal divine order is to provide a model of what the community can and should look like when that order is perfectly adhered to by community members. Its eventual downfall therefore cannot be explained by means of its inherent, systemic flaws but must be the consequence of a diabolical enemy depicted, at best, as an instrument of divine wrath sent to punish the people or leaders who have sinned, which is to say, failed to perfectly adhere to the revealed order. This narrative fits the mold of

[82] Smith 2003: 214.
[83] Ibid.: 215–16.
[84] Ibid.: 179.

the traditional theodicy, defined in the *Encyclopaedia of Religion* as "the effort to defend God's justice and power in the face of suffering. Theodicies . . . are specific explanations or justifications of suffering in a world believed to be ruled by a morally good God."[85]

But without the pretensions to universality of a divine order, depictions of the Golden Age in national mythologies tend to be more ambiguous, such that we recognize another internal contradiction pointing to the ambivalence that the myth functions to resolve. Although at times, as has been noted, national myth will anachronistically attribute a distinctly national form of horizontal solidarity to the Golden Age and a nationalist sentiment to those figures depicted as defending it, at other times it evidences a far more nuanced conception of history than most scholars are willing to credit, representing with unexpected accuracy those aspects of the age that would distinguish it from a genuinely national society. Even at its purported high point, the society is depicted as rife with class divisions, in which factions placing their own interests above loyalty to the nation are the norm and notions of national solidarity, as such, simply did not exist. Indeed, such sentiment is represented as precisely what the purported Golden Age was lacking that rendered it unable to withstand the challenge of aggressors, who, while portrayed as barbaric and uncivilized in most respects, are also frequently depicted as having prevailed because of their superior capacity relative to the in-group for group solidarity.

For just as the *axis mundi* assumed a different character in the age of nations, linking not the divine and earthly realms but rather the members of the imagined community across time and space, so too would the concept of theodicy undergo transition into terms functional to modern forms of social organization. The modern nation has no imperative to retain the notion of a just and good God. But it does have to explain how a society that represented the pinnacle of national–cultural expression could possibly lose its cohesion in the face of challenge. Traditional theodicy explains suffering in relation to sin. But, in a national context, sin does not amount to violation of a divinely ordained order. The ultimate nationalist sin is disunity. The defeat and the negative state of affairs following from it are depicted as having been caused by the failure of the community to achieve the ideal of unity and horizontal loyalty under the signifiers of the common culture. And these failures are seen as having been built into or, at the very least, allowed for by the very fabric of the society that is consequently destroyed.

<hr>

[85] Green 2005: 9111–21.

Contrary, then, to what one might expect, the Golden Age is rarely characterized in national mythology as a *perfect* era, and in key respects it can even come across as inferior to the national present, or at least to the potential national present. If it were perfect, the explanation for its eventual fall would be unsatisfying from the standpoint of the present need for national mobilization, for if even the perfect society can fall, then what's to say our present efforts will not also be in vain? Although the defeat is depicted as a tragedy, the destruction of a society of unequaled virtue and value, it is, paradoxically, a tragedy made possible by the iniquities of the society that was defeated. And it is not the case that one narrative is in ascendance at some times, the other at others, or that some aspects of the mythic heroic age fall into the former category and other, rarefied elements in the latter. On the contrary, in most cases, these two narratives appear almost effortlessly in tandem, without the need for any special explanation or complex formula to justify this otherwise apparent contradiction or enable its widespread acceptance.

An expressedly ambivalent attitude to the purported Golden Age is evident in Israeli approaches to the Second Temple period and the Western Wall, with the means for a transition from traditional to national theodicy already built into traditional Jewish sources. As we have seen, accounts of the Wall, both traditional and modern, tended to stress two conflicting themes: that of glory and durability and that of destruction and degradation. In traditional accounts, the size of the stones was said to reflect the glory of David and Solomon, and their survival over time was described as symbolic of the eternal nature of God's promise to Israel. At the same time, however, the destruction of the Temple was explained according to the same theodicy framework one might expect from any religious system that made reference to a transcendent deity, established through the prophetic tradition. Catastrophe was the wages for violations of the covenant, and this incorporated such events into history in such a way as to vindicate the notion of God's perfect justice at the center of the belief system. Theodicy also gave rise to eschatology in the notion that the wickedness of the people and of the age must run its course so that the righteousness of God will be vindicated in the age to come. In the traditional construction of history, the righteousness of God's judgment could not be questioned. As tragic as the event is perceived to be, traditional sources all imply an acceptance of God's justice in allowing it to happen. The sinfulness of the people provides an explanation that allows for such a conclusion, and the necessity of the destruction as a step toward a future restoration in glory, one that would justify God's action by ultimately demonstrating his faithfulness, provided another.[86]

Both of these notions would retain their force even after God was removed from his central role in the construction of history, to be replaced by national equivalents. The sins of the people seen to have caused the disaster would no longer be sins against the divine covenant but rather sins against the nation such as disunity and violations of common cultural values; the promised future restoration in glory would not come as a result of divine intervention but rather by means of national mobilization through the Zionist endeavor. These reinterpretations were facilitated by the fact that traditional explanations for the destruction of the Second Temple, unlike that of the First, were varied and conflicting. It was clear in the prophetic tradition that the First Temple had been destroyed because of the sin of idolatry, practiced collectively by the nation and its leaders. But rabbinic authorities contemporary to the destruction of the Second Temple were hard pressed to find comparable sins in their more recent history that could serve even metaphorically as equivalent. The abstract notion that the destruction was a punishment for sin retained its power, even if specific sins with specific atonements could not be named, because any deviation from this clear and morally coherent prophetic tradition implied the attribution of an unacceptable injustice to God. The effort to preserve this formula in ancient times produced explanations such as that attributed in the Talmud to Rabbi Yohanan ben Torta: "Why was the first Temple destroyed? Because of three factors: idolatry, fornication, and bloodshed. But why was the Second Temple, in which people were occupied with Torah, the commandments, and deeds of loving-kindness, destroyed? Because it housed causeless hatred."[87] Causeless – which is to say, in-group – hatred was an explanation particularly amenable to reinterpretation into national terms centuries later because it could be supplemented through historical sources such as Josephus, which documented factional fighting between Jewish groups during the Judean revolt as both a practical and spiritual cause of the defeat:

The rebels failed to read the political picture of the times correctly, and their revolt was doomed to failure. To this must be added the fact that the zealot fanatics were divided even amongst themselves and spent a great deal of time and energy on internal factional fighting as well as conducting a struggle against the more moderate elements in the population. The result was an abysmal failure paid for

---

[86] Stone 1981: 196–200.
[87] Talmud, bYoma 9b; yYoma 1:138c; tMen 13:22; quoted in Goldenberg 1982: 523.

by untold numbers of victims, tens of thousands of whom died in vain, and by the destruction of the Jewish people's religious and spiritual symbol – the Temple.[88]

A similar dynamic is evident in the case of Greece, given that the very term "byzantine" has entered into language as an adjective to describe a complex factionalized politics, with the connotation of elaborate scheming and intrigue in which political power or favor stands as the highest value.[89] What is interesting, however, is the frequency with which such a connotation appears in Greek nationalist literature, though the ambivalence this would imply toward one of Greek national mythology's most pivotal Golden Ages is obscured by the manner in which scholars tend to bifurcate the Greek nationalist movement into two competing streams: the Byzantine–Orthodox and the classical–revolutionary.

Traditional historiography, with its focus on salvation as the ultimate value, viewed history not as history of the people but of the faith, with insiders to the group defined as Orthodox Christians, not ethnic Greeks, and events judged according to their value to the continuity of the community of the faithful. Thus, although the fall of Constantinople was a defeat, it was no great tragedy insofar as the traditional theodicy identified it as the consequence of sin, punishment for which was just and good insofar as it served toward the goal of salvation. The view of the Orthodox Patriarchate was best summarized in the *Paternal Exhortation* issued in 1798: "Our Lord in his infinite mercy and wisdom, in order to keep yet untainted the holy and orthodox faith of us the pious, and in order to be the salvation of all, raised from nothing this mighty kingdom of the Ottomans over the kingdom of us the Romans, which had begun in some wise to fall away from its orthodox beliefs."[90]

Revolutionary nationalists such as Adamantios Korais rejected this formula, of course. Identifying the national Golden Age with classical Athens, he viewed the Byzantines as no better than foreigners, successors to the Romans as occupiers. In his view, the Byzantine Empire fell "not from divine providence, but from the impudent folly of the Greco-Roman Emperors. They, quite unlike the prudent Kings of Russia, having trampled the laws, burdened their subjects with insupportable taxes, polluted the Imperial court with murders and massacres of their relatives, and having been transformed from kings into theologians . . . gradually increased the power of the contemptible province of the Turks until they sat them

[88] Ben Dov 1983: 26.
[89] "Byzantine." Dictionary.com Unabridged (v 1.1). Random House, May 30, 2008. Available at <Dictionary.com http://dictionary.reference.com/browse/byzantine>.
[90] Quoted in Politis 1998: 10; see also 5–6.

on the very throne of Byzantium."[91] The defeat is here depicted as having been brought on by the system under which the nation was governed at the time, which placed little value in ethnocultural sovereignty when this could be sacrificed in the interests of power and wealth. An even clearer statement of this national theodicy is evident in a comment made by Ioannis Pringos on the Russo-Turkish war in 1773, "May the Lord God have mercy on us to set us free, for that we lost our kingdom through our sins. But I say: through our ungovernability . . . the whole of Europe is guilty of like sins; yet they keep their own countries, because they have taken care to keep their own countries. If the *Romaioi* too had taken care, they would not have lost theirs."[92]

But the continued relevance of such sentiments, even through the subsequent merging of the competing discourses into a continuous and inclusive narrative of Greek national identity, is best illustrated by the fact that they appear frequently during this period even in the literary works of authors and poets more generally associated with the Byzantine–Orthodox stream of nationalist thought. Alexandros Papadiamantis is celebrated as an icon of the Orthodox construction of Greek identity, to the point where he has been venerated at the level of a modern saint.[93] Between April and October 1884, the last and longest of Papadiamantis' historical novels, *The Gypsy Girl*, was serialized in the newspaper *Akropolis*. Set against the backdrop of the fall of Constantinople between April and May of 1453, this work explicitly contends with conflicting notions of how the relationship between Greek national identity and the Byzantine past should be framed. And although the work is often presumed as endeavoring to legitimate the Byzantine past, according to Robert Peckham who examines it extensively in the article "Papadiamantis, Ecumenism and the Theft of Byzantium," this assumption serves to obscure what is in fact a complex dialectic. Papadiamantis depicts the tension between classical and Byzantine conceptions of nationhood as having been a factor in the fall of Constantinople, represented in the Orthodox population's inability to decide whether to compromise with Rome as a means out of their predicament.

The main protagonist of the story is George Gemistos Plethon (fancifully placed in the narrative given that the historical Plethon died a year before the events depicted). Plethon is represented as a Western-oriented

---

[91] Quoted in Politis 1998: 10.
[92] Quoted in Politis 1998: 6.
[93] The hymns he wrote have been recorded by the Greek Byzantine Choir and his skull is preserved as a relic in the central church of Skiathos (Peckham 1998: 92–3).

humanist seeking to revive Greece by appeal to the culture of its ancient, classical past. Although branded by the narrator as a pagan apostate, this stigma clearly does not extend to any denial or disavowal of his link to the Greek *ethnos*. On the contrary, the narrator also contends that "he was one of the few who had a consciousness of nationalism and his heart burned with patriotism."[94] Although, at first glance, the anachronistic appeal to nationalism might be what strikes one as interesting in this line, what is most interesting is that if, indeed, the ideology was to be anachronistically inserted into a depiction of the defeat of Byzantium, why then would it be associated with this representative of the ancient pagan past and identified as a minority position? According to the narrator, Plethon, as a young man, had devised a new system of government that had it been implemented might well have averted the catastrophe of the defeat. This problematizes the straightforward dichotomies of East versus West, Orthodoxy versus Humanism. Instead, these sometimes antagonistic ideologies appear to coexist simultaneously in the Orthodox community on the eve of the disaster. Neither side of the controversy over union with Rome is presented as unequivocally correct, whereas Plethon's ideological Hellenism, explicitly representative of an emergent Greek nationalism, is challenged by the clerics in the narrative as a rejection of the ecumenical ideal.[95]

Peckham represents Papadiamantis, in this work, as the first writer of fiction to engage with Kostantinos Paparrigopoulos' conception of a tripartite model of cultural continuity. The year of its publication was also the year that Politis first coined the term *laografia* for the study of Greek folklore. Thus, in Papadiamantis we can see the ideological underpinnings of Paparrigopoulos and Politis stripped bare of their scholarly historicism through translation to the level of myth and imagination, with the figure of Plethon standing in the medieval Byzantine period, looking back to the ancient classical and, in so doing, prefiguring a modern nationalism. The character is both "last of the Hellenes, in the sense of pagans of the classical age, and the first of the Greeks, in the sense of modern nationalists,"[96] with the story taking place at the pivotal moment of the fall of the medieval age, thereby establishing an unbroken, if precarious, continuity of identity.

[94] Quoted in Peckham 1998: 97–8.
[95] Peckham 1998: 98.
[96] Ibid.: 95–7.

These struggles between divergent interpretations are reflected metaphorically in the figure of Aima, the orphan "gypsy girl," whose frustrated ability to recollect a coherent narrative of her past is explicitly
identified by the narrator as an allegory for that of the nation. As symbolic representative of the nation, and ultimately surrogate victim, the
conflicting narratives that are never resolved mark her as the quintessential crosser of boundaries. According to one version, she is linked to the
capital through royal lineage; according to another, she was conjured
forth by Plethon; and yet another maintains that she is the product of a
union between Apollo and a mortal woman. Each myth conveys a different message, and the fact that the mystery is never resolved suggests that
the truth lies in the ongoing tension between them, with a series of dreams
invoked to fill in the gaps in the incomplete narration, suggesting the pivotal role of imagination in the construction of national history.[97] "Like
Aima's childhood, the nation's narration is lost in inscrutable myths of
origin.... Aima's efforts to recover the submerged secret of her origin
are connected to the nation's strivings to recuperate its multiple historical identities. If *The Gypsy Girl* ends with the act of recollection frustrated, and Aima's origins are nowhere convincingly explained, it is worth
recalling Renan's celebrated remark of 1882, two years before the publication of Papadiamantis's novel, that the nation's identity is founded as
much upon an act of collective amnesia, as upon an abundant legacy of
remembrances."[98]

Peckham sees it as paradoxical that the protagonists appear to stand
at the edge of the nation they symbolically represent; but this is precisely
what enables them to serve as boundary crossers and thus as suitable
symbolic victims at this pivotal sacrificial moment for the nation. Aima,
whatever her origins, has been raised by gypsies, with gypsies at the time
representing the quintessential rootless outsiders, disengaged from their
host societies as juxtaposed to the settled social life of the national ideal.
They are wild and autonomous and offer a blank slate in terms of any
political or literary history of their own. This association places Aima on
the boundary between insider and outsider – she is not a gypsy herself but
was associated with them while excluded by the society she represents;
she is illiterate yet retains memories of a former literacy. Plethon, as
well, is described in the opening pages as an "Egyptian" who passes

[97] Ibid.: 99.
[98] Ibid.: 100–1.

either for "a Jewish merchant or a vagabond gypsy."[99] After frustrated attempts to reclaim the girl, Plethon finally succeeds in bringing Aima to his sanctuary near Sparta, where he plans to initiate her into his pagan rites, revitalizing Byzantium on the brink of its destruction through a resuscitation of ancient Greek culture in the classical Greek heartland away from the Roman capital. At the last moment, however, before Plethon is able to celebrate the girl's marriage to a young gypsy named Machtos, the couple is fatally crushed in Plethon's cave by a marble statue of Artemis in an apocalyptic earthquake that accompanies the City's subjugation.[100]

Kostis Palamas also incorporates the image of the gypsy in his epic work surrounding the fall of Constantinople. Anthony Hirst cites *The Dodecalogue of the Gypsy* as a key example of the "equivocal" attitude held by Greek poets toward the Byzantine heritage during the ascendancy of the Great Idea. "The picture which it offers of the City is a disparaging one. The Gypsy speaks of a corrupt city, incapable of its own defense and richly deserving its impending fate . . . The Byzantium of the *Dodecalogue* serves as an image of decadent civilization which must be destroyed before any good can come of it."[101] Classical Greece doesn't fare much better, though not so much because of its inherent systemic flaws as because of the principle that "there is no future in clinging to the past." The protagonist's utopian vision, rather, is of a world ruled by science and humanism, where cultures of the past and national boundaries are transcended. The poems of C. P. Cavafy also tend to reflect a nuanced political picture of Byzantium, depicted as a state divided against itself. Cavafy viewed the Byzantine period less as a Golden Age than as a period heroic only insofar as it was the one in which the suffering and divisions of his nation (or race) were most clearly reflected.[102]

Papadiamantis, Palamas, and Cavafy are generally identified as having been heretics to the classicist conception of Greek national identity considered standard at the time, embracing instead Byzantine and Orthodox historical and cultural elements in their narrative of continuity.[103] But it is simplistic to draw lines quite so sharply in such terms. Although it may be the case that certain figures at certain times may have favored one narrative over the other, it is clear that in literary descriptions of Byzantium,

[99] Ibid.: 103–4.
[100] Ibid.: 94–5.
[101] Hirst 1998: 108–9.
[102] Ibid.: 112–13, 117.
[103] Beaton 1998: 133–4.

even among its reputed proponents, its glory is almost invariably synonymous with corruption; both internal in the sense of its own systemic failures and external in the sense that these failures were the cause of its ultimate if inevitable decay and conquest. It would be more accurate to say that the merging of narratives that forged the modern national identity retained an ambivalent attitude to both historical periods. The presence of two such clearly distinct "Golden Ages" associated with two distinct ideological models of nationhood simply served to enable easy resolution of the ambivalence toward each period by means of reference to the other.

At times, this trait of disunity is identified as a perpetual flaw in the nation itself and thus one that will characterize any society that has governed it, thereby explaining its historical failures. Revolutionary France rediscovered the Gallic period as a time of the people, progenitor to a succession of revolutionaries fighting against foreign aristocratic domination, with 1789 serving as a high point in a long battle between Franks and Gauls. But Wolfgang Schivelbusch observes that although this identification persisted into the late 19th century, it adopted a more ambivalent tone, with the notion that the defeat of the Gauls under Vercingetorix by a more civilized and cohesive Rome under Caesar had been a historical necessity in order for France as such to be born. In the language of one republican reformer, "the Gauls lacked the quality of discipline essential to national greatness. They were incapable of following orders and subordinating their personal and group interests to the greater good.... Rancor and anarchy destined the Gauls to fall prey to a better organized and more disciplined nation. Rome's victory over the Gauls, thus, was ultimately the triumph of civilization over barbarism."[104]

In the conclusion to his study of the role of Joan of Arc in French national memory, Winock connects this narrative to the Joan of Arc myth. Arguing that "a certain idea of France" can be found to underlie the rhetoric of all factions vying for possession of her memory, it is a narrative that demonstrates the persistent need to express through the national mythology both national glory and a sense of the nation's inherent failings that prevent it, through successive events in history, from realizing that glory. The history of the nation is miraculous; France is represented as one of a very few civilizations that have dominated world history, whether as eldest daughter of the Church (for Catholics) or as birthplace of the Revolution and the Rights of Man (for republicans).

[104] Francois Correard, quoted in Schivelbusch 2003: 166–7.

Thus, it belongs to the category of the sacred, a "chosen" nation. However, the nation has nonetheless always been divided. As Winock puts it, "the war between the Armagnacs and the Burgundians was merely a belated revival of ancient divisions among the Gauls in the days of Caesar and Vercingetorix. Anarchy is consubstantial with France, be it tribal, feudal, intellectual, or popular, and of the left or the right. An inexpugnable individualism (of persons or groups) has constantly hindered the country's defense and weakened its social cohesion. What is more, opposition between two camps, religions, or parties has been a persistent feature under all regimes."[105] But if this disunity is endemic to the character of the nation, its solution is exceptional and must constantly be renewed in order to be effective. France's providential mission can be fulfilled only through the periodic intervention of savior figures who will repeatedly incarnate in a perpetual effort to unify a France divided unto itself. Joan of Arc comes across as one manifestation of such a savior figure. As in the Kosovo myth, it is the Christian salvation drama that is taken as the literary model, though again this is translated into national terms; Joan's ultimate defeat and demise are the inevitable end to the story, brought about by the failure of the nation to stand by her example, inevitable because of that nation's perpetually divided character.[106]

Similar sentiments can be found in the works of historians and literary figures of the Czech national revival, specifically relating to myths of martyrdom and defeat. František Palacký, while sentimentalizing "patriotic" high points in Czech history, nonetheless appeared to criticize what he deemed to be the essential Czech character as inimical to lasting national unity in a number of telling ways, namely: "their obstinacy, perfervour, and, above all, religious quarrelsomeness."[107] He presented Bohemian culture prior to the defeat at White Mountain as under an ongoing process of Germanization that was less the fault of the Austrian Empire as it was of the Czech Estates; a notion further popularized by Alois Jirasek, who was influential in putting a literary flare to Palacky's conception of history. Many of the heroic figures of the Czech past, while praised by Jirasek for their achievements for the nation, are at the same time criticized as laboring under a debilitating Germanophilia, depicted as a causal factor leading to the feudalization and division of the nation. Although most subsequent national historians would portray

---

[105] Winock 1998: 475–6.
[106] Ibid.: 476–8.
[107] Pynsent 1994: 177.

White Mountain as the quintessential national disaster, they would also pick up on this theme that the disaster was made possible only by the weakness of Czech society itself. Radl portrayed what was defeated at White Mountain as a Bohemia "living on local squabbles between a backward nobility and backward towns," while according to Karasek, pre–White Mountain Czech history amounted to a "psychological process of racial decay.... The Czechs were no longer capable of fighting and regaining their independence.... Foreign ideas so tyrannized the nation's natural resistance that the Czechs left their country and then, abroad, for the sake of those same ideas, abandoned their nationality and fused forever with alien elements."[108] Tomáš Masaryk would ultimately pick up on this line, identifying White Mountain as having occurred as a consequence of lack of unity among morally unsound nobles, though the common people were the chief sufferers of the consequent counterreformation.[109]

Pynsent portrays such views as amounting to a critical rejection of the White Mountain myth. But when we compare them with similar ambivalent sentiments toward the destroyed Golden Age expressed in other national defeat myths, they come across as necessary refinements to the prenational memories of these events in order to make them better able to serve national ends. As Sayer notes, the development of the White Mountain myth during the national revival coincided with a reframing of Czech national identity as distinguished through notions of language and race, rather than religion. The "sacred instrument" of the Czech language was seen as having been kept alive among the country people, thereby enabling the survival of the *narod* whereas the wealthy, urbanized classes were "Germanized" in the centuries following White Mountain. This contained, in Sayer's words, "more than a hint of society's upper echelons being bought off, of their having sold their mother tongue that was their birthright for the mess of pottage represented by imperial favor and favors."[110] Selling out to a foreign culture (although, interestingly, not its religion) is connected to the maintenance of hierarchical privilege inimical to defense of a horizontally structured nation, whereas the "simple people" who kept their language are elevated to the epitome of the democratic nation, and distance from this class is transformed into a mark of foreignness.[111]

---

[108] Quotes from Pynsent 1994: 175–7.
[109] Pynsent 1994: 181.
[110] Sayer 1998: 118.
[111] Ibid.: 118–19.

Even in Ghana, where the anticolonial element to the defeat myth leaves open the prospect of attributing that defeat entirely to the ruthlessness and technological superiority of the enemy colonizer, elements of the national theodicy are evident in both scholarly and popular historical accounts. To begin with, accounts of the conflict neither downplay nor attempt to rationalize the fact that one of the grievances that sparked the Asante into war, although subordinate to the issues surrounding the Golden Stool, was the abolition of slavery in Asante territory by British authorities. This is even highlighted as a moral indictment of traditional Asante society relative to that of Britain.[112]

Although Boahen, in his history of the Yaa Asantewaa War, claims that the Asante failed "because the odds were too much against them," the primary explanation he cites for this disparity is "internal disunity." "The Asante fought this War as a divided nation – those who remained loyal to and fought in defence of the Golden Stool and those who were pro-British."[113] He then proceeds to list those tribes and leaders who assisted the British in their victory but stresses that "worse still" was the fact that "most of the young, influential and rich commoners of Asante also sided with the British," not only fighting on their side but also revealing war tactics and betraying Asante hideouts leading to arrests. These people are described as petty officials, traders and "bullies," with the petty crimes they committed against their subjects enumerated.[114] Their collaboration is clearly connected to their wealth and status, and their selfish desire to acquire or maintain such wealth and status within the framework of the traditional hierarchy, even at the expense of the nation's collective sovereignty. The critical flaw that renders the community incapable of self-defense in the face of the challenge of the Other invariably relates to its failure to live up to a per se national ideal: It is disunity, hierarchy, and the vertical nature of authority, along with lack of widespread allegiance to the principle of national–cultural sovereignty, or even, at times – and sometimes quite contradictorily – the failure of an obstinate people to conform to values associated with industrial modernity: economic industriousness and growth, representative government and civic responsibility, and principles of in-group equality superseding differences of class, gender, religion, or politics.

---

[112] See, for example, Asirifi-Danquah 2002: 3.
[113] Boahen 2003: 154.
[114] Ibid.: 156–7.

The Traitor

One of the most popular vehicles for the expression of this ambivalence toward the institutions that characterized the Golden Age is the figure of the Traitor. Curiously, this is one of the most common characters in the national defeat myth. Lazar and Miloš Obilić have their Vuk Branković; Lāčplēsis has his Kangars; the Armenian tragic hero Vartan Mamikonian has his Vasag Sewny. In each case, these names have entered their respective languages as synonyms for treachery. Even where a traitor figure might not be named as a character in the story, the concept of the defeat being ultimately the fault of an individual insider violating national–cultural solidarity tends to appear somewhere in the mythology. Certain well-known Greek folk songs on the fall of Constantinople contain the image of a traitor who turned the keys of the City over to the Turks, allowing it to be taken.[115] The ubiquity of this element, along with its often clearly fabricated insertion into the myth, indicates its unique capacity to serve a particular function, as does the fact that from the standpoint of narrative coherence, it would appear to be entirely redundant. The defeat can already easily be explained by either the overwhelming power and ruthlessness of the enemy Other/or by the willing and heroic self-sacrifice of the Savior. Yet, in a quite contradictory manner, the myth often nonetheless suggests that despite these factors, the defeat still would not have been suffered if not for the specific actions of the traitor and the disease internal to the society that spawned him.

The Traitor serves to personify, by means of a straightforward narrative, the flaws in the social structure of the heroic age that prevented it from being a true and lasting vehicle for national mobilization. At the same time, he reinforces, by negative example, the principle that mere possession of the traits that define the boundaries of the ethnic group is insufficient for membership and acceptance to the emergent national community. This points to yet another interesting paradox. One would expect that the highlighting of the role of the Traitor would tend to come from the more ethnic exclusivist elements of national-political culture and, indeed, we do see such rhetoric associated with the effort to cleanse what is perceived as national impurity. But, at the same time, this narrative motif depends on a decidedly civic framework of national identity, whereby individuals who might otherwise share all of the ethnic signifiers

---

[115] Herzfeld 1982: 132.

of language, culture, religion, or descent are nonetheless expelled as outsiders for their failure to identify with the nation. Whereas the character of the Sacred Executioner facilitates the setting of ethnically defined boundaries, the character of the Traitor, in contrast, reinforces the notion that ultimately "mingled blood" trumps "kindred blood." Identification with the signifiers that define the nation must be voluntary as well as ascribed, and the ultimate distinction between insiders and outsiders comes down to willingness to identify with the totem in its foundational moment of sacrifice. Failure to participate in a ritual that must by its nature project unanimity means effective expulsion.

Thus, the Traitor, too, is surrogate victim and boundary crosser. Just as the enemy Executioner is mirror image to the Savior, the Traitor is mirror image to the Hero. As the Hero is the model of self-sacrifice in the name of the national ideal, the Traitor is a negative model representing concupiscence and disregard of group interests in the name of self-interest. Distinct from the Executioner, who must be an outsider in order to be seen as dealing the society its final blow, the Traitor whose actions make this calamity possible is, like the Hero, an insider to the community according to whatever signifiers are relevant to defining community boundaries. His refusal to identify with the Savior at the moment of sacrifice is the only thing that sets him apart, a refusal that is often depicted as informed by his position in the stratified traditional society and his selfish desire to maintain the prerogatives of that position at the expense of submission to the democratic national ideal epitomized by the Savior's act of renunciation.

The Traitor in the national mythology rarely acts as an instrument of divine judgment, but neither is he dismissed as driven by a motiveless, diabolical evil. The circumstances that place him in a position to act against the common interests of the national community, and the motivation that drives him to do so, are frequently attributed to the flawed structure of the society itself. His actions, although dishonorable in their selfishness, are portrayed as entirely sensible in their social context, merely perpetuating the social stratification and factional in-fighting already prevalent in the ambivalent Golden Age that prevented it from being a vehicle for true national fulfillment. He is simply following the imperatives of his role rather than transcending and violating those imperatives in the interests of national solidarity.

In the Kosovo myth, the hostility felt toward the norms of the feudal society, inimical to a national solidarity characterized by a horizontal loyalty to the culture, is directed against the image of Vuk Branković, whose treason because of his alleged flight from the battlefield serves as a negative example representing the inability of Serbs to unite, both at the battle itself and on an ongoing basis. In fact, the historical Branković went on to resist Ottoman encroachment longer than any other Serbian noble, holding on to his territorial autonomy until becoming a vassal only in 1392. Even then, he was not a particularly loyal one. He did not take part in Bayezit's later Balkan campaigns of 1395 and 1396, as did Stefan Lazarević and other vassals in the region, and was finally deposed by the Turks and put in prison, where he died.[116]

His transformation into the myth's traitor-figure was, however, a development that rapidly followed the events themselves. All of the basic narrative elements were apparently present in the sources used by the Benedictine historian from Dubrovnik who wrote *Il Regno degli Salvi* in 1601. This text cites both Vuk Branković and Miloš Obilić by name, juxtaposing the treacherous and loyal lords according to the classic structure whereby the traitor accuses the hero of disloyalty before the battle and, stung by the false accusation, the hero vows to assassinate the sultan and prove his loyalty.[117] Virtually all of the epic songs would incorporate this element in some form or another, even those whose narrative focus was Lazar and the Kosovo Covenant. The contradiction is particularly evident in *The Downfall of the Serbian Empire*, the best-known statement of the Kosovo Covenant tradition; for even after Lazar chooses the heavenly kingdom, gives his soldiers communion, and sends them knowingly to defeat, at the threshold of the disaster, the narrative suddenly appears to change its mind and declare:

> Then Lazar would have overwhelmed the Turks,
> May God strike Vuk Branković dead!
> He betrayed his father-in-law at Kosovo.[118]

An assertion that seems even more absurd in light of the fact that the poem immediately goes back to the Kosovo Covenant paradigm in describing the conclusion of the battle as foreordained, according to divine plan:

> Then the Turks overwhelmed Lazar,
> And the Tsar Lazar was destroyed,
> And his army was destroyed with him,
> Of seven and seventy thousand soldiers.

[116] Velikonja 1998: 26; Malcolm 1998: 65–7.
[117] Bogert 1991: 176; Malcolm 1998: 66.
[118] Cited in Bogert 1991: 184.

> All was holy, all was honourable
> And the goodness of God was fulfilled.[119]

Vuk Branković demonstrates that the mere fact that one is part of the ethnic community does not automatically qualify one for membership to the nation. The latter requires a common and equal allegiance to the culture above all else, and thus one must also take part in the communion of the totem feast. One must stand in solidarity, identifying with the same symbolic ideal; therefore, Vuk Branković's failure to identify with Lazar at the critical moment of defeat and sacrifice effectively disqualifies him, and anyone like him, from full participation. It is made explicit in several of the Kosovo songs that the battle is a pivotal moment that will serve to distinguish between true insiders and outsiders, expressed most clearly in the curse spoken by Lazar against prospective traitors. This constant theme is repeated twice in *Musić Stefan* and found in similar terms in numerous other songs and poems:[120]

> Lazar exhorted us like this:
> Whoever is a Serb, and of Serbian blood
> And he comes not to fight at Kosovo
> May he never have any progeny
> His heart desires, neither son nor daughter;
> Beneath his hand let nothing decent grow
> Neither purple grapes nor wholesome wheat;
> Let him rust away like dripping iron
> Until his name shall be extinguished.[121]

Although on the one hand we have seen Lazar represented in the Kosovo myth as the undisputed leader of the army at Kosovo and, therefore, by extension of Serbia as an imagined nation, it is clear that the myth does not consequently obscure the decentralized nature of power characteristic of the feudal period nor the tendency of leaders to form alliances

[119] West 1982: 911. It is interesting to note that according Rebecca West's account, her guide does not translate the section of the poem that describes the battle but merely summarizes it as "a long passage, very muddled, about how gallantly the Tsar fought and how at the end it looked as if they were to win, but Vuk Brankovitch betrayed them, so they were beaten." It seems that he was well aware of the implied contradiction.

[120] For example, in *Pieces from Various Kosovo Poems*: "Whoever will not fight at Kosovo / May nothing grow that his hand sows: / Neither the white wheat in his field, / Nor the vine grapes on his mountain," or in *The Battle of Loznica*: "Who betrays us, may summer betray him / May he have no harvest of white grain / May his old mother never look on him / May his dear sister never swear by him" (Koljević 1991: 138, n. 10).

[121] Cited in Gorup 1991: 114.

and conduct diplomacy without regard for any kind of national principle. Even in the myth, Lazar does not preside over a national society. Much as the feudal society is glorified as the height of cultural achievement, the myth is surprisingly frank in identifying its structure as inimical to cultural solidarity, and the Serbian leadership, at least as an abstraction, is depicted as more than willing to violate key cultural norms such as religion in the name of maintaining their own authority. The "treason" of Vuk Branković offers the clearest symbol of the willingness of Christian leaders to cooperate with the Turks when it suited their purposes, and this element enters into virtually any retelling of the Kosovo myth.

One of the immediate results of the Ottoman conquest symbolized by the Battle of Kosovo was the loss of Serbia's nobility through war, conversion, and migration. Although this development was on the one hand stunting to the nation's cultural development, it was also, on the other, a necessary step toward the formation of a national society whereby loyalty was transferred from the Serbian feudal polity to the Serbian culture as defined and codified by the church. When oppression did occur, it was felt equally by all remaining members of the cultural community, engendering a sense of social homogeneity, equality, and solidarity. It is only under circumstances in which the feudal elite no longer exists that the feudal society can be idealized in contrast to current oppression. The effect of the Kosovo myth was to symbolically wipe away all remnants of the feudal system so that a national society could be forged in its place that could, in turn, idealize it. Thus, the symbolic leaders of the old system are divided between martyrs and traitors. The only figures from the Kosovo story who come to be revered are those who choose to die, voluntarily removing themselves from their positions of privilege and authority through acts of sacrifice and struggle that enable their transformation into saintly heroes to the national culture, symbolic reinforcers of norms inimical to those that characterized the society they once ruled in life. On the other hand, those who remain alive, retaining their feudal privilege and authority, however much they might be a part of the common culture or *ethnie*, are removed from the national communion and therefore become legitimate targets against whom struggle for national fulfillment may be waged.

We see this formula applied again in the contest within French national culture over the memory of Joan of Arc. Although the English, or foreigners in the abstract, might play the role of Executioner, no less and sometimes even greater importance is placed on the identity of the internal Traitor. Voltaire's condemnation of Joan's killers was not directed at the English but rather at the Inquisition in France: the 9 doctors of the Sorbonne and 35 priests and monks presided over by Bishop Cauchon. Although this, on the one hand, served his anticlerical agenda, it also subtly serves a national one as well, providing an explanation for the defeat in terms consistent with the national theodicy that lies not in the power of the enemy but in the failure of the nation to live up to the ideal represented by the totemic victim. "It is difficult to conceive how we dare call any other people barbarous after the innumerable horrors of which we ourselves have been guilty."[122] But although Cauchon provided anticlerical revolutionaries with a symbol of the *ancien régime* to blame for national defeat, Catholic France did not shy away from this focal point either, if only because Cauchon provided a convenient scapegoat by which the church as a whole could separate itself from responsibility and thereby identify itself with the nation. In 1894, when the canonization process began in Rome and Joan was declared "Venerable," the archbishop of Aix declared, "We admit that she was sent to her death by a bishop . . . a bishop who was no longer French in the slightest because he had sold himself to the English":

. . . But Pope Callistus III avenged the Virgin of Domrémy. He ordered a revision of her trial. He dismissed and nullified the sentence as the most monstrous since Pilate's. We are still waiting for as much to be done for the countless innocent victims condemned by the revolutionary tribunals.

Bishop Cauchon is no more one of ours than Judas was, because we have repudiated him in a most authentic and solemn judgement. Cauchon was the precursor of Voltaire, who profaned our brightest and purest national glory.[123]

Even in the eyes of this clerical author, Cauchon ceases to be French – despite whatever ascriptive credentials of language, religion, descent, and territory he might possess – entirely because of his conduct vis-à-vis Joan of Arc and the English, just as Judas ceased to be a Christian through his conduct toward Jesus and the Romans, though in this case because he valued his allegiance to his hierarchical station above that to the nation. Further, we see that just as association with the totem allows for a political faction to identify itself with the nation, so too does association with the Traitor enable that political faction to expel its opponents from the nation, whatever claim those opponents might

---

[122] Quoted in Gildea 1994: 155.
[123] Quoted in Winock 1998: 450.

have to insider status. This conflict continued to play out through French national history, as illustrated by this excerpt from communist wartime propaganda:

In the fifteenth century France, at war for a century, divided and devastated, fell under the foreign yoke. Then, as now, there was a party of treachery, in the pay of the invader.... But the masses burned with patriotic faith... and a humble peasant girl of Domrémy, Joan of Arc, put herself at the head of the party of resistance, fought the climate of resignation that surrounded the Dauphin, and set a courageous example in the freedom struggle that finally drove out all foreign troops from the soil of the Fatherland.... Communist and other patriots who are fighting to deliver the country, who are gunned down by the Hun and their lackeys, are in the tradition of Joan of Lorraine, while the 'collaborators', the men of Vichy, Laval, Pétain, Darlan and co., are in the tradition of Bishop Cauchon.[124]

Whatever tradition of the Joan myth the protagonist came from, Cauchon was always the anti-Joan. Inevitably banned from being considered as French, he invariably lacked whatever qualities the protagonist associated as integral to Frenchness. This was taken to a literal extreme by the racist anti-Semitism of certain nationalists such as Raoul Bergot, who determined via circular logic that Cauchon had to have been of another race, un-French in his essence, else he would not have been able to betray the national cause in the name of an alternative principle. Thus followed the conclusion: "Cauchon had Jewish blood in his veins." Constructing a dubious genealogy, he concludes, "Cauchon did not betray his country. He was obeying the instincts of his origins. Before belonging to a country, a man belongs to his race."[125]

We have seen Ghanaian national history represent the Yaa Asantewaa War as an all-Asante effort, with Yaa Asantewaa's status as legitimate leader and symbol of the nation left without doubt. Yet lack of unity among the Asante is neither forgotten nor denied. The fact that many principalities concluded separate treaties with the British and remained allied with them throughout the war, either in their own interests or as a consequence of animosity toward the Kumasi leadership lingering from the civil war, is recognized in almost every retelling of the history, both popular and scholarly. The presence of significant traitorous elements among the Asante is an element of the narrative that is in no way downplayed. On the contrary, Boahen notes that the issue of betrayal is highly

---

[124] Quoted in Gildea 1994: 164.
[125] Raoul Bergot, *Jeanne D'Arc et l'histoire moderne*, quoted in Winock 1998: 465.

emphasized in the oral traditions.[126] Although he is himself concerned to list as many states and kings as possible that fought for the Golden Stool, even to the point of including a few that at least would have, had circumstances allowed for it, he provides as well a parallel list of those who betrayed the Asante cause by siding with the British, informing on Asante war tactics and, most significantly, assisting in their efforts to locate and acquire the Golden Stool.[127]

Symbolic among the list of traitors were the names Yaw Awua, his servant Kwadwo Asumen, and most centrally Kwame Tua; and Boahen notes that many of his oral accounts suggest that defeat would not have been suffered if not for the betrayal of these figures. "Whites won because Kwame Tua, Yaw Awua and other Asantes betrayed the Asantes."[128] Kwadwo Asuman is said to have accompanied the British on the March 31 expedition to locate the Golden Stool that led to the opening of hostilities.[129] Kwame Tua developed a widespread reputation as the single most devoted collaborator in aiding British attempts to locate the Golden Stool[130] and in ultimately betraying the location of Yaa Asantewaa herself and leading the contingent of British forces that captured her.[131] In return, he was rewarded by the British with the office of Gyaasewahene, although he was never able to claim it effectively. This office had been previously held by one of the hero figures of the war, Opoku Mensa, who, along with the Gyaasewa people, showed allegiance to the Golden Stool by acting decisively to conceal it and keep it hidden for the intervening decades.[132] Just as Opoku Mensa, who was executed by the British, serves to symbolize those who wished to restore the traditional status quo, Kwame Tua, depicted as unsuccessfully claiming the former's traditional prerogatives, symbolizes those willing to collaborate with outsiders further to discarding that traditional society in the face of the challenges of modernity. However, as time went on and the colonial state became more established, it became clear that more and more Asante identified with the latter category, as evidenced by the fact that when the Golden

---

[126] Boahen 2003: 159.
[127] Ibid.: 158–9, 166–73.
[128] Cited in Boahen 2003: 158.
[129] McKaskie 2000: 78–81; Boahen 2003: 35.
[130] Ibid.: 85–7.
[131] Boahen (2003: 144–5) includes this detail in his account, though he goes on to note that the evidence suggests it to be fanciful.
[132] McKaskie 2000: 90.

Stool was accidentally happened upon by ordinary Asantes in 1921, their reaction was to desecrate it by dismantling it for its material value.[133]

In the final analysis, it serves the interests of the nation that the heroes, praised for defending the traditional order, end the story dead or in exile; whereas the traitors, reviled for their accommodation with modernizing forces, live on, if unable to enjoy their ill-gotten gains and thereby claim the totem's prerogatives. As with the Zealots of Masada, the Serbian nobles who fought at Kosovo, and the 27 Czech aristocrats executed in Starometske Square, the greatest heroes of the nation are those representatives of the glorious golden age who obligingly remove themselves from history with minimal fuss, leaving history and the national soul to the "common people." The greatest traitors are, by contrast, those who stubbornly insist on their continued place in it, remaining as an aggravating remnant of a period of disunity, socioeconomic stratification, and religiocultural heterogeneity; one clearly lacking in the sense of common destiny and purpose provided by the national principle.

"Without death there is no resurrection"

The function of many of the previously mentioned elements – the sacrificial hero–model, the traitor, the ambivalent Golden Age, and the national theodicy – can be demonstrated through examination of the role of Kosovo symbolism in one of the most influential works of Serbian national literature: *Gorski Vijenac* [The Mountain Wreath], written by Prince Bishop Petar Petrović-Njegoš, ruler of Montenegro during the second quarter of the 19th century. *The Mountain Wreath* is one of those texts that seems to evoke entirely different meanings to those inside the national tradition than to those outside of its particular myth–symbol framework. To insiders, it is a straightforward story of good against evil, with the moral that all people must do their part in the ongoing struggle against tyranny and oppression; for outsiders, it is difficult to read as anything other than an elegant glorification of genocide. The epic relates the story of a massacre of Muslims that allegedly took place on a Montenegrin hilltop village on Christmas Eve in the late 17th century, and it is remarkable for its anti-Muslim epithets, its merging of religious identity with nationalist aggression, and its exaltation of violence as the path to national integrity. Yet it has been cited in the past even by secular and universally oriented pragmatists within the nation, such as Yugoslav

[133] Ibid.: 93.

dissident Milovan Djilas, as a metaphorical expression of a noble struggle for a just cause. Andrew Wachtel notes with some amazement that the first time the ethnic nationalist implications of the work were critically discussed in public in communist Yugoslavia was in 1984.[134]

Just as Yitzchak Lamdan's poem was not about the fall of Masada, *The Mountain Wreath* is not about the Battle of Kosovo, neither does it even take place in the territory of Kosovo. But the fact that images of Kosovo permeate the narrative throughout is testament to the power of these images within Serbian culture as sources of both commonly understood metaphor and of inspiration. In this poem, Kosovo is not an event in history but rather an ongoing state of affairs keeping the Serbian nation enslaved. Njegoš refers to Kosovo as "borba neprestana," an unremitting struggle.[135] The introduction to the epic begins with a dedication to Karadjordje, the leader of the first Serbian uprising against Ottoman rule in 1804, and closes by invoking Miloš Obilić, thereby linking the expected rebirth of the nation in continuity with the moment of its destruction.[136] As Djilas put it, for Njegoš, "Kosovo as an event hardly exists, but its tragedy permeates every act, every thought, and the national being; it is felt from verse to verse throughout the entire work as a fateful misfortune imposed on the Serbs from on high":

Kosovo is the height of misfortune, but neither the beginning nor the end, rather, the constant destiny of the Serbs.... Supreme and immutable laws are at work under which our misfortune was conceived long before Kosovo, because our [elite] departed from the higher eternal order.... Evil and misfortune are our lot, as well as the struggle against them.... Our national existence is permeated with our principal calamity; it was our own leaders who opened the gates of our woe to an alien faith and rule. Our unhappy people drag and shake off their chains, but always alone and weak, disunited and irresolute.[137]

The narrative centers around the figure of Bishop Danilo and his Arjuna-like internal struggle over the necessity of violence. Danilo laments the conquests that have been made by Islam and, noting that Montenegro might still be free, worries that it remains threatened less by armed conquest than by a gradual weakening from within through conversion. Yet although he is convinced of the necessity of violence in order to effect the rebirth of his nation, he is torn by the realization that the Muslims

---

[134] Wachtel 2004: 144.
[135] Bogert 1991: 180.
[136] Wachtel 2004: 133.
[137] Quoted in Schwartz 2000: 46–7.

in question are Montenegrins, his blood relations. Although the pivotal event of the narrative is the massacre itself, its tension revolves around the question of whether Danilo will continue to equivocate or whether he will ultimately adhere to the unanimous will of the collective.[138]

The sense of national theodicy – of defeat and degradation being the wages of disunity and, in particular, the disunity of the feudal elite – is expressed in a song sung early in the poem during a communal dance, the Kolo, which serves in the manner of a Greek chorus to express the sympathies of the group and audience:

> Our God hath poured His wrath upon the Serbs,
> For deadly sins withdrawn His favour from us:
> Our Rulers trampled underfoot all law,
> With bloody hatred fought each other down.
> Tore from fraternal brows the living eyes:
> Authority and Law they cast aside,
> Instead chose folly as their rule and guide!
> And those who served our kings became untrue,
> Crimson they bathed themselves in kingly blood!
> Our noblemen – God's curse be on their souls –
> Did tear and rend the Kingdom into pieces,
> And wasted wantonly our people's power.
> The Serbian magnates – may their name rot out! –
> They scatter'd broadcast Discord's evil seed,
> And poisoned thus the life-springs of our race.
> Our Serbian chiefs, most miserable cowards,
> The Serbian stock did heartlessly betray.
> Accursed be Kossóvo's Evening Meal;
> Far better had it been if from that hour
> Our magnates all had disappear'd for aye!
> If only Milosh still remain'd unto us,
> With his two valiant Pòbratims,
> Then Serb would be with Serb to-day.
> Thou Brankovitch, of stock despicable,
> Should one serve so his Fatherland,[139]

National and religious theodicy merges, as the disunity of the feudal elite is identified both in a practical sense as the state of affairs that prevented a unified defense, opening the door to Turkish conquest, and, at the same time, as the sin that brought the wrath of God on the nation. The song goes on to speak derisively of those leaders who, after squandering the nation's potential, converted to Islam, betraying their Serbian heritage in

---

[138] Wachtel 2004: 133–4.
[139] Nyegosh 1930: 79–83.

contrast to "those who still held true to Christian faith, Who with abhorrence thought of bonds and chains, All such as these took flight to mountains gray, To wane and perish and pour out their blood, 'Mid mountains, trust and heritage to guard, Our sacred Freedom and our glorious Name.... In bloody combats falling day by day, For sake of Honour, Faith, and Freedom dear;"[140] The dichotomy is thus established between the Christians who remained faithful to Kosovo, symbolized by Obilić, and the Muslims who, through their conversion, betrayed Kosovo in the manner of Vuk Branković. Throughout the poem, the memory of Miloš Obilić is invoked more than that of any other heroic figure. *The Mountain Wreath* gave shape to the notion of Obilić as the ideal Christian hero, a symbol of freedom. Serbs were to understand, in the face of centuries of Ottoman rule and the symbols of the Kosovo story, that to kill a foreign tyrant was the noblest of acts.[141]

How, then, does "Muslim" come to stand in for "tyrant"? Although the Ottoman Empire may have been multiethnic and multireligious, with an impressive degree of religious toleration and community autonomy relative to other imperial regimes, the millet system still relegated non-Muslim communities to a subordinate class. As the Empire was in decline, and oppression and stratification increased, memory of this second-class status behind Muslim citizens engendered sentiments that, when translated into a national context, placed not individuals but rather religious communities into categories of those who had betrayed the nation, collaborating with the oppressor as symbolized by their conversion, and those who had resisted as symbolized by their perseverance in their faith regardless of the resulting disadvantages.[142]

Miloš Obilić comes through in *The Mountain Wreath* as exemplar of those who would not compromise, in that he is depicted as having accepted the ultimate disadvantage – death – over dishonor and therefore as an ideal of self-effacing loyalty in contrast to self-interested betrayal; an ideal that provided a model of behavior with which one could identify. On the night before taking part in the massacre, all of the 30 or 40 figures depicted in the story claim to see the same vision of Miloš Obilić in their dreams,[143] a powerful expression of this symbol as a common and unifying heroic ideal. Earlier in the story, a character asks a group of

[140] Ibid.: 86–7.
[141] Emmert 1989: 9–10; 1990: 124.
[142] Cohen 2001: 5.
[143] Nyegosh 1930: 197–8.

"Turks" (the term used in the poem to refer to Muslims, who in this case are, in fact, fellow Slavs), "With what will you appear before Miloš, And before all other Serbian heroes, Whose names will live as long as the sun shines."[144] In effect, though they might reap the benefits of their conversion in this life, their betrayal of the totem disqualifies them from participation in the eternal and primordial nation. Speaking in reference to the Battle of Kosovo, one character says to a Slavic Muslim:

> Were we not there together on that day?
> I wrestled then, and still I wrestle now,
> But thou hast ever traitor been, both first and last;
> Thyself hast thou dishonour'd 'fore the world:
> Thou hast denied the faith of all thy fathers:
> And hast enslaved thyself to strangers![145]

In the mythic register of the poem, it is this continuing division between Christian patriots and Muslim collaborators that keeps the nation from achieving its freedom, just as it caused it to lose its freedom at Kosovo. In effect, if Vuk Branković is Kosovo's Judas, then in *The Mountain Wreath*, Muslims take on the role of the Jews as Christ killers. And as with the crucifixion, the defeat at Kosovo is not merely an event in history but also a perpetual tragedy producing an ongoing state of affairs. Vuk Branković can be blamed for the historical defeat, but the ongoing state of affairs also requires a scapegoat found in those who perpetually re-enact his betrayal through their adoption of the conqueror's religion in the interests of maintaining their status.

The Montenegrin leaders are eager to massacre the converts, but the conflicted Danilo, in an effort to forestall the bloodshed, calls for a meeting in which the Muslims are asked to revert back to their "Fathers' Faith" so as to enable a unified national defense. The Muslims counter with what might appear to the uninitiated as a message of reconciliation, reflecting a desire for peaceful coexistence that is flatly rejected by the Christian warrior–heroes.[146] The characters then take an oath of solidarity before the attack, amounting to a preemptive curse on traitors, comparable to those found in the poems of the Kosovo cycle cited earlier, prescribing effective national excommunication to anyone who does not

---

[144] Quoted in Mihailovich 1991: 150.
[145] Nyegosh 1930: 93.
[146] Ibid.: 110–26.

participate fully in the massacre.[147] The massacre itself is described by
one of the participants as follows:

> We put them all unto the sword,
> All those who would not be baptiz'd;
> But who paid homage to the Holy Child
> Were all baptiz'd with sign of Christian Cross,
> And as brother each was hail'd and greeted.
> We put to fire the Turkish houses,
> That there might be nor stick nor trace
> Of these true servants of the Devil!
> From Cettigné to Tcheklitche we hied,
> There in full flight the Turks espied;
> A certain number were by us mow'd down,
> And all their houses we did set ablaze;
> Of all their mosques both great and small
> We left but one accursèd heap,
> For passing folk to cast their glance of scorn.[148]

News of these exploits finally moves Danilo to "weep for joy." But the
story does not end there. The massacre does not conclude and there is
no denouement but rather the final scene depicts one of the participants
lamenting the loss of his favorite rifle, longing to go back into the fray.
The Christian warrior heroes of the poem declare their efforts to be
unfinished and that they will not cease until they or the "Turks" are
exterminated.[149]

As disturbing reading as *The Mountain Wreath* might be, understanding the role of this text in Serbian national mythology requires viewing it
not just in light of the Srebrenica massacre of 1995 but also in comparison with texts such as the Book of Joshua in Judeo–Christian mythology
or the Bhagavad Gita in Hindu nationalism. All of these texts, on the
surface, glorify a moment of conquest, war, or genocide. A more universal message and moral can be discerned only if one is implicitly familiar
with the deeper meanings of the various symbols employed within the
particular myth–symbol system.

The underlying message of *The Mountain Wreath* is the glorification
of the horizontal brotherhood of equals depicted as characteristic of the
patriarchal society, in contrast to the privilege enjoyed by the dominating

---

[147] Ibid.: 199–201.
[148] Ibid.: 209.
[149] Schwartz 2000: 46.

Muslim authorities who stratified the society according to religion. Virtually all images of social privilege are scorned in the poem, including those of Christian societies, even the Serbian feudal society before Kosovo. The derision leveled against the disloyal and disunited Serbian elite during the Kosovo Battle is a reflection of this ethic. Lazar and the sacrificial element of the Kosovo myth receives little attention, as the ideal that one is meant to emulate is not one of suffering but of active struggle, embodied in Miloš Obilić.

Obilić comes through as one of the few Serbian aristocrats worthy of commemoration, and only because he symbolizes those who, in holding to their Christian identity, relinquished their elite status making common cause and sharing a common fate with the oppressed Serbian masses. In contrast, conversion to Islam is seen not simply as a betrayal of religious principles important to the culture but as the means by which the traitorous elements of the Serbian elite were enabled, after Kosovo, to preserve the privileges of status inimical to the horizontal form of social organization that the poem idealizes, preventing the nation from flourishing as a nation. In other words, it is not Muslims as such that are despised but rather what Muslims represent as an abstract principle: the surrender of national solidarity and its corollary in-group equality in the name of maintaining hierarchical dominance. Within a cultural system in which these meanings are implicitly understood, the destruction of such elements offers an essentially democratic message, symbolizing the victory of justice and social equality over the symbols of tyranny against which one must struggle for cultural independence.

The image of the massacre as a purifying act, symbolic of an uncompromising struggle against tyranny, comes through both explicitly and metaphorically. Before leaving the negotiation, one of the Muslims, along with one of the Montenegrins, observes a fight between two cockerels. The Montenegrin wishes victory to the smaller, the "Turk" to the larger, "Wherefore else should God give size? He is bigger: let him have more power!"[150] In light of this and other expressions of Muslim dominance, the offer of truce appears less as an opportunity for peace and reconciliation and more as a temptation to quietly acquiesce to domination and the stratification of the society. Just before the massacre, a blind, elderly abbot, revered by the people for his obvious piety yet who shows none of Danilo's hesitation, expresses this notion that struggle against such domination, even against impossible odds, is the ongoing responsibility

---

[150] Nyegosh 1930: 134–5.

of every generation, necessary to ensure the continuity of the nation and the hope of ultimate redemption:

> The Man defender is of Wife and Child;
> Altar and Hearth a People must safeguard,
> And Honour is a Nation's sacred charge!
> Each generation must its burden bear,
> New needs call forth from man new powers;
> 'Tis in such struggle Genius is forged.
> The Oppress'd do rise against th' Oppressor:
> The stroke calls forth a flash from out the stone;
> Lacking that stroke, imprisoned still the spark!...
> Is not the Real more puzzling than the Dream?
> When man on Earth doth merit name of Honour,
> He hath had right to start as pilgrim here,
> Missing such name, how deep his fall may be!
> O generation mine, created to be sung!
> From Age to Age shall muses vie
> To bring thee wreaths that cannot die;
> What ye by deeds proclaim shall poets teach,
> In songs that shall be sung down deathless years.
> O generation mine, most dread is thine ordeal!
> One part of thee all renegade hath been,
> And pervert is become to Mammon,
> Sure Nemesis already on it falls,
> For what is Bosnia? What Albania's half? –
> If slaves to Islam brothers of your blood?
> United all, there's toil enough for you:
> It is your lot and call to bear the Cross,
> Alike to strive with brethren and with strangers.
> The thorny crown is sharp, sweet after be the fruit!
> Except by way of death was never resurrection.[151]

The massacre thus comes through as a reenactment of the blood sacrifice ritual, with its suitable surrogate victims. The fact that the Muslim victims are both Serbs and Turks – the former by descent, the latter by volition – makes them fitting sacrifices, in that they are threatening boundary crossers that can represent the resented forces of coercive power both foreign and domestic. Thus, the massacre can be seen to both avenge and renew the Kosovo sacrifice, purging the community of its internal divisions through the unanimous direction of rage at its surrogate victims. "Like the *Odyssey*, *The Mountain Wreath* will end with the hero's return to the home that had seemingly been lost: in this case, however, the home

---

[151] Ibid.: 194–6.

is the unity of national life that was lost at Kosovo, and the hero is a collective rather than an individual."[152]

"Except by way of death was never resurrection." This fascinating line could amount to a near-explicit recognition of the totem secret, indicating that perhaps the totem secret is far more poorly kept than the talents Freud attributes to the unconscious would suggest, and supporting Gellner's notion that nationalism is religion, in the Durkheimian sense of societal self-worship, stripped of its camouflage. Yet, as such, it can have two conflicting yet equally valid meanings. On the one hand, the very notion of resurrection requires the purported event of a death that the resurrection serves to supersede. Without death, resurrection is not resurrection but rather birth, or invention. At the same time, however, this line, in its context, implies what has been argued all along: that generative rebirth demands blood sacrifice, that a ritual of violent death is a necessary element toward ensuring the continuous renewal of social existence.

"The thorny crown is sharp, but sweet thereafter be the fruit." The "sweet fruit" of communal unity can be achieved only through the "thorny crown" of unanimous violence applied to the appropriate surrogate victims, on the one hand close enough to the community to be a valid recipient of that community's self-directed hostility, and on the other sufficiently distant to carry the resulting violence away from the community without threat of reciprocation leading to social breakdown. These victims are killed not because they represent an external threat. Rather, they personify the internal discord and disunity inherent to any society, blamed for that society's failure to bring the individuals that compose it to a state of perfect fulfillment, both historically and up to the present moment.

---

[152] Wachtel 2004: 134.

5

Implications to Politics and Diplomacy

In 1971, *Newsweek* journalist Stewart Alsop reported the complaint of a top U.S. State Department official who said that Israeli Prime Minister Golda Meir's "Masada complex" was undermining efforts to reach a compromise with the Arabs. Two years later, Alsop reported Meir's response:

... She suddenly turned and fixed me with a basilisk eye. "And you, Mr. Alsop," she said, "you say that we have a Masada complex."

"It is true," she said. "We do have a Masada complex. We have a pogrom complex. We have a Hitler complex."

Then she gave a small, moving oration about the spirit of Israel, a spirit that would prefer death rather than surrender to the dark terrors of the Jewish past.[1]

Meir explicitly connects Masada with pogroms and the Holocaust, linking in continuity the anti-Jewish violence that purportedly caused the end of Jewish sovereignty in ancient times with that of modern times that justified Zionism as a movement effecting its restoration. In doing so, she identifies these violent episodes as bookends enclosing a long period of oppression never to be repeated. But she also embraces the notion that this perception of history amounts to a "complex," albeit one that can and should inform her political decisions and assessments.

Defending the Totem: Defeat Monuments as Axis Points

We tread on dangerous ground when we endeavor to extrapolate widespread psychological effects with a potential impact on political

---

[1] Quoted in Zerubavel 1995: 209.

decision making from a narrow category of cultural myths culled from a
limited set of texts. A society is a reality *sui generis* to be studied in its own
right, not simply the sum of the individuals who compose it, and therefore one must guard against the trap of psychoanalytic reductionism,
whereby sociopolitical phenomena are essentialized into an element of
individual psychology and a society is treated as though it were a patient
suffering from a collective disorder. Nonetheless, we must consider the
possibility that the placement of a particular sort of symbol at the center
of a communal mythology might have an aggregate effect on how members of that community are socialized, rendering them more inclined to
adopt certain attitudes and engage in certain behaviors that in turn have
the capacity to shape public opinion and policy. Certainly, the obvious
importance of these texts to the national culture has led to introspection
along these lines within societies that elevate symbols of defeat in their
national mythologies.

Along with the decline of the Masada myth in Israel came an effort at
self-criticism within the society, in which scholars began to examine the
effects of the elevation of this event to the status of a national symbol.
Israeli social psychologist Daniel Bar-Tal has proposed that it generates
what resembles a pathological state, referring to the "Masada Syndrome"
defined as "a state in which members of a group hold a central belief that
the rest of the world has negative behavioural intentions toward that
group," stressing, as well, that this expectation can be self-fulfilling.[2]
Masada came to represent an omnipresent threat throughout Jewish history; a symbol not only of the defeat in 73 C.E. but also of pogroms,
the Holocaust, of what would have awaited Israel had it not won the
Six Day War, and of what still awaits it should it lose its position of
relative strength. It became a powerful symbol of a people that dwells
alone, a people that can rely on no one but themselves; a central tenet of
Israel's civil religion, as well as a belief key to mass mobilization in the
name of distinctly national goals.[3] In a 1973 column in the newspaper
Ha'Aretz, Israeli historian Benjamin Kedar argued that this attitude can
be dangerous when it distorts the vision of those in power:

It is desirable that a political leader have a sense of history. But he would be better
off devoid of all historical sense rather than to cling compulsively to a specific
image from the past and act as though it were literally applicable to him and his
situation in the present. For in that case reality is not grasped as it actually is but

---

[2] Zerubavel 1995: 211.
[3] Liebman and Don-Yehiya 1983: 149.

according to its degree of correspondence to preconceptions drawn before the fact from the past.... In this context, the recollection of Masada is less an inspiring model than an obfuscating obsession, a complex that could pervert moral criteria. For if in fact our situation is as desperate as Masada's, the lines of demarcation between forbidden and permitted begin to waver.[4]

One would imagine that a symbol of defeat would provide a community with a conceptual framework for accepting and coping with defeat. And, indeed, such symbols do accomplish this purpose in non-national symbol systems, as we have seen in the cases of traditional Judaism and the prenational Greek Orthodox Church, providing a theodicy to reconcile acceptance of an ongoing state of subjugation with continuity of the community and the continued efficacy of its core beliefs. But reinterpreted to serve the needs of a national form of social organization, they become foundation myths; pivotal moments of birth that, as such, cannot be repeated. The defeat does not mark an end but rather the moment when the ongoing struggle for fulfillment, a struggle that is itself the nation, began. Therefore, a repetition of the defeat would serve to mark the surrender of the struggle, the failure of the national mission, in effect, the dissolution of the nation itself. When every challenge confronted by the nation-state is viewed through the prism of a struggle between survival and destruction, middle ground becomes blurred. Behavior that would normally seem unacceptable becomes tolerable as necessary self-defense, not just of life but of a principle that is viewed within the national meaning system as higher than one's own mortal existence. Violence comes to be seen as a form of "vaccination," a mythic dynamic described by Roland Barthes whereby momentary evil is justified by the rationalization that it serves to prevent a greater and more permanent evil.[5] The effect is often that those responsible for setting Israeli foreign policy are inclined to discount the position of strength that the nation-state finds itself in as a regional power, instead seeing the Jewish state as inherently in the stranglehold of superior forces and thus compelled to conduct itself with what Robert Alter referred to as "a sacred sense of desperation."[6]

The Masada complex has its Serbian parallel in what Serbian sociologist Jovan Cvijić termed the "Dinaric Personality," formed through the blending of the Serbian patriarchal society with the epic folk tradition.

---

[4] Kedar 1982 provides an English translation of this article. Another article critical of this aspect of Israeli political culture is Alter, "The Masada Complex," *Commentary* 56 (July 1973): 19–24.
[5] Discussed in relation to the Serbian myth–symbol system in Velikonja 1998: 35.
[6] Alter 1973: 24.

The key characteristic of this personality lies in the blurring of distinctions between the mythic past and current reality: "Every Dinaric peasant considers the national heroes as his own ancestors . . . in his thoughts he participates in their great deeds and in their immeasurable suffering. . . . He knows not only the names of the Kosovo heroes but also what kind of person each one was and what were his virtues and faults. . . . For the Dinaric man to kill as many Turks means not only to avenge his ancestors but also to ease their pains which he himself feels."[7] Serbian psychotherapist Zoran Milivojević adds that another characteristic is "a feeling of spite [*inat*] or defiance [*prkos*]. We are really masters in that. Defiance always appears when someone important or stronger is regarded as having a negative image of us. By means of spite we convey a practical demonstration of our identity, thereby conveying that we are 'someone'. When you look at our national history we see that it is full of 'no' – from 'no' to the Turkish empire, to 'no' to Austria-Hungary, 'no' to Hitler and Stalin, to Europe, to the NATO pact."[8] In this register, Kosovo is not simply a medieval battle but rather what Njegoš termed an "unremitting struggle." Should that struggle cease to be "unremitting," the nation would dissolve along with it. This inclines toward the perception of any external threat as a mortal one, again blurring the lines between the permissible and the forbidden. When the myth is activated, it produces a sense that the nation is continually on the verge of destruction or dissolution, which leads to a chronic wartime mentality inclined toward the perception of all nonconformists as traitors or enemies and a mistrust of compromise as a form of vassalage. "Taken to its extreme, this feeling of historical victimization is often expressed in delusions of persecution and also the rectitude of one's cause, or what has been comparatively termed a 'paranoid style of politics.'"[9]

But even taking aside the possibility of such mass psychological effects, the mere recognition of the totemic role that symbols of defeat can occupy under certain conditions should influence our understanding of the character that political conflicts involving those symbols can assume. If a symbol amounts to the nation's effective if not purported foundation myth, a threat to it threatens the very foundations of the nation. Understanding this will help to explain why nations might react more explosively to the violation of some symbols rather than others, enabling policy makers to

---

[7] Quoted in Emmert 1990: 134–5.
[8] Quoted in Cohen 2001: 285.
[9] Cohen 2001: 81.

better predict what sorts of impulses will lead to violent reactions. For a fundamental aspect of the totem as the symbolic embodiment of sovereign violence is that it cannot be seen to lose. This is not the same as saying that it cannot be defeated, but defeat must be transformable into a sort of moral victory for which the continued presence of the totem at the defining head of the group affords it an aura of durability – immortality, as it were – even in the face of catastrophe.

Desecration of the totem amounts to a claim over its killing authority, an act that threatens the entire social contract and therefore the group.[10] Taboos only need exist in order to prevent individuals from doing what they would otherwise desire to do: to touch or destroy the totem, to appropriate its power. That an outsider, unaffected by these taboos, should be able to attack or appropriate the totem in a manner that should only be possible for the entire community in its unanimity is unthinkable, in that it threatens to expose the illusory nature of the restraints that prevent individuals within the community from doing likewise. Violations of the totem must be avenged unanimously by the community in order to obscure the envious desire felt by each member to mimic the violation. The impulse to vengeance reflects an awareness that if the violation were not avenged, desire to imitate it would take hold in other members of the community, leading to the community's dissolution. Thus, conflicts over totem symbols will take on a sacred character of desperation, as impossible for outsiders to comprehend as is the unanimity of purpose generated by such conflicts. It is only a select set of symbols within a given community that will have this unanimous and unifying appeal, but any conflict in which such symbols are a factor will take on a different character to one in which they are not.

In an article for the *New York Times* titled "Independence for Kosovo," historian Noel Malcolm, further to his general outlook on conflict in the Balkans as the result of political manipulations rather than "ancient hatreds," dismissed the mythic and religious connection of Serbs to Kosovo as an irrelevant factor to the resolution of the conflict. Downplaying the importance of Kosovo's "holy sites," he claimed that Milošević's real interest in the territory was economic, involving "the rich mines of the Trepca district and their associated factories and power plants."[11] While I would not venture to speculate on Milošević's personal motives, it is difficult to believe that the near-universal support

---

[10] Marvin and Ingle 1999: 76.
[11] Malcolm 1999a.

for his policy on Kosovo across the Serbian political spectrum, which Malcolm also highlights, could be aroused solely by images of mines and power plants. Malcolm refers to the rationalization that Serbia should have sovereignty over Kosovo's churches and monasteries as "a pious fiction," noting that surveys before the war showed Serbs to be "the most nonreligious population in the former Yugoslavia." But the importance of these churches and monasteries lies more in their status as national monuments than in their function as religious shrines, and national religiosity is expressed in a different way than its traditional counterpart. It is not measured by the frequency with which one attends services but rather lies in the commitment to keep the monument within the boundaries of the nation's sovereign territory. Just as nationalists desire to be governed by those of their own culture, so too must symbols that represent mythic objects and figures incorporated into the national communion enjoy the same rights. To allow the battlefield of Kosovo Polje to be ruled by outsiders is to permit Lazar and Miloš Obilić to live under the subjugation to which they refused to submit in their own lifetimes and to allow the medieval monasteries to be incorporated into a foreign polity is to do the same to Milutin and Stefan Dušan. So long as objects that serve as totemic symbols of the national communion remain in a state of domination, the nation cannot be truly free.

The ancient hatreds versus modern manipulations debate with regard to Kosovo continued on the pages of *Foreign Affairs* when Aleksa Djilas published a review of Malcolm's book, *Kosovo: A Short History*, that alleged that the historian was affected by an anti-Serb bias.[12] Malcolm responded that he was not "anti-Serb but anti-myth" and that the impression of bias stemmed from the fact that Serbs simply had more myths in relation to Kosovo than any other people.[13] But at issue is not merely the quantity of myths a nation has but also their character. The Serbs are the only people for whom the territory of Kosovo embodies their foundation myth, which is why it is understandably difficult to distinguish between being anti-Serb and being anti-myth in this case. If a nation, as an imagined community, amounts to the sum total of myths and symbols that serve to unify and reify its distinct social order, there is little perceptible difference, at least from the perspective of an insider, between opposing the nation's foundation myth and opposing the nation itself. This is something that Djilas, being an insider to the Serbian myth–symbol system,

---

[12] Djilas 1998.
[13] Malcolm 1999b.

appeared to implicitly understand but could not articulate, seeing as it is hardly an intellectual argument. Malcolm's suggestion that the resolution to the Kosovo conflict lay in the Serbs recognizing that their national myths were dangerous and historically inaccurate, and thereby letting them go and permitting Kosovo's Albanian majority the independence they desired, amounted to a demand that they discard their collective memory, deny their identity. Telling a Serb to simply give up on Kosovo is tantamount to telling him to stop being a Serb.

By now there should be no illusions that a slogan like "Masada shall not fall again" speaks to a desire to defend the strategically insignificant site of the mountain itself. What it really means is "Israel shall not fall again." Ever since the publication of Lamdan's poem first made this analogy explicit, carrying through to the use of the symbol to encourage national mobilization, Masada became a symbol of the national vision itself. As much as the purpose of this work is to explore the question of how and why this happened, such an explanation is important only because of the need to fully grasp the implications of the fact that it has happened. And if understanding the psychological dynamics that underlie this equation serves to explain why certain symbols develop this quality for certain nations under certain circumstances, the reactions of communities to threats or attacks against such symbols can be better understood, perhaps even predicted, rather than simply dismissed as irrational and, as such, a factor that cannot be accounted for in international relations and diplomacy. I would speculate, for example, that even the most cynical, left-leaning academic fully versed in Josephus, who questions the historicity of the mythic narrative and decries the problematic of the resulting "Masada complex," would be just as unlikely as anyone else within the national tradition to advocate or accept the surrender of the site to a foreign polity, especially an enemy, were this ever to be a realistic possibility, at least so long as he or she identified in any way as Zionist. To do so would represent the surrender and dissolution of the Jewish state itself, through the severing of the tie to antiquity it requires for its legitimacy, the dissolution of a nodal point that serves to encapsulate and represent a wide range of core national myths, images, and values. Fortunately, such a territorial concession has never been suggested since the founding of the state, so it is an issue we may never have to confront. However, this issue does encroach on politics with regard to the Western Wall.

According to Jewish tradition, the presence of the Temple afforded a sanctity to the whole of the city of Jerusalem, right up to its outer walls. However, the Temple grounds were holier than the rest of the city, and on the grounds, various barriers marked increasing levels beyond which only certain categories of people could go at certain times, until one reached the focal point, housed in the Holy of Holies, into which only the High Priest could go, and only on one day each year. Such increasing levels of numinous power as one approaches the *axis mundi* are described by Eliade as characteristic of religious shrines. And aside from the stratification of society incompatible with a national ideology implicit in the Temple tradition, the *axis natio* of the Western Wall exhibits a similar dynamic. Although anyone can visit the Wall at any time, there is a definite sense that norms of behavior change as one crosses the threshold into the plaza, then again as one crosses the barrier into the section of the plaza closest to the Wall designated as a synagogue. These stages can be viewed as a national equivalent to the increasing levels of holiness experienced as one approached the original Temple. In the informal section of the plaza, various groups can interact; men and women, tourists and locals, Jews of various religious persuasions along with non-Jews, children, and adults, and so on. In the synagogue section, men and women are separated. The free availability of various ritual items enforces a sense of being in a different place where different rules apply, while at the same time giving the impression that the site is open to all.

The notion of increasing levels of sanctity as one approaches the center has political implications as well, as demonstrated by a poll conducted during the early stages of the Oslo peace process, which revealed that 80% of Israelis at the time were not willing to contemplate negotiation with the Palestinians over the future of Jerusalem. When asked to specify what was meant by this, by identifying whether various sites and areas were considered "important to you as part of Jerusalem," an astonishing 91% of respondents identified the Western Wall as "very important," with another 8% citing it as "important." This result remained remarkably consistent across the political spectrum, showing slight variation only in the distribution between "important" and "very important." Although 100% of respondents associated with religious parties cited the Western Wall as "very important," 85% of Labor voters did so, with 13% identifying it as merely "important." Even among supporters of the smaller, secularist Meretz party, to the left of Labor, 72% cited the Western Wall as "very important," with another 18% identifying it as "important." By comparison, and as a further illustration of the political implication of these decreasing levels of national sanctity, the total number of respondents who identified the rest of the Jewish Quarter of the Old City as either "very important" or "important" to them as part of Jerusalem was

79% and 15%, respectively. For new Jewish neighborhoods outside of
the Old City, the results were 75% and 20%; 34% and 25% for the
non-Jewish quarters of the Old City; whereas non-Jewish areas of down-
town Jerusalem showed results of only 24% and 21%.[14] Intransigence
increases as one approaches the axis point, both physically and conceptually, to the point where the number opposed to compromise over the
Wall itself reflects a rejection of the notion across the whole of the Zionist
political spectrum.

At the same time, however, the very universality of the symbol renders it a potent image at times of political conflict, employed as a litmus test of political legitimacy. This is illustrated by a political cartoon
produced by the right-wing cartoonist Oleg around the same time as the
just-mentioned poll, which depicted then Prime Minister Yitzchak Rabin,
standing at the Western Wall dressed in the accoutrements of traditional
Jewish prayer and addressing the edifice, "I know I previously pledged
I will not go down from the Golan; that I will not give up Aza; and, in
addition, that I will not talk to the PLO; Now, I swear that forever I will
never abandon *you*." Although the message of the cartoon might be controversial, the point of interest is that the message is nonetheless clear to
anyone who reads it from within the Zionist symbol system: Each broken
promise is portrayed as an incremental betrayal of the national values,
which will lead inevitably and in stages to what is depicted and widely
understood as the ultimate capitulation, the surrender of the Western
Wall. Not everyone within the Zionist political spectrum would consider
Rabin's earlier compromises as betrayals, neither would they agree that
they would inevitably result in the loss of the Wall. But all would recognize the surrender of the Wall as symbolic of the abandonment of the
nation's core values, and the suggestion that Rabin could not be trusted
not to entertain such a compromise is meant to place him outside the
bounds of political acceptability.

What must be recognized is that although there are many political
issues relating to the relationship between territory and identity that
remain matters of intense dispute within Israeli society, the notion that
the Western Wall must remain under Jewish sovereignty is entirely uncontroversial. It is acknowledged even by those of the Zionist left who are
otherwise willing to entertain far-reaching territorial compromises. It is
acknowledged even by radical secularists who, although they may have
nothing but disdain for the religious character of the site, nonetheless

---

[14] Segal et al. 2000: Appendix A-2, 243–4.

place great importance on the fact that traditional Jews are free to practice their religion there unmolested. Israelis who have no personal desire
to visit the Wall, and who might never do so in their lives, nonetheless
need to know that they can if they so choose, or at least that those Jews
who are inclined to do so can on the nation's behalf, in much the way
that Serbs who might never see Kosovo Polje must know that it and the
Serbs who do choose to live there remain in the same state of freedom
they desire for the nation as a whole. Therefore, no leader, on the left or
the right, who wishes to retain the support of the nation, could entertain
the prospect of willingly surrendering these sites. Although Israelis have
proven increasingly willing to consider compromise over Jerusalem, at
least with regards to some of its lesser layers of sanctity, compromise
over the national Holy of Holies remains beyond the realm of what is
imaginable. Neither would it be an exaggeration to say that this will
always be the case, for in order for this condition to change, the Zionist
myth–symbol system would have to change so radically that it would
become an entirely different identity.

This introduces obstacles to peace negotiations, for although allowing
the Temple Mount to remain under Muslim religious sovereignty has not
caused significant ideological difficulties over the past four decades, dividing the city according to the principle of national territorial sovereignty
presents practical complications. Proposals over the division of Jerusalem
have not only to determine a way of placing an international boundary
through the middle of the walled Old City but in such a way that the
platform of the Haram would be located in one national polity while its
retaining wall remains in another.

But the news should not be interpreted as all bad. For although our
model has the potential to identify and explain a narrow set of sites and
symbols over which a nation might be expected to be intransigent to
the point of fanaticism, it also, by extension, has the potential to show
that this same nation is just as liable to be more accommodating than
expected over sites and symbols outside of that narrow set. We have
seen, for example, that beyond a small religious–nationalist constituency,
the Temple Mount itself is largely irrelevant if not abject to Israel's mainstream political culture. Yet the expectation, sensible on its face, that the
Jewish national movement must ultimately seek to assert sovereignty over
the Jewish religion's holiest site has been at the core of several political
misunderstandings, often to the point of violent conflict.

In September of 1996, the opening by Israeli authorities of a second
alternative entrance to a tunnel that allowed tourists and worshippers

access to excavations of the Western Wall sparked violent protests on the part of Palestinians that ultimately left 80 Palestinians and 15 Israelis dead. The protests were driven by a perception that has been a consistent factor in conflict over the site: that any challenge to the status quo represented the thin end of a wedge, leading to the assertion of more far-reaching Jewish claims over the Temple Mount. The fear was that this move was part of a secret agenda by Israeli authorities to excavate under the Dome of the Rock and thereby undermine it – both physically, in terms of causing the platform to collapse, and metaphorically in terms of challenging Muslim historical claims to sole sovereignty over the site – fueled by hyperbolic rumors that "the Jews are attacking the Haram al-Sharif."[15] From the point of view of Israelis, however, such a disproportionate reaction to such a trivial action that in practice affected only the Western Wall fed stereotypes of the intransigence and paranoia of the Other.

Although several explanations can be offered for the eventual breakdown of peace negotiations, the event that is widely deemed by both sides to have sparked descent into open violence was Likud leader Ariel Sharon's September 2000 visit to the Haram. Sharon can be said to have brilliantly manipulated both sides' lack of understanding of the other. Fully aware that his visit would be perceived by Palestinians as an assertion of sovereignty, a violent reaction was expected. Yet for Israelis, most of whom take for granted that they desire no effective sovereignty over the site, this reaction once again fed perceptions that the Palestinians were eager to seize on any pretext to violently reject the proposals for peaceful coexistence that were simultaneously on offer from Prime Minister Ehud Barak at the Camp David summit.[16] Five months later, Sharon was elected prime minister and the Palestinians were in the midst of their "Second Intifada," tellingly referred to as the "Al-Aqsa Intifada" for the site where it began and the shrine that was perceived as being defended.

Heroes and Saviors and the Autocratic Democrat: The Career of Slobodan Milošević

A comparable dynamic is evident in Serbian attitudes toward Kosovo, where the sense of sanctity increases as one conceptually approaches the

[15] Enderlin 2003, 53–8.
[16] Ibid., 284–97.

focal point: the field of Kosovo Polje where the medieval battle took place. Lesser levels of sanctity are attributed to other points conceptually related: the remnant Serbian communities surrounding the site, the medieval monasteries built at the height of the Nemanjić Empire, the territory of Kosovo as a whole, and, finally, other Serbian minority communities throughout Yugoslavia whose plights are seen as comparable to as well as the consequence of the mythic defeat. This sanctity is not dependent on political orientation, and though liberal elements of Serbia's political spectrum might phrase their interest in Kosovo in secular democratic terms relating to their concern that the rights of minorities (read: Serbs) in the region be protected, the notion that Kosovo must remain in some way connected to Serbia is uncontroversial throughout Serbian political culture. Willingness to defend Kosovo is the litmus test that defines the suitability of a leader to act on behalf of the nation not just with regard to Kosovo's territory but in other situations as well.

It is only in light of this that one can even begin to appreciate the extraordinary opportunity that was presented to Slobodan Milošević as a Serbian politician in a position to represent himself as the unique defender of Kosovo. Numerous scholars have commented on how central mobilization of the Kosovo myth was to Milosevic's rise to power. In particular, his campaign for the rights of Kosovo Serbs, beginning with his unexpectedly forceful defense of protestors at a meeting in 1987 where he uttered the iconic line "No one is allowed to beat you!,"[17] the revocation of Kosovo's autonomous status, and his orchestration of massive celebrations for the 600th anniversary of the battle in 1989.[18] As one commentator put it:

By taking a decisive leadership role at the time of his 1987 intervention in the affairs of Kosovo and the 'anti-bureaucratic revolution', Milošević was able to implant himself in the consciousness of a wide section of Serbian opinion. He became a *supra-political* figure whose actions were not judged by normal political criteria and whose popularity was largely detached from the reputation of the political organization of which he was the leader. Although his standing as a modern political icon suffered from a process of ongoing decline in the eyes of particular groups such as the urban population, he maintained a high

---

[17] As rendered by Dragović-Soso (2002: 208) and Cohen (2001: 63), in its immediate context it was an apparently spontaneous expression of support for the protestors against the police, already a striking position for a representative of the ruling party to adopt. However, it was sometimes imbued with deeper historical implications when it was repeatedly rebroadcast on Radio-Television Belgrade, and has been translated impressionistically at times by commentators and journalists to reflect these implications.

[18] Cohen 2001: 97–100.

degree of loyalty among a certain core of the electorate in spite of the increasing economic misery in Serbia and the failure of his national policies. Milošević's support remained strongest among the rural population and industrial workers of Serbia whose political loyalties were determined more by the attraction of 'symbols of power' than by the merits of policy in the civic marketplace of ideas.[19]

But this is not to suggest, as some commentators have, that Milošević's continued popularity – indeed, his political survival over a decade that saw the overthrow of nearly every other communist regime in Eastern Europe – was a direct product of his activation of atavistic Serbian ethnic myths in the political arena. If that were all that was needed, there were plenty of nationalist leaders who appealed to these myths more overtly in the course of advocating equally aggressive measures over Kosovo. And although these figures may have had their followings, none of them was able to penetrate the political mainstream in the same manner, but they were widely perceived as primitive, dangerous, destabilizing influences, and indeed were portrayed as such in Milošević's own political rhetoric.[20] Milošević's appeal lay rather in his unique positioning to manage the ambivalence that such ethnic myths evoke. He did not invoke Kosovo imagery and advocate for the defense of Kosovo Serbs in the name of the ethnic tradition but rather for the continued stability and modest reform of the modern socialist state; it was not, at least at first, portrayed as a struggle for Greater Serbia but rather for the preservation of the multinational Yugoslavian framework *against* the forces of reactionary nationalism that threatened it.

By using the issue of the Kosovo Serbs as a means to associate himself with symbols that were universal to Serbian national identity, Milošević was able to stand out from other communist party leaders and appeal to a wider constituency that included anticommunists and the nationalist intelligentsia. Through his ability to associate himself with national symbols that crossed ideological boundaries, he set himself up not just as a political leader but also as a national figurehead, above the political structures and institutions he led and beyond the reach of mundane political criticism. In this way, he was able not only to remain in power, along with his party and ruling elite, but also to maintain his inordinate level of authority through the whole of the following decade. This was

[19] Thomas 1999: 425–6.
[20] Gagnon 2004: 46–7; see also his analysis of the rhetoric surrounding the 1990 elections (97–100).

despite numerous policy failures and increasing democratization pressures in Serbian society, which prior to the upheavals of the late 1980s had been assessed as one of the most promising in terms of its capacity to develop democratic institutions.

The contemporary experiences of other Eastern European countries had demonstrated that under normal conditions, the nationalist vision could enable diverse opposition groups to unite, if only temporarily, against the regime, after which the collapse of the coalition would bring with it the seeds of democratic pluralism. But in Serbia, the ruling party co-opted nationalist discourse in the interests of mobilizing the political energies of the population as communism was collapsing, thereby denying the opposition a platform over which to unify. Thus, the transition from one-party totalitarianism to pluralism was arrested, leaving a system in which weak democratic institutions mixed uneasily with authoritarian structures left over from the communist period, all of which were overshadowed by the influence of Milošević whose authority relied on the suprapolitical status he had acquired in part through his activation of the Kosovo myth.[21]

This was possible in part because of the nature of the Serbian myth and in part because of the manner and timing of Milošević's exploitation of it. Unlike the socialist partisan symbols employed by communist Yugoslavia, which referred to a divided wartime past and therefore could appeal to only a particular segment of the population, Kosovo was a unifying symbol. It had different meanings to different segments of Serbian political culture, but the fact that the symbol itself did not inherently contain any particular political or doctrinal position only added to its status as a common signifier that transcended the considerations of party politics and could therefore be used to bolster any policy. It was a symbol that merged the norm of a princely, autocratic leader with the glorification of a horizontally configured national society. It was a symbol that could be applied both to Serbian particularism, to a pan-Yugoslavian idea, or, as increasingly became the case, to a blending of these two principles. And it was a symbol that focused the nation on uniting against external enemies, tending toward a siege mentality in which opposition is equated with victimization, internal dissent with treason and defection, and compromise with surrender. As Lenard Cohen observes in his study of Milošević, "central to the myth is the notion of heroism, both a heroic figure who although lonely and misunderstood on the eve of battle will

---

[21] Thomas 1999: 3–4.

single-handedly sacrifice his life against superior odds to achieve glory, and also the heroic existence of the Serbian army, which is willing to offer resistance to a superior force no matter what the cost."[22]

But although much has been made of the role of the Kosovo myth in facilitating Milošević's rise to and hold on power, there has been comparatively little consideration of the role of that same myth in his eventual fall; or, more accurately, of the extent to which his fall may well have been built in to the manner of his rise. For although appeal to Kosovo might be a reliable way to mobilize support in a Serbian national political context, one must not forget that the Kosovo narrative can have only one possible ending: the self-sacrifice of the autocrat and his earthly kingdom in favor of the kingdom of the spirit. This was a sacrifice that Milošević was ultimately unwilling to make.

There was widespread consensus among diplomats who encountered Milošević during the 1990s that he was by and large a pragmatist, with little personal concern for the ideal of Greater Serbia beyond the point to which this notion could be used to serve the interests of enhancing and maintaining his personal authority. As British negotiator David Owen observed, "there is a ruthlessness and a pursuit of power for its own sake about Milošević that underpins the pragmatism that otherwise seems so neatly to characterize Milošević's political personality.... Milošević carries his nationalism lightly and it does not intrude in an offensive manner in conversations with foreigners. He has used nationalism for the purpose of gaining and holding power but his economic attitudes are those of a man fully conscious of international realities."[23] This could be used to their advantage, as the proper combination of incentives and threats had been known to turn Milošević from a belligerent into a force for moderation. It was, for example, air strikes against Bosnian Serbs in 1995 that brought Milošević to the negotiating table to agree to the Dayton Accords, and his capitulation did little significant damage to his broader base of support.[24] The territory of Bosnia or Krajina, although no

---

[22] Cohen 2001: 101.

[23] Owen 1995: 135.

[24] Although it should be noted that this move prompted Bosnian Serb leaders to condemn Milošević in terms that compared him to Vuk Branković. For example, Tomislav Nikolić wrote in *Velika Srbija*, "The Serbian nation remembers Vuk Branković as the greatest traitor in their history. Apart from the folk-songs there is no reliable evidence that Vuk Branković was a traitor or that he was the chief commander of the Serbian army at the battle of Kosovo. You, Mr. Milošević, are the greatest traitor in history. You are the commander of the Serbian armies ... all that has happened to us has happened under your command and the blame for it must fall on your head"(quoted in Thomas 1999:

doubt of great significance to the Serbs who lived there, did not hold the same symbolic value to the nation as a whole as did Kosovo. Therefore, although Milošević could enhance his prestige with nationalist segments of the population through his support for Serbs in Bosnia and Croatia, he could also compromise without seriously damaging his nationalist reputation, preserved through his continued association with Kosovo's more universal symbols. However, in his book detailing his experiences in the negotiations over Bosnia, Owen noted that Kosovo was a very different situation:

On almost every occasion that we met I would at some stage raise Kosovo, and when I did I knew I was striking a jarring note. Over Kosovo the polite mask sometime broke and we would be in an ugly confrontation. It was as if he knew this was the area of his most indefensible behaviour on which he was personally vulnerable.... It was on Kosovo that Milošević had risen to power and in the process had spoken for almost all Serbs, who genuinely believed Tito had sacrificed their interests for the sake of keeping the Albanians quiet... yet Milošević will know that Kosovo could be his undoing.... I have often likened him to someone who has jumped onto the tiger of nationalism and is finding it hard to get off again without the tiger eating him.[25]

Owen's observations about the coming conflict in Kosovo would prove accurate for, to take his metaphor further, Kosovo was not merely another portion of the tiger's anatomy, it was the heart of the beast. Milosevic could not dismount without its devouring him, and he knew it. NATO leaders, however, were not so farsighted. When violent insurrection in Kosovo began in earnest under the Kosova Liberation Army (KLA) in 1997, they failed to consider the possibility that their dealings with Milošević under these conditions would be any different than they had been over Bosnia. It was the perception of Milošević as a self-interested pragmatist, as well as a dictator who held sole decision-making authority, that made it reasonable to assume that he would back down at the last minute or, at worst, after a brief and token assault provided him with sufficient pretext to do so without losing face. A press statement by NATO Secretary-General Javier Solana neatly summarized the misperceptions that led to this failure of diplomacy: "we have no quarrel with the people of Yugoslavia who for too long have been isolated in Europe because

242). This serves as example of the use of the universal symbols of Kosovo to express a local Bosnian-Serb message. It is also interesting to note that Nikolić's questioning of the factual accuracy of the epics does not interfere with the force of the symbol.
[25] Owen 1995: 137.

of the policies of their government. Our actions are directed against the repressive policy of the Yugoslav leadership."[26]

The perception of Yugoslavia as a simple authoritarian state with Milošević as its dictator, acting in defiance of popular will, caused NATO leaders to ignore the complexities of Serbian politics and to disregard the unique symbolic role that Kosovo played in Serbian national identity, thereby failing to credit how these factors combined in a way that was crucial to Milošević's hold on power. Because Milošević's authority depended on his suprapolitical status as national figurehead, which he enjoyed by virtue of his association with these national symbols, he could not be expected to take any action that would threaten that association so long as he wished to remain in power. Thus, the expectation that Milošević would easily allow himself to be seen as capitulating under pressure over any issue relating to Kosovo, even pressure of the sort that may have worked when other issues were at stake, was highly unrealistic. It was possible in Serbia, as in Israel, to compromise over some of the lesser areas of sanctity. Although this would antagonize the nationalist right increasingly as these compromises approached the symbolic center, much as the Israeli right was aggravated by any prospect of negotiation over Jerusalem, so long as Milošević's identification with the universal focal point remained secure, his status as a national icon was not threatened. But having come to power as the defender of Kosovo, he could not be seen to betray it without undermining the very reason for his being in power in the eyes of a core segment of the population whose support he did, in fact, require to maintain his legitimacy and capacity to stifle opposition. When presented at the Rambouillet Conference with terms that demanded that Serbia relinquish effective sovereignty over the whole of the territory of Kosovo, he knew he could not submit to them without losing the symbolic status of national leader he required to maintain his political authority as head of the national state.

Because of these misperceptions, NATO's intervention served to exacerbate the very humanitarian catastrophe it was meant to prevent. Once the Rambouillet talks dissolved and it became clear that military action was inevitable, the Serbian government responded in a way that NATO leaders neither anticipated nor prepared for, launching a preemptive offensive against the KLA with the objective of clearing the southern and western parts of Kosovo bordering on Albania and Macedonia, while

---

[26] Quoted in Judah 2000: 234.

imposing ruthless internal security throughout the province. The operation resulted in more than 800,000 Albanians fleeing the province, and tens of thousands more were displaced internally.[27] Whether the expulsion of the Albanian population was the goal of Serbian forces or the unlamented effect of the escalation of their offensive against the KLA, there was undoubtedly a link between the NATO bombing of Serbia and the actions of Serbian forces in Kosovo. If the goal of Serbian forces was the expulsion of the Albanians, the bombing gave them a cover and a pretext they would not otherwise have had to carry it out. If their aim was the destruction of the guerrillas by any means necessary, then their operation had to be escalated drastically before NATO air power became available to deny them the use of heavy weapons. Although Serbian forces were clearly the instrument of the refugee crisis, NATO's coming war was a proximate cause.

Some Western leaders expressed a hope that even if Milošević would not give in, the hardship caused by a heavy and sustained bombing campaign would provoke the democratic opposition to overthrow him.[28] This was perhaps the clearest illustration of their naïveté, for the centrality of Kosovo to the Serbian national myth was such that the territory's symbolic importance transcended conventional political ideologies and formations, influencing the internationalist left as much as the nationalist right. It was true that by the late 1990s domestic dissatisfaction with the regime was already widespread, and protests in the winter of 1996–1997 had proved the existence of a large and active pro-reform constituency. However, repression in Kosovo had not been an issue during those protests.[29] Even if it had been, nothing would have done more harm to the democratic opposition than to be seen as attacking the leader who had set himself up as the defender of Kosovo at the very moment the epic battle over the territory was being refought. It would have placed them in the role of betrayer of the nation, an association from which the opposition, and possibly their pro-democracy platform, would not have easily recovered.

Instead, the opposite occurred, and the war created a wave of patriotic fever in which the differences among the nation, the regime, and the leader blurred in the face of a common external enemy, resulting in a mood of national solidarity to the benefit of the ruling regime. NATO

---

[27] McGwire 2000: 10, 17.

[28] Judah 2000: 228–9; Gagnon 2004: 125.

[29] McGwire 2000: 4.

was playing the perfect role in Milošević's mythic drama, as the oncoming Turks against his Lazar, in effect substantiating the perception cultivated by the regime that Serbia was besieged by hostile forces of an inherently antagonistic international system with which the democratic opposition was in collusion. Any opposition, according to this model, would have been equated in the popular imagination with the treason of Vuk Branković. Both independent and state media presented a patriotic message during the bombing campaign, and even after the war, the opposition was nearly unanimous in its condemnation of NATO's intervention and its endorsement of the need to keep Kosovo as a part of Serbia. Any condemnations voiced against Milošević were not over his determination to keep Kosovo but rather were phrased in terms of his failure to defend it appropriately, either by his eventual capitulation or through the heavy-handed policies that had unnecessarily provoked the crisis in the first place.[30] As late as February 1999, an opinion poll in the opposition paper, *Dnevni Telegraf*, showed that 37% of the population was willing to defend Kosovo by force "under any circumstances," and when terms were ultimately accepted by Milošević, a comparable proportion of the Serbian parliament voted against ratifying them.[31]

But just as striking as the unanimity behind the regime generated by the bombing were the mobilization and revitalization of opposition almost immediately following the end of hostilities. In light of this, it is more plausible to conclude that it was not Milošević's stubborn resistance to NATO that contributed to his ultimate fall from power just over a year later but, on the contrary, his eventual capitulation that contributed to the loss of his status as national icon, rendering him subject to judgment on the basis of standard political criteria to which his record could not measure up. Although the terms Milošević signed on June 9 were marginally better than those offered at Rambouillet,[32] paying lip service to the principle that Kosovo would technically remain a part of Yugoslavia, their key provisions were an "immediate and verifiable" end to the violence and repression, withdrawal of Serb military and police forces from the province, the deployment of 50,000 foreign troops under a UN flag, the safe return of all refugees, and the establishment of an

---

[30] Cohen 2001: 285, 320.
[31] McGwire 2000: 19.
[32] Changes in Serbia's favor were that the NATO force in Kosovo would be joined by a token Russian contingent, and the clause that had ostensibly caused Milošević's rejection of Rambouillet, relating to transit rights through Serbia for NATO troops, was no longer included (Robertson 2000: 418).

"interim administration" for Kosovo under the auspices of the Security Council.[33] One can only wonder if, on being presented with these terms, Milošević thought of those lines from Karadžić's *Pieces from Various Kosovo Poems*:

> We cannot both of us be ruler,
> Send every key to me and every tax,
> The keys of gold that unlock the cities,
> And the taxes on heads for seven years,
> And if you will not send these things to me,
> Then come down to Kosovo meadow,
> We shall divide up this land with our swords![34]

Milošević handed over the keys, choosing dishonorable vassalage to preserve his earthly kingdom, over continued hopeless resistance to preserve his autonomy in the heavenly one, and with the signing and implementation of these terms, Serbia surrendered effective sovereignty over the territory of Kosovo.

Several commentators noted that postwar opposition to the regime took on a very different tone than had the student protests of 1996–1997, evident in the fact that government propaganda now began to look desperate, stressing contradictory themes in an effort to recapture the familiar ground of Kosovo rhetoric. On the one hand, Milošević claimed glorious victory in the struggle against NATO, while at the same time resolving to reverse the defeat and regain Kosovo as soon as possible. Another common theme was the importance of stopping "traitors," a loosely defined group that essentially included anyone who appeared to oppose the state's postwar goals as the regime defined them.[35] But the loss of Kosovo had broken the ruling regime's monopoly over the legitimate use of nationalism, giving the opposition a means to unite that had been denied them over the previous decade. Milošević was no longer a symbol of Serb patriotism, either to the people or, just as significant, to the army. Stripped of the aura of personal authority that had enabled him to wield inordinate influence over the institutions of power, his ability to fix elections or enforce his rule in the face of opposition by means of his security apparatus was severely weakened. Dissent was no longer psychologically equivalent to treason, and opposition candidate Vojislav Koštunica was able to plausibly combine his Western-oriented and democratic outlook

---

[33] Alexander 2000: 437.
[34] Quoted in Koljević: 129.
[35] Cohen 2001: 316–17.

with an unsullied nationalist reputation. Unlike Milošević, he had preserved his heavenly kingdom: He had unreservedly condemned NATO attacks on Yugoslavia and supported the government's refusal to accept the Rambouillet terms.

Given the capacity of the regime to manipulate the results, Koštunica's first-round victory in the elections of 2000 was nothing short of overwhelming, reflecting Milošević's clear loss of mandate to exercise state power in a democratic polity. Most striking is the estimate made by opposition leaders that some 80% of the military vote, normally a safe reservoir of support for the ruling party, went to Koštunica. Despite the official release of figures that suggested the need for a run-off vote, the Serbian Orthodox Church, which had always had a love–hate relationship with the Milošević regime, recognized Koštunica as "president-elect." Even more damaging, the ultranationalist Serbian Radical Party (SRS), that had run its own candidate for the presidency and had been a part of Milošević's ruling coalition, recognized Koštunica as first-round victor according to its data, declaring that it would not participate in a run-off. Milošević persisted in his demand for a run-off election in a speech on state television in which he tried to appeal to nationalism but succeeded only in looking desperate. Mass demonstrations, which his security apparatus refused to suppress, ultimately compelled him to resign.[36]

Many of those who have commented on the role of the Kosovo myth in Milošević's rise to and hold on power have extrapolated from this the notion that the Kosovo myth draws Serbs to seek autocratic savior–leaders in the model of Lazar, such as Milošević attempted to be. And, indeed, we have observed in the preceding chapters that the notion of the savior–hero inherent to the defeat myth conditions nations to seek extraordinary saviors in the present in order to rescue them from a state of inherent decay. But when we consider the role of the Kosovo myth in Milošević's fall as well, we find that this is only half the story. For we have also observed in the preceding chapters that the Kosovo myth, and the myth of defeat in general, is ultimately a myth about the *destruction* of autocracy, both Serbian and Ottoman, in favor of a democratic ethos. Thus, autocratic leaders are glorified only as long as they can present themselves as adhering to a national ideal absolutely inimical to an autocratic system or society.

[36] Ibid.: 409–23.

Although this might seem ironic and contradictory, Milošević was not the first Serbian politician to run up against this problem. Both the Karadjordjević and Obrenović dynasties invoked Kosovo, portraying themselves as presiding over the resurrection of the nation just as Lazar had presided over its ritual sacrifice, while at the same time stressing their own humble origins further to the nationalist ethic.[37] But every Serbian leader who has attempted to walk the tightrope of the Kosovo myth – setting himself up as a "people's monarch," a princely defender of social equality – has managed to maintain this balance for only a handful of years. He would fall from grace once his inability to achieve national fulfillment was exposed, an inability engendered in part by his own position of privilege and evident desire to maintain it, after which his regime would be remembered only as the next in a long history of coercive formations that served to stifle the Serbian national character and destiny.

In the case of Milošević, his defense of Kosovo Serbs and his "anti-bureaucratic revolution" are often seen as two separate pillars of his rise to power, appealing to and thereby forging a coalition between nationalist and reformist constituencies. In fact, they are intrinsically connected; any defender of Kosovo has to, by definition, also be a champion of the people against the system. In presenting himself as the aristocrat (or, more appropriately, the apparatchik) of the people, Milošević tapped into a primordially human myth with a distinctly Serbian character. What he failed to appreciate was that this myth is only the prelude to its protagonist's eventual sacrifice; the aristocrat of the people truly joins the people only when he voluntarily removes himself from history in the name of their cause. Once he ceased to be a defender of Kosovo, Milošević was no longer a man of the people; merely another bureaucrat clinging to the prerogatives of his hierarchical authority in the manner of Vuk Branković, rather than sacrificing himself as a good leader should at such a moment in favor of the equality and horizontal solidarity of his people. The immediate result conformed to James Frazer's description of the precarious place of the sovereign in cultural myth:

The sovereign . . . exists only for his subjects; his life is only valuable so long as he discharges the duties of his position by ordering the course of nature for his people's benefit. So soon as he fails to do so, the care, the devotion, the religious homage which they had hitherto lavished on him cease and are changed into hatred and contempt; he is dismissed ignominiously, and may be thankful if he

---

[37] Malcolm 1998: 79.

escapes with his life. Worshipped as a god one day, he is killed as a criminal the next. But in this changed behaviour of the people there is nothing capricious or inconsistent. On the contrary, their conduct is entirely of a piece. If the king is their god, he or she should also be their preserver; and if he will not preserve them, he must make room for another who will.[38]

Milošević activated the Kosovo myth, with himself in the role of Lazar's spiritual successor, recognizing it as the fastest and most reliable way to acquire the power associated with the symbolic status of leadership in the Serbian nation. But he could not play out the myth to its logical completion. Unable to achieve complete national fulfillment and thereby finish the job Lazar had begun, his only other option was to sacrifice himself and his nation in the attempt, and Milošević, the self-interested pragmatist, had no genuine interest in martyrdom. All he could do was forestall the inevitable for as long as possible by maintaining, by any means necessary, the perceived equation between his regime and the core principles of the nation; and, though he would do so through compromise when he could, he was not unwilling to resort to warfare, ethnic cleansing, and even the devastation of his own nation once it was the symbols of Kosovo itself that were at stake. But when NATO intervention confronted Milošević with the stark option of either surrendering Kosovo or effecting his own destruction, he chose the earthly kingdom and, once he had capitulated, he ceased to be the symbolic leader of the nation but became rather a symbol of the privilege and stratification of society such as had caused the original defeat. Stripped of his symbolic status, his regime was relegated to merely the latest in a long line of Serbian misfortune, and few were sorry to see him go.

Enemies and Traitors: Defining Insider–Outsider Boundaries

The elevation of a particular symbol of defeat to a position of centrality within a national mythology also introduces significant restraints into how the distinction between insiders and outsiders to the nation can be defined. Not only must insiders be capable of identifying with the savior-hero in his moment of sacrifice, but if one can be associated with the enemy Other – whether by descent, religion, class, culture, or politics – one is thereby rendered ineligible for full membership in the national communion. We have already seen how this has had an impact on Muslims perceived through the framework of the Kosovo myth as

[38] Frazer 1994: 171.

"Turks" and therefore relegated to outsider status despite commonalities in language and descent. Similar rhetoric can be found in post–World War II Czechoslovakia, where the law leading to the expropriation and expulsion of Germans passed on May 19, 1945, referring specifically to "Germans, Hungarians, traitors and collaborators," was justified by communist officials and official demonstrations with the slogan "we will redress Bílá hora."

Here again, local Germans were outsiders not simply because they were not Czech or Czech speaking. Rather, they were associated, through the White Mountain myth, with the Czech nobility who, having failed to share the fate of the 27 lords executed on Staromestske Square, allowed themselves to be "Germanized" as a class, adopting the language and culture of their Habsburg overlords in order to maintain their privileges in defiance of the principle of national solidarity with the Czech masses. This rhetoric proved useful to communist authorities, providing a distinction between national insiders and outsiders that equated social class with national treachery. Not only could "German" be equated with "traitor," but also the propertied classes in general could be equated with "German," thereby expelling them to the margins of the nation and blurring the limits of what could or could not be done to them. With the Other standing as a symbol of the antinational, the prenational, attacks on the Other were thereby fulfillments of the nation, enabling communist leaders to claim nationalist credentials much as they would later do in Serbia. The redistribution of agricultural land and nationalization of industry from German owners to the Czech state thus came across as a transition from aristocratic hierarchy to national equality, implemented under the slogan of "redress for Bílá hora," affording these measures a broad nationalist popularity leading to communist victory in the elections of 1946.[39]

It is here that the double-edged nature of nationalism manifests around symbols of defeat. There is an optimism, even a utopianism, inherent in the sacrificial myth in that it offers the possibility that through sacrifice, evil can be expunged from society, and this enables genuine altruism and self-sacrifice in its adherents. However, because the complete fulfillment promised by a utopian project must inevitably fail – because, as we have observed, no social system can satisfy the fundamental lack engendered by the very fact of socialization – the resulting elements that will inevitably fall short of the promise of fulfillment must be attributed to an outsider, and the neutralization or elimination of those elements becomes a part of

[39] Sayer 1998: 241–5.

the utopian program if utopian discourse is to sustain itself. Of course, this need not be as catastrophic as it sounds. Physical extermination or expulsion is merely the most extreme form of such an effort at neutralization. And although one might speculate that it is inevitable for the program to eventually reach such an extreme because all other efforts to resolve lack and achieve utopia will fail, in fact a distinction between insiders and outsiders is a necessary element of any social group, and distinctions reinforced through the choice of a particular symbol of defeat need not necessarily lead to the projection of violence or hostility. They could also serve as a force for effecting in-group solidarity and restraining civil conflict, unifying a diversity of cultural and political groups within the nation by distinguishing them collectively from an abstract external Other too distant geographically or historically to pose a credible threat or, more significant, to be threatened by the persistence of the myth.

Ghana, as one of the more successful and stable multiethnic national states in Africa, illustrates this dynamic. The Yaa Asantewaa myth serves to direct the attentions of the collectivity toward an Other external in both time and space: the British during the colonial period. This may partially explain why a historical memory specifically associated with Asante ethnicity nonetheless has been adopted in both elite and popular circles as a unifying Ghanaian national myth. Although Yaa Asantewaa was distinctly Asante, and the defeat was a defeat of Asante provinces rather than of the whole Ghanaian polity, she can also be represented as a proto-Ghanaian or even pan-African patriot, depending on the context, when juxtaposed against the enemy she was fighting. One might even go so far as to speculate that the elevation of such a symbol to national status has thereby contributed to the easing of ethnic tensions and the relative decline of ethnicity as a factor in national politics, compared to neighboring states that remain embroiled in ethnic animosity.

On the other hand, the lack of a common defeat myth, and hence common conceptions of insider–outsider boundaries, can contribute to explaining the peaceful dissolution of Czechoslovakia in 1993, illustrating as well the primacy of myth over language as a basis for defining national boundaries. For whatever signifiers the boundaries of national identity may be based on, the members of the nation so defined have to recognize a common totemic authority in order for the identity to perpetuate itself. As a consequence, the pan-Slavic ideal that encouraged secular nationalists of the 19th and 20th centuries to develop a myth of common

Czechoslovak nationhood on the basis of linguistic commonality ultimately could not overcome the separate identities that had been forged as a consequence of divergent histories, illustrated by the radically different historical axis points recognized between the two groups, including different defeat myths. Jan Hus was not a Slovak hero and *Bílá hora* was not a Slovak tragedy. During this period, Slovakia had been incorporated into the kingdom of Hungary for over a millennium; hence, the *bêtes noires* of Slovak national sovereignty were not Germans but Hungarians.

This was a key difference preventing a lasting commonality between Czechs and Slovaks, transforming Slovakia into an authentically separate nation as opposed to simply a regional and cultural subdivision on par with Bohemia and Moravia. Bohemians and Moravians could identify alike with a sovereignty destroyed at White Mountain and restored through Czech nationality. But to incorporate Slovakia as well into a national communion with a premodern pedigree, Czechs would have to go back as far as the defeat of the Great Moravian Empire in the 10th century, an effort that was attempted at times but never plausibly able to eclipse White Mountain as the pivotal moment. To do so would have been to consign the golden age of Jan Hus and the Kingdom of Bohemia to the period of "Darkness" and lack; something Czechs were unwilling to do even in the name of maintaining a larger state, because this would have served to shift the locus of totemic authority away from Prague and toward... well, the fact that no one is quite sure where the capital of Great Moravia was located illustrates the further problem of the lack of an adequate matrix of symbols and monuments from which such a myth could be constructed and commemorated.[40]

This is not to say that Czechs and Slovaks could not exist under a single state formation; clearly, they could and, for a time, they did. But this was considered by neither party as a necessary state of affairs. Despite linguistic commonality, the two groups, first, could be clearly recognized as separate nations under separate totemic authorities embedded in their separate historical mythologies; and, second, they were fortunate in that these myths did not implicate one another as the nation's enemy Other. Thus, their sovereignty could be expressed in their free choice to either remain in or separate from a Czechoslovak state, without either state of affairs being perceived by significant numbers on either side as an unconscionable injustice.

[40] See Sayer 1998: 170.

A similar case might be proposed in response to any lingering fear in Turkey that the continued centrality of Constantinople to Greek national identity reflects a lingering and intractable Greek irredentism.[41] Although hyperbolic depictions of the aggressive and uncivilized behavior of the Ottomans during the capture of Constantinople and the consequent *Tourkokratia* warrants their depiction as an Other of the worst possible kind, this ultimately serves as a necessary device to enable the nation to accommodate modern political realities. We have observed that brutal sacrifice at the hands of a brutal executioner ultimately does the nation a service. In this case, the capture of Constantinople provides a narrative to justify relocating the locus of Greek national–cultural identity back to the classical heartland of mainland Greece and the Greek islands, an area corresponding to both the present-day boundaries of the modern nation-state and the alternative Golden Age of Hellenic antiquity.[42] One need only imagine the upheaval that would be involved in relocating it back again to understand that the image of Constantinople is as dangerous to the integrity of Greek national identity as it is pivotal to it. It remains an important axis point, but its importance lies as much in its absence as its presence. The construct of Greek national identity could persist indefinitely with sovereignty over Constantinople as nothing more than a vague, unfulfilled aspiration; indeed, longer than it could with it as a concrete political agenda. Were *hē Polis* ever to indeed be "ours once more," that construct as it has evolved over the past two centuries would be thrown into disarray.

Thus, although many of the implications of symbols of defeat to politics and diplomacy might appear bleak – with such symbols standing as predictors of mass psychological complexes, fanatical irredentism, mass support for totalitarianism, and fossilization of boundaries leading to potential ethnic cleansing – this is inevitably only half the story. For any model that endeavors to explain when and how nationalism can become violent and intransigent has its flip-side: It can also suggest when and how it will not. For beyond the narrow set of symbols that might be expected to generate intransigence for reasons now explained, a nation may well be more conciliatory than its reputation suggests in relation to other national symbols whose lesser importance is now better understood.

---

[41] Millas (2004: 54) notes that such a concern can still be found in some Turkish textbooks that characterize Greeks as maintaining a grand plan with the intention of re-creating the Byzantine Empire at the expense of Turkey.

[42] Soysal and Antoniou 2002: 65.

Although symbols of defeat might glorify heroic martyrdom of an eerily fascist variety, we find that they only do so as long as they are perceived to be in the service of a democratic ethos of social equality and horizontal solidarity. And although these symbols may serve to fix insider–outsider boundaries, clarity of such boundaries can generate unity within a society or effect peaceful separation between societies as often as it exacerbates intergroup or interstate conflict. The nature of a group's defeat myth may well enable us to predict and understand where boundaries are located and why, and a community that alters its emphasis from one defeat myth to another may in so doing shift or broaden boundaries to accommodate changing circumstances.

6

Exceptions

Although it is hoped that this work has served to demonstrate how common it is for nations to elevate symbols of defeat to the center of their mythologies, as well as suggesting what the ubiquity of this myth can tell us about the construct of the nation in general, we cannot conclude without acknowledging numerous cases that do not fit this pattern. One would be hard pressed, for example, to find a prominent image of defeat in the mythologies of the United States, Russia, or China,[1] and having just named three of the most powerful nation-states in the world, which between them incorporate about a quarter of its population and territory, one can hardly argue that the centrality of the defeat myth is a universal phenomenon. What is universal is the need for any society to commemorate sacrifice, and although the defeat myth may serve as a convenient means for the modern social construct of the nation to manage this function, it is not the only means, and it is a mechanism that will prove more convenient for some varieties of nations in some circumstances than others.

---

[1] Recalling the narrow definition of "defeat" employed for the purposes of this work, which includes only those myths or symbols "that serve to commemorate a moment at which the nation, or a predecessor community with which the nation identifies itself in continuity, suffered or is perceived to have suffered a military conquest represented as a historical turning-point leading directly to a period of subjugation or domination, the effects of which are to at least some degree seen as enduring up to the present day." See Introduction.

Imperial Nations

Indeed, one might even speculate that it is the very size and power of the United States, Russia, and China that render them exceptional. For if our theory holds that the convenience of symbols of defeat as a means to commemorate sacrifice is the product of the particular relationship between culture and organization posited by Gellner as characteristic of the modern nation, it stands to reason that this will differ among nations that are compelled by circumstance to negotiate this relationship differently. As noted in Chapter 1, Gellner defined nationalism as "a political principle which maintains that similarity of culture is the basic social bond."[2] But there remains a discrepancy between this and our functional definition of a national discourse, elaborated in Chapter 3 as "the system of myth, symbol, and ritual that serves to channel human violence so as to legitimate and enable social existence in the context of modernity," as there may be principles other than a perceived common culture capable of organizing such a system of violent authority in the modern context.

It is those nations that best conform to Gellner's model – nations that asserted their sovereignty in the face of decaying multicultural empires – that are therefore the best candidates for the elevation of symbols of defeat because these will experience most acutely the need to rationalize an earlier lack of a sentiment linking their national culture to political organization, and thus the effective nonexistence of the nation, during the imperial period. On the other hand, nations that reject the norm linking culture to political organization, that form through an effort to construct or reconstruct a multicultural imperial polity in a manner consistent with the forms of the modern bureaucratic state – that is, nations defined by any imperial–universal aspirations, past or present, or that are the product of the successful consolidation of an imperial into a national polity – will have little use for a defeat myth, because this will only serve to call into question the unity or efficacy of the national project.

The United States would be an example of such a nation with pseudo-imperial aspirations, openly defining itself as the product of a modern revolutionary principle of universal applicability and therefore capable of uniting culturally diverse individuals in a common political project. The lack of such a project in the distant past is not a problem that requires explanation; neither does the defeat of this project at any point in the

[2] Gellner 1997: 3.

past provide the community with a cathartic resolution of ambivalence. The efficacy of an imperial or "missionary" national principle[3] is better demonstrated through a narrative of its unbroken success and spread; hence, memories of defeat, if they are commemorated at all, are not elevated to positions of centrality but rather treated as something abject, more as one might expect setbacks to be recalled. The Vietnam War Memorial is not a towering monolith bearing an inscription calling on all true Americans to avenge past wrongs. It rather has been likened to a scar on the complexion of the capital, commemorating a seemingly senseless loss in a quiet and dignified corner of the National Mall.

This is not to say that our theory does not apply to such nations in any respect, for although their members might not experience ambivalence toward the structures of any premodern predecessor community in a perceived "Golden Age," they will experience ambivalence toward the restrictions of social order in general, universal to the human condition. Hence, my theory as to the importance of the commemoration of sacrifice to the maintenance of social order remains effective for these nations as well. It is simply the case that defeat, in such cases, does not resolve the sacrificial crisis. In *Blood Sacrifice and the Nation*, Carolyn Marvin and David Ingle examine some of the symbols and mechanisms that do so in the American case, from reverence for the image of the flag and the text of the Constitution, to the possibility that the actual renewal of sacrifice through periodic warfare stands as a necessary mechanism for ensuring the continuity of the society.[4]

For nations that have formed not from the dissolution of empires but rather from their consolidation into a single state with a unifying national ideology, symbols of defeat can stand to create more psychological problems than they solve, even in cases where these nations do look back to an ambiguously defined "Golden Age" and simmer with a sense of historical injustice. For in such cases, it may be difficult to find a historical moment that can be unambiguously represented as the defeat of the whole, multifaceted nation. More often, historical memories of defeat tend to reflect the defeat of one element of the nation at the hands of another in the course of imperial consolidation; thus, to elevate them as foundational moments would effectively relegate to the role of

---

[3] Krishan Kumar discusses the notion of a third "missionary" form of national identity, in addition to the standard "civic" and "ethnic" varieties, in his study of *The Making of English National Identity* (2003: 30–2).

[4] Marvin and Ingle 1999.

outsider and executioner some element defined by the normative ideology as integral to the nation, and on which the integrity of national boundaries depends.

China presents us with an example of this problem. Several recent commentators have remarked on the importance of "humiliation" as a theme in Chinese national discourse, and much of this discourse conforms to the model of the defeat myth, identified as the product of imperialist invasion facilitated by the corruption of the domestic ruling class with "national salvation" being the logical corrective. However, the difficulty in anchoring this sense of lingering grievance to a particular historical moment has also been noted. Hostility cannot be unambiguously directed against the forms of the premodern imperial monarchy because it was this institution that unified the country under a common administration, ideology, and written language, defining as well the extent of its territorial boundaries. Neither can the conquest of an indigenous (Han) dynasty by a foreign (Mongol or Manchu) one be commemorated as the pivotal transition from sovereignty to national servitude, as these ethnic categories are among the "Five Races" identified as integral elements to the civic nation. Even modern defeats by European colonial powers are not without controversy, threatening to throw an unwanted light on cultural and political divisions within the purported national communion, because China was never formally conquered and colonized.

Political factions within the nation, even those with hegemonic aspirations, do not encounter difficulty with the problem, appointing narratives of humiliation that mark turning points that unambiguously identify their external enemies as executioners and their internal opponents as traitors. But none of these narratives have gained a permanent hold in the nation as a whole. The Communist Party of China had no difficulty defining a "Century of Humiliation" as beginning with the First Opium War in 1840 and concluding with the founding of the People's Republic of China (PRC) in 1949, whereas the Nationalist Party version saw humiliation as beginning with Russian expansion into Siberia in the 17th century with the founding of the PRC as merely a continuation of Russian imperialism. These divisions are evident in the failed attempts to fix a "National Humiliation Day" for the nation. For a time, such a commemoration was ritualized by the Republican government subsequent to the acceptance of Japan's "Twenty-one Demands" in 1915, though even then it was disputed whether the day should be commemorated on May 7 when Japan issued the demands, thereby stressing external aggression, or May 9 when the Chinese president accepted them, stressing internal weakness.

In 2001, when the PRC's National People's Congress passed a resolution to establish a National Humiliation Day, neither of these dates was suggested but nor could the Congress ultimately agree on a date. They were torn between dates that stressed Japanese aggression (such as July 7, the date of the invasion of 1937) or Western imperialism (such as September 7, the date of the Boxer Indemnity of 1900).[5]

Russia could be taken as another case of a large nation forged from the imperial unification of a multiplicity of cultures in which an ethos of a glorious destiny thwarted by a tragic fate pervades national history.[6] Yet it would be difficult to appoint a particular place or moment in history to symbolize this sense of frustration without alienating significant political or cultural groups that the nation must embrace as insiders. The concept of the nation having suffered and overcome the "Tatar yoke" appears from time to time, but only among a certain ideological subset of the nation, salient only within circumscribed geographical boundaries far narrower than the nation-state as a whole. Certainly, it is less than salient to those with palpable Tatar ancestry who nonetheless identify as insiders to the wider Russian nation.

Much the same could be said for the mythology of pan-Arab nationalism. Parallel to the Chinese concept of "humiliation," Arab national history incorporates the notion of "stagnation," in which a golden age of cultural, political, and scientific achievement at the height of the Umayyad and Abbasid Caliphates is interrupted by centuries of cultural decline effected by a lack of political sovereignty and unity, to be reversed by a renaissance of national consciousness in modern times. However, it is difficult for Arab nationalism to confidently identify a turning point to mark the transition between sovereignty and stagnation without threatening the integrity of the very pan-Arab identity the myth is designed to reinforce. As with China's successful imperial nationalism, the defeats contained in the myth–symbol matrix of an aspiring pan-nationalism will invariably be defeats suffered by one part of the purported nation at the hands of another part, or at least defeats that privilege one contending narrative of national belonging over another. Regardless, it is difficult in such cases to find an historical aggressor who can unambiguously be identified as an outsider by all elements of the national culture.

---

[5] Callahan 2004: 204–11; for a literary analysis of the phenomenon during China's republican period, see Tsu 2005.
[6] See McDaniel 1996.

A nationalist historian of Christian background such as Edward Atiyah might identify the fall of Cairo to the Ottomans in 1517 as the unambiguous turning point to servitude, just as he might identify the corrective renaissance as beginning with the arrival of Napoleon in 1798.[7] But the lack of mass appeal of these dates as moments of commemoration may stem from the centrality of Islam to the character of the nation and its purported Golden Age, and hence the implausibility of identifying a moment of conquest at the hands of another Muslim empire as a national tragedy leading to a period of effective servitude. However, the lack of national sentiment and political unity among the Arabs at the time of contact with Western imperial powers was too evident for instances of defeat and humiliation during this period to be appointed as dramatic turning points either. One might even speculate that it is for this reason that Arab nationalism seized so tenaciously on Zionism as an external enemy, and the defeats of 1948 and 1967 as markers of identity, for these finally provide specific moments in time during which the nation as a whole can be depicted as having been defeated by clearly defined outsiders, thus symbolizing the state of moral–cultural stagnation that national mobilization seeks to reverse.

But it is in Britain that we find the partial exception that thereby serves to effectively prove the rule. For English history does contain a pivotal symbol of defeat: the Battle of Hastings, 1066. Here is a moment explicitly depicted as one in which a foreign force permanently conquered and subjugated a local indigenous one, and it is clearly elevated as a key foundational moment in the national mythology, tellingly referred to through the very title of the satire, *1066 And All That*, as one of only two memorable dates in English history.[8] Yet in no other respect does this myth conform to the model described in the preceding chapters. The defeat is not depicted as any great tragedy, a historical injustice crying out for correction, but simply as a matter of course in the teleological progress of English history. King Harold is no salvific martyr, and William the Conqueror and the Normans do not take on the roles of hated outsiders playing executioner. There is no traitor, little sense of a golden age destroyed, and hence no aspiration for its future restoration.

If one visits the English Heritage site where the battle took place, the audio-guide one is given allows the tourist to enter a different code at

---

[7] Thus connecting the rise of modern nationalism to contact with the West; Atiyah 1958: 45, 68, 73.

[8] Seller and Yeatman 1975; the other being 55 BCE, the date of the first Roman invasion under Julius Caesar.

each point on the tour of the battlefield in order to hear the perspective of either a Norman or an Anglo-Saxon participant in the battle. At the end of the tour, both narrators, while still advocating staunchly for the justice of their side, concede that in the final analysis, it didn't really matter who won because there remains no distinction between Norman and Anglo-Saxon today, nearly 1,000 years later. This sentiment is reinforced by a plaque adjacent to the spot where King Harold died: "This stone has been set in this place to commemorate the fusion of the English and Norman peoples which resulted from the great battle fought here in 1066." The peculiarity of this representation becomes evident when contrasted to the multiple cases of defeat myths examined in the preceding chapters. Could one imagine an audio-guide at the site of Masada in Israel providing the option of the Roman point of view on the last battle against the Zealots ("those backwards religious fanatics just couldn't understand the value of Roman civilization")? Could one imagine a plaque at Kosovo Polje celebrating the battle as marking the foundation of the Serbian nation through a fusion of Slavic Orthodox and Ottoman cultural elements?[9]

The answer to this conundrum lies in the convergence between nation and empire particular to British and English history, for the unions of Great Britain and the United Kingdom and the project of the British Empire were at their height at precisely the time when the ideology of nationalism was being defined and gaining salience throughout the rest of Europe and the world. The "missionary" nationalism of Britain therefore depended on an ideology that fundamentally rejected the principle that common culture was the basis of political legitimacy, else how could the diverse ethnocultural groups of Great Britain be united in common purpose to project their values and power over the diverse ethnocultural groups of the British Empire? Hastings could not be commemorated in the same way as most nations commemorate their national defeats because if it is considered a great historical injustice for *them* to conquer and to rule *us*, then what right do *we* have to conquer and to rule, say, India and Africa – or, for that matter, Scotland and Wales?

Indeed, there was a period in English history when the Battle of Hastings was perceived roughly according to the model elaborated in this work. During the English Civil War, prior to the unions and the Empire, when the idea of nationalism was at best in its infancy and hardly a major sociopolitical force, the concept of the "Norman yoke," of Anglo-Saxons reclaiming their original freedoms from foreign Norman oppressors, was

[9] See Asari et al. 2008: 8.

prevalent. It persisted only in the rhetoric of radicals up until the 19th century, disappearing almost completely in England by the time the ideology of nationalism was in full bloom elsewhere in Europe.[10] It is in this rhetoric that we see what the cultural and political content of a more narrow English national myth might have looked like had it followed the trajectory of a typical nationalism. But the radical revisionist agenda implied by the defeat myth, of throwing off the strictures of the premodern imperial and hierarchical social order as a foreign imposition on the nation, did not appeal to the mainstream political culture of England in the 19th and early 20th centuries, even on an unconscious level. The strictures of the premodern imperial and hierarchical social order were serving the nation quite well, thank you very much. England never waged nationalist war against the symbols of its own stratified, heterogeneous agrarian past in the course of its transition to a modern industrial nation, because these constructs were essential to the institution of empire that was, in turn, pivotal to the sense of national pride and glory at the time that nationalism as a European ideology was in ascendance. Hence, constructs such as the British monarchy and aristocracy were retained, in form if not substance, as totems of the national social order.

Nations Without States

At the opposite end of the spectrum is another category of nation that negotiates the relationship between culture and organization in a manner that differs from Gellner's ideal-type. Just as nations that dominate a quasi-imperial state or system must reject the principle that common culture is the basis of political legitimacy, so too must nations that are comfortably incorporated into such a state or system. Given our functional, discursive definition of the nation, we will define a nonstate nation not simply as a nation that does not possess its own independent state but also as a nation that does not even aspire to state sovereignty; a nation for which state sovereignty is not a factor in their construction of national identity. For, although our definition of the nation recognizes the affinity between the constructs of nation and state, it also recognizes that exceptional nations could exist, able and content to express their distinctiveness and cultural autonomy within the institutional framework of a multinational state dominated by another national group. A system of myth, symbol, and ritual might nonetheless organize loyalties and define

---

[10] Kumar 2003: 48.

insider–outsider relationships relating to a community of violent authority, embodied in either regional substate administrations, or even, lacking this, in instruments of civil society distinct from formal government.

The Frisians identify as a nation on the basis of a distinct language and history of state sovereignty. Yet their population and territory is currently incorporated into other national states, primarily The Netherlands, and has been for centuries with little in the way of any political movement for national unification or independence. Friesland was conquered by Albert, Duke of Saxony, in 1498, and any number of battles further to this conquest could have been appointed as the pivotal turning point between national sovereignty and servitude, complete with conniving nobles to round out the narrative. But this defeat goes uncommemorated in either the landscape or calendar of the Frisian nation. Instead, the annual Frisian national holiday commemorates the Battle of Warns, September 26, 1345, in which the Frisians were victorious over the Dutch. Warns is also commemorated with a monument at the site of the battle that bears the inscription "Better to be dead than a slave."

The national history of Wales contains several moments and monuments that could be designated as the pivotal turning point between independence and incorporation into a London-dominated Britain, each featuring figures that could serve as the national savior–hero. The most popular of these is Owain Glyndŵr, who led the last successful Welsh rebellion against the English in 1400–1415. The Glyndŵr narrative conforms to the model described in this work in numerous respects: A hero with a reputation for great physical strength and prowess, he is also a boundary crosser who on the one hand was an indirect descendant of the royal lineage but on the other is supported by the masses and chosen as their leader.[11] He refuses to submit to his enemies when offered a pardon, preferring instead to continue resistance to English encroachment, even against impossible odds.

However, this is where the similarities end. Despite the potential that this narrative would appear to offer, it is difficult to identify it as a case of a symbol of defeat, for of all of the sites and stories associated with Owain Glyndŵr, one would be hard pressed to find a monument or event identified with the moment of his defeat. Elisa Henken surveys a comprehensive list of landmarks in Wales named for Glyndŵr, but a location associated with military defeat is not among them. On the contrary, Henken observes

---

[11] Henken 1996: 51. Henken also notes the importance of his reputation as a "trickster" and social outlaw, juxtaposed against that of the noble and warrior: 89–107.

that "the sites perhaps most closely associated with Glyndŵr's military activities are those places said to have been destroyed by Glyndŵr in the fierceness of battle,"[12] stressing his strength and ferocity in victory, not defeat, and that he was especially destructive, vengeful, and powerful.

Historical defeats were suffered by Glyndŵr and thus many sites or historical moments exist that could be appointed as the pivotal locus of defeat, no less arbitrarily than in many of the cases previously examined. Yet this is not done; no battlefield, castle ruin, execution site, or grave stands as the focal point of commemoration. Rather, it is his successful resistance to the encroachment of the dominating imperial power, his calling of a parliament, and his brief maintenance of a genuinely sovereign Welsh state that is recalled and celebrated, not that state's eventual and final fall. Glyndŵr's decline comes through in the mythic narrative as gradual, and his death goes essentially unrecorded even in legend and speculation. Indeed, the most popular legend holds that Glyndŵr never died but rather that he and his men remain sleeping in a cave, awaiting the appropriate time when they are needed to return and fight again to restore the land to its former glory.[13] In effect, the narrative goes directly from a myth of resistance to an eschatological myth of restoration and return, bypassing almost entirely the myth of decline and defeat.

Glyndŵr's ultimate departure from the historical scene without any reliable moment or place to mark his death leaves a myth of his continued dormition comparable to those of other national eschatologies. But lacking a dramatic end point, this myth of dormition serves to symbolize the continued durability of the nation even during times of domination, without necessarily requiring the rectification of any moment of defeat that, if uncommemorated, can hardly be elevated as a historical injustice that Welsh honor exists to redeem. As counterintuitive as it may seem, it may well be that images of victory over the Other are as cathartic to nations comfortable under the domination of that same Other, as are images of defeat at the hands of the Other to nations seeking to assert their autonomy against a symbolic enemy. The Frisians and the Welsh do not experience the need to commemorate an historical injustice, demanding mobilization to effect its revision. Although both identify as distinct nations, neither evidence widespread dissatisfaction with current institutional arrangements but rather seek to mobilize national sentiment to defend and preserve their distinct culture under the political status quo.

[12] Henken 1996: 126; see also 146–60.
[13] Ibid.: 23, 70–88.

The commemoration of victory and successful resistance reinforces the sense of distinctiveness, for if the nation was never defeated, if the savior–hero simply fades unvanquished from history, then the independence they defended can be perceived as still existing in spirit, regardless of whatever institutional arrangements might prevail in practice, to which they can therefore freely acquiesce without shame.

Again, it is in Britain that we find the partial exception whose very ambiguity serves to prove the rule. Scotland stands as an interesting test case, in which two contending interpretations of national identity put forward two conflicting interpretations of a pivotal national symbol: one as representing triumph, the other as defeat. The symbol in question is the national hero William Wallace, and one need only turn to the summary provided on the dust jacket of Nigel Tranter's 1975 book, *The Wallace*, to see just how neatly his story conforms to the mythic framework described in the preceding pages:

Here is the epic story of a young man of lofty stature but not very lofty birth who, driven to desperation and tears by the savagery and indignities perpetrated upon his fellow countrymen and women, as the policy of Edward Plantagenet, Hammer of the Scots, took upon himself to challenge almost single-handed the might of the greatest military machine in Christendom; and who by indomitable courage, shrewd strategy, brilliant tactics, sublime faith and a kind of holy impatience, raised a stricken and leaderless nation to self-respect again and, in absence of its king, became its acknowledged head as well as its saviour; and then was shamefully betrayed.[14]

In short: A hero of ambiguously humble or low aristocratic birth shuns comfort and privilege and chooses to stand for the plight of the masses. Possessed of extraordinary virtue and physical prowess, he takes on *de facto* kingly authority and leads his people in defense of their sovereignty against overwhelming odds. He is brought down not only by the overwhelming force and ruthlessness of a named enemy (Edward I and the English) but also by the perfidy of his own nobility who, in contrast to the common people, fail to stand by him in the pivotal hour, symbolized by the treachery of an iconic traitor (Menteith). Violently executed by the enemy, he becomes a martyr and a symbol of inspiration for his people to successfully regain their sovereignty and, with the onset of nationalism in the 19th century and up to the present day, is widely commemorated in both official monument and banal advertisement (to say nothing of Hollywood film), a universal national symbol enlisted

---

[14] Quoted in Morton 2001: 144–5.

as champion of a diversity of causes across the whole of the political spectrum.[15]

More could be said about Wallace as yet another case study of a national defeat myth. Of particular interest is the manner in which the theme of betrayal is frequently taken as an indictment not just of the nobility at the time but also of the very principle of social stratification.[16] Indeed, much could be made of the ambivalence suggested by the portrayal of Robert the Bruce; a clear symbol of Scottish sovereignty who could be said, in the context of the Wallace myth, to simultaneously embody both the figure of the aristocratic traitor and the avenging popular hero in the same historical personage.[17] But of more immediate interest is the fact that as nationalism developed in the 19th century, the myth of Wallace proved perplexingly unthreatening to British Unionist interests, to the point where it was often invoked enthusiastically as a heroic image even by such an arch-Tory and Unionist as Sir Walter Scott, advocating an assertive Scottish ethnonational identity within the framework of the British state. Lord Rosebury, Scottish secretary, promoter of the bill to establish the Scottish Office in 1885, and prime minister briefly upon Gladstone's death – another enthusiast for all things Scottish who remained deeply committed to the Union – commemorated the 600th anniversary of the Battle of Stirling Bridge at a banquet for 300.[18] And in 1929, statues of Wallace and Bruce were unveiled on the esplanade of Edinburgh Castle by the Duke of York, later King George VI, on the 600th anniversary of the city's Royal Charter of 1329. In part, this appropriation of the Wallace myth by the British establishment was made possible by the very ambiguity, just discussed in reference to England, allowed for by the persistence of premodern imperial forms in a modern national society. The fact that premodern allegiances were dynastic rather than national in character allowed British monarchs to claim Wallace's allegiance on dynastic grounds. After all, the monarchy that Wallace had resisted had been of a different dynasty, and all British monarchs since the Stuarts have been direct descendants of Robert the Bruce.[19]

---

[15] See Morton 2001: esp. 21, 28, 53–61, 109–10.

[16] Morton (2001) quotes Thomas Carlyle to the effect that "the nobles of the country (Scotland) have maintained a quite despicable behaviour since the days of Wallace downwards – a selfish, ferocious, famishing, unprincipled set of hyenas, from whom at no time, and in no way, has the country derived any benefit"(59).

[17] See, for example, Morton 2001: 96–103.

[18] Morton 2001: 52.

[19] Ibid.: 83–4.

But of deeper significance is the fact that there are, in effect, two William Wallaces. There is the Wallace who was victorious over the English at the Battle of Stirling Bridge, and there is the Wallace who was defeated at the Battle of Falkirk, betrayed, and then executed in London. The Wallace of Falkirk tended to be invoked by more radical elements of Scottish political culture, those seeking a revision of the sociopolitical status quo such as the Chartists and the instigators of the Glasgow riots in the early 19th century.[20] In contrast, liberal and conservative unionist elements of the political culture tended to focus on the Wallace of Stirling, where the National Wallace Monument was eventually constructed in 1869 with the full approval and participation of the British establishment.[21]

It is precisely this paradox, that unionists tended to stress Wallace as a symbol of victory over England, whereas radicals identified him as a symbol of defeat at the hands of England, that demonstrates the circumstances under which a symbol of defeat is effective. The commemoration of Wallace at Stirling not only allowed for a reenactment of national pride and autonomy but also, on the flip-side, obscured many of the themes prevalent in most defeat myths that came to the fore when Wallace was commemorated at Falkirk. Scotland under Wallace at Stirling was united; Falkirk was "lost because of disunity."[22] At Stirling (and Bannockburn), one could celebrate the Scottish dynastic heritage of what later came to be the united British monarchy. At Falkirk, one could condemn the perfidious nobility who chose to support English dynastic claims over the cause of national autonomy. Falkirk, the lost battle, gave the Wars of Independence a sense of unfinished business, begging for a present-day victory to undo the historic defeat. But the victory at Stirling renders Wallace's eventual defeat and martyrdom merely a prelude to the immediate follow-up victory and assertion of Scottish sovereignty at Bannockburn under Robert Bruce. Stirling, therefore, was a moment that, when reinforced in monument and reenacted in ritual, represented a state of perpetual independence, even for a Scotland comfortably settled within the Union. This sentiment can be read into the writings of many liberal, devolutionist yet still pro-Union Wallace enthusiasts of the 19th century. James

---

[20] Eriksonas 2004: 141–2.
[21] Morton 2001: 78–9; Eriksonas 2004: 159–60.
[22] As put by the anonymous author of *The Life of William Wallace: The Scots Patriot* in 1808; quoted in Eriksonas 2004: 141.

Moir, in the introduction to *Sir William Wallace: A Critical Study of His Biographer, Blind Harry*, writes:

Had the result of Edward's war in Scotland been to make him its lord, we might have had today a Scottish Home Rule Question as difficult to settle as the Irish one. The aggression of Edward only helped to consolidate Scotland and make the country not a geographical expression, but a nation. Dr Arnold of Rugby points out that the battles of Bannockburn and Orleans, in both of which the English were defeated, were really blessings for England. The one secured the independence of Scotland, the other put an end to the English pretensions to a continental sovereignty. The conquest of Ireland, on the other hand, was complete, with the result that the Irish have always been dissatisfied with their position, whereas the Scots can look back to the Wars of Independence with pride, and can feel that when the Union took place it was between equals, and not between a conquered and a conquering nation.[23]

This reference to Orléans brings to mind the parallel of Joan of Arc, who might also be considered a borderline example for the purposes of this study insofar as, much as in the case of William Wallace, the question remains ambiguous as to whether she qualifies as a symbol of defeat or of victory; not simply because of the ambiguity present in all defeat myths, whereby military defeat is transformed into moral victory, but also in the sense that different elements of the nation might prefer to focus on one element of the narrative as opposed to another. Traditional elements of French political culture, content with the status quo, have tended to focus on the Joan of Orléans; her victory in restoring the French crown. It was the French Revolution, the turmoil of the mid-19th century, the defeat of 1871, and the Second World War that transformed her failure to take Paris and her martyrdom in Rouen into something more than just the dénouement to the story.

Indeed, a nation need not be inordinately large and powerful or small and powerless in order to serve as such an exception. It need only have some reason to reject the ethnonationalist model – representing either a principle depicted as transcending the conceptual boundaries of the national–cultural community or one that is content with a relatively low level of self-assertion. Similarly, we find that not all nonstate nations will necessarily favor victory narratives over defeat. We have already observed that what works for Caledonia does not always play in Catalonia, as modern Catalan nationalism was born in a moment of political opposition

[23] 1888: 60–1; quoted in Morton 2001: 118.

to the state. The demonstrations of 1977 were able to incorporate commemoration of the fall of Barcelona into a broader Spanish rather than simply Catalan narrative precisely because these demonstrations reflected a struggle to correct an historical injustice rather than to perpetuate an ongoing state of affairs. Yet after the restoration of democracy to Spain, the fact that modern Catalan nationalism found its roots in this moment of protest and maintained such an unequivocal moment of defeat as its rallying point rendered problematic the incorporation of state-centralist elements of Catalan political culture into the celebrations of its national day, in contrast to the ease with which a victorious Wallace or Glyndŵr could be incorporated into a unionist paradigm of Scottishness or Welshness.

One could even go so far as to suggest this as another indication of the utility of this theory as a predictive model: that the extent to which a nation elevates defeat rather than victory points to the extent to which the national identity incorporates significant revisionist demands. Although, once again, this does not mean that the model is capable only of predicting intolerance and intransigence. For just as we can predict not only when perturbations against symbols will but also will not provoke a violent response, we can assess how the placement of particular symbols within a national myth–symbol framework might indicate either the presence or lack of a feared hostile intent. Take, for example, the Albanian national hero Skanderbeg, similar to Owain Glyndŵr in the sense that he is credited for securing and presiding over the last period of Albanian sovereignty against the Ottoman Empire in premodern times. But also like that of Glyndŵr, his mythology tends to focus on his success in carving out and maintaining an independent state in the face of imperial aggression, with the manner of his death and his state's eventual collapse to Ottoman rule left largely ambiguous and uncommemorated. The lack of any symbolic moment of injustice calling for revision could lend support to the views of scholars such as Paulin Kola, who dispute the widespread salience of irredentist myths of "Greater Albania," so feared in the region and by the international community.[24]

[24] Kola 2003.

Conclusions

"Would you be good enough," our delightful interlocutor inquired eagerly, "to tell me what news there is of Mother Prague, the City of a Hundred Towers?"

"It is growing, my friend," I replied, pleased at his interest, and in a few words outlined to him the prosperous growth of our golden metropolis.

"What joyful tidings these are," the Newt said with undisguised satisfaction. "And are the severed heads of the decapitated Czech nobles still stuck up on the Bridge Tower?"

"No, they haven't been for a long time," I said, somewhat (I admit) taken aback by his question.

"That is a great pity," the Newt observed sympathetically. "That was indeed a precious historical relic. It is a pity crying to high Heaven that so many splendid memorials have perished in the Thirty Years' War! Unless I am mistaken, the Czech land was then turned into a desert drenched with blood and tears. How fortunate that the genitive of negation did not die out then as well! It says in this book that it is on the point of extinction. I am deeply distressed to learn it, sir."

"So you are fascinated also by our history," I exclaimed joyfully.

"Certainly, sir," the Newt replied. "Especially by the disaster of the White Mountain and the three hundred years of servitude. I have read a lot about that in this book. No doubt you are very proud of your three hundred years of servitude. That was a great period, sir!"

"Yes, a hard period," I agreed. "A period of oppression and grief."

"And did you groan?" our friend inquired with keen interest.

"We groaned, suffering inexpressibly under the yoke of the savage oppressors."

"I am delighted to hear it," the Newt heaved a sigh of relief. "That is exactly what it says in my book. I am happy to find it is true...." – Karel Čapek, *War with the Newts*[1]

---

[1] Čapek 1999: 148–9.

In the penultimate chapter of his last, posthumously published book on the subject of nationalism, Ernest Gellner posed a question that evocatively expressed what he identified and what remains widely understood as "perhaps the major debate which has arisen in the theory of nationalism of late": Do nations have navels?[2] Given his view of the nation and nationalism as fundamentally modern constructs, dependent on modern instrumentalities such as industrialization, mass literacy, and the state, can nations nonetheless legitimately claim descent from premodern predecessors and, if so, under what conditions?

It may be possible, however, to carry Gellner's metaphor further, for the question he was really posing was not whether nations have navels but rather whether they have parents, the "navel" being merely the concrete evidence of parentage. It is rather this work that deals directly with the existence, nature, and significance of the navel itself. For what is a navel but a shriveled remnant that serves no biological purpose other than as a tangible reminder that the organism was not created *ex nihilo* but rather physically severed from the body of the parent? In much the same way, we have seen that images of defeat, the relics and rituals associated with them, the myths and symbols surrounding them, serve to legitimate the connection between modern nations and the premodern ethnic communities with which they identify, an association that is vital to the perception of the nation as immortal and primordial. To a corporeal being, a navel is redundant, little more than a curiosity. But to an imagined community – a community whose existence and continuity depends on its being imagined and the manner in which it is imagined – it could well be the most vital of organs. For regardless of whether a nation's parentage is genuine or invented, any community that even claims descent must support the plausibility of this claim through commemoration.

Using Anthony Smith's ethnosymbolic model that identified the key distinctive features of a national mythology, we locate the importance of a myth of decline in its ability to explain the inglorious present with reference to an idealized, heroic past that national mobilization is meant to restore in the undefined future. As Benedict Anderson observed, the reason why nations must locate themselves with reference to a primordial past lies in their having displaced the transcultural dynasties that

---

[2] Gellner 1997: 93.

preceded them as systems of order and thus taken on the role of traditional, universal religious systems in providing the individual with a sense of ultimate meaning in the face of his or her own mortality. To sacrifice one's autonomy to the interests of the nation, an individual must believe that his or her sacrifice is undertaken in the name of something greater than himself or herself, and that in making such a sacrifice the individual is assured a place in something that his or her own meaning system deems immortal.

Myths of defeat provide models of heroes who have made such sacrifices, while the fact that the nation continues to live on in spite of the defeat to commemorate the heroic act serves as concrete proof that those who altruistically choose suffering or death on behalf of the nation do not do so in vain. Because a common willingness on the part of individuals to sacrifice for the national society is precisely what makes the imagined community real, the willingness of those mythical heroes to sacrifice even in the face of hopelessness is depicted as precisely what enabled the community to persevere in the face of defeat, just as continued such commitment by the nation will enable it to survive adversity today. The individual, even when not called on to make personal sacrifices, must therefore identify on an ongoing basis with the sacrifices of those who came before – much as the Christian identifies with the suffering of Christ, formally acknowledging those sufferings as having been undertaken on his or her behalf – symbolically indicating that his or her own sense of ultimate meaning derives from the same source for which the heroes willingly sacrificed, thus binding the community across space and time through a common signifier collectively acknowledged through a system of public patriotic ritual, symbol, and myth.

But as important as the sense of continuity provided by a tangible association to a parent *ethnie* is to a nation, it must also be remembered that the cutting of the umbilical cord is an equally necessary element to the creation of an autonomous being. The nation must, of necessity, represent something very different in form and function from its parent *ethnie*. Hence, the navel serves a dual purpose, both as a reminder that the organism was once bound to a parent and as evidence of the moment at which these bonds were severed. Necessary as both purposes are, they produce conflicting sentiments, the former generating a sense of identity with the parent and longing for the ideal it represents, the latter an assertion of autonomy. Myths and symbols of heroic defeat can successfully serve both conflicting purposes at once, glorifying the symbolic ideal while depicting its necessary and ongoing destruction.

It is here that we find our explanation for the exceptional role that such symbols often play as the very nodal points of a national mythology. Images of the premodern "Golden Age" take on the role in the collective memory attributed to the Freudian image of the Father: a symbolic ideal that serves to enforce submission to social norms, a distinct order of law and morality to which individuals must submit in common in order to be a community. In doing so, this symbol comes to represent the community's unique values, its authentic voice, its ideal self. But entering into a social order necessitates a loss. The individual must be disconnected from direct experience and unrestrained fulfillment of desire, and placed into an alienating world in which desire can be expressed only in terms of representations and fulfilled through the mediation of social norms. Thus, these symbols become both the means and the obstacle to fulfillment, and commemoration must at the same time express both continuity and discontinuity with the ideal; continuity with a noble parentage, but at the same time discontinuity with the norms inimical to a national form of social organization that characterized the parent's generation.

The memory of the Father is a necessary element to a national mythology, but it must be kept in mind that the Father can better serve the nation as a memory than as an actual living force exerting authority over the community. For the horizontal form of social organization characteristic of the modern nation to be formed, the leaders, defenders, and symbolic focal points of the agrarian hierarchical state must be killed and seen to be killed. Only after they have been removed can the values they represented and the order they imposed be reinterpreted in national terms, as models and symbols of service to the nation that thereby becomes the new focus of loyalty and source of authority. Then can they once again be loved, not as leaders but as symbols of the norms necessary to the maintenance of the "brother clan" to which the ethnic community must continually adhere in order to maintain the principle of in-group equality necessary to a national form of social organization.

The ambivalence felt toward the symbolic ideal is one that has to be resolved, and images of defeat offer such resolution through their unique ability to simultaneously represent in a single symbol conflicting impulses all of which are integral to the structure of a national form of social organization. Much like the very concept of "the nation" itself, these signifiers give meaning to a broad range of symbols, myths, and values that are otherwise not only heterogeneous but also often in conflict with one another. Myths and symbols of defeat provide, on the one hand, a banner around which to rally for national mobilization in the name of the restoration of the ideal that was defeated, while at the same time offering concrete evidence that the ideal is no longer in place to compromise that very sense of national solidarity.

Durkheim saw the function of religion as being to reify the social order. But Gellner noted that in the age of nationalism, this camouflage is discarded and the society worships itself openly. If religion and the nation are different forms that serve the same essential function, it stands to reason that constructs serving similar functions will be present in both, even if they might be radically different in appearance to the point where they are unrecognizable as related phenomena. We have even noted instances in which concepts such as salvation, martyrdom, eschatology, and theodicy, present in their traditional forms in the source texts of myth as documented by the prenational *ethnie*, are reinterpreted to suit a modern national context.

Eliade theorized that religious man required concrete points in space and time where the boundaries between the immanent and transcendent realms could be bridged, coining the term *axis mundi* for such points of contact. Nations require such points as well, though it is not the gulf between heaven and earth that must be bridged in this case. Rather, contact must be maintained between all purported members of the imagined community past, present, and future. Because this contact is maintained only with the bounded community and not with any universal transcendent, I have suggested the alternative term *axis natio* for symbols that reinforce this connection. The sacrifice of national savior–martyrs does not serve to mediate between the human and the divine; rather, they sacrifice out of commitment to the integrity of the cultural community, thereby becoming exemplars for the society to revere symbolizing the lesser renunciations it requires in common of all its members on an ongoing basis in order for the group to remain a group in the face of temptation and adversity. The Golden Age is not an age of perfect divine order but rather the wellspring from which the boundaries of the culturally authentic are defined, though, at the same time, an age characterized by a society inimical to national ideology and forms of social organization. National saviors and heroes, therefore, while encapsulating the ideals and values of the appointed Golden Age, ultimately serve their nations by selflessly removing their own unnatural presence from history. Their mirror images, in the form of external enemies and internal traitors, selfishly remain as irritating remnants of autocracy and social stratification.

The sins that bring about suffering are not sins against a divine order as in the traditional theodicy. Rather, the only true sins recognized by the national theodicy, sufficient to render comprehensible any historical or present-day lack of national sovereignty and fulfillment, are sins against signifiers of community solidarity and violations of the principle of in-group equality.

Recognition of the ambivalence that lies at the root of national identity, as indicated by the prominence of symbols of defeat and the dynamics of their elevation in national mythologies, has the potential to shed light on numerous seemingly irresolvable disputes in the area of nationalism studies. Or, more accurately, it can explain why these disputes are irresolvable by their nature, reflecting as they do contradictions inherent to the construct of the nation itself. Is the nation a novel form of sociopolitical organization generated by the forces of modernity, or does it reflect the transformation of continuous and enduring ethnic communities? To what extent is it a voluntary community, Renan's *plébiscite de tout les jours*, or an organic construct built around inevitable notions of ascriptive culture and purported descent? Is nationalism more a forward-thinking ideology inclined to encourage altruism, community cohesion, and democratic stability; or backward-looking, inclined to incite violence and fanaticism, to justify autocracy and oppression? And is ethnic conflict generally the result of "ancient hatreds" ingrained in the mythologies of the contending communities, the instrumental machinations of unscrupulous elites manipulating and exacerbating otherwise minor difference, or the inherent incompatibility of disparate modes of social organization between groups preventing meaningful communication and coexistence?

The answer, in nearly every case, is "all of the above." Not because these are reconcilable positions or because compromise between them is possible, but rather because the nation is better seen as a complex and continuously adaptive system of diverse and often contradictory myths, symbols, and values, which as such will take on a bewildering multiplicity of forms but ultimately exist to serve a common function: to transform the disorganized capacity for violence of a collection of individuals into unanimous submission to the collective violence of the modern political community. Any such system will contain ambivalence; in general, toward the norms of society that serve as both the means to comfort, security, and identity while at the same time standing as obstacles to individual autonomy and direct experience; and, in the particular case of the nation, toward memories of a prenational past from which identity is constructed around the principle of cultural authenticity, yet that represent forms of social organization at odds with those that must be rationalized to ensure growth and stability in the context of modernity. Such a system must be held together by certain nodal symbols, such as the symbols of defeat we have examined that, like the keystone of an edifice, are able by their distinct form and placement to absorb and resolve contrary forces that would otherwise collapse the structure. As a result, threats to these nodal symbols are quite genuinely threats to the community itself and will be met with a level of fanatical resistance impossible for outsiders to the system to comprehend.

Far too often in diplomacy, international relations, and even scholarship, the attachments of individuals and groups to national symbols such as lead to violent conflict are dismissed to the realm of the irrational, an unpredictable element of human nature that as such cannot be taken into account. The contrary approach that rejects this dismissal of ethnic conflict to "ancient hatred" and acknowledges the role of human agency in constructing ethnic and national identity has the benefit of being both compassionate and historically accurate. National mythologies are constructed and reconstructed according to the social needs of the present, and external influences can therefore affect whether a given myth or symbol serves to spark ethnic hatred or intercommunal cooperation.

Nevertheless, this approach too can tend to a form of dismissal, as it invites the false implication that these attachments are therefore superficial, easily transcended, and thus of little account to negotiating instrumental solutions to the conflicts in question. However, we dismiss the significance of these symbolic attachments at our own peril. It does not automatically follow from the modern, manufactured, or even manipulated nature of symbols that they lack lasting salience to the communities that revere them. For these myths and symbols have a rationality to them; under ordinary circumstances, they serve a function pivotal to the maintenance of social existence on which all human individuals rely for stability and meaning. Attachment to them is not the cause of violence; rather, they are necessary to the function of containing and restraining a community's violence. Unrestrained violence occurs only when these symbols are threatened and thereby lose their efficacy in fulfilling this function. Only once this function is understood can we begin to model the structure of national identity in terms of the relationships among its component myths, symbols, and rituals in such a way as to enable diplomatic interventions to navigate around such existential threats to the integrity of the societies concerned.

Nations will not discard their founding myths simply upon being shown that they are of modern fabrication because they are not dependent on historical accuracy, or even on the more nebulous category of "authenticity" but rather on the sense of meaning that the individual requires for rationalizing and comprehending prevailing modes of social existence and organization. Academics can pontificate all they want about the relative modernity of nations. As true as this is historically, it does not permit us to dismiss the primordialist position, if for no other reason than that it is the position of nationalism itself; a position frequently reinforced by pivotal myths and symbols of defeat that both commemorate the nation's necessary link to a primordial past and channel its animosities toward outsiders.

Given that nations are imagined communities – communities formed by perception – the perception that nations, along with their "ancient hatreds," are primordial is ultimately more important than the historical reality that they are not. Failure to credit the depth of these sentiments can only lead to misperceptions that will, in turn, result in diplomatic failures. The 20th century was full of events – in Europe, Africa, the Balkans, and the Middle East – that served to illustrate just how costly such diplomatic failures can be. When they lead to escalations of violence in already bitter ethnic conflicts, this cost is measured in property, homes, and lives.

Bibliography

Akyeampong, Emmanuel. (2000). "Asante at the Turn of the Twentieth Century." *Ghana Studies* 3: 3–12.

Alexander, Klinton W. (2000, Spring). "NATO's Intervention in Kosovo: The Legal Case for Violating Yugoslavia's National Sovereignty in Absence of Security Council Approval." *Houston Journal of International Law*, 22(3): 403–50.

Alter, Robert. (1973, July). "The Masada Complex," in *Commentary* 56: 19–24.

Anagnostopolou, Sia. (2002). "'Tyranny' and 'Despotism' as National and Historical Terms in Greek Historiography," in C. Koulouri (ed.), *Clio in the Balkans: The Politics of History Education*. Thessaloniki, Greece: Centre for Democracy and Reconciliation in Southeast Europe.

Anderson, Benedict. (1991). *Imagined Communities: Reflections on the Origin and Spread of Nationalism*. New York: Verso.

Aner, Zeev. (1983). "The Struggle for the Wall," in Meir Ben-Dov, Mordechai Naor, and Zeev Aner (eds.), *The Western Wall (HaKotel)*, Raphael Posner (trans.). Jerusalem: Ministry of Defense Publishing House, Chap. 6, pp. 121–38.

Aron, Raymond. (1967). *Main Currents in Sociological Thought II: Durkheim, Pareto, Weber*. London: Weidenfeld and Nicolson.

Asari, Eva-Maria, Daphne Halikiopoulou, and Steven Mock. (2008). "British National Identity and the Dilemmas of Multiculturalism." *Nationalism and Ethnic Politics* 14.1: 1–28.

Asirifi-Danquah. (2002). *Yaa Asantewaa: An African Queen Who Led an Army to Fight the British*. Kumasi: Asirifi-Danquah Books Ltd.

Atiyah, Edward. (1958). *The Arabs*. Edinburgh: Pelican.

Bakić-Hayden, Milica. (2004). "National Memory as Narrative Memory: The Case of Kosovo," in Maria Todorova (ed.), *National Memory in Southeastern Europe*. London: Hurst & Co.

Balcells, Albert. (1996). *Catalan Nationalism: Past and Present*. Basingstoke, UK: Macmillan.

Beaton, Roderick. (1998). "'Our Glorious Byzantinism': Papatzonis, Seferis, and the Rehabilitation of Byzantium in Postwar Greek Poetry," in David Ricks and Paul Magdalino (eds.), *Byzantium and the Modern Greek Identity*. Centre for Hellenic Studies, King's College London, 4. Aldershot, UK: Variorum, pp. 132–40.

Ben-Dov, Meir. (1983). "From the Temple to the Western Wall," in Meir Ben-Dov, Mordechai Naor, and Zeev Aner (eds.), *The Western Wall (HaKotel)*, Raphael Posner (trans.). Jerusalem: Ministry of Defense Publishing House, Chap. 1, pp. 11–38.

Ben-Yehuda, Nachman. (2002). *Sacrificing Truth: Archeology and the Myth of Masada*. New York: Humanity Books.

Ben-Yehuda, Nachmann. (1995). *The Masada Myth: Collective Memory and Mythmaking in Israel*. Madison, WI: University of Wisconsin Press.

Beyer, Peter. (1994). *Religion and Globalization*. London: Sage.

Billig, Michael. (1995). *Banal Nationalism*. London: Sage.

Boahen, A. Adu. (2003). *Yaa Asantewaa and the Asante–British War of 1900–1*. Oxford: James Curry.

Bogert, Ralph. (1991). "Paradigm of Defeat or Victory? The Kosovo Myth vs. the Kosovo Covenant in Fiction," in Wayne S. Vucinich and Thomas A. Emmert (eds.), *Kosovo: Legacy of a Medieval Battle*. Minneapolis, MN: University of Minnesota Press, Chap. 10, pp. 173–88.

Brempong, Arhin. (2000). "The Role of Nana Yaa Asantewaa in the 1900 Asante War of Resistance." *Ghana Studies* 3: 97–110.

Breuilly, John. (1993). *Nationalism and the State*. Manchester, UK: Manchester University Press.

Breuilly, John. (1996). "Approaches to Nationalism," in G. Balakrishnan (ed.), *Mapping the Nation*. London: Verso, pp. 146–74.

Brown, David. (2000). *Contemporary Nationalism: Civic, Ethnocultural & Multicultural Politics*. London, UK: Routledge.

Burkert, Walter. (1983). *Homo Necans: The Anthropology of Ancient Greek Sacrificial Ritual and Myth*. Berkeley, CA: University of California Press.

Burkert, Walter. (1996). *Creation of the Sacred: Tracks of Biology in Early Religions*. Cambridge, MA: Harvard University Press.

Calhoun, C. (1997). *Nationalism*. Buckingham, UK: Open University Press.

Callahan, William A. (2004). "National Insecurities: Humiliation, Salvation, and Chinese Nationalism." *Alternatives* 29: 199–218.

Čapek, Karel. (1999). *War with the Newts* [Ewald Osers (trans.)]. North Haven, CT: Catbird Press.

Cohen, Lenard J. (2001). *Serpent in the Bosom: The Rise and Fall of Slobodan Milosevic*. Boulder, CO: Westview Press.

Connor, Walker. (1978). "A Nation is a Nation, is a State, is an Ethnic Group, is a...," *Ethnic and Racial Studies* 1(4): 379–88.

Connor, Walker. (1994). *Ethnonationalism: The Quest for Understanding*. Princeton, NJ: Princeton University Press.

Conversi, Daniele. (1997). *The Basques, the Catalans, and Spain: Alternative-Routes to Nationalist Mobilisation*. London: Hurst & Co.

Davies, Alan. (2008). *The Crucified Nation: A Motif in Modern Nationalism.* Portland, OR: Sussex Academic Press.

Day, Lynda R. (2000). "Long Live the Queen! The Yaa Asantewaa Centenary and the Politics of History." *Ghana Studies* 3: 153–66.

Djilas, Aleksa. (1998, September/October). "Imagining Kosovo: A Biased New Account Fans Western Confusion." *Foreign Affairs* 77(5): 124–31.

Djordjevic, Dimitrije. (1991). "The Tradition of Kosovo in the Formation of Modern Serbian Statehood in the Nineteenth Century," in Wayne S. Vucinich and Thomas A. Emmert (eds.), *Kosovo: Legacy of a Medieval Battle.* Minneapolis, MN: University of Minnesota Press, Chap. 14, pp. 309–30.

Donkoh, Wilhelmina J. (2001). "Yaa Asantewaa: A Role Model for Womanhood in the New Millenium," in *JENdA: A Journal of Culture and African Women Studies*, Vol. 1.1.

Dragović-Soso, Jasna. (2002). *Saviours of the Nation: Serbia's Intellectual Opposition and the Revival of Nationalism.* Montreal: McGill University Press.

Durkheim, Emile. (1971). *The Elementary Forms of the Religious Life.* London: Allen & Unwin.

Eliade, Mircea. (1959). *The Sacred and the Profane: The Nature of Religion*, Willard R. Trask (trans.). London: Harcourt, Brace.

Emmert, Thomas A. (1989). "The Kosovo Legacy." *Serbian Studies* 5(2): 5–32.

Emmert, Thomas A. (1990). *Serbian Golgotha: Kosovo 1389.* New York: Columbia University Press.

Encyclopedia Judaica. (1972)."Av, Ninth of," Vol. 3: pp. 935–7. Jerusalem: Keter Publishing House.

Enderlin, Charles. (2003). *Shattered Dreams: The Failure of the Peace Process in the Middle East, 1995–2002* [Susan Fairfield (trans.)]. New York: Other Press.

Eriksonas, Linas. (2004). *National Heroes and National Identities: Scotland, Norway and Lithuania.* Brussels: P.I.E.-Peter Lang.

Frazer, Sir James. (1994). *The Golden Bough: A History of Myth and Religion.* London: MacMillan.

Freud, Sigmund. (1946). *Totem and Taboo: Resemblances Between the Psychic Lives of Savages and Neurotics* [A. A. Brill (trans.)]. New York: Vintage Books.

Freud, Sigmund. (1991). "Group Psychology and the Analysis of the Ego," in *Civilization, Society and Religion*, Penguin Freud Library, Vol. 12. Harmondsworth, UK: Penguin Books.

Friedland, Roger, and Richard D. Hecht. (1991). "The Politics of Sacred Place: Jerusalem's Temple Mount," in Jamie Scott and Paul Simpson-Housley (eds.), *Sacred Places and Profane Spaces: Essays in the Geographies of Judaism, Christianity and Islam.* Westport, CT: Greenwood Press, pp. 21–61.

Gagnon, V. P. (2004). *The Myth of Ethnic War: Serbia and Croatia in the 1990s.* Ithaca, NY: Cornell University Press.

Gellner, Ernest. (1983). *Nations and Nationalism.* Oxford, UK: Blackwell Publishers.

Gellner, Ernest. (1985). *The Psychoanalytic Movement: The Cunning of Unreason.* Evanston, IL: Northwestern University Press.

Gellner, Ernest. (1997). *Nationalism.* London: Weidenfeld & Nicolson.

Giddens, Anthony. (1986). *Durkheim*. London: Fontana Press.

Giddens, Anthony. (1990). *The Consequences of Modernity*. Cambridge, UK: Polity Press.

Gildea, Robert. (1994). *The Past in French History*. London: Yale University Press.

Girard, René. (1977). *Violence and the Sacred* [Patrick Gregory (trans.)]. Baltimore, London: The Johns Hopkins University Press.

Girard, René. (1987). "Generative Scapegoating," in Robert G. Hamerton-Kelly (ed.); *Violent Origins: Walter Burkert, Rene Girard and Johnathan Z. Smith on Ritual Killing and Cultural Formation*. Stanford, CA: Stanford University Press.

Goldenberg, Robert. (1982). "Early Rabbinic Explanations for the Destruction of Jerusalem." *Journal of Jewish Studies* 33: 517–25.

Gorenberg, Gershom. (2000). *The End of Days: Fundamentalism and the Struggle for the Temple Mount*. New York: Free Press.

Gorup, Radmila J. (1991). "Kosovo and Epic Poetry," in Wayne S. Vucinich and Thomas A. Emmert (eds.), *Kosovo: Legacy of a Medieval Battle*. Minneapolis, MN: University of Minnesota Press, Chap. 6, pp. 109–22.

Green, Ronald M. (2005). "Theodicy," in *The Encyclopedia of Religion*, 2nd ed. Detroit, MI: Macmillan Reference, Vol. 13, pp. 911–21.

Guibernau, Montserrat. (1996). *Nationalisms: The Nation-State and Nationalism in the Twentieth Century*. Cambridge, UK: Polity Press.

Guibernau, Montserrat. (2004). *Catalan Nationalism: Francoism, Transition and Democracy*. London, New York: Routledge.

Ha'Cohen, Rabbi Mordechai. (1983). "Sanctity, Law and Customs," in Meir Ben-Dov, Mordechai Naor, and Zeev Aner (eds.), *The Western Wall (HaKotel)*, Raphael Posner (trans.). Jerusalem: Ministry of Defense Publishing House, Chap. 4, pp. 79–98.

Hayes, Carleton. (1931). *The Historical Evolution of Modern Nationalism*. New York: Macmillan.

Hechter, Michael. (1975). *Internal Colonialism: The Celtic Fringe in British National Development, 1536–1966*. London: Routledge.

Henken, Elisa. (1996). *National Redeemer: Owain Glyndŵr in Welsh Tradition*. Cardiff: University of Wales Press.

Herzfeld, Michael. (1982). *Ours Once More: Folklore, Ideology, and the Making of Modern Greece*. Austin, TX: University of Texas Press.

Hirst, Anthony. (1998). "Two Cheers for Byzantium: Equivocal Attitudes in the Poetry of Palamas and Cavafy," in David Ricks and Paul Magdalino (eds.), *Byzantium and the Modern Greek Identity*. Centre for Hellenic Studies, King's College London, 4. Aldershot, UK: Variorum, pp. 105–17.

Hobsbawm, Eric. (1992). *Nations and Nationalism Since 1780: Programme, Myth, Reality*. Cambridge, UK: Cambridge University Press.

Hobsbawm, Eric, and Terence Ranger. (1983). *The Invention of Tradition*. Cambridge, UK: Cambridge University Press.

Hubert, Henri, and Marcel Mauss. (1964). *Sacrifice: Its Nature and Functions* [W. D. Halls (trans.)]. Chicago: University of Chicago Press.

Hutchinson, John. (2005). *Nations as Zones of Conflict*. London: Sage.

Huxley, George. (1998). "Aspects of Modern Greek Historiography of Byzantium," in David Ricks and Paul Magdalino (eds.), *Byzantium and the Modern Greek Identity*. Centre for Hellenic Studies, King's College London, 4. Aldershot: Variorum, pp. 15–23.

James, Paul. (1996). *Nation Formation: Towards a Theory of Abstract Community*. Thousand Oaks, CA: Sage.

Josephus. (1981). *The Complete Works of Josephus* [William Whiston (trans.)]. Grand Rapids, MI: Kregel Publications.

Judah, Tim. (2000). *Kosovo, War and Revenge*. New Haven, CT: Yale University Press.

Kaplan, Robert D. (1993). *Balkan Ghosts: A Journey Through History*. New York: St. Martin's Press.

Kauffmann, Eric. (2002). "Modern Formation, Ethnic Reformation: The Social Sources of the American Nation." *Geopolitics* 7(2): 99–120.

Kauffmann, Eric. (2008). "The Lenses of Nationhood: An Optical Model of Identity." *Nations and Nationalism* 14(3): 449–77.

Kedar, Benjamin Z. (1982). "The Masada Complex." *Jerusalem Quarterly* 24: 57–63.

Kedourie, Elie. (1966). *Nationalism*. London: Hutchinson & Co.

Kedourie, Elie (ed.) (1971). *Nationalism in Asia and Africa*. London: Weidenfeld & Nicolson.

Kitromilides, Paschalis. (1989). "'Imagined Communities' and the Origins of the National Question in the Balkans." *European History Quarterly* 19(2): 149–94.

Kitromilides, Paschalis. (1998). "On the Intellectual Content of Greek Nationalism: Paparrigopoulos, Byzantium and the Great Idea," in David Ricks and Paul Magdalino (eds.), *Byzantium and the Modern Greek Identity*. Centre for Hellenic Studies, King's College London, 4. Aldershot: Variorum, pp. 25–33.

Kola, Paulin. (2003). *The Search for Greater Albania*. London: Hurst & Company.

Koljević, Svetozar. (1991). "The Battle of Kosovo in Its Epic Mosaic," in Wayne S. Vucinich and Thomas A. Emmert (eds.), *Kosovo: Legacy of a Medieval Battle*. Minneapolis, MN: University of Minnesota Press, Chap. 7, pp. 123–40.

Kumar, Krishan. (2003). *The Making of English National Identity*. Cambridge: Cambridge University Press.

Kwadwo, Osei. (2004). *An Outline of Asante History, Part I.*, 3rd ed. Kumasi: Cita Press Ltd.

Lamdan, Isaac. (1971). "Masada," in Leon I. Yudkin, *Isaac Lamdan: A Study in Twentieth-Century Hebrew Poetry*. Ithaca, NY: Cornell University Press.

Liebman, Charles S., and Eliezer Don-Yehiya. (1983). *Civil Religion in Israel: Traditional Judaism and Political Culture in the Jewish State*. Berkeley, CA: University of California Press.

Lieven, Anatol. (1993). *The Baltic Revolution: Estonia, Latvia, Lithuania and the Path to Independence*. New Haven, CT: Yale University Press.

Maccoby, Hyam. (1982). *The Sacred Executioner*; London: Thames and Hudson.

Maccoby, Hyam. (1992). *Judas Iscariot and the Myth of Jewish Evil*. New York: Free Press.

Majstorovic, Steven. (2000). "Autonomy of the Sacred: The Endgame in Kosovo," in William Safran and Ramon Maiz (eds.), *Identity and Territorial Autonomy in Plural Societies*. Portland: Cass.

Malcolm, Noel. (1998). *Kosovo: A Short History*. London: Macmillan.

Malcolm, Noel. (1999a, June 9). "Independence for Kosovo." *New York Times*.

Malcolm, Noel. (1999b). "Is Kosovo Real?: The Battle Over History Continues." *Foreign Affairs* 78(1): 130–4.

Markovic, Marko S. (1983). *The Secret of Kosovo; in Landmarks in Serbian Culture and History*. Pittsburgh, PA: Serb National Federation.

Marvin, Carolyn, and David Ingle. (1999). *Blood Sacrifice and the Nation: Totem Rituals and the American Flag*. Cambridge: Cambridge University Press.

McDaniel, Tim. (1996). *The Agony of the Russian Idea*. Princeton, NJ: Princeton University Press.

McGwire, Michael. (2000). "Why Did We Bomb Belgrade?" *International Affairs* 76(1): 1–23.

McKaskie, T. C. (2000): "The Golden Stool at the End of the Nineteenth Century: Setting the Record Straight." *Ghana Studies* 3: 61–96.

Mihailovich, Vasa D. (1991). "The Tradition of Kosovo in Serbian Literature," in Wayne S. Vucinich and Thomas A. Emmert (eds.), *Kosovo: Legacy of a Medieval Battle*. Minneapolis, MN: University of Minnesota Press, Chap. 8, pp. 141–58.

Millas, Hercules. (2004). "National Perception of the 'Other' and the Persistence of Some Images," in Mustafa Aydin and Kostas Ifantis (eds.), *Turkish-Greek Relations: The Security Dilemma in the Aegean*. London: Routledge.

Mojzes, Paul. (1994). *Yugoslavian Inferno*. New York: Continuum.

Morton, Graeme. (2001). *William Wallace: Man and Myth*. Stroud, UK: Sutton Publishing.

Nairn, Tom. (1981). *The Break-up of Britain: Crisis and Neo-Nationalism*. London: Verso.

Naor, Mordechai. (1983a). "The Wall in Accounts of Travelers and Visitors," in Meir Ben-Dov, Mordechai Naor, and Zeev Aner (eds.), Raphael Posner (trans.), *The Western Wall (HaKotel)*. Jerusalem: Ministry of Defense Publishing House, Chap. 3., pp. 63–78.

Naor, Mordechai. (1983b). "The Wall in the Six-Day War," in Meir Ben-Dov, Mordechai Naor, and Zeev Aner (eds.), Raphael Posner (trans.), *The Western Wall (HaKotel)*. Jerusalem: Ministry of Defense Publishing House: Chap. 7, 139–58.

Noy, Dov. (1983). "Folk Tales About the Western Wall," in Meir Ben-Dov, Mordechai Naor, and Zeev Aner (eds.), Raphael Posner (trans.), *The Western Wall (HaKotel)*, Jerusalem: Ministry of Defense Publishing House, Chap. 5, pp. 99–120.

Nyegosh, P. P. (1930). *The Mountain Wreath* [James W. Wiles (trans.)]. London: Allen & Unwin.

Obeng, Pashington. (2000). "Yaa Asantewaa's War of Independence: Honoring and Ratifying an Historic Pledge." *Ghana Studies* 3: 137–52.

Owen, David. (1995). *Balkan Odyssey*. Harcourt, Brace.

Özkırımlı, Umut. (2010). *Theories of Nationalism: A Critical Introduction*, 2nd ed. New York: Palgrave-Macmillan.

Peckham, Robert Shannan. (1998). "Papadiamantis, Ecumenism and the Theft of Byzantium," in David Ricks and Paul Magdalino (eds.), *Byzantium and the Modern Greek Identity*. Centre for Hellenic Studies, King's College London, 4. Aldershot, UK: Variorum, pp. 91–104.

Peckham, Robert Shannan. (2001). *National Histories, Natural States: Nationalism and the Politics of Place in Greece*. London: Tauris.

Perica, Vjekoslav. (2002). *Balkan Idols: Religion and Nationalism in Yugoslav States*. New York: Oxford University Press.

Peters, Francis E. (1986). *Jerusalem and Mecca: The Typology of the Holy City in the Near East*. New York: New York University Press.

Politis, Alexis. (1998). "From Christian Roman Emperors to the Glorious Greek Ancestors," in David Ricks and Paul Magdalino (eds.), *Byzantium and the Modern Greek Identity*. Centre for Hellenic Studies, King's College London, 4. Aldershot, UK: Variorum, pp. 1–14.

Popovich, Ljubica D. (1991). "The Battle of Kosovo (1389) and Battle Themes in Serbian Art," in Wayne S. Vucinich and Thomas A. Emmert (eds.), *Kosovo: Legacy of a Medieval Battle*. Minneapolis, MN: University of Minnesota Press, Chap. 13, pp. 227–308.

Pynsent, Robert B. (1994). *Questions of Identity: Czech and Slovak Ideas of Nationality and Personality*. Budapest, London: Central European University Press.

Robertson, Geoffrey. (2000). *Crimes Against Humanity: The Struggle for Global Justice*. London: Penguin Books.

Roshwald, Aviel. (2006). *The Endurance of Nationalism*. Cambridge: Cambridge University Press.

Rovira, Marta. (2006). "Symbols and the National Representation of the Past," unpublished paper presented at the 16th Annual ASEN Conference, *Nations and Their Pasts*, London School of Economics, March 28–30, 2006.

Sayer, Derek. (1998). *The Coasts of Bohemia: A Czech History*. Princeton, NJ: Princeton University Press.

Schaffer, Rabbi Shaul. (1975). *Israel's Temple Mount: The Jews' Magnificent Sanctuary*. Jerusalem: Achva Press.

Schivelbusch, Wolfgang. (2003). *The Culture of Defeat: On National Trauma, Mourning, and Recovery* [Jefferson Chase (trans.)]. New York: Metropolitan Books.

Schwartz, Stephen. (2000). *Kosovo: Background to a War*. London: Anthem Press.

Segal, Jerome M., Shlomit Levy, Nadar Izzat Sa'id, and Elihu Katz. (2000). *Negotiating Jerusalem*. Albany, NY: State University of New York Press.

Seller, W. C., and R. J. Yeatman. (1975). *1066 and All That*. London: Magnum Books.

Shargel, Baila. (1979). "The Evolution of the Masada Myth," *Judaism* 28: 357–71.

Smith, Anthony D. (1991). *National Identity*. London: Penguin Books.

Smith, Anthony D. (1998). *Nationalism and Modernism*. New York: Routledge.
Smith, Anthony D. (1999). *Myths and Memories of the Nation*. New York: Oxford University Press.
Smith, Anthony D. (2003). *Chosen Peoples: Sacred Sources of National Identity*. Oxford: Oxford University Press.
Soysal, Yasemin Nuhoglu, and Vasilia Lilian Antoniou. (2002). "A Common Regional Past? Portrayals of the Byzantine and Ottoman Heritages from Within and Without," in C. Koulouri (ed.), *Clio in the Balkans: The Politics of History Education*. Thessaloniki, Greece: Centre for Democracy and Reconciliation in Southeast Europe.
Stavrakakis, Yannis. (1999). *Lacan and the Political*. New York: Routledge.
Stone, Michael E. (1981). "Reactions to the Destruction of the Second Temple: Theology Perception and Conversion." *Journal for the Study of Judaism in the Persian, Hellenistic and Roman Period* 12: 195–204.
Sullivan, Lawrence E. (1987). "Axis Mundi," in *The Encyclopedia of Religion*. London: Collier Macmillan, Vol. 2, 712–13.
Thomas, Robert. (1999). *The Politics of Serbia in the 1990s*. New York: Columbia University Press.
Tomashevich, George Vid. (1991). "The Battle of Kosovo and the Serbian Church," in Wayne S. Vucinich and Thomas A. Emmert (eds.), *Kosovo: Legacy of a Medieval Battle*. Minneapolis, MN: University of Minnesota Press, Chap. 12, pp. 203–26.
Tsu, Jing. (2005). *Failure, Nationalism, and Literature: The Making of Modern Chinese Identity, 1895–1937*. Stanford, CA: Stanford University Press.
Velikonja, Mitja. (1998). "Liberation Mythology: The Role of Mythology in Fanning War in the Balkans," in Paul Mojzes (ed.), *Religion and the War in Bosnia*. Atlanta, GA: Scholar's Press.
Vilnay, Zev. (1973). *Legends of Jerusalem: The Sacred Land, Vol. 1*. Philadelphia: The Jewish Publication Society of America.
Wachtel, Andrew B. (2004). "How to Use a Classic: Petar Petrović-Njegoš in the Twentieth Century," in John Lampe and Mark Mazower (eds.), *Ideologies and National Identities: The Case of Twentieth-Century Southeastern Europe*. Budapest: Central European University Press, pp. 131–53.
Wasserstein, Bernard. (2001). *Divided Jerusalem: The Struggle for the Holy City*. New Haven, CT: Yale University Press.
West, Rebecca. (1982). *Black Lamb and Grey Falcon*. New York: Penguin Books.
Wilks, Ivor. (2000). "Asante at the End of the Nineteenth Century: Setting the Record Straight." *Ghana Studies* 3: 13–59.
Winock, Michel. (1998). "Joan of Arc," in Pierre Nora (ed.), *Realms of Memory, Vol.3: Symbols*. New York: Columbia University Press, pp. 433–82.
Yadin, Yigael. (1966). *Masada: Herod's Fortress and the Zealots' Last Stand*. London: Weidenfeld and Nicolson.
Yadin, Yigael, and Gerald Gottlieb. (1969). *The Story of Masada (Retold for Young Readers)*. New York: Random House.
Zerubavel, Yael. (1994, Winter). "The Death of Memory and the Memory of Death." *Representations* 45: 72–100.

Zerubavel, Yael. (1995). *Recovered Roots: Collective Memory and the Making of the Israeli National Tradition.* Chicago: University of Chicago Press.

Zimmer, Oliver. (2003). "Boundary Mechanisms and Symbolic Resources: Towards a Process-Oriented Approach to National Identity." *Nations and Nationalism* 9(2): 173–93.

Index

Printed in Great Britain
by Amazon

72341943R00174